THE CHALLENGE OF SOCIAL INNOVATION IN URBAN REVITALIZATION

Spatial Planning Group - Faculty of Architecture
Delft University of Technology

THE CHALLENGE OF SOCIAL INNOVATION IN URBAN REVITALIZATION

Paul Drewe , Juan-Luis Klein, Edward Hulsbergen (eds)

Techne Press

Design/**Science**/Planning

Series Editor:
Dr. I.T. Klaasen, Faculty of Architecture (Spatial Planning), Delft University of Technology, The Netherlands, I.T.Klaasen@tudelft.nl

Editorial Board:
Prof. dr. P. Drewe, Emeritus, Faculty of Architecture (Spatial Planning), Delft University of Technology, The Netherlands
Prof. ir. J.J. Jacobs, Faculty of Industrial Engineering, Delft University of Technology, The Netherlands
Prof. dr. P. Roberts, Department of Civic Design (Regional Planning), University of Liverpool, United Kingdom
Dr. T. Poldma, Associate Professor, School of Industrial Design, Faculty of Environmental Planning, University of Montreal, Canada
Prof. dr. A. van der Valk, Land Use Planning Chair, Wageningen University, The Netherlands

The Challenge of Social Innovation in Urban Revitalization / edited by Paul Drewe, Juan-Luis Klein, and Edward Hulsbergen
2008, Amsterdam, 272 pages
ISBN: 978-90-8594-018-0
Keywords: Social innovation, urban revitalization, integrated area approach, multiple deprivation, active citizen participation

Translation: Magee & Nguyen Associées, Montréal (Québec); Chapters 2 and 11
Lay-out: Marieke Rombout
Editing Assistance: Ina Klaasen, Lisette Rueb, and Danielle Wijnen
Cover Design: Iwan Kriens and Jan Willem Hennink

Published and distributed by Techne Press, Amsterdam, The Netherlands
www.technepress.nl

This publication is produced within the frame of the research program of the Delft Center for Sustainable Urban Areas and financed by the Chair of Spatial Planning. Translations were funded by the Department of Urbanism, Faculty of Architecture Delft University of Technology, The Netherlands.

Copyright © 2008 by the authors, unless otherwise stated. All rights reserved. No part of this publication may be reproduced or stored by any electronic or mechanical means (including copying, photocopying, recording, data storage, and retrieval) or in any other form or language without the written permission from the publisher.

Contents

Introducing The Challenge of Social Innovation in Urban Revitalization   9
Paul Drewe

Part I Theory

1   Social Innovation at the Territorial Level: from Path Dependency to Path Building   17
Jean-Marc Fontan, Juan-Luis Klein and Diane-Gabrielle Tremblay

2   Social Innovation and Urban Regeneration from the Perspective of an Innovative Milieu Analysis   29
Andrée Matteaccioli

3   Social Innovation: an Institutionalized Process   51
Denis Harrisson

4   The Agile State, an Organizational View on Spatial Development Policy in The Netherlands   63
Roy G. Mierop

5   Combating Poverty in Europe and the Third World: Social Innovation in Motion   87
Pasquale De Muro, Abdelillah Hamdouch, Stuart Cameron and Frank Moulaert

Part II Cases

6   Local Development as Social Innovation: the Case of Montreal   103
Juan-Luis Klein, Jean-Marc Fontan and Diane-Gabrielle Tremblay

7   Social Innovation, Spatial Transformation and Sustainable Communities: Liverpool and the 'Eldonians'   117
Peter Roberts

8   Bottom-up in Gouda East: Design Atelier R&M Activity Center   135
Edward D. Hulsbergen

9   Urban Development and Self-help Activities in León, Nicaragua   151
Jan Bredenoord, in co-operation with Desiree van de Ven and Patricia Ardiles

10	Battling the Digital Divide from the Bottom-up in Lima, Peru Ana María Fernández-Maldonado	167
11	The URBAN Initiative or the EU as Social Innovator? Paul Drewe	183
12	The Urban Renewal Program of Caisse des Dépôts et Consignations: Innovative Action to Regenerate French Towns and Cities Pierre Narring	197
13	The Case of Jerusalem: a Study in Complexity Rami Nasrallah and Amin Amin	215
14	Thinking about Transfer from the Mondragón Experience Hervé Grellier, Jean Michel Larrasquet, Sain Lopez Perez and Luxio Ugarte	235
	Cross-Case Analysis Paul Drewe, Edward Hulsbergen and Juan-Luis Klein	251
	Reference Index	261
	Geographical Index	267
	About the Authors	269

Introducing The Challenge of Social Innovation in Urban Revitalization

Paul Drewe

> *'The solution of social problems lags behind technology because we have not organized the same sharp search for new ideas'*
> *(J.R. Platt, The Step to Man, 1966: 132)*

Setting the scene

Social problems, especially persistent ones, ask for new ideas or social innovations. One of the most persistent problems is how to make the worst off population groups as well off as possible. It is hard to believe that the mythical entity of 'the market' would be able to achieve distributional justice.

Innovation – according to the dictionary – is 'the introduction of something new' or, more important, 'something that deviates from established doctrine or practice' (Webster's). Social innovations, unlike technological innovations, are not necessarily commercially successful as they are rather oriented toward the public interest or social cohesion for that matter. The lofty goal of *'la ville solidaire'* as the French call it, is a multidimensional ambition: requiring a rethinking of solidarity (Paugam, 2007). Urban revitalization is only one, albeit vital and urgent focus. *Innovation*, as it is understood in this book *"is a social and territorial construction, whose production and effects depend on local and global socio-economic contexts that are conflict ridden and hierarchical. From this perspective, the territory mediates and structures arrangements of production actors, organizations and decision makers, thus allowing for the emergence of specific innovation cultures but that are not isolated from nor independent of more global contexts"* (see Chapter 1, by Fontan, Klein and Tremblay, page 17 in this book).

Focusing on urban revitalization or regeneration, social innovation constitutes a challenge. Urban revitalization has been on planning and political agendas for many decades. But what is the state-of-the-art? The URBAN Community Initiatives seem to be fairly representative. Between 1994 and 2006:
- 190 programs (urban areas) have been selected in the 15 EU member states
- targeting 5.2 million inhabitants
- with € 1.6 billion of funding allocated, and
- a total investment of € 3.38 billion.

Starting from the diagnosis of multiple deprivation, the EU has advocated an integrated area approach with active citizen participation. One may question the real impact of URBAN, but its rationale or basic philosophy still seems convincing (see chapter 11). Reading the evaluation reports (GHK, 2003 and Commission of the European Communities, 2002), however, one is left with the feeling that the evaluators (maybe 'straitjacketed' by the methodology prescribed by the European Commission) lack the discernment and understanding with which to penetrate the heart and essence of the problem. How can one, for example, explain that the evaluators have not in any way signaled the 'explosive' situation in the French suburbs? After all, the 'riotous' or 'revolting' Clichy-sous-Bois or Aulnay-sous-Bois (among others) have been among the 'troubled' urban areas selected for URBAN. This is not to imply that this kind of 'sensitive' areas are exclusively a French phenomenon. Violent outbursts only underline the gravity or urgency of the problem. The problem of multiple deprivation or social exclusion also exists without them.

URBAN intended to organize citizen participation in the development and implementation of programs. The individuals affected by severe deprivation were not to be treated as passive objects of intervention. The problem of urban deprivation was supposed to be tackled 'at grass root level'. It is not only the French experience that casts serious doubts on effective citizen participation within URBAN (although the experience across the 190 urban areas is not uniform).

Urban regeneration is not only a matter of land use, built environment or social housing. New ideas are desperately needed. Even if cities view themselves as 'competing' with each other, 'success' is not only be measured in terms of competitive economic and built environment outcomes, but rather to be evaluated in terms of social benefits and costs and their distribution among citizens.

How to deal with the challenge of social innovation in urban revitalization?
The book is organized in three parts:
- theoretical guidelines or ways of conceptualizing the creation of new ideas
- selected cases of social innovation related to urban regeneration
- cross-case analysis.

Theory

Five promising theoretical avenues are introduced in Part I:
- the territorial effects of social innovation (Chapter 1)
- innovative milieu analysis (Chapter 2)
- the role of institutions in innovation (Chapter 3)
- the agile state (Chapter 4)
- networking within and across cities (Chapter 5).

Fontan, Klein and Tremblay, in Chapter 1, start from technological innovations: the founding analyses of Schumpeter's entrepreneur-innovator and Veblen's view on the role of technology. Social innovation, however, implies a renewed concept of innovation, moving from the cyclical to the spatial effect. It is about social experimentation and power relationships as well as the construction of social innovation networks. Social innovations are three-dimensional. They cover the social milieu (prior to the innovation, during and following its implementation), the territory and a cyclical temporal dimension. Social innovation systems belong to geographical spaces ranging from the global to the local space via intermediary, continental, national and regional spaces. Hence social innovation is not limited to local space.

Matteaccioli, the author of Chapter 2, has been a member of the former research group GREMI, *Groupe de Recherche Européen sur les Milieux Innovateurs* (see for example Camagni & Maillat, 2006). She has also dedicated a book to Aydalot, the inventor of the very concept of innovative milieu as a pioneer of spatial economics (Matteaccioli, 2004). The innovative milieu analysis, according to GREMI, focuses on technological innovation. In Chapter 2, it is applied to social innovation and urban revitalization discussing three points. Firstly, there are points of convergence between urban-community based organizations and the innovative milieu. Both are based on partnership or negotiated, marked by an emerging logic of learning and a territorial logic: but with different aims. Secondly, innovative milieus, associated with social innovation, can produce externalities favorable to urban regeneration. And, finally, social innovation - seen from an innovative milieu angle – can make a difference in the case of social exclusion through unemployment. But – according to Matteaccioli – there are limits facing multiple segregation, especially in the face of urban problems of an ethno-cultural nature as in the case of the French *banlieues*.

Harrison, in Chapter 3, sheds light on the institutional aspects of the social innovation process. According to the neo-institutional approach, an institution is a regulative, normative and cognitive system. Institutions tend toward inertia. But how is change or innovation then possible? To answer this question, Harrison refers to Hollingworth's five hierarchical levels of institutionalization in society. Innovation read 'building legitimacy'. Social innovation is not only a matter of efficiency, but also of social capital, social networks, sharing and the feeling of participating in the development of democracy. Those who innovate are those who succeed in transforming their institutional environment, concludes the author of Chapter 3.

Mierop, in Chapter 4, deals with the State as far as it is responsible for spatial development policy in the three-tier political system of the Netherlands which involves central, regional and local levels. How to increase the State's flexibility in coping with changes imposed by a sometimes turbulent environment: in order to conduct an effective spatial development policy. The means to create an agile organization include: demand-oriented performance; changeability of the organization; culture; leadership; and, application of ICT. Culture stands for four behavioral aspects: responsible entrepreneurship; strong external orientation; high degree of mental flexibility of staff members; and, achievement-oriented behavior. (A.T. Kearny, 2004; Mierop & Bastiaansen, 2002) The challenge to create an agile government, to prove that it is not an oxymoron, goes beyond the Dutch context.

The final theoretical contribution relates to network dynamics both in the Third World (international co-operation networks) and in Europe (network initiatives to combat social exclusion in large cities). De Muro, Hamdouch, Cameron and Moulaert view social innovation as a multidimensional concept. The dimensions cover: aim of the initiative; change in the organization of the initiative; role of 'special agents' (leadership, creative individuals); role of 'path dependency' and of structural constraints; and, how to overcome the tensions between normativity and reality. Networks to combat social exclusion in urban Europe and in developing countries (in especial Africa) are examined, following a common grid. The European cases are compared in terms of innovative vision, innovative delivery, innovative institutional organization, innovative process, and innovative scalar effect. Chapter 5, in fact, presents a mix of theoretical reflections and case studies, thus providing a link between Parts I and II. The European project comprises 16 case studies in 10 cities in 6 countries: Newcastle (United Kingdom), Milan (Italy), Brussels (Belgium), Vienna (Austria), Naples (Italy), Lille (France), Berlin (Germany) and several initiatives in Wales (United Kingdom). Dealing also with developing countries, Chapter 5 provides additional information complementing our two cases within a Third World context, i.e. León, Nicaragua (Chapter 9) and Lima, Peru (Chapter 10).

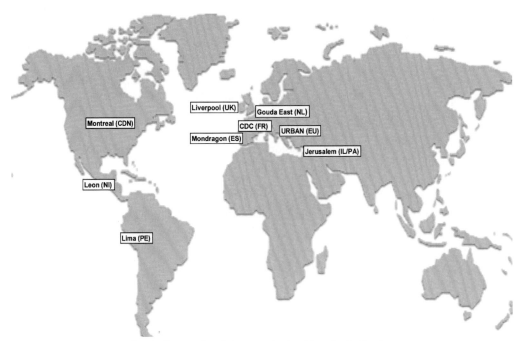

Illustration 0.1: Cases in *The Challenge of Social Innovation in Urban Revitalization*

Cases

Selecting the case studies for this book, we have emphasized diversity, "looking forward and backward and in all directions" (Platt, 1966: 134). There simply is no royal road leading to social innovation in urban revitalization. Nine cases have been selected as shown in the map:
These cases will be analyzed and evaluated in part II.

The first three of them are about urban revitalization in a Western context: two large cities and medium-sized one:
- Montreal (Chapter 6)
- Liverpool (Chapter 7)
- Gouda (Chapter 8).

Having read Klein and Fontan (2003) about socio-economic conversion in Montreal, has in a way become the source of inspiration for the entire book, together with the work of CRISES. Klein, Fontan and Tremblay present an updated version of the story of the Angus Technopole.
The Liverpool case is not only about the Eldonian Village project, a successful action of residents against demolition and re-housing. Roberts also provides a link with the recent British approach of sustainable communities. See Office of the Deputy Prime Minister (2003) and Roberts (2003).

One may be surprised by the inclusion of Gouda in the book. What is so special about this medium-sized city in the Netherlands presented by Hulsbergen? A joint Dutch-Moroccan activity center is of special interest as it deals with what Matteaccioli has referred to an ethno-cultural urban problem not uncommon in the Netherlands (Penninx, 2006). Chapter 8 builds on Hulsbergen and Vellinga (2001).

In the subsequent two cases we switch to a Third World context.
- León (Chapter 9)
- Lima (Chapter 10)

In the 1980s, the Dutch government and Dutch municipalities have been engaged in Nicaragua until the US boycott. Of the many city links only one has survived: Utrecht (together with Zaragoza and Hamburg) and Bredenoord are still working in and supporting León. See Chapter 9 and also Bredenoord (2005) about urban development in a precarious economic context.

The so-called digital divide is not an exclusive Third World phenomenon. It is on the political agenda in the Western world (Drewe, Fernández-Maldonado & Hulsbergen, 2003). But the case of Lima, presented by Fernández-Maldonado, demonstrates that the digital divide can be tackled successfully from the bottom up through an ingenious, informal approach to the use of ICT in everyday life. Chapter 10 is based on a PhD Thesis (Fernández-Maldonado, 2004).

Next, we have selected two uncommon approaches of the State as social innovator:
- the EU's URBAN Community Initiative (Chapter 11)
- the French *Caisse des Dépôts et Consignations* (Chapter 12)

URBAN, presented by Drewe has already been referred to at the outset. The program is about an intervention at the European level vis-à-vis 15 member states and selected urban areas. The *Caisse des Dépôts et Consignations* (CDC) is a unique banker since 1816, able today to act as a pioneer investor in projects in the 'public interest' such as the Urban Renewal Program: comprising 100 projects over five years. Narring writes about an internal CDC evaluation of this program.

The final cases are very special ones:
- Jerusalem (Chapter 13)
- Mondragón (Chapter 14).

Amin and Nasrallah present an article that builds on their current PhD research. Their 'study in complexity' is about a dialogue and cooperation between Israeli and Palestinian NGOs, non-governmental practitioners, academics and civil society activists focusing on scenario building. This venture has started in 1996 with foreign support and has already been widely published (see, for example, Friedman & Nasrallah, 2003; Misselwitz & Rieniets, 2006). Another special case is the Mondragón Co-operative Corporation, a unique model of socially innovative business founded in 1956. In the final case, Grellier, Larrasquet, Lopez Perez and Ugarte deal with transfer from the Mondragón experience to other countries around the world.

Cross-case analysis

The final part of the book is dedicated to cross-case analysis. Each of the nine cases is analyzed in a nutshell following a framework which reflects the theoretical avenues introduced in part I and is inspired by the work of CRISES, the *Centre de Recherche sur les Innovations Sociales*.

References

A.T. Kearny, 2004, *The Agile Government is not an Oxymoron*, Executive Agenda, Vol. VII, N° 1, pp.57-65.

Bredenoord, J., 2005, *Urban Development Strategies in León Nicaragua*, Dutch University Press, Amsterdam.

Camagni, R. & D. Maillat (eds), 2006, *Milieux innovateurs, théorie et politiques*, Economica Anthropos, Paris.

Commission of the European Communities, 2002, *The Programming of the Structural Funds 2000-2006, an Initial Assessment of the Urban Initiative*, Brussels.

Drewe, P., A.M. Fernández-Maldonado & E.D. Hulsbergen, 2003, Battling Urban Deprivation: ICT Strategies in the Netherlands and in Europe, *Journal of Urban Technology*, Vol. 10, N° 1, pp.23-37.

Fernández-Maldonado, A. M., 2004, *ICT-related Transformation in Latin American Metropolises*, PhD Thesis, Series Design / Science / Planning, Delft University Press / Techne Press, Delft / Amsterdam.

Friedman, A. & R. Nasrallah, 2003, *Divided Cities in Transition*, Jerusalem Berlin Forum, Jerusalem.

GHK, 2003, *Ex-post Evaluation Urban Community Initiative (1994-2000)*, Brussels & London.

Hulsbergen, E. & B. M. K. Vellinga, 2001, *Buurtvernieuwing door actief burgerschap, R&M Gouda Oost als casus en experiment*, Stichting Habitat Platform, Den Haag.

Klein, J.-L. & J.-M. Fontan, 2003, Reconversion économique et initiative locale, l'effet structurant des actions collectives; in Fontan, J.-M., J.-L. Klein & B. Lévesque (eds), *Reconversion économique et développement territorial*, Presses de l'Université du Québec, Sainte-Foy, pp.11-33.

Matteaccioli, A., 2004, *Philippe Aydalot, pionnier de l'économie territoriale*, L'Harmattan, Paris.

Mierop, R. & C. Bastiaansen, 2002, *De actieve overheid*, LEMMA, Utrecht.

Misselwitz, P. & T. Rieniets, 2006, *City of Collision. Jeruzalem and the Principles of Conflict Urbanism*, Birkhäuser, Basel, Boston & Berlin.

Office of the Deputy Prime Minister, 2003, *The Sustainable Communities Plan*, London

Paugam, S. (ed), 2007, *Repenser la solidarité. L'apport des sciences sociales*, Presses Universitaires de France, Paris.

Penninx, R., 2006, Après les assassinats de Fortuyn et de Van Gogh : le modèle d'intégration hollandaise en déroute?, *Critiques internationales*, Vol. 4, N° 33, pp. 9-26.

Platt, J.R., 1966, *The Step to Man*, John Wiley & Sons, New York, London & Sydney.

Roberts, P., 2003, Sustainable Development and Social Justice: Spatial Priorities and Mechanisms for Delivery, *Social Inquiry*, Vol. 73, pp. 228-244.

Part I
Theory

1 Social Innovation at the Territorial Level:
from Path Dependency to Path Building

Jean-Marc Fontan, Juan-Luis Klein and Diane-Gabrielle Tremblay

Introduction

The concept of innovation has been traditionally restricted to technology or the technical field. Until the 1990s, almost no one talked about social innovation except, in certain cases, to refer to the likely effect on society of the emergence of technical innovation, although Schumpeter and Veblen presented wider views (Tremblay, 1989, 1995). The analysis stopped there. Thus, this Chapter aims to broaden the analysis of innovation by examining its social dimension, a notion that has recently come into use in the trends of 'new economic sociology' (Lévesque, Bourque & Forgues, 2001) and 'new socio-economic geography' (Benko & Lipietz, 2000) and has inspired important pieces of work from a territorial perspective (Gertler & Wolfe, 2002; Fontan, Klein & Tremblay, 2005; Moulaert & Nussbaumer, 2005). From this perspective, innovation is not considered to be the simple mechanical insertion of technical novelty into production. It is embedded in society (Klein & Harrisson, 2007). It is essential to examine this link in order to understand the different dynamics of development which take place in territories which, while certainly specific and local, are related to global processes. We argue that the continuous presence of society must be taken into account throughout the 'process of innovation production', starting with the invention (in both technical and social fields), the different mechanisms leading to its institutionalization, the necessary efforts to construct the social usage of the invention, and ending up with its social and territorial diffusion. This process leads to an institutional 'path building' which is necessary to achieve social transformation.

In this Chapter, our analysis of the role of society in innovation processes consists of an overview, indeed a summary, of the different perspectives developed to study the innovation process. We suggest an approach that will allow us to revisit the different stages marking the evolution of the concept of innovation. The Chapter is divided into four parts. Firstly we will review the bases laid by Schumpeter's (1935) and Veblen's (1899) founding analyses while pointing out the lack of a specific examination of innovation by the classical social analysts. Secondly we will address innovation from the perspective of evolutionary economists. We will reconstruct an explanation of social innovation as a cognitive process confronted with localized social resistance, thus posing the problem of social and territorial diffusion of innovation. We will then focus on the renewal of the concept of innovation, a renewal initiated by authors whose conceptual and methodological framework considers innovation as a social process with multiple phases and facets. We will round off concludes by emphasizing the strong link between sociality, territoriality and market and building new institutional paths that allow social actors to redesign the society from the local to the global.

Our assumption is that innovation is a social and territorial construction, whose production and effects depend on local and global socio-economic contexts that are conflict ridden and hierarchical. From this perspective, the territory mediatizes and structures arrangements of production actors, organizations and decision makers, thus allowing for the emergence of specific social innovation processes, that are not isolated from nor independent of more global contexts, but can inflect their local effects.

Innovation and society: founding analyses

It must first be specified that the works by classical analysts of society and its evolution did not focus much on the notion of innovation. This lack of interest is explained, in our view, by the deterministic and linear conception of social change held by these authors. This conception, against which Braudel (1985) rebelled, was held by important authors such as Durkheim, Weber, Spencer and Marx. It was only toward the end of the 19th century that the concept of innovation entered into the language of sociology in an indirect way. This occurred when the notion of 'imitation' was used by Tarde (1890) who explained that societies evolve through the daily accumulation of inventions - 'innovations'- which gradually alter the lot of human behavior. According to Tarde, the distinctive feature of human beings is to imitate fellow human beings and therefore when a new behavior appears, it entails an 'epidemiological' reaction whereby 'the innovation' is imitated as soon as conditions permit. However, Tarde did not dwell on the conditions of this imitation and this vision remained marginal. It was not until the analyses by two trail-blazing authors, namely Schumpeter and Veblen, that a more comprehensive conceptualization of innovative processes emerged.

Schumpeter's entrepreneur-innovator

Schumpeter's main contribution to the analysis of innovation is the entrepreneur-innovator. He borrows his vision of the entrepreneur or business leader from the notion of *Führershaft* which refers to the fact that in all fields of social activity, the leader has a special role. The abilities of this leader essentially amount to initiative and will. By transposing this notion into the field of economics, Schumpeter derives from it the notion of entrepreneurship and entrepreneur. Entrepreneurship is the act of achieving and the entrepreneur is the agent who carries out new combinations of production factors (Tremblay, 1989).

For Schumpeter, the entrepreneur-innovator is not the inventor himself but the one who introduces this invention into the firm, the industry, the economy, that is, strictly speaking, the person responsible for its diffusion. In Schumpeter's view, economic society is run by human decisions, those of entrepreneurs, and not by ideologies or abstract social classes. This is what basically distinguishes his theory from the deterministic and macro-social perspectives mentioned above. Thus, change stems from the concrete exercise of a function and not from the function per se, which means that when somebody is an 'entrepreneur', it is because he implements new combinations; he creates a context through which the framework of social intervention broadens and is transformed. Only this act of entrepreneurship corresponds to the role and function of an entrepreneur. Schumpeter constructs his analysis in the economic environment and sees an actor-innovator in anybody who can implement a new combination of arrangements in a firm, an organization with an economic vocation (Tremblay, 1989).

From this perspective, the function of the entrepreneur consists in overcoming a series of obstacles. According to Schumpeter, innovation is a creative response to these obstacles. Three major types of resistance to innovation can be identified. First, the entrepreneur-innovator acts in a context of uncertainty, that is, given the information that he has, he is not sure that his project will be successful. He may use retrospective data, but these bring little certainty since nobody is using them the way he suggests. The second type of obstacle appears to be fairly obvious and was described by Schumpeter in 1935 as follows: "It is objectively more difficult to innovate than to use what is usual and proven". Lastly, the third type of obstacle - in our view, the most important - involves the reaction of the social milieu to the innovation, or 'to anybody who wants to innovate'. (Schumpeter, 1935; translations, quoted in Tremblay, 1989). Thus, Schumpeter said: "It is not enough to produce satisfactory soap, it was also necessary to induce people to wash"[1]. This metaphor still applies to the present day since it raises the issue of the social construction of usage of the invention, which is the specific feature of innovation.

Although Schumpeter's works have made it possible to isolate the role of the entrepreneur as a key agent of change in economic organizations, he did not broaden the role of the entrepreneur to other types of actors in the social, political and cultural spheres. To grasp the full complexity of the recognition of usage, the link must be made between Schumpeter and Veblen's works.

Veblen and the role of technology

Veblen (1899) makes an important contribution to the economic analysis of innovation, but especially to the global and interdisciplinary examination of this subject. For Veblen, as for Schumpeter, technology or, in his words, 'the state of the industrial arts', is the key and determining economic factor in social evolution. What Veblen meant by 'technology' can be summed up in two series of elements: on the one hand, a system of tools, instruments and machines, and on the other, what we consider to be the most important aspect – know-how. Veblen also used the terms 'intangible assets', 'collective assets' and 'immaterial wealth' while referring to this technical know-how that he deemed to be more important than the tools and instruments which make up physical capital. Veblen viewed technology as an "indivisible possession of the community at large, whereas the instruments created by this technology can become one person's individual property" (Corbo, 1973; Tremblay, 1989, 1995).

For Veblen, technology will only be effective if it finds the appropriate material conditions, if the required material forces are available, and if it is located in an appropriate diffusion or 'propagation environment'. To a certain extent, Veblen's theory is thus imbued with a certain degree of 'technological determinism'. However, Veblen brings other forces into play which will contribute to tone down this determinism that tends to be emphasized. Among these other forces is 'culture'. Indeed, Veblen views technology not as a static reality but as a dynamic reality 'that continuously evolves and whose effectiveness depends on a number of specific conditions'. "Although it is true that technology influences culture, it is also true that culture can facilitate as well as inhibit the effectiveness and progress of technology" (Corbo, 1973: 295; translation, quoted in Tremblay, 1989). Once again, we are getting closer to a global rather than a purely economic vision of technology.

Thus, to sum up, for Schumpeter, innovation lies in the process that leads to the generalization, even the creation of the social usage of invention. Although the entrepreneur is in charge of constructing the usage, he does so by creating on his own something that the inventor did not have, which in itself also constitutes an invention. In this respect, Veblen completes and even goes beyond Schumpeter's analysis by bringing out the effects of reciprocity between technique/technology and the social environment. For him, not only do technologies have an effect on the cultural and institutional environment, but this institutional environment itself exerts an effect on the technologies and innovations being developed. Thus, a form of reciprocity of effects exists between the social context and the technologies (or innovation, a term that we prefer but Veblen hardly uses).

The evolutionary approach: from cyclic to spatial effect

As we have just seen, Schumpeter and Veblen's works constitute important background for the development of an analysis which embeds innovation in society. However, it was the 'evolutionary' economists who completed their work by proposing a global vision of innovation. For this movement, innovation is a *process* (Freeman, Clark & Soete, 1982), a process which transmits and receives impulses, connects new technical ideas to the markets (Le Bas, 1995), a process of problem solving, a learning process which brings into play knowledge, skills, competencies, know-how, capacities and abilities (Tremblay, Fontan, Klein & Bordeleau, 2002; Tremblay, Chevrier & Rousseau, 2004).

Cyclic effect of innovation

According to evolutionary economists, the innovation process occurs in an organization or a firm; thus, their vision is closer to that of Schumpeter (Dosi, 1988). For Schumpeter, at first small or medium-sized firms were the initial sites of innovation, whereas the concentration of capital over the years has given rise to the domination of large firms and their research and development departments. However, for the evolutionary economists, these two places (small and medium size enterprises and large enterprises) do not necessarily succeed one another in time but can, on the contrary, coexist.

This seems to correspond better to today's reality in which, depending on the sectors and the degree of maturity of the sector involved, it is in some cases Small and Medium Sized Enterprises (SMEs) and in other cases large enterprises which dominate the innovation process. Moreover, these two innovation regimes can be explained by the phase a given industry is going through (Dosi, 1988). As observed by Dosi, when an industry is in an emerging phase (for example, multimedia, biotechnology, optronics, etc.), innovation tends to proceed by trial and error. Entrepreneurs take risks and new technologies appear, leading to the creation of new enterprises. On the contrary, during the maturity phase -- for example, the steel and automobile sectors - where markets are quite saturated and generally oligopolistic, technological changes and innovation in general constitute one of the, if not the main, weapons of competition.

The revitalizing potential of an innovation thus does not last forever. It runs out, which explains technological revolutions as well as the appearance of new technological cycles and the obsolescence of former technologies. As explained by Vernon (1974), whose analysis is similar to that of Dosi (1988), the revitalizing potential of an innovation is closely related to the life cycle of a product. Vernon's works show that there are five phases to a product initiated through innovation: novelty, growth, maturity, standardization and decline.

The revitalizing effect of innovation is felt during the first phases when the manufacturing of the new product creates new market opportunities, attracts capital and thus generates new enterprises, including small ones, where new usages and types of product are developed. The creation is subsequently replaced by mass production with stricter and more intensified standards, and the revitalizing potential of the innovation diminishes. Based on his analysis of the United States, Vernon put forward an explanation of the effect of innovation on economic development. According to this explanation, development is linked to the capacity of a country, or a regional or local milieu, to specialize in the manufacturing of products which are still in their first phases and then to withdraw from it as the cycle advances in order to redirect its economic specialization toward other emerging products. It thus paves the way for a new development strategy centered on the capacity to innovate, where growth depends on the specialization in the first phases of goods production, although R & D can be costly in some sectors and standardization in mature sectors can compensate the costs.

The spatial effect of innovation

As highlighted by the evolutionary perspective, innovations have an effect on temporal dynamics. However, they also have a major effect on the territory. This spatial effect is due to the fact that an innovation stems from the combination of the technical invention with a community's organizational and economic capacity to develop it. Yet, this combination is a specific phenomenon. As Perroux (1955, in 1986) indicates, innovation does not appear everywhere or at the same time. It appears in specific places where it brings about changes in the methods of production and therefore of consumption, where it changes production standards and from where it is diffused.

Perroux puts the diffusion of innovation in the context of a process which brings into conflict production and consumption practices induced by innovation on the one hand with, on the other hand, a community's potential to adapt to them. But to adapt to innovation does not simply mean to imitate it, as suggested by Rostow (1960) in his study on the stages of economic growth. It also and especially refers to the voluntary actions taken jointly by entrepreneurs and organizations to appropriate the innovative process, develop it, extend it, and generate a recurrent dynamic capacity. This obviously implies various types of innovation (Perrin, 1985).

Thus, a question arises: How can a milieu adapt so as to create productive groups capable of taking advantage of the effect of innovations? To pose this problem means to turn the question around. Thus, we must examine how communities react to the diffusion of an innovation. Rather than considering what effect the innovation has, we must consider how to move over to the new production practices induced by an innovation, either by specializing in the types of production that have a revitalizing potential, or by putting forward social conditions that allow the community to innovate (Hillier, Moulaert & Nussbaumer, 2004; Fontan, Klein & Tremblay, 2005).

Based on evolutionary analysis, innovation is thus viewed as a social process that is linked with technologies or technical systems, as well as with the products market and the labour market (Le Bas, 1995). This process is therefore uncertain, although not entirely so. The firm acts as an interface between these elements, mediating and making choices within the context of this set of social facts of which it is part. According to this vision, the diffusion of new production practices induced by innovation occurs through changes in production standards – changes that are passed on from firm to firm, and thus from place to place, through their productive interrelations. This diffusion is carried out within the boundaries of the firms which contribute to the innovation-induced production and is then generalized across the industries which include combinations of firms and actors.

The systemic territorialized effect of innovation

The diffusion of change is accompanied by or confronted with social changes which are related to the social structure and the cultural characteristics of the different milieus. These changes have to do with the communities' ability to adapt to the technological change induced by the different types of innovation and to appropriate them, thus in turn generating a recurrent capacity to develop innovations and produce growth. The combination of social changes which include the organizational and social structure of a community as well as the capacity to get in step with the innovations diffused throughout the industries, are conditions for the emergence of production systems characterized by innovation in specific regions and milieus (Lundvall, 1988; Wolfe, 2002).

Several studies have addressed the relationships between innovation and territory in this type of place by using the notions of innovative milieus (Aydalot, 1986; Maillat, 1992), industrial district (Becattini, 1991; Piore & Sabel, 1984), technopole (Benko, 1991), and regional innovation system (Braczyk, Cooke & Heidenreich, 2003; Doloreux & Revilla Diez, 2007). In all cases, despite the different approaches, these notions have been used to designate the methods of arranging a community's technology, territory and organizations. The result is communities where production and society are interlinked by configuring territorial production systems. The co-ordination of the different phases of these systems and the control of the regularity of their functioning are not subject to pre-established rules and hierarchical mechanisms, but on the contrary are subjected to both the automatic play of the market and to a system of social sanctions imposed by the community. Territorial proximity allows the territorial system of firms to rely on economies of scale linked with the entire production process while not loosing their flexibility and adaptability to the vagaries of the market owing to the segmentation of this process.

The agglomeration effect of these territorial systems encourages the establishment of local forms of co-operation so as to collectively take charge of a series of individual production problems and thus ensure local governance. Therein lies the synergy induced by this type of system. This synergy is made possible by the fact that firms are part of comparable production processes and the goal of the established collective learning processes is to solve common difficulties. The implementation of these solutions means new infrastructures and is expressed through the will to strengthen the partnerships between the large enterprises, SMEs, institutions of higher learning (universities, research institutes), local authorities (municipalities, local organizations) and government institutions.

The analysis of the relationships between innovation and territory highlights the systemic effect created by the strengthened links between the economic, social, political and cultural actors sharing the same geographical space within a context of reticular interrelations constructed at the global level. The place is more than a localization, it is a system. There is a 'place effect' which directs the action of actors. This effect is economic, political, social, cultural and ideological. It is the effect of place which leads to the hierarchical structuring of local systems, the structuring of the local, as a result of the territorial arrangements of stages and actors of a globalized network (De Bresson & Amesse, 1991; Holbrook & Wolfe, 2002).

Renewal of the concept of innovation: toward social innovation

Recent work on the theme of 'Innovation and Society' complements the approach of evolutionary economists and authors who have drawn on their work. Thus, writings on social innovation seen as social experiences aiming at finding new solutions to unsolved social problems (Chambon, David & Deverey, 1982; Lévesque 2007), on technical innovation seen as the result of social practices and experiences (Flichy, 1995), on organizational innovation seen as a creative transgression of established rules (Alter, 2000), or those on social innovation seen as creative strategies and processes fostering inclusion and combating poverty in integrated areas (Moulaert & Nussbaumer, 2005; Nussbaumer & Moulaert, 2007) reflect the emergence of a new approach to innovation. Rather than explaining the links between innovation and economic growth (Amable, Barré & Boyer, 1997), this new approach seeks to understand the heterogeneous innovation processes that bring about civil-society-based social changes at the meso- social and micro-social levels (Fontan, Klein & Lévesque, 2003).

The renewal of the concept of innovation is also related to the rediscovery of the works by Polanyi (1944), who redefines the field of what constitutes economics. It should be recalled that Polanyi defines the economy as a dynamic set of social processes which are continuously being transformed and from where stem forms of integration based on reciprocity (symmetric logic), redistribution (centralizing logic) and exchange (market logic). Within this set of processes, innovation can be seen to be characterized by a dual movement of appropriation and localization. The appropriation movement is associated with the process of defining the social usage of the invention, and thus with its ownership and the standards relating to the generalization of its usage. This appropriation process is generally carried out through negotiation but also sometimes through imposition. The localization movement, on the other hand, corresponds to any physical change of place.

We associate this movement with territorialization, that is, the definition of the spatial framework of innovation, which includes embedding territories in a spatial hierarchy. A spatial hierarchy specific to the field targeted by innovation is established, since the social usage implies a different connection between social elements, that is, transferring material and immaterial objects. The territorialization movement in turn structures the methods of social reproduction by taking action on the existing flows, that is, by reinforcing, reducing, directing and redirecting them (Fontan, Klein & Tremblay, 2005). As was pointed out above, there are many links between innovation and territory, but these links take place in a context of the redefinition of social hierarchies and power relationships.

Social experimentation and power relationships

In the mid 1970s, the French journal *Revue Autrement* initiated an examination of the concept of innovation within the context of power relationships. This endeavor involved thinkers for whom social innovation refers to new social experiments, formal and informal. Innovation was mainly examined from the political angle by giving it a particular function, that is, as a tool for social change. This was how the notion of 'social innovation' was introduced into the examination of innovation. According to Chambon, David and Deverey (1982), this notion has the following three facets:

1. The first is explanatory in nature. Social innovation is not unwarranted but the product of a need, a desire, an aspiration, or a quest for solutions to a social problem. It is important to note that this response is constructed locally. For the authors concerned, the local level is the best place for the emergence of social innovation. It does not stem from new mechanisms or processes introduced by the large organizations or institutions, but from localized and localizable actions. In this sense, although a government policy cannot be considered as a social innovation, it can be treated as the appropriation by the State of an innovation proposed at the local level.

2. The second aspect is moral and political in nature. Innovation is politically oriented and aims to improve the quality of life. It appears in response to what is viewed as the incompetence of large social institutions which are seen as incapable of ensuring this quality. The political project is based more on 'doing things differently' than on the authoritarian and hierarchical model of large institutions. Innovation, viewed in this way, does not necessarily mark a break with the large institutions, which allows it to move up the institutional system and provoke changes within it. This is what Morin presented as 'the deviancy which becomes a trend' (Revue Autrement, 1976: 110).

3   The third aspect is economic in nature, that is, for innovations to last, they should be supported financially. The greater the financial needs, the greater the likelihood that the State has to finance the social experiment. Thus arises the issue of the difficult relationship between social innovation and the State.

To ensure recognition of the social usage of an innovative experiment, Chambon, David and Deverey's (1982) analysis of the tactics used by social innovators describes a strategy of 'bypassing', that is, of getting around obstacles so as to connect the entrepreneur, in Schumpeter's sense, to the policy makers. This means that the social innovator will bypass any obstacle between himself and the place of power. The individual or group innovator thus seeks to gather all the means that can be used to influence any decision maker. The purpose of his action is to establish a relationship of trust with a decision maker in order to reduce any areas of discomfort and uncertainty which prevent his proposals or requests from being recognized by policy makers.

Thus, the social entrepreneur sets out to tame social networks of influence. In this respect, what is extremely important for us is not so much the particular type of strategy used by an actor but the significance of this strategy, namely the idea of mobilizing resources to get round the obstacles so that a 'decision' that can modify the framework of action in society (a new law, new standards) can emerge. The construction of social usage or the crystallization of social innovation is fuelled with solutions formulated to find an effective response to the conflict that pits the social entrepreneur against a hostile milieu. Thus, the challenge is to diffuse and achieve recognition of the legitimacy of a 'concept' or a 'social project', for example, the insertion firms in the early 1980s, fair trade in the early 1990s, and the altermondialist demands since the mid 1990s.

A parallel can be established here with the social resistance mentioned by Veblen. To overcome resistance, the social entrepreneur uses a network that is not constructed randomly but is directly linked to the decision-making chains that are favorable to him. This network is constructed not because the targeted actor - for example, the elected official who has become a minister - is socially inclined toward novelty but because there is political capital to be gained in this recognition. The politician and the innovator play the political capital card, seeking to reinforce it through strategic alliances. The mediation between the innovator and the lawmaker is not fuelled with generosity but with convergent interests and compromises.

Construction of social innovation networks

In the tradition of Mead's interactionalist perspective of sociology (1935), the works by Lazarsfeld, Berelson and Gaudet (1944) and by Katz and Lazarsfeld (1955), to mention only these scholars, highlight the fact that information exchange does not occur without social screening. Information is exchanged between a transmitter and receiver of a message based on a prior recognition of the usefulness of the information by an opinion leader, an influential and significant person for the message receiver. The communication circuit includes a share of doubt, mistrust, fear of novelty or a share of incommunicable information. The opinion leader is then perceived as a positive or negative mediator who either makes it possible to clear up or to confirm doubt, or even to interpret the information in such a way that the message either can or cannot get through.

The observed two-step-flow of communication implies that the construction of the social usage of an invention will benefit greatly from going through the intermediary of opinion leaders. The social entrepreneur who wishes to see his invention diffused establishes a relationship with the opinion leaders in question. This last point introduces the contribution of Latour (1988) and Callon (1989) through their research on the close association between innovation and reticulation. According to Callon, innovation is not the result of a clever instinct stemming from the brain of a single person. On the contrary, technical or scientific innovation is a process in which a great number of actors participate, each collaborating in their own way in the production of what, afterwards, seems to be a unique product.

Innovation is thus developed through the transformation of instinct. It pertains to process and not to an established fact. It takes shape with the contributions of each of the actors involved in the innovative process. These contributions are not made without conflict. There are negotiations between more or less convergent and sometimes divergent viewpoints, thus innovation is developed in the negotiation of an agreement or an understanding. As stated by Callon, technical innovation is information that is created gradually as negotiations are conducted between the actors attached to networks within hierarchical innovation systems.

Conclusion: toward a path building perspective

To study innovation is to explain a process with dimensions that become determining factors and eclipse others, depending on the specific innovation studied. Though certainly technical and economic, the innovation process is just as social as it is political and obviously has a cultural impact. To study an innovation is to shed light on the social, technical, economic, political and cultural characteristics that are put forward by individual and collective actors. This set of factors is significant in that it occurs in a specific place and time. Therefore, it is important to take into consideration both the territory and the temporal dimension. We hypothesize that innovation is conditioned by a social context. Therefore, for us, the dynamic of social innovation brings into play actors who hold positions within a set of institutional arrangements in territorial settings. Since these groups, as demonstrated by Hollingsworth and Boyer (1996), are structured on the basis of different but complementary regulatory modes of social systems, social innovation operates on the basis of these regulatory levels (Klein & Harrisson, 2007). Therefore, reference can be made to the existence of a set of social innovation systems that belong to geographical spaces ranging from the global space to the local space, transiting through the intermediary spaces (continental, national and regional). We are thus faced with a spatialized map linking a combination of innovation systems, some of which are moreover cross-border. Thus, innovation cannot escape from the institutional determinism and the social system which embeds it, which makes it 'path dependent'. However, institutional arrangements can be changed and innovation paths steered in new directions. Our vision of innovation emphasizes the social construction of innovation and the processes and interrelations which come into play at all levels, facing the past paths and building new paths, that means new arrangements of social actors and institutions, creating new milieus by the effect of socially innovating actions.

References

Alter, N., 2000, L'innovation ordinaire, Presses universitaires de France, Paris.
Amable B., R. Barré & R. Boyer, 1997, Les systèmes d'innovation à l'ère de la globalisation, Economica, Paris.
Aydalot, Ph., 1986, L'aptitude des milieux locaux à promouvoir l'innovation; In: Federwish, J. & H. Zoller (eds), Technologies nouvelles et ruptures régionales, Economica, Paris, pp. 41-58.

Becattini, G., 1991, Italian Districts: Problems and Perspectives, *International Studies of Management & Organization*, Vol. 21, and N ° 1, pp. 83–90.

Benko, G., 1991, *La géographie des technopôles*, Masson, Paris.

Benko, G. & A. Lipietz (eds), 2000, *La richesse des régions*, Presses universitaires de France, Paris.

Braczyk, H.J., P. Cooke & M. Heidenreich (eds), 2003, *Regional Innovation Systems*, Routledge, London.

Braudel, F., 1985, *La dynamique du capitalisme*, Champs Flammarion, Paris.

Callon, M., 1989, *La science et ses réseaux*, La Découverte, Paris.

Chambon, J.L., A. David & J.M. Deverey, 1982, *Les innovations sociales*, PUF, Paris.

Corbo, C., 1973, *Les théories épistémologiques et sociales de T.B.Veblen (1857-1929): clefs pour une lecture de Veblen*, PhD Thesis, Université de Montréal.

De Bresson, C. & F. Amesse, 1991, Networks of innovators, *Research Policy*, Vol. 20, pp. 363-379.

Doloreux, D. & J. Revilla Diez (eds), 2007, Clusters and regional innovation systems. Special Issue of *Int. J. Entrepreneurship and Innovation Management*, Inderscience Enterprises, Vol. 7, N° 2/3/4/5.

Dosi, G., 1988, The Nature of the Innovative Process; In: Dosi, G.C., N. Freeman, G. Silverberg, & L. Soete (eds), *Technical Change and Economic Theory*, Pinter, New York, pp. 221-238.

Flichy, P., 1995, *L'innovation technique*, Éditions La Découverte, Paris.

Fontan, J.-.M., J.-L. Klein & B. Lévesque, 2003, *Reconversion économique et développement territorial: le rôle de la société civile*, Qc. Presses de l'Université du Québec, Québec.

Fontan, J.-M., J.-L. Klein & D.-G. Tremblay, 2005, *Innovation socioterritoriale et reconversion économique. Le cas de Montréal*. L'Harmattan, Paris, Collection Géographies en liberté.

Freeman, C., J. Clark & L. Soete, 1982, *Unemployment & Technical Innovation: A Study of Long Waves & Economic Development*, Pinter, London.

Gertler, M.S. & D.A. Wolfe, 2002, *Innovation and Social Learning*, Palgrave, London.

Hillier, J., F. Moulaert & J. Nussbaumer, 2004, Trois essais sur le rôle de l'innovation sociale dans le développement territorial, *Géographie, Économie, Société*, Vol. 6, N° 2, pp.129-152.

Holbrook, J.A. & D.A. Wolfe (eds), 2002, *Knowledge, Clusters and Regional Innovation*, McGill-Queen's University Press, Montréal and Kingston.

Hollingsworth, J.R. & R. Boyer, 1996, *Contemporary Capitalism, the Embeddedness of Institutions*, Cambridge University Press, Cambridge.

Katz, E. & P.F. Lazarsfeld (eds), 1955, *Personal Influence: The Part Played by People in the Flow of Mass Communications*, Free Press, Glencoe, Ill.

Klein, J.-L. & D. Harrisson (eds), 2007, *L'innovation sociale*, Presses de l'Université du Québec, Québec.

Latour, B., 1988, *La vie en laboratoire*, Paris, La découverte.

Lazarsfeld, P.F., B. Berelson & H. Gaudet, 1944, *The People's Choice*, Duell, Sloan & Pearce, New York.

Le Bas, C., 1995, *Économie de l'innovation*, Presses universitaires de France, Paris.

Lévesque, B., 2007, L'innovation dans le développement économique et le développement social; In Klein, J.-L. & D. Harrisson (eds), *L'innovation sociale*, Presses de l'Université du Québec, Quebec, pp. 43-70.

Lévesque, B., G.L. Bourque & E. Forgues, 2001, *La nouvelle sociologie économique*, Desclée de Brouwer, Paris.

Lundvall, B.A., 1988, Innovation as an interactive process; from user-producer interaction to the national system of innovation; In: Dosi, G., C. Freeman, R. Nelson, G. Silverberg & L. Soete (eds), *Technical Change and Economic Theory*, Pinter, New York, pp. 349-369.

Maillat, D., 1992, Milieux et dynamique territoriale de l'innovation, *Canadian Journal of Regional Science*, Vol XV, N° 2, pp. 199-218.

Marty, A.G., 1955, *Analyse critique de l'oeuvre de Joseph Schumpeter*, Ed. Montana, Bruxelles.

Mead, M.,1935, *Sex and Temperament in Three Primitive Societies*, Morrow, New York.

Moulaert, F. & J. Nussbaumer, 2005, Defining the Social Economy and Its Governance at the Neighbourhood Level: A Methodological Refelction, *Urban Studies*, Vol 42, N° 11, pp. 2071-2088.

Nussbaumer, J. & F. Moulaert, 2007, L'innovation sociale au coeur des débats publics et scientifiques; In Klein, J.-L. & D. Harrisson (eds), *L'innovation sociale*, Presses de l'Université du Québec, Quebec, pp. 71-88.

Perrin, J.C., 1985, Redéploiement industriel et aménagement du territoire: le cas français; In: Boisvert, M. & P. Hamel (eds), *Redéploiement industriel et planification régionale*, Faculté de l'aménagement, Université de Montréal, Montréal, pp. 69-92.

Perroux, F., (1955) 1986, Note sur la notion de pôle de croissance; In: Savoie, D. & A. Raynauld, 1986, *Essais sur le développement régional*, Presses de l'Université de Montréal, Montréal, pp. 27-37.

Piore, M. & C.F. Sabel, 1984, *The Second Industrial Divide*, Basic Books, New York.

Polanyi, K., 1944, *The Great Transformation*, Holt Rinehart, New York.

Revue Autrement, 1976, Vol. 5, Special issue on social innovation.

Rostow W., 1960, *Les étapes de la croissance économique*, Le Seuil, Paris.

Schumpeter, J. A., 1935, *Théorie de l'évolution économique*, Dalloz, Paris.

Tarde, G., 1890, *Les lois de l'imitation*, Félix Alcan, Paris.

Tremblay, D.-G., 1989, *La dynamique économique des processus d'innovation*, PhD Thesis in economics, Université de Paris 1.

Tremblay, D.-G., 1995, La multidimensionnalité du phénomène de l'innovation: une réalité abordée par les économistes institutionnalistes; In: *La recherche sur l'innovation; une boîte de Pandore?*, Cahiers de l'Acfas, N°. 83, pp. 79-113.

Tremblay, D.-G., C. Chevrier & S. Rousseau, 2004, The Montreal Multimedia cluster: District, Cluster or Localized system of production?; In: Wolfe, D.A. & M. Lucas (eds), 2004, *Clusters in a Cold Climate: Innovation Dynamics in a Diverse Economy*, McGill-Queen's University Press and School of Policy Studies, Montreal and Kingston, pp 165-194.

Tremblay, D.-G., J.-M. Fontan, J.-L. Klein & D. Bordeleau, 2002, The Development of the Relational Firm : the Case of the Multimedia City in Montréal; In: Holbrook, A. & D. Wolfe (eds), 2002, *Knowledge, Clusters and Regional Innovation: Economic Development in Canada*, Mc Gill Queens Univ. Press, Toronto-Montréal, pp. 161-185.

Veblen, T., 1899, *The Theory of the Leisure Class: An Economic Study of Institutions*, The Macmillan Company, New York.

Vernon, R., 1974, *Les conséquences économiques et politiques des entreprises multinationales*, Robert Laffont, Paris.

Wolfe, D.A., 2002, Social Capital and Clusters Development in Learning Regions; In: Holbrook, A. & A. D. Wolfe (eds), Knowledge, Clusters and Regional Innovation, McGill-Queens University Press, Toronto-Montreal, pp. 11-38.

Note

1 This is an excerpt of Business Cycles (pp. 243-244) taken up again in Marty (1955: 92) and quoted in Tremblay (1989).

2   Social Innovation and Urban Regeneration from the Perspective of an Innovative Milieu Analysis

Andrée Matteaccioli

Introduction

In the context of the recession in the 1970s and 80s, which was related to the shift in spatial dynamics, Aydalot (Matteaccioli, 2004) put forth the hypothesis that territory, as both the context of and an actor in its own development, can generate a creative dynamic within itself and that there is "a driving force behind the territory that gives rise to the innovative process" (because) "the company is not an isolated agent but, rather, is part of the 'milieu' (environment) that makes it work. The past history of territories, their collective behaviors and the consensus that structures them are all major components of innovation" (Aydalot, 1986:10). Aydalot introduced the concept of the 'innovative milieu' which GREMI[1] defines as "a territorialized whole in which interactions between economic agents develop through the learning processes stemming from multilateral transactions which generate externalities that are specific to innovation, and through the convergence of such learning processes towards increasingly effective forms of joint resource management" (Maillat, Quevit & Senn, 1993:6). Innovation is no longer solely attributable to companies, as the official economy had determined it to be since Schumpeter. Indeed, "the innovative company does not just appear from nowhere", as wrote Aydalot. It needs a dynamic relational environment within the territory where it is located which, through its organizational mode and method of operation, generates externalities that are specific to innovation.

The urban area and the innovative 'milieu' are not one and the same: "While the innovative milieu and the city share some common elements, such as proximity and the capacity to be connected to the outside world and to the system of governance, cities are much more complex systems than non-urban innovative 'milieus' (…), due to their diversified economic activity, a more restricted physical environment, greater redundancy in relations and the tendency towards metropolitisation. All of these factors differentiate the city from the innovative milieu" (Camagni, 2000).

However, under the aegis of GREMI, the interaction between urban dynamics and the dynamics of innovative milieus has been studied by comparing innovative milieus which have been integrated into metropoli, such as those specializing in high fashion/creative design and finance in Paris (Matteaccioli & Tabariés, 2000) or those specializing in communication and fashion in Milan (Camagni, Galbiati & Pompili, 2000), and by comparing the interactions between innovative milieus and various urban contexts in, for example, three Swiss cities (Corolleur, Boulianne & Crevoisier, 2000) or two Italian cities (Bramanti, Senn & Tamisari, 2000) and, again, by examining the impact that the transformation of urban space has had on the production system, for example in Ghent (Belgium) (Drewe, Allaert & de Klerck, 2000), in Evora (Ferrao, 2000) or in the cities of the Rhône-Alpes region (Rousier, 2000). These studies have shown that the revival of cities in the West has been based on the discovery of new forms of interaction between urban actors, public/private partnerships, participatory decision-making, and the implementation of new co-operative instruments, all of which enable the development of a shared vision for the future of the local community.

This has led to the emergence of a conceptual framework in which the city is understood as a place of interaction having both a material component (physical structures) and a social component, as accounted for in the definition of the city as "a social and material unit: a social unit made up of a set of interrelated social functions which, through the convergence of products and information, play a major role in material and non-material exchanges; a material unit, on the other hand, characterized by a certain density as well as a continuity in physical structures in which can be observed a series of opposing constituents (city-center, urban periphery, private/public spaces, etc.)" (Rémy & Voyé, 1992:8).

This relational approach to the city is distinct from the traditional notion in which the city was defined by the concept of an urban area. The city is much more than a compact geographical space containing 'stocks of resources' generated by specific urban functions. It is, rather, the space in which various urban functions are connected. This fundamentally relational approach to the city reveals a strong convergence between the urban area and the innovative milieu and allows us to shift, along with Camagni, adapting his earlier statement, toward a view in which the city, "whose destiny is to be a trans historical archetype and an effective way of organizing socio-economic interaction, can be interpreted as a particular form of innovative milieu, in an urban context, represented by its vast deployment of transversal externalities throughout local activities and local heritage development, with a synergetic dynamic element represented by powerful collective learning processes and the construction of a local identity" (Camagni, 2004).

This synergetic dynamic, opening up new horizons for a dynamic of creation, characterizes the innovative approach to both local innovative 'milieus', and innovative urban systems involved in social innovation experiments aimed at urban regeneration. However, each of these approaches has its own specific characteristics. Innovative milieus involve a dynamic of resource creation which is carried out through a truly dynamic territorial organization which can be considered as the appropriate context for creativity (technological, organizational and even that relating to heritage promotion[2]) on the part of the economic actors who, in interaction with one another, make up this milieu. Cities, and metropoli in particular, being 'immense living milieus' forced to continuously adapt to a global reality that is constantly changing, involve a dynamic in which very diverse local initiatives are created, grouped together under the generic term 'social innovation', which Cloutier defines as: "an intervention initiated by social actors to respond to an aspiration, meet a need, suggest a solution, benefit from an opportunity or propose new cultural trends. These innovations, when combined, can, over the long-term, attain a level of social effectiveness that goes beyond the scope of the initial project (companies, associations, etc.) and represent a challenge to the established social equilibrium. They thus become a source of social transformation and can contribute to the emergence of new models of development" (Cloutier, 2003). Based on these themes of 'social innovation and transformation', researchers at CRISIS[3] are studying social innovation from the standpoint of three areas of focus. One of these, involving 'social innovation centered on territory'[4] concerns the "role of social actors and their innovative practices in contemporary territory-based reconstruction projects; the emergence of social networks and their ties to new forms of territoriality; the relationships between companies, social actors and local political bodies; and local identities and their ties to economic and social development and modes of territorial governance" (Cloutier, 2003).

Faced with the problems caused by the offshoring of existing activities, such as massive unemployment, huge disparities between well-to-do neighborhoods and disadvantaged ones, the destruction of traditional living environments, and crime, which are affecting large formerly industrial cities and in particular those districts that are out of step with new technologically-oriented production modes in the midst of tertiarization within a globalized economy, new forms of collective action are emerging, which could become an organized social movement capable of putting an end to the process of marginalization and/or segmentation and which could, through 'the configuration of social arrangements', contribute to urban regeneration.

Given that a creative and dynamic territorial organization exists in both cases, the first oriented toward renewed social action, the second toward technological innovation or the development of heritage-related resources, why not approach social innovation from the standpoint of urban regeneration based on the 'innovative milieu'? This approach would allow us to highlight their points of convergence and, possibly, bring forth an analysis based on socially innovative milieus. It would also allow us to specify to what extent the type of governance found in innovative milieus enables urban functions to produce externalities which are favorable to social innovation and vice versa. Finally, it would allow us to examine the relevance and limitations of social innovation, in the face of urban problems, from the perspective of an innovative milieu approach. These three points will be examined below.

Points of convergence between urban community-based organizations and the innovative milieu and their contribution to the analysis of negotiated processes

Social innovation responds to a need to restore social balance within large cities where glaring disparities continue to increase between well-to-do neighborhoods and disadvantaged ones in terms of living, working and employment conditions in the context of intensified global competition. This need is so pressing that these internal problems are penalizing the competitiveness of these cities. In some districts that have suffered from de-industrialization, a fierce desire to catch up has given rise to action and experiments, advocated by actors from civil society, which reflect a major change in the types of action led by social movements. In order to respond to the increasing mobility of capital, industrial off shoring and a spatial re-orientation of investment which has led to unemployment, local actors in these deprived districts are engaging in collective action which is different from the traditional claim-based action that characterized the workers' movements and that, with a view to redistributing wealth, focused on wage increases and a reduction in working hours. These actors from civil society are inventing new modes of action that reconcile local economic development with the needs of the population in these districts in terms of jobs and the working and living environment. Achieving this dual goal can lead these actors to engage in community action and development (Klein & Fontan, 2003) which respect both local entrepreneurs and the local population, and which are based on the principle of compromise and agreement. This gives rise to the institutionalization of negotiation as a new mode of action within community-based organizations, and to emphasizing what unites the parties, while qualifying what divides them.

This involves a change in the mode of social organization of cities, which is not far-removed from the mode of organization of the innovative milieu. The latter is characterized by three emerging features (Matteaccioli, 2004). The first is organizational in nature (innovation networks), the second is procedural and learning-oriented (the ability to improve knowledge and know-how 'along the way' and the third is territorial (actors identifying with their territories). It may be hypothesized that the concept of the innovative milieu is relevant for the study of, and perhaps for enriching the concept of social innovation in the context of the regeneration of an urban territorial system.

Partnership-based organizations within community-based urban structures are like innovative milieus, but with different aims

The recourse to the partnership-based type of organization that characterizes innovative milieus dates from the 1970s and 80s, when companies were confronted with the challenge of industrial decline and/or a change in the status of innovation. The rapid obsolescence of innovation (the traditional 30-year life-cycle having dropped to a maximum of three years), associated with the speed of technological progress and therefore with the cost of research in the face of the rising force of global competition, obliged companies, including the largest among them, to end their practice of working individually, organizing themselves instead into networks. Innovative milieus are characterized by the emergence of a partnership-based mode of organization among the actors of innovation, who share the common goal of advancing their scientific and technical knowledge and know-how in order to create advanced technologies which will allow them to gain a competitive edge in the market. Innovation networks are composed of innovative companies and actors involved in training and research who, together, share the goal of creating a product. Added to this are the territorial communities that wish to set such a project in motion or support it. These networks are open to the extraterritorial world, to the extent that the scientific and technical community is mainly international, but the more sophisticated the project and the more it involves specific knowledge that exists only in the virtual realm and calls on non-coded knowledge, the greater the extent to which co-operation between these actors requires geographical and cultural proximity. The ability of these networks to develop scientific, individual and social relationships within the territory fosters the development of effective co-operation. These innovation networks do not exclude traditional market relations, but their ties are essentially back-of-the-market relations which bring together all the synergy-creating forms of contact such as direct relationships between companies and research centers, scientific and technical collaborations, highly sophisticated scientific material put at the disposal of SMEs through public research centers, and also the incubation phenomenon that develops on account of the professional experience and the know-how contained in the technical culture of the region.

Social actors, on the other hand, have been confronted with the challenge of off shoring which has made strikes less and less effective. A major change has therefore taken place in their behavior. Klein and Fontan (2003) have demonstrated that, as incubators of social innovation, the Community Economic Development Corporations (CEDCs) in Quebec and more specifically in Montreal (Canada), have had a structuring effect on the economy and the city by strengthening the capacity for development and structural adaptation in formerly industrialized districts through the mobilization of social actors, no longer on the basis of ideological or political considerations, but by implementing collective restructuring actions. These social actors aim to defend the urban territory as a living and working milieu, through economic development that creates companies and jobs, and no longer by clinging to plants that date from the first wave of industrialization. Aware of the transformations brought about by globalization, of which the main requirement is competitiveness (flexibility and mobility), they have worked to create companies and jobs that are adapted to the new economy, through the construction of social innovation networks which support economic development and technology creation in order to gain a competitive edge, through the "creation of a space in which an increase in societal value can be achieved" (Fontan, Klein & Tremblay, 2005:20). This is what these authors call 'social-territorial innovation'.

In order for co-operation to develop between these actors with diverging interests (associations representing the community, companies and public institutions), and in order for them to successfully achieve their goal, which constitutes a collective asset, it is necessary to construct social innovative networks. These are not constructed randomly, but rather are directly tied to the decision-making networks that will work in their favour. When communication within these networks involves a measure of doubt, mistrust and fear of anything new, or again, a measure of incommunicability as regards information, this leads the actors within these networks to combine traditional confrontational strategies with the new registers of action involving compromise and agreement.

Emergence of a logic of learning within social innovation networks, geared toward conflict resolution and participation in strategic decision-making

The actors involved in innovative milieus adopt a partnership-based organizational approach which, "by adapting know-how" (Perrin, 1991:346), allows for the advancement of knowledge and know-how, because these actors no longer proceed by exchanging ready-made, turnkey knowledge in the market, but rather work together toward a common goal (an innovative project) outside of the market. They proceed by trial and error, and through a collaborative process of research and experimentation. This is a procedural approach which becomes concrete 'along the way' through a process of 'interactive learning' based on scientific and technical co-operation, or a process of 'learning by learning' through which skills are improved. The individuals involved are motivated by a constant desire to learn and they look for all kinds of situations through which to increase their knowledge, 'by doing, by using, by searching'. As opposed to a Fordist mode of production, in which only established knowledge and know-how were required for work, these actors participate in experiments and collectively carry out initiatives which lead them into a logic of advancing knowledge.

The initial and determining goal of co-operation, which is a specific characteristic of social innovation networks, is the acquisition of knowledge and know-how, so as to create a culture of negotiation "which allows for conflict resolution and even forces synergy to arise between the actors" (Camagni, 2004), by making them participate in strategic decision-making, and defining and collectively implementing development projects. It is through negotiation, dialogue and participation in collective decision-making that their 'negotiating know-how', their 'consultation know-how' and their 'participation know-how' develop. It could be said that social innovation itself consists in a learning process. The actors involved in social innovation work to improve their knowledge and know-how, insofar as the new cognitive logic prevails. This is why it is in their interest to turn toward learning modes that are specific to innovative milieus, and which consist in working out rules and agreements, for example, learning to negotiate so as to initiate a co-operative effort and to bring it to a successful completion; in 'institutional learning' which aims to eliminate obsolete institutions, transform inadequate ones and create new ones to stimulate innovation; and in 'organizational learning' which allows the actors in organizations to better co-ordinate their actions. Companies among themselves and/or in relation to other actors involved in social innovation must learn to step beyond the usual barriers of confrontation and discuss common institutional problems, learn from one another and seek collective solutions. Through interactive learning, as in innovative milieus, knowledge and know-how are created collectively which none of the participants had individually at the outset, before embarking on this co-operative process. These learning processes are all the more effective in that they foster the development of cumulative learning processes within the milieu.

Within innovative milieus, learning processes essentially aim at scientific and technological progress, and only involve negotiation when the partners of the technological innovation networks come from different scientific and professional cultures or have different ideas on the way in which to conduct an innovative scientific and technical process or, again, concerning how to divide up the profits of the innovation. In the community structures that result from the construction of social innovation networks, learning how to resolve conflicts and tensions that arise between socio-economic actors takes on a predominant role, given that these actors, from the very outset, have diverging interests.

Emergence of a territorial logic in carrying out negotiated or partnership-based processes

Territory plays a role as a "factor of collective identity in the success of collective action", [...in particular in the case of] "the structuring of an alternative path of redeployment [which] is the result of processes in which local initiatives contribute to the configuration of social arrangements that make collective entrepreneurship possible, constructing a symbolic identity and defining an agenda that takes collective interests into account" (Klein & Fontan, 2003:12). These authors emphasize in particular the role of territory in negotiation procedures, pointing to the specificity of these, given that the culture of confrontation persists to a significant extent even within partnership-based governance. While they speak of 'social arrangements' which allow for the construction of a symbolic identity and of a context of associativity, it is difficult to see how a process of self-identification and self-contextualization involving local partners vis-à-vis their territory operate in negotiated processes. It appears that, in this respect, the contribution of GREMI is significant (Matteaccioli, 2004).

Early on, Aydalot (1986) noted the importance of the innovative milieu (rather than simply of proximity itself) as an 'incubator of innovation', which allows techno-productive creation to develop in a continuous and cumulative fashion. Planque (1991) introduced the notion of 'agreement' in the territorial economy, linking together members of the local economic 'milieu' and leading to relations of 'trust' which are necessary for the development of long-term multi functional innovative co-operation. Perrin (1997), after analyzing the emergence of a logic of territorialization by referring to the notion of 'territorial contextuality'[5], created the term 'territory/identity' and studied how the processes of self-identification and self-contextualization involving actors vis-à-vis their territory intervene in the way that negotiated processes are carried out, in particular between the partners of an innovation network. The notion of contextuality (Perrin, 1995) at the territorial level allows for an analysis of how the innovative milieu brings in components of an emotional nature and those relating to self-identification that contribute to the emergence of partnership-based behaviors and learning behaviors that become determining factors from a procedural perspective with respect to the creativity of the territorial system, when the goal is technological innovation, the development of heritage-related resources or even social innovation.

According to Perrin, it is not the organization (and therefore the network) which ensures solidarity among the actors, but rather, first and foremost, trust: trust both in the skills of future partners and that they will play fair in transactions or negotiations. "It is from the moment that trust becomes stronger than mistrust that the reflex of co-operation can come into play" (Perrin, 1997; Matteaccioli, 1999). This was the case in the Swiss Jura region (Maillat, Crevoisier & Lecoq, 1993), where the milieu in which the people who lived and worked knew each other well, either directly or by reputation, made it easy to identify potential partners that could be trusted, based on pre-existing interpersonal relationships. Quite the reverse was true in Barcelona (Sole-Parellada & Barcelo-Roca, 1993) and in the Avignon-Marseille-Nice region (Planque, 1993), where local partnership-based networks had trouble forming, due precisely to a lack of trust between local actors who, in the case of Barcelona, even preferred to associate with foreign actors rather than with fellow Catalonians.

However, emotionality is characterized by its fickleness. If a conflict erupts between two or more partners during the course of a negotiated process, the risk of reversal is a threat to the smooth progress of the negotiations. "It is up to the protagonists who oppose one another to decide whether or not they should persevere in the joint action despite the clashes that this process gives rise to" (Perrin, 1997). The force which leads them to reach an agreement is collective self-identification vis-à-vis their territory, which brings the local actors, who are stakeholders in the negotiations, to move closer together in spite of different social and professional cultures and to find grounds for agreement in order to come up with a strategy for long-term technological creation or a sustainable economic development plan, or else to deal with the question of dividing up the profits of their co-operation. It is the self-identification of the various actors vis-à-vis the territory which allows their points of view to come together, despite the distinctiveness of their ideas and the ambivalence of individual and conjunctural interests. This self-identification is based on their sense of belonging to the same representational space and to the same cultural and techno-productive whole, and on the fact that the partners refer to the same system of shared values which are specific to the milieu and have the collective will to create for themselves and the rest of the world an image that includes high-standard know-how and amiable social relations. Conflicts and crises can thus be overcome through a process of collective identification which appears to have a smoothing effect on tensions.

Perrin also points out that this rise in awareness can be an elusive phenomenon. Sharing the same culture within the territorial community is not always enough to create cohesion within it. A good system of governance based on partnership must aim to strengthen self-identification through what he has called self-contextualization, that is, the creation of spaces for intercommunication which act as interface structures between the actors involved, within which these actors learn to reconcile their different points of view based on the creation of a common destiny among the various partners. This has been the case in the *Pôle de l'Optique* (optics center) situated in the *Cité Scientifique* in the southern part of the Ile-de-France region which, over a twenty-year period, has succeeded in forming a veritable 'micro innovative milieu', strengthened by the creation of 'Optics Valley', an association which is in the process of constructing a truly territorial identity through the development of an awareness, on the part of all the actors involved, of their membership in this *Pôle* as a territorialized socio-economic configuration, deeply-rooted in its territory and capable of taking control of its own future. The creation of Optics Valley, has allowed the *Pôle de l'Optique* to benefit from a space for interconnection which enables the actors to get to become acquainted with one another. Designed as "a means of increasing the visibility of the *Pôle de l'Optique* with regard to the outside world, it has also been able to help construct the *Pôle*'s identity for all the actors who participate in it, creating a common destiny among the various partners which should increasingly be based on shared values and common ideas, in both professional and social terms" (Decoster, Matteaccioli & Tabariés, 2004).

The construction of spaces for self-contextualization within which actors learn not only to become better-acquainted with the potential and needs of one another in order to arrive at a consensus on strategic choices and decision-making, but also in order to foster the development of co-operative and learning-oriented behaviors and to generate a dynamic of creation, is very important. This is all the more true given that adopting a strategy aimed at attracting exogenous companies carries the risk, past a certain threshold, of diminishing the initial sense of identity.

Highlighting the points of convergence between the modes of organization of innovative milieus and social innovation networks leads to extending the analysis to include a look at how the type of governance found in innovative milieu can allow the various urban functions carried out by the city to take social innovations into account and contribute to urban regeneration, and vice versa.

To what extent does the type of governance found in innovative milieus associated with social innovation allow for urban functions to produce externalities which are favorable to urban regeneration?

Camagni points out that, increasingly, the type of governance found in innovative milieus refers to urban governance which is based on the mobilization of numerous initiatives: "The revival of cities that has been observed in the West over the last decade has been based on the discovery of new forms of interaction between urban actors, public/private partnerships, the participation of citizens in decision-making, and the implementation of new co-operative instruments, all of which enable the development of a shared vision for the future of the local community" (Camagni, 2000).

Through its externalities, the city carries out functions which are favorable to an innovative approach to the innovative milieu: it plays a supportive role for economic activity geared toward the potential development of technological innovations and provides services to companies; it connects the local to the global by setting up information, communication and trade networks linking the urban space to the international space; it contributes to enhancing the image of the urban space through the collective representations of the various actors, thus fostering, through a rise in awareness of their collective experience, the emergence of processes which generate the creation of ideas and the transformation of the behaviors and cultures that motivate them; and lastly, it organizes the framework within which the citizens of the urban space live and within which its economic environment develops. The challenge is to understand how these urban functions foster a more extensive structuring of the social realm through the modes of governance brought into play.

Governance centred on the technopolitan structuring of the city: a 'model' in which social innovation is integrated into a research process and involves quality relationships between the various actors

In the context of heightened competitiveness in the global production system and of evolving technologies, it is in the interest of the social-economic partners of districts that are undergoing industrial redeployment to agree on a strategy which, while being focused on the creation of companies and jobs, gives precedence, as much as possible, to the areas of excellence in which the local production system should specialize or diversify, in order to gain a competitive edge.

A public/private mode of governance, such as that which forms in urban innovative milieus, fosters the implementation of a technopolitan agreement based on networks of co-operation through which institutional learning processes develop that are implemented through working out rules and agreements, such as, for example, a code of conduct for the various participants in the partnership-based network, with the aim of discouraging opportunistic behaviors. Working out rules and agreements and learning to negotiate are examples of social innovation which are part of and contribute directly to the type of governance found in innovative milieus. The local/urban system is regulated through the direct control that the actors exert on one another. The role of the public actor is reduced, but, nevertheless, does not disappear altogether. Relinquishing all forms of state control, it acts as an initiator and is one partner among others. However, depending on the local milieu, the importance given to social initiatives varies, as is seen through the following two examples.

In Charleroi (Belgium) (Quevit & Van Doren, 2000), the public actor developed voluntaristic policies intended to reach sufficient numbers of players in the technological and economic fields to position companies and research centers in co-operation-based partnerships at the European level, so as to involve the local industrial infrastructure in the globalization of the economy in a positive way. Social innovation, for the public actor that takes up such an initiative, involves encouraging partnership-based behaviors geared toward training so as to develop the supply of a highly-qualified, university-educated labour force in the field of science and technology, encouraging co-operation between universities, higher educational institutions and companies, helping teachers keep their knowledge of advanced technology up-to-date, and developing the supply of a local professional qualification. In this partnership-based and collective mode of governance, the public actor acts as the co-ordinator of territorial development rather than as the guardian or director. It was this process of bringing institutions or organizations up to date which constituted, in this case, real behavioral social innovation.

In Grenoble (France), social innovation has been more widely distributed across the whole of society. It has consisted in the emergence of a specific social culture. In the 1960s, the urban environment was able to develop a culture which was conducive to the propagation and renewal of the innovative spirit based on detectors of innovation and the creation of a 'founding' organization with the task of proposing a valid outlook for a desirable future for local activity in the eyes of the public concerned" (De Bernardy & Loinger, 1997). Created by key local development actors, this quasi-institution worked to earn the trust of people involved in new fields, by creating opportunities to meet with them. Moreover, Grenoble was able to produce research work which was converted into a wealth of local productivity, thanks to individuals and networks that came in part from the region and in part, as of the end of the 19th century, from outside the region, and that co-ordinated their efforts within the city. This example demonstrates the importance of a system of governance in which the innovative milieu and the urban environment are entwined to create a more complex system than the innovative milieu alone, in particular on a social level. While urban planners generally favour communities of researchers/engineers and their potential synergies, here, it is the social and cultural practices which have developed within the city that are considered to be the genesis of new practices and that, when combined with scientific and technical capabilities, have allowed for an increase in the local capacity for innovation. There is, in the capacity of this mode of governance to mobilize social and cultural practices, a social innovation which is complementary to technological innovation and which most certainly contributed to the vitality of the production system, which is highly influenced by research. This model of mobilizing social and cultural practices in the city has, in a way, created a socio-economic milieu that is conducive to propagation and which, in turn, has generated externalities which are specific to innovation. In this milieu, as a territorialized whole, interactions between economic and local agents have developed through the lessons they have drawn/learning processes that have stemmed from multilateral transactions. This has undeniably fostered the technopolitan structuring of the city, to the extent that today, Grenoble is one of the most competitive European hubs of nanotechnology. However, in Grenoble, as in Charleroi, the social dimension of those who are left to fend for themselves has been overlooked.

Skillfully linking districts undergoing industrial redeployment to the global economy in a metropolitan context

Districts, within metropoli, that embark upon a process of industrial redeployment are highly exposed to the constraints of the global production system, which is itself undergoing constant change. Like the innovative milieu, the urban environment that is undergoing industrial redeployment needs to bring in knowledge from the outside, collaborate with technically advanced companies (Fontan, Klein

& Tremblay, 2005: 154) wherever they may be found provided that they have the required skills, follow the evolution of the markets, export new goods and services, and reduce the gap that separates them from the whole metropolis to which they belong, because the latter, in terms of technology and the production of services with high added value, is in step with the global competitive production system and with other metropoli. At the same time, however, this openness puts the district at risk of operating for the sole profit of outside spaces. The challenge is to link the local to the global in a skilful way.

For D. Maillat, the ability to skillfully achieve this connection is linked to the capacity of the innovative milieu to "develop a competitive edge for the milieu, that is, intangible resources (such as know-how), relational capital, 'trust' capital, the capacity to co-operate, and the ability to understand changes in the environment and decide on common strategies that serve to activate a development dynamic with regard to the territorial production system" (Maillat, 1996). To this could be added, following Fontan, Klein and Tremblay (2005:154), that successfully linking the local to the global is also tied to a capacity to develop "socio-territorial capital" (which) "includes both a set of resources and a dynamic (…) of tangible and intangible resources that a community can mobilise (…) within a territorial framework (…) where individuals and groups are put in contact with each other through informal and formal mechanisms of interaction (…) in order to create social cohesion". Adopting a mode of governance based on partnership and the resolution of social conflict is the classic example of social-territorial capital that not only makes it possible to 'ensure the well-being of citizens', but also becomes a factor in attracting exogenous companies. For the territory that mobilizes it, this mode of governance becomes a competitive edge for the milieu compared to spaces where the social climate is characterized by demands. On the other hand, a mode of governance based on partnership and conflict resolution carries the risk of being just an externality, a simple location factor for the companies that come to set up shop in the district that is undergoing industrial redeployment. If this is the case, it is possible that no particular 'milieu' phenomenon will emerge, especially if the companies in question have a propensity toward predatory and/or nomadic behavior. It is therefore advisable to combine this mode of governance based on the resolution of social conflict through negotiation with a 'milieu' approach that sufficiently develops technical and economic synergies within the territory to attract companies which, while carrying out a strategy of externalization[6], become deeply rooted in the territory through numerous networks of scientific and technical co-operation, and contribute to its structuring.

This approach should be facilitated by the indirect synergies that stem from specific externalities related to metropolization, since metropoli are the new economic and financial control centers in the world and constitute the fundamental framework for the current dynamics of innovation. It can be said that, for civil society, social innovation consists in its capacity to tame and bend market forces and geopolitical constraints to its own advantage, while leaning on the metropolis. As Fontan, Klein and Tremblay (2005:20) wrote, "a city has the power to increase its capacity to govern and to concentrate resources within a single territory, when its population proves itself to be innovative".

Governance based on promoting the city's image and on the system of representations

The new governance must, through the use of symbols, produce a coherent, distinctive and positive global 'image' of the city or milieu. Social innovation can consist in a policy of reviving the collective memory of a place, so as to restore, for the city or local milieu, its past history. Highlighting its architectural, artistic, historical or cultural heritage greatly contributes to developing its positive image. There is nothing like heritage to restore the collective feeling etched in the memory of place, even when the image that a territorial community has of its past is not particularly appealing or is even repulsive. This was the case, for example, in Charleroi (Quevit & Van Doren, 2000) which, in the 1980s and 90s, succeeded in replacing its image as a 'black country' (old heavy industry), with the image of a region that is technologically advanced (biotechnology, high-tech ceramic industry, etc.) It developed externalities aimed at offering a convivial living environment (cleaning up industrial wasteland, safety contracts, urban renewal, etc.) while facilitating economic activity (developing zones of economic activity outside the city, creating an international hub of scientific activity), and linking the local to the global (regional airport, widespread dissemination of information technology, etc.). This image of a modern city that is open and convivial greatly contributed to the development of partnership-based behaviors. But there was also the whole range of whatever strengthened the system of collective representation (senses of belonging, solidarity, trust, territorial preference and collective identification, through museums, heritage preservation, architectural renovation, organizing meetings, etc.) which allowed for the promotion of local know-how, contributed to the revival and transformation of an industrial culture and successfully strengthened the city's viability.

The technopolitan structuring of the city, the linking of the local to the global via the metropolis, and the promotion of the city's image all fit into an instrumental logic by which the well-being of its inhabitants is taken for granted simply on account of the mode of governance found in innovative milieus. Developing the city's image through urban renewal and by highlighting points of interest such as its architectural heritage, museums and festivals, has an impact at a social level in terms of the well-being of its inhabitants and recognition of their capabilities. Promoting heritage contributes to social development. According to Greffe (2004), it is "the means by which its inhabitants can regain confidence in the prospects for development and for community living in the place where they live, an incentive to develop new projects, stemming the exodus of young people". It is also a way for the city's inhabitants to "make themselves actors of their own destiny; to allow them to associate with one another through the dissemination of the values and references that they share".

Taking social innovation into account in the analysis of urban functions completes or at least sheds new light on the analysis of the type of governance found in innovative milieus, by demonstrating their positive impact on urban regeneration. However, the existence of persistent unemployment and growing violence in former industrial districts raises the question of the possibilities and limitations of an approach based on social innovation and on the innovative milieu, unless, as a simple 'milieu', it allows for a new perspective.

The relevance and limitations of social innovation in the face of social, economic, ethnic and cultural urban problems from the perspective of an innovative milieu analysis

Large cities are affected by the growing segregation between people living downtown and those living in the urban periphery, which may be close by or farther away. This segregation is dual in nature. On the one hand, a 'classic' spatial segregation can be observed which is essentially linked to socio-economic causes. It is expressed through "the exclusion of part of the labour force from their status as workers, in particular when it comes to a labour force which is not highly or not at all qualified" (Dadoy, 1998). On the other hand, the rise of a new form of spatial segregation can be observed which is also due to economic causes, but to which are added problems related to ethno-cultural integration. The spatial cohabitation of poor unemployed people who are native to the country and people of immigrant origin who are also affected by unemployment has played a part in obscuring this ethno-cultural phenomenon, to which the rise in insecurity and violence is drawing increasing attention. These two forms of segregation/exclusion lead us to wonder about the relevance and limitations of an approach based on social innovation and the innovative milieu.

Contributions of social innovation and an innovative milieu approach, in the face of exclusion through unemployment

In the de-industrialization-restructuring phase of the economy, linked to the off shoring and technological change which caused massive and structural unemployment, spatial segregation has taken on a particularly social character. The poorest inhabitants have continued to make a living from precarious jobs in the most dilapidated areas of large cities, while those who can, have left the city to live in the outskirts. As new industrial and tertiary activities have been established in abandoned industrial wasteland, luxury housing projects have been built, in which the wealthiest inhabitants have settled. Thus, alongside a very poor but residual population, city centers have once again become home to a well-to-do population, thus giving rise to a phenomenon of gentrification, with the outskirts of the city being occupied by the middle classes. This spatial segregation has resulted in an income disparity, which is becoming more pronounced as unemployment rises. In the Parisian region, for example, while the unemployment rate is 10 percent for the whole metropolis, it rises to 20 percent in former working class suburbs and the sensitive housing estates that surround the city center.

Social policies have been implemented, some aimed at bringing social solutions to unemployment at the national level, through various social assistance benefits; others in the form of social innovations focused on the individual that aim at helping people acquire knowledge, change their representations and learn new co-operation skills in order that they may be better prepared to hold a job. According to Lallemand (2001), the problem of unemployment among the underprivileged classes cannot be solved simply by acquiring new know-how and new knowledge; the solutions will come from a learning process aimed at equipping individuals to solve their own problems, whatever they may be. This integrated approach, which mainly consists in the growth and development of individuals, is based on autonomy and taking responsibility for oneself. Auclair and Lampron (1987) point out that through the reorganization of services and/or work, learning processes, autonomy, personal development and motivation, notions are discovered which link the well-being of each to the well-being of others. This type of social innovation based on the individual concerns people who are maladjusted and who need to improve their self-esteem, regain confidence in themselves, and take responsibility for their own well-being in order to be better prepared to confront the world and/or the labour market. This is very positive on an individual level, but has little impact on structural unemployment which concerns thousands of unemployed workers, and even less impact on unemployment that is tied to ethno-cultural causes. On the other hand, economic restructuring experiences based on social innovation in the context of a set of challenges that are closely related to those of innovative milieus (such as in Pittsburg in the United States, Montreal in Quebec, Canada or the Northside in Ireland) have had very encouraging results.

The study by Sabel (1996) on the Northside, a former industrial zone which has been deeply affected by unemployment, demonstrates how social innovation, with the aim of transforming the territory on the basis of a partnership-based and cognitive mode of organization, deeply-rooted in the territory, was carried out. Describing the process of the transformation of this territory, he highlights the importance of co-operation efforts between unemployed workers, who set up a programme designed to create new businesses, and the heads of local businesses, in particular SMEs, "which allowed the former to benefit from the experience of the latter". These co-operation efforts were based on a structure of mutual assistance which allowed them to improve their management skills and form trade networks at the local and international levels and which gave rise to "the implementation of a process of co-operation, mutual exchange and learning within the territory that was advantageous for each of the partners involved and contributed to the territorial transformation of production, and the supply and demand of work". At the same time, he demonstrates the effect of the transformation of solidarity behaviors and collective learning processes on the antagonism that existed between the traditional classes: "the analysis of the process of transformation of the production system through the transformation of the behavior of actors, their mode of co-ordinating work and the adoption of new rules of conduct, reveals the positive impact of strong local solidarity on partnership-based behaviors and collective learning behaviors, in that they allow the rifts between the traditional social classes to be overcome" (Sabel, 1996). By totally transforming the behaviors of employees and entrepreneurs, moving them toward dialogue, social innovation paved the way for a new mode of peaceful conflict resolution, job creation and regional development. This process, however, required trust on the part of the parties involved, and the capacity to refer to the idea of a higher unit that tied them together and that was stronger than their individual conjunctural interests. This coherence ensued from the realization that "the implementation of a process of co-operation, mutual exchange and learning within the territory was advantageous for each of the partners involved" (Sabel, 1996). This experience is entirely in keeping with the challenge facing the 'innovative milieu', which consists in grasping territorial development on the basis of interactive association between partnership-based, cognitive and territorial logics, even when the new jobs do not necessarily lead to technological innovations.

The study by Fontan, Klein and Tremblay (2005) on three districts surrounding the core of the metropolis of Montreal (Ville-Saint-Laurent, Le Faubourg des Récollets, and Rosemont), which all experienced decline starting from the 1950s and 60s after becoming involved in a process of de-industrialization and off shoring, describes three cases of economic restructuring based on socio-territorial innovation and partnership. The most innovative of the three, however, was most certainly the district of Rosemont, which opted for a strategy based on the social movement that brought together representatives from civil society in the local community and the union movement to face one of the largest Canadian companies, Canadian Pacific Railway (CPR). CPR, which specialized in the production and repair of railway equipment (engines and railway cars), had employed 6000 workers in the post-war era, but was down to a mere 1000 employees at the time they closed down the plant between 1976 and 1980, leaving behind 500,000 square metres of industrial wasteland near the urban center of Montreal. The challenge was how to achieve the rehabilitation of the site in the context of economic, social, urbanistic, and environmental constraints. A very tough negotiation process was initiated between the two parties.

Klein and Fontan (2003) explain that two opposing plans came up against one another, one introduced by the Community Economic Development Corporation (CEDC) representing local citizens, which aimed to maintain the industrial vocation of the site and create jobs by attracting outside companies, in particular in the environmental field; the other by CPR, the owner of the industrial site, which intended to build a housing development on it. The protagonists emphasized the role of the territory throughout the negotiation process[7] because, despite its limited financial means, the CEDC (or rather its spin-off organization, the Société de Développement Angus (SDA)) managed to negotiate on an equal footing with CPR. Indeed, the SDA, recognized and supported by various levels of government in Quebec (Pro-Est, *Chambre de commerce* de l'Est de Montréal, the provincial government in Quebec), became a major player (Klein & Fontan, 2003) in local governance. At the end of a period of adversarial negotiations, the protagonists arrived at a consensus which resulted in the ownership of half of the site being transferred to the SDA, which is currently in the process of creating a science park, called the Technopole Angus, which specializes in resolving environmental problems[8], and in biotechnology. The other half of the site, which remained the property of CPR, was set aside for its housing project. These authors also point out that the negotiation process combined mechanisms for dispute resolution and bargaining based on a balance of power that weighed in favour of the community structure and against industrial interests. They interpret this as having been fair to both sides: it was, they say, "the right of governance of a rehabilitation project involving a property held by a company that had incurred an 'ethical' debt to the community that allowed it to prosper for approximately 60 years" (Klein & Fontan, 2003:27). What was new about this partnership-based approach to adversarial negotiations, was putting the emphasis on what united the parties while qualifying what divided them. New forms of partnership-based governance thus emerged which can be referred to as 'social arrangements', and which were facilitated by the fact that the protagonists had an investment in the long-term economic, social and cultural well-being of their territory, based on the fact that they identified with it and belonged to it, such that, despite their diverging interests, they succeeded in coming to an agreement: starting out as protagonists, even antagonists, they became partners. The collective interest prevailed over individual interests. In this case, the collective interest of all the protagonists was considerable, involving the viability, sustainability and regeneration of their metropolis, especially in a context of heightened competitiveness, in particular between Montreal and Toronto. Klein and Fontan (2003:27) point out, moreover, that the various actors adopted a development strategy that was based on the creation of companies that would be able to create local jobs for underprivileged citizens. The means they used involved attracting private companies and setting up collective companies that could benefit from the support of private companies. In order to achieve this objective, the promoters of the project succeeded in establishing a synergetic relationship between actors from the district concerned and actors from outside the area. These actors were from both the public and private sectors, including universities, training centers, unions and research centers, "thus expanding the pool of resources that could be mobilized." Through the SDA, the development strategy consisted in using local organizational, human and financial resources based on a sense of local identity, in order both to counter the earlier trend of companies leaving the districts surrounding the downtown core and to attract exogenous companies. Furthermore, the SDA took great pains to familiarize the local population with "post-Fordist production dynamics (networking, innovative milieus) (…) that could help develop the community base".

This experience, along with the other two[9] in Montreal, all involved territorial action that was intended to attract investment and develop entrepreneurship. All three cases were characterized by partnership arrangements and a shared strategic vision, that is, the creation of companies and jobs. They shed light on coalitions between classic economic actors (the entrepreneurial elite and public and private organizations) with the aim of restructuring metropolitan economies, but also demonstrate that the social actor (civil actor) can be an important protagonist, such that action on the part of each of these three types of actors is essential for the restructuring of a territorial economy.

The study of social innovation centered on the local milieu, in both the Irish cases and those in Montreal, demonstrates that interaction between partnership-based, cognitive and territorial logics is a determining factor in the process of transforming and restructuring the territory. On the other hand, the essential difference between social innovation and the innovative milieu most certainly concerns the strategy adopted and the type of innovative actors involved. For territories that aim at technology creation, the key partners are companies (large companies and SMEs that are technologically advanced), scientific actors (knowledge centers, basic and applied research centers, and technical centers) and the public actor, who plays the role of 'facilitator' in setting up partnership-based networks. For territories that aim to attract companies and jobs, the innovation is primarily social in nature and allows for the introduction of a new type of actor and a new approach, that is, the civil actor and a community-based approach that involves social coherence within the district concerned.

However, what is the relevance of social innovation when, in districts in the urban periphery of metropoli or even of mid-sized cities, two types of populations are juxtaposed or even entwined, one being a socially homogenous working class population, and the other an immigrant population which is culturally and ethnically almost homogenous?

Limitations of social innovation in the face of economic, social, ethnic and cultural segregation from the perspective of an innovative milieu approach

Over the last 30 years, the urban landscape in Europe and, in particular in France, has been altered by the arrival of an increasingly large immigrant population, which has settled in the poorest neighborhoods and areas. This new segregation is also social to the extent that the new population is threatened by the growing precariousness of employment (the average rate of unemployment is around 20 and even 40 percent for young people in sensitive areas of the Parisian metropolis), but no more so than that of populations that are native to the country living in these areas. On the other hand, a deep cultural division is forming between the former middle classes in these near-urban areas and the new residents, due to the increasingly substantial demographic weight of the latter (they make up over 90 percent of the population in sensitive housing developments) and to the fact that a number of these new residents, young people in particular, have been perpetrating repeated acts of violence and incivility. It would undoubtedly be distorting the truth to impute these acts of violence to young people from immigrant populations alone. However, what is certain is that overall, the image of these suburban areas and neighborhoods/housing estates has declined. An ethno-cultural divide has been added to the purely socio-economic divide related to unemployment and the growing precariousness of employment. These two divides, interacting with one another, are expressed, in formerly working class suburban areas, by the juxtaposition of culturally and ethnically distinct communities and, in sensitive neighborhoods in these suburban areas, by the departure of the old-stock middle classes who, when they can, move to suburban areas that are farther and farther away from the downtown core. To what extent can social innovation resolve these problems? Is it possible to come up with a diagnosis by considering the problem in terms of the innovative milieu?

Failure of urban renewal policies and those aimed at social integration through economic means

The political leaders of European countries who have endeavoured to resolve the problem of insecurity in cities over the last 20 to 30 years have, by and large, diagnosed the problem to be 'civil' insecurity resulting from social segregation due to three movements: the relegating of the most troubled populations to social housing neighborhoods, the gentrification of downtown neighborhoods through the arrival of upper classes and intellectuals, and peri-urbanization, by which a large part of the middle class leaves the sensitive districts, moving to detached housing in surrounding areas that are farther and farther away and are less socially distinct. The policy that has been put in place (in response to this situation) has been urban renewal.

Today, this policy has given way to a social mix policy. Bernard (2005) has observed that, in Berlin, a 'mild' urban renewal policy put in place at the start of the 1980s, with the goal of protecting and renovating older districts, modernizing housing while respecting social concerns, has, since 2002, in particular in the neighborhoods of former East Berlin, been replaced by a 'self-help' construction support programme, in which inhabitants contribute 20 percent to the project, thus allowing for the rehabilitation of several buildings. Swinnen (2005) has demonstrated that the current policy involves a set of measures which, in various ways depending on the country studied (The Netherlands, Belgium or Sweden), focus on the supply of housing, the social mix of the population, and promoting social mobility in disadvantaged neighborhoods. In France, Rieu (2005), describing the urban renewal plan put in place by the *Agence Nationale de la Rénovation Urbaine* (ANRU) (national urban renewal agency), which was created in 2003, points out that this plan is at odds with the city's traditional policy, which focused on the demolition and reconstruction of certain districts. The city's new policy involves achieving social integration through economic means by using integration charters that focus on training the local population, on creating clearly defined urban zones that benefit from tax exemptions for businesses that set up there and create jobs, and on housing and living environments, in partnership with local communities whose goal is to achieve a social mix.[10]

This 'social mix' model, introduced as a 'new model for urbanity and living together' within which different socio-professional groups are supposed to live side by side and intermingle has, however, failed. Even in the opinion of the *Plan de l'Urbanisme Construction et Architecture* (PUCA, 2005), "the public measures taken to support a social mix have symbolic significance only; they have no real effect on the phenomenon. States and cities have not managed to effectively combat the processes of exclusion. (…) Approaches to the problems of rectification that dominated for approximately 20 years seem to have exhausted themselves and new approaches to these phenomena are being sought". Even the promotion of social mobility in disadvantaged neighborhoods, which involves encouraging the middle classes to settle in these neighborhoods, is not a solution, because the social mix of populations has been widely rejected by old-stock populations that are better-off.[11] Perhaps, then, the relevance of the diagnosis should simply be called into question. Duyvendak (2005) noted that in the three countries studied (The Netherlands, Belgium and Sweden), "socio-cultural differences and the question of ethnic segregation and the integration of immigrants are taking on increasing significance in the social mix debate".

The diagnosis of ethno-cultural urban problems from the perspective of an innovative 'milieu' analysis

It is hard to see how the concept of the 'innovative milieu', with its set of challenges as a territory that carries the potential for a creative dynamic, its reticular organization aimed at bringing skills together and helping them progress, and its local actors who are deeply rooted in the history and the long-term survival of collective representations, could be relevant for grasping the problems of social, ethnic and cultural segregation within the sensitive districts and housing estates in large cities. On the other hand, in the concept of the 'milieu' itself, the definition of which was borrowed from Maillat[12], there are elements that can be taken up to describe this new territorial reality. In particular, it is the idea "of a spatial whole that shows a certain unity, even coherence that is reflected by identifiable behaviors and a specific culture that generates 'coded' attitudes and behaviors that form the basis of a certain organization and regulation of the milieu". These elements characterize former working class suburbs and housing estates where new immigrant populations have settled. Despite the diversity of ethnic groups, they are united by feelings of resentment toward Western society which give them a sense of belonging to a coherent whole in terms of issues relating to minorities and ethnic communities within society, and this coherent whole coincides with what they now consider to be their territory.

Looking at these neighborhoods from the perspective of an 'milieu' has the advantage of heightening an awareness that, even though these territories are only pseudo-milieus, they are spaces of 'self-identification and self-contextualization' which, through the behavior of the people living in them, become specific social, ethnic and cultural enclaves in relation to the metropolis as a whole and the nation as a whole. The problem is even more serious given that this type of self-identification has led to violent behaviors in these areas which can be seen in the rise in delinquency, riots, an increase in the traffic of illegal substances[13] and all sorts of incivility causing widespread insecurity.

In a chapter devoted to the integration crisis, Tandonnet (2003:148) mentions 200 'forbidden housing estates' identified by the *Renseignements généraux* (the security branch of the police force) in France in 2000 (compared to 132 in 1998 and 67 in 1993), 30 of which are being 'particularly monitored'[14] and which have "become territories that are exposed to violence and arbitrary behavior, where the police and public and private services have a lot of difficulty intervening (…). Setting cars on fire in these housing estates is not just an ordinary crime. Gratuitous, and designed specifically to cause harm, this act, carried out in a way that belongs more to terrorist logic than regular delinquency, expresses the nihilism of a generation of inhabitants from immigrant families who have largely remained on the fringes of French society" (Tandonnet, 2003:149). As early as 1999, Finkielkraut attributed the overwhelming responsibility of insecurity "to young people from immigrant families". He expressed the view that "looking to unemployment as an explanation, to the despair caused by exclusion, is these days an invitation to crime, (…). It is important to resist the sociological argument."[15]

In spite of a certain success in the area of social integration in France, which is, however, limited to individual cases such as mixed marriages, social ties, sporadic manifestations of tolerance, and the social and professional success of many immigrants (30 percent of people of Algerian descent born in France before 1968 have become middle or senior managers)[16], the riots that wrecked havoc over a period of a little more than three weeks in October and November 2005 in sensitive suburban areas of the Parisian metropolis and in a great many large and mid-sized cities in France, confirmed the ethno-cultural argument. Whatever the reasons for the violence, which some people attributed to racial discrimination, hiring discrimination and access to social housing, and others to lacking immigration and integration policies, academic failure, delinquency, the refusal of parents to shoulder their responsibilities, a rise in these housing estates of a Mafia-like economy based on the traffic of cannabis, a state of anomie that is conducive to Islamic discourse, or a 'culture' of hatred and violence, "these two points of view represent two sides of the same reality, that is, the difficult coexistence of populations with different origins, which seriously threatens national unity in the long term" (Tandonnet, 2003:149). This involves problems of a political nature which go way beyond the scope of the socio-economic approach to economic regeneration in metropolitan urban districts. Nevertheless, urban regeneration cannot take place as long as these problems are not resolved. Approaching them solely in socio-economic terms will only provide very partial solutions and may even make them worse.

The community-based development of socio-territorial capital through the mobilization of the local community (civil society) was behind the economic restructuring and urban regeneration of Montreal. Our colleagues in Quebec state that this "socio-territorial capital can be developed through various types of social, cultural, economic and ethnic actors, to name a few, thus making it a major social and territorial challenge". The ethnic factor, therefore, does not in itself prevent the economic restructuring of a metropolitan district. However, these authors add that, "this socio-territorial capital leads to development when the actors can work together to develop it and when the logics of intervention that they use have the same aim" (Fontan, Klein & Tremblay, 2005:154). But which aim?

The aim, it could be said, is 'living well together', as described by a contemporary philosopher, Mourral, reflecting on the past and future of Europe: "It is important to understand," she says, "the essence of the urban development. It is a 'moral organization', the goal of which is 'living well'. It is quite an art to run an economy, which is a healthy activity if, indeed, its goal is 'living well'" (Mourral, 2004:53). How can coherence, unity, and meaning be restored within urban society, allowing its citizens to live well? It could be said that it is this culture of living well in the urban development, that a governance freed from the egocentricity, nihilism and ethical relativism of which we have been prisoners for so long, must help us rediscover. However, two realistic preconditions are necessary. The first is of a demographic nature: culturally foreign populations cannot be assimilated as long as new waves of immigrants continue to arrive, which implies immigration that is chosen rather than simply put up with. The other is of an educational nature: due to the influence of culture in any given social group, it is important, as was done for the successive waves of immigrants who were very well assimilated up to approximately 30 years ago, to make it a priority to teach new generations of citizens from immigrant families, as well as new immigrants themselves, the language, history and civilization of their new country and to help them to like and respect these aspects of their new home. It will thus be possible, perhaps, to see the emergence in our cities of a context in which society is in motion, functioning, united by a sense of solidarity, a shared destiny, and a collective project.

References

Auclair, R. & C. Lampron, 1987, Approche intégrée: une innovation dans la dispensation des services sociaux, *Service Social*, Vol. 36, N° 2/3 pp. 315-341, as quoted by J. Cloutier, Qu'est-ce que l'innovation sociale?, CRISES, Etudes théoriques collection, N° ET0314, November 2003.

Aydalot, Ph., 1986, Préface; in: Aydalot, Ph. (ed.), *Milieux Innovateurs en Europe,* GREMI, Paris, p. 10.

Bernard, H., 2005, Rendre les habitants responsables de leur habitat: le cas de Berlin, PUCA conference paper, Recherche urbaine: confrontations européennes, November 17-18, Paris.

Bramanti, A., L. Senn & M. Tamisar, 2000, Le milieu des services logistiques et le rôle de l'environnement urbain: une comparaison entre Milan et Vérone; in: Crevoisier, O. & R. Camagni (eds), *Les milieux urbains: innovation, systèmes de production et ancrage*, GREMI-IRER-EDES, Neuchâtel.

Camagni, R., 2000, Avant-propos; in: Crevoisier, O. & R. Camagni (eds), *Les milieux urbains: innovation, systèmes de production et ancrage*, GREMI-IRER-EDES, Neuchâtel.

Camagni, R., 2004, Natural and Cultural Resources and the Role of the Local Milieu: towards a Theoretical Interpretation; in: Camagni, R., D. Maillat & A. Matteaccioli (eds), *Ressources naturelles et culturelles, milieux et développement local*, GREMI-IRER-EDES, Neuchâtel.

Camagni, R., M. Galbiati & T. Pompili, 2000, Urban Structural Dynamics and Innovative Milieux: the communication and the fashion production systems in the metropolitan area of Milan; in: Crevoisier, O. & R. Camagni (eds), *Les milieux urbains: innovation, systèmes de production et ancrage*, GREMI-IRER-EDES, Neuchâtel.

Cloutier, J., 2003, *Qu'est-ce que l'innovation sociale?*, CRISES, Etudes théoriques collection, N° ET0314.

Corolleur, F., L.M. Boulianne & O. Crevoisier, 2000, Ville et innovation: le cas de trois villes de Suisse occidentale; in: Crevoisier, O. and R. Camagni (eds), *Les milieux urbains: innovation, systèmes de production et ancrage*, GREMI-IRER-EDES, Neuchâtel.

Dadoy, M., 1998, L'innovation sociale, mythes et réalités: l'innovation en question, *Education permanente*, Vol. 134, pp. 41-53, as quoted by J. Cloutier, Qu'est-ce que l'innovation sociale, CRISES, Etudes théoriques collection, N° ET0314, November 2003.

De Bernardy, M. & G.Loinger, 1997, Technopolis and Serendipity. The Adjustment Effects Created by Nancy-Brabois and ZIRST Technological Parks: a Comparison; in: Ratti, R., A. Bramanti & R. Gordon (eds), *The Dynamics of Innovative Regions: the GREMI approach*, GREMI, Ashgate Publ., Aldershot.

Decoster, E., A. Matteaccioli & M. Tabariés, 2004, Les étapes d'une dynamique de territorialisation: le pôle optique en Ile-de-France, *Revue Géographie Economie Société*, Vol. 6, N°4, pp. 383-413.

Drewe, P., G. Allaert & P. de Klerck, 2000, Towards an urban innovative environment in the city region of Gent; in: Crevoisier, O. & R. Camagni (eds), *Les milieux urbains: innovation, systèmes de production et ancrage*, GREMI-IRER-EDES, Neuchâtel.

Duyvendak, J.W., 2005, Gentrification, mixité sociale, exclusion, PUCA conference paper, Recherche urbaine: confrontations européennes, Paris, November 17-18.

Ferrao, J., 2000, Innovative Milieux in Small Cities – An Attainable Utopia? The Case of Evora, Portugal; in: Crevoisier, O. & R. Camagni (eds), *Les milieux urbains: innovation, systèmes de production et ancrage*, GREMI-IRER-EDES, Neuchâtel.

Fontan, J-M., J-L. Klein & D-G. Tremblay, 2005, *Innovation socio-territoriale et reconversion économique: le cas de Montréal*, L'Harmattan, Paris.

Greffe, X., 2004, Le patrimoine dans la ville, Ressources naturelles et culturelles, milieux et développement local; in: Camagni, R., D. Maillat & A. Matteaccioli (eds), *Ressources naturelles et culturelles, milieux et développement local*, GREMI-IRER-EDES, pp. 19-43.

Klein, J-L. & J-M. Fontan, 2003, Reconversion économique et initiative locale: l'effet structurant des actions collectives; in: Klein, J-L., J-M. Fontan & B. Lévesque (eds), *Reconversion économique et développement territorial: le rôle de la société civile*, Presses de l'Université du Québec, Québec, pp. 11-33.

Lallemand, D., 2001, Les défis de l'innovation sociale, Issy-les-Moulineaux, ESF éd., as quoted by J. Cloutier, Qu'est-ce que l'innovation sociale?, CRISES, Etudes théoriques collection, N° ET0314, November 2003.

Maillat, D., 1996, Milieux innovateurs et nouvelles générations de politiques régionales, *Cahiers de l'IRER*, N° 9604, IRER-Université de Neuchâtel.

Maillat, D., O. Crevoisier & B. Lecoq, 1993, Réseaux d'innovation et milieux innovateurs; in: Maillat, D., M. Quévit & L. Senn (eds), *Réseaux d'innovation et milieux innovateurs: un pari pour le développement régional*, GREMI-IRER-EDES, Neuchâtel.

Maillat, D., M. Quevit & L. Senn, 1993, Réseaux d'innovation et milieux innovateurs; in: Maillat, D., M. Quévit & L. Senn (eds), *Réseaux d'innovation et milieux innovateurs: un pari pour le développement régional*, GREMI-IRER-EDES, Neuchâtel.

Matteaccioli, A., 1999, Auto-organisation et émergence des milieux innovateurs, RERU, 1999, N° 3, pp. 489-511.

Matteaccioli, A., 2004, *Philippe Aydalot, pionnier de l'économie territoriale*, L'Harmattan, Paris.

Matteaccioli, A. & M. Tabariés, 2000, Dynamiques urbaines et milieux innovateurs dans la métropole parisienne: les milieux de la finance et de la haute couture; in: *Les milieux urbains: innovation, systèmes de production et ancrage*, O. Crevoisier & R. Camagni (eds), GREMI-IRER-EDES, Neuchâtel.

Mourral, I., 2004, *Une sagesse pour l'Europe*, Editions de Paris.

Perrin, J-C., 1991, Réseaux d'innovation-milieux innovateurs-développement territorial, *RERU*, N° 3/4.

Perrin, J-C., 1995, Apprentissage collectif, territoire et milieu innovateur: un nouveau paradigme pour le développement, Politicas de inovação e desenvolvimento regional e local; in: *Actas do encontro realizado em Evora*, Nov. 1995, coordenação: João Ferrão, Ed. do Instituto de ciencias sociais da universidade de Lisboa pp.103-130.

Perrin, J-C., 1997, *La dynamique des milieux: convention, auto-identification, auto-contextualisation*, mimeo.

Planque, B., 1993, Réseaux d'innovation et milieu régional: un cas méditerranéen; in: Maillat, D., M. Quévit & L. Senn (eds), *Réseaux d'innovation et milieux innovateurs: un pari pour le développement régional*, GREMI-IRER-EDES, Neuchâtel.

PUCA (Plan Urbanisme Construction Architecture), 2005, Conference program Recherche urbaine: confrontations européennes, Paris, November 17-18.

Quevit, M. & P. van Doren, 2000, La dynamique des milieux innovateurs dans un contexte urbain de reconversion industrielle, le cas de Charleroi, Les milieux urbains: innovation, systèmes de production et ancrage, IRER-EDES, Neuchâtel, pp. 115-143.

Rémy, J. & L. Voyé, 1992, *La ville: vers une nouvelle définition?*, L'Harmattan, Paris.

Rieu, P., 2005, Le plan de rénovation urbaine de l'Agence Nationale de la Rénovation Urbaine, PUCA conference paper, Recherche urbaine: confrontations européennes, Paris, November 17-18.

Rousier, N., 2000, Dynamiques urbaines et milieux innovateurs en région Rhône-Alpes: Lyon, Grenoble, Annecy; in: Crevoisier, O. & R. Camagni (eds), *Les milieux urbains: innovation, systèmes de production et ancrage*, GREMI-IRER-EDES, Neuchâtel.

Sabel, C., 1996, Irlande, partenariats locaux et innovation sociale, OECD, as quoted by J. Cloutier, *Qu'est-ce que l'innovation sociale*, CRISES, Etudes théoriques collection, N° ET0314, November 2003.

Sole-Parellada, F., & M. Barcelo-Roca, 1993, Evolution et restrictions de la configuration réticulaire du milieu: le cas de Barcelone; in: Maillat, D., M. Quévit & L. Senn (eds), *Réseaux d'innovation et milieux innovateurs: un pari pour le développement régional*, GREMI-IRER-EDES, Neuchâtel.

Swinnen, H., 2005, Institut Verwey-Jonker in Utrecht, Un état des lieux des politiques et des recherches sur la mixité sociale et la gentrification aux Pays-Bas, en Belgique et en Suède, PUCA conference paper, Recherche urbaine: confrontations européennes, Paris, November 17-18.

Tabariés, M., 2005, *Les apports du GREMI à l'analyse territoriale de l'innovation: 20 ans de recherches sur les milieux innovateurs*, MATISSE-CNRS-Université de Paris I, Cahiers de la Maison des Sciences Economiques, n°.18.

Tandonnet, M., 2003, *Migrations: la nouvelle vague*, L'Harmattan, Paris.

Notes

1   GREMI (*Groupe de Recherche Européen sur les Milieux Innovateurs*) (European research group on innovative milieus), which was created in 1984 by Philippe Aydalot and has formed an association since 1986, initially included approximately 20 teams of European and North-American researchers who wished to explore the appearance of new spatial dynamics in developed countries.

2   In the mid 1980s, GREMI took an interest in the relationship between technical progress and territory, centred on the notion of the 'innovative milieu'. It then moved on to study the organization, emergence and evolution of the innovative milieu, followed by the interactions between territorial dynamics and urban dynamics. Finally, it examined the development of heritage-related resources in terms of the innovative milieu in the early 2000s. (cf. M. Tabariés (2005), "Les apports du GREMI à l'analyse territoriale de l'innovation: 20 ans de recherches sur les milieux innovateurs," MATISSE-CNRS-Université de Paris I, Cahiers de la Maison des Sciences Economiques, N° 18.

3   CRISIS, (*Centre de Recherche sur les Innovations Sociales*) (Research center studying social innovation), an inter-university organization which mainly studies and analyzes 'innovation and social change'.

4   The other two areas of focus are: social innovation centred on individuals and their living conditions, and social innovation centred on the company.

5   To say that partnership-based behaviors and learning behaviors become territorialized means that they "become deeply rooted" in their territory. J-C. Perrin explains the idea of becoming deeply rooted by referring to concept of the 'contextual organisation' of territory: "For a particular individual, territorialisation is a way of becoming established in a natural environment that consists in settling down in it in a relatively permanent way. At the level of a social group, a collective self-identification takes place such that the various actors have a sense of belonging to a coherent whole." (…) The territory is therefore "a specific territorialised socio-economic configuration having a certain unity linked to the actors' senses of belonging to a shared representational space, and to a shared cultural and techno-productive whole" (Perrin, 1997).

6   When a company carries out the opposite strategy of internalization, and relies on its subsidiary or on SME subcontracting for inter-firm agreements in order to gain an 'edge' in the market, it tends to use the milieu, whether it is innovative or not, as a supplier of location factors that are adapted to the chosen function.

7   And this was even more the case given that, in order to be in step with the constraints of globalization, these structures of partnership-based governance are increasingly oriented toward technological development and high value-added services. The result will undoubtedly be that the more these corporations evolve toward technological creativity or even the development of urban heritage, the more they will adopt the negotiation modes that were referred to earlier, with regard to innovative milieus.

8   The site was contaminated due to the former activity of Canadian Pacific Railway.

9   Ville Saint-Laurent (Canada) opted for a partnership strategy among representatives from the business sector and the main private and government institutions and universities, focusing on private leadership, globalization and the development of the high-tech sectors. *Le Faubourg des Récollets* went through a restructuring process based on a government project, working with and involving tensions with local and social actors, in order to find solutions to meet needs that were not covered by the market.

10 The most recent measures adopted by the government, following the riots that took place in October and November 2005 in a great many cities in France, consist in strengthening the policy aimed at achieving a social mix (higher financial penalties for communities that refuse to allocate 20 percent of their housing stock to social housing; increased financial assistance for the creation of educator positions and the creation of companies and jobs in sensitive areas).

11 The municipalities in middle class suburbs prefer to pay fines rather than build social housing on their territory.

12 D. Maillat, in the Encyclopédie d'Economie Spatiale, defines the concept of milieu as a "spatial whole, having a territorial dimension that corresponds to a geographical space that has no a priori boundaries, that does not correspond to a given region in the usual sense of the word, but that shows unity and coherence that are reflected in identifiable and specific behaviors and a technical culture understood as the development, transmission and accumulation of practices, knowledge and know-how, standards and values related to an economic activity. These different elements generate 'coded' attitudes and behaviors which form the basis of the organization and regulation of the milieu."

13 Drug networks also exist in 'rich' neighborhoods and are not solely made up of inhabitants of immigrant origin from sensitive neighborhoods.

14 P. Rieu (ANRU) points out that the 2003 map of areas classified as ZUS (sensitive urban areas), which was completed in 2005, refers, for the whole of France (including the DOM-TOM, with 34 ZUS), to 751 isolated recently urbanized districts experiencing social difficulties and where there are few businesses, including 190 high-priority districts. (PUCA conference, "*Recherche urbaine: confrontations européennes*", Paris, November 17-18, 2005).

15 Le Figaro Magazine, January 30, 1999.

16 Le Figaro, January 31, 2003.

3 Social Innovation: an Institutionalized Process

Denis Harrisson

Introduction

There are many challenges posed by social innovation to researchers who seek to understand its processes. One of them consists of grasping the factors which explain the diffusion of social innovation given that its contributing components seem to be interlinked in a complex whole. Exploring the links between *organization* and *institution* is a means to explain the structuring of new relations between actors and the ways in which rules are transformed. We will first try to understand the connection between the concepts of organization and institution. Organization can be temporarily defined as the locus of production of co-ordinated activities with a view to achieving expected results. Institution refers to a construct enabling actors to interact in predefined situations which provide stability to the relations. The institution consolidates social relations and makes the relationships between agents predictable and controllable. An organizational form is institutionalized when the actors identify with it and recognize its legitimacy. However, what happens to these links when the organization goes through a period of *social innovation*? How do the rules, norms, conventions and institutional systems interact with each other when activities are designed and implemented by the actors in order to innovate through a process which transforms organizational rules?

The social innovation process

Social innovations such as partnership between employers and unions, social housing, community kitchens, community-enterprise services, voluntary associations and co-operatives are diffused in organizations with more or less success, depending on the economic sector, the organization's management approach, the context of implementation and the dynamic at play between the actors. It is when social innovations are widely diffused that the institutionalization of the organizational form leads to a degree of stability and brings new meaning to the relations. From then on, the organization's work no longer merely involves applying rules according to the state of relations inside the organization but also involves remodeling the organization by bringing into play the broader social structures which support social institutions. External factors such as the market, technical procedures and technologies, laws (the law), and social conventions and norms also come into play. Our approach is based on a diachronic perspective of the organization in which agents compete with each other but negotiate, clash with each other but know how to co-ordinate their activities and use institutions, in order to better understand the interdependence of these agents.

Institutions refer to the nature of the different types of organization involved in the innovation process and their different co-ordination methods. Institutions provide resources, thereby reducing uncertainties. In order to fully grasp the innovation process, the coherence and hierarchy between the systems and sub-systems of basic institutions must also be understood. Tensions exist between institutional systems and inconsistencies exist between systems of rules.

Studies on the processes of organizational transformation, that is, all the sequences of activities led by innovative actors, have hardly helped to conceptualize and theorize social innovation. Indeed, classic organizational theories consider change from the viewpoint of adaptation (contingency theory, Woodward, 1965) or evolution (ecological theory, Lawrence & Lorsch, 1967). Moreover, studies dealing with organizational transformation focus more on the morphology of the post-bureaucratic and post-Fordist organization which maintains or breaks continuity with the bureaucratic and hierarchical organizational form widely diffused in large organizations.

In addition to organizational morphology, a second dimension emerges, concerning the way in which innovation is produced, that is, the speed of transformation, the sequences of activities implemented, decision making, communications, and co-operation and resistance between the actors –in brief, the analysis of the process (Pettigrew, 1985; Callon, 1992; Barnett & Carroll, 1995; Van de Ven & Poole, 1995; Alter, 2003). This second level of analysis of organizations is highly consistent with organizational action as viewed by Weber (1995) and Simon (March & Simon, 1958). Examining a process means taking note of a negotiation between the actors involved. This perspective helps to describe the progression leading actors to agree with each other, to co-operate, to confront each other in a given organizational form despite differentiated interests, based on an institutionalized relational itinerary. The role of institutions in this process will be examined in depth from two angles: (a) the form taken by the organization is harmonized with the basic institutions of a given society; and (b) the process which gives rise to a new organizational configuration is in keeping with the principal patterns of institutionalized relations among actors, groups and individuals. We have thus selected the neo-institutional approach which adds a cognitive dimension and a representation of the social order whose underlying logic guides the action. Cognition adds to the regulative and normative dimensions of the institution which are already known by sociologists and have been well documented. Thus, social actors first of all attempt to find meaning in the situation in which they find themselves. They thus interpret and construct reality in the arenas in which they meet, while taking social rules into account.

Organizations, institutions and the trend toward isomorphism

Organizations respond to numerous co-ordination and collaboration problems based on their institutional arrangements. Thus, organizations structure institutional properties in concrete contexts. Organizational practices are in fact exposed to strong pressures which are legitimized, at times coercive and often normative, and which provide guidance concerning appropriate ways to organize economic activities. Organizational forms reflect not only the rationalities of efficiency and techniques, but also underline the ceremonial adoption of myths and rules which are 'taken for granted' by the actors who appropriate them. Actors in an organization are motivated not only by the criteria of optimum productivity, but also by a system of meaning where normative rules are developed. Alter (2003) shows that users improve the inventions introduced as defined by Schumpeter (1931, in 1967) and develop rules of use which are unexpected, more efficient or deviate from the initial meaning. Innovations are created, integrated and diffused, used, rejected or renewed because they are created by actors driven by social logics. A successful innovation is one that incorporates a multiplicity of actors discovering a variety of uses and types of usefulness. It is in this context that organizations borrow a form modeled by institutions which are represented in a set of cognitive, normative and regulative structures.

In this respect, Powell and DiMaggio challenge Weber's theory of convergence in organizational forms toward those that are most effective. Is convergence not instead the result of institutional pressures toward one form rather than another, regardless of its real effectiveness? This is referred to by the authors as *organizational isomorphism* (Powell & DiMaggio, 1991). This involves a constraining process which encourages an organization to resemble other organizations which are facing the same environmental conditions. Thus, legitimization activities are those which comply with common ideas and not those which are most effective. There are three mechanisms of legitimization: (a) coercive isomorphism through policies or rules of law; (b) mimetic isomorphism when an organization reacts to uncertainty by imitating another organization; (c) normative isomorphism when an organization changes following the integration of agents who introduce new ideas, beliefs or norms to the organization's actors. This last mechanism of legitimization is thus similar to innovation networks through which the ideas carried by innovative actors are disseminated from organization to organization through a process of knowledge circulation and communication. This last mechanism lends itself better to the analysis of social innovations. In fact, social innovations have not achieved the legitimacy conferred by laws and the law. They are the result of interactions between agents who move from one organization to another and convey innovative knowledge and ideas. Social innovations first construct their legitimacy based on values and knowledge long before formal rules. Innovation involves a continuous game of exchange of ideas on the *content*, the *context* and the *process*. Thus, decision making is not the product of rational debates but is first of all formed by the interests and commitments of individuals and social groups, as well as by bureaucratic forces, changes in the external environment and manipulations of the structural context by the actors.

The neo-institutional approach

There are several conceptions of the institution which nevertheless concur in their rejection of the atomist premises of social processes. The neo-institutional approach was created in reaction to the perspective of rational choice and behaviorism which is based on individualism, by which an individual makes choices based on his preferences and beliefs which are formed according to available information (Abell, 1995). The rational choice theory recognizes the existence of institutions, but rejects the motivating nature of them with regard to action because institutions are not derived from motivated behavior. In other words, institutions constrain and thus cannot serve as a starting point of action. An institution comprises a set of more or less harmonized rules which convey the meaning and determine the action. According to Scott, institutions are composed of "...cognitive, normative and regulative elements that, together with associated activities and resources, provide stability and meaning to social life. Institutions are transmitted by various types of carriers- cultures, structures and routines- which operate at different levels of jurisdiction" (Scott, 2001: 48).

Institutions are the result of human activity but not necessarily the result of a conscious conception. Institutionalists are interested in the way in which action is structured and through which social alignments and arrangements are created, by favoring systems of shared rules which constrain the capacities of actors to optimize their choices and to favor some groups and options (Commons, 1931; DiMaggio, 1988; Selznick, 1996).

Cognitive aspects dominate the neo-institutional approach. Thus, knowledge is made up of values, norms and attitudes but also of scripts, 'ready made accounts' (taken-for-granted behaviors) and rules. People take action because they have perfectly integrated the scripts which become routines and even rituals. However, social arrangements derive from daily activities in which the manifestations are often ambiguous and erroneous, little understood by each other and only partially explained. Thus, in rules, there is an implicit clause which leaves room for negotiation and innovation in the face of unexpected circumstances. According to Merton (1949, in 1973), innovation lies in the impossibility for certain actors to achieve the legitimized social goals with the means available to them. They must therefore create new ones. Everyday acts exist only through the eyes of others and do not consist of the act itself. It is the interaction between the agents present in the situation which defines the nature of the act and governs its institutionalization. Institutions can also be viewed as a renunciation of an integration of innovative actions by state instrumentalization of civil society (Laville, 2005). They reflect the relations of domination, the inequalities between social groups, and the relations between the public authorities and social actors. The most common use of institutions leads to them being understood as a mode of 'legalization', i.e. a mode of governance with constraints, aspirations and resources of a legal nature. Let us review one by one the elements of the definition of institutionalism (Scott & Christensen, 1995; North, 1990; Powell & DiMaggio, 1991).

An institution is a *regulative system*. The law and administrative rules belong to this system and there is obligation. Some actors have power and impose their view on others through coercion, control and sanctions. All institutions have a set of more or less harmonized rules which determine the action of agents. Public powers are structured in this way. The industrial relations system is represented as a set of procedural rules stemming from collective bargaining and labor law. Within this classic approach to institutions, the rules regulate the managerial practices of the workforce. The institutional dimension exceeds the organization when the rules help to stabilize the relations between actors. Rules of law and conventions provide points of reference for action beyond the limits of the groups to which individuals belong. The institutional dimension thus regulates the organizational dimension which corresponds more to the mechanisms of co-ordination. In this context, the state is recognized as a strong institution and one which is hard to challenge.

An institution is a *normative system*. Social arrangements are significant only if they are based on obligations which are understood by each agent, as Durkheim meant by moral beliefs. What matters here is the awareness of the role to be played in a given situation and the desire to behave according to the expectations of others. The conduct of agents is internalized as standards. Thus, a new world of labor regulation cannot easily be imposed through force. Durkheim reminds us that a rule is acceptable only if it is legitimized vis-à-vis a great number of agents who will submit to it. Members of a group are subject to the rule which is maintained only if it is based on a state of opinion founded on customs (Durkheim, 1995). Unlike Durkheim, who refuses to consider the actor's conceptions or descriptions because they are viewed as being too vague to be sociological conceptions, interactionists turn these descriptions into the object of sociology. While some interactions produce meanings which serve as stabilized references, other interactions must be negotiated again at each new meeting. In this respect, the norms of a system possess a considerable margin of interpretation.

An institution is a *cognitive system*. This most recent conception of the institution is composed of cognitive elements which view social reality as a constructed whole. The institution appears to be historically given to others when there is objectivity, i.e. a crystallization of forms which goes beyond the preferences of the actors. The objectivity of institutions deepens and consolidates the relations; it takes hold and cannot change easily. The institutional world is thus experienced as a natural order but it is socially constructed as a reality made up of external and coercive events. The neo-institutional approach underlines the importance of roles, ideas, knowledge systems, beliefs and rules in the structure of organizations but also that of cognitive processes and social symbols. The innovation process reflects the power and organized interests of actors who rally around solution proposals.

However, the interests or intentions of actors are not organized in an automatic and transparent way but are defined and take shape in an institutional way. The institution has two meanings: (a) a situation in which shared knowledge defines what has meaning and consequently shows what actions are possible; (b) a phenomenological process through which certain social relations and actions end up being taken for granted by the actors. According to Garfinkel (1967), the shared views of a situation are produced in interaction, but once produced, they are perceived to be objective and external to the actors as a natural order and not as a human construction. From this perspective, institutions are not only a conglomeration of rules or sets of norms but also knowledge systems. Tacit rules, informal organization and prescribed work show that the interpretation of a particular rule by actors in the situation can only be understood through this third dimension of institutions (Reynaud, 1985, in 1997). Social innovation must carve out a place for itself in this predominating pre-established institutional framework. The innovation must then be diffused. Creation and diffusion are possible only if this institution withdraws and some components of this institutional system are deconstructed and this break is also legitimized.

Thus, habits, routines and tacit knowledge embedded in formal qualifications are also the medium of institutional rules. The neo-institutional approach therefore focuses on the cognitive and cultural explanations as well as on the properties of supra-individual units which cannot be reduced to direct consequences of individual motives. When a situation is recognized as being appropriate for institutionalization, the actor no longer seeks alternatives since he has developed preferences which are identified with an obligation on his part and on the part of others. This means internalization which opens the door to ritualization. It is at this point that the rule becomes external to the actors who only retain the obligation, forgetting its premises and the reasoning which gave rise to the requirement. These rules, norms and knowledge systems are obstacles to social innovations. When embarking on a change process, the actor does not automatically abandon these rituals but reproduces and protects them and, if necessary, will abandon or transform them based on the new emerging situation. Thus, his action is not motivated only by the constraint or norm but by this cognitive dimension according to which the actor appropriates the formal rules anew and then changes them while, at the same time being understood by others and comply with their expectations. Given that this is how social innovations are realized, let us examine this process.

Role of institutions in innovation

Organizations permeated with institutional rules and norms are subject to inertia. However, tensions continuously exist in organizations which originate in the diversity of representations and logics of action carried by a diversity of actors. An organization's system of rules stems from technical requirements, to which is added a political dimension represented by an unceasing fight for power recognition, numerous demands for new powers, new bases of authority or new forms of participation. These tensions are opportunities for social innovation. They show disagreements and variations in relations between the actors and encourage change. But, how is change then possible?

Hollingsworth (2000) completes the role of institutions in innovation processes by distinguishing five hierarchical levels of institutionalization in society. Each level possesses a degree of institutional embeddedness which deepens according to the hierarchical level. At the first level are performance and results. This involves taking account of the organization's goals which are measured in terms of expected results. When the results are not met, this may mean a problem of adaptation, malfunction or a clash of logics. A negative performance may be a sign that the organization cannot go on without a profound change in its rules. The opportunity to innovate is thus provided. Results are not merely the sheer product of technical constraints but also the opportunity to reconfigure the foundations of power in the organization.

At the second level, organizational forms are created in order to achieve the performance and results of the first level. Organizations tend to model themselves after similar organizations in their area of activity, which are perceived to be successful or legitimate. The ubiquity of some forms of structural arrangements thus flows from the process of mimetism rather than from a model of efficiency. Organizations adjust without seeking solutions to their problems. If it were only a matter of determining the organizational form based on the optimization of interests of the dominant coalition in the organization, institutions would undoubtedly not develop forms so similar to each other in a given society. Organizations resemble one another because they are under the influence of institutions and not because they are in pursuit of optimal productivity. An organizational form which meets the productivity goals while integrating legitimized rules is soon diffused according to the principles of mimetism. Structural components of an organization are institutionalized when the latter has attained a special character through the emergence of distinct forms, processes, strategies, visions and competencies from organizational interactions and their adaptation. Institutionalization is realized when patterns exist which are socially integrated, ordered and stable, stemming from activities which were originally unstable and poorly organized (Selznick, 1996).

Context cannot be ignored when considering social innovations. It is often identified with what is external to the organization and what escapes from the influence of internal actors. However, context is more than just a background. It is the result of decisions which are made elsewhere, in other organizations, the sum of which form the social, economic or political environment which greatly affects the actors' capacity to take action in a given organization. Context thus stands out as a set of environmental variables which are interwoven in actors' internal relations and form a system. The organization's internal context depends on all past decisions which structure current relations between the actors.

A context exists to serve reproduction where laws and hierarchy are considered. A context exists to serve innovation where the market and information technologies are favored while the welfare state is weakened (Esping-Andersen, 2002). The context acts as a set of constraints but also highlights innovation resources. Innovation emerges when certain types of problems cannot be solved within existing institutions. Actors must take action and find innovative solutions to their problems, given the institutional void. In order to change, a number of innovative responses exist which were created at the theoretical level, but whose diffusion pits actors against each other, fighting over the consequences which respond only to the demands of the other's logic. There is a gap between identifying an isolated problem and institutionalizing a solution which is standardized to the whole society or a sub-system of this society. A great number of responses emerge at the outset. Actors propose solutions based on their interests, expectations, desires and identity as the solution gives meaning to them while being at times concerned with the consequences that the proposed solution will have for the other members of their group and other social categories. Actors develop a cognitive repertory which can be spotted or alternative strategies enabling comparisons, by evaluating the solutions which comply with the various standards of desirability.

At the third level are institutional sectors, such as the education system, the legal system, the industrial relations system and the corporate financing system which are distinct in each society but linked by a rule of coherence which makes it difficult to transfer them from one society to another. An institutional system can change only if the other sectors also change. These sub-systems are interdependent, in particular through institutional arrangements of co-ordination methods. For example, labor relations run across all organizations such that labor relations in organizations, such as those in the healthcare system and those in the education system, resemble one another. Then, at the fourth level are institutional arrangements which are important for co-ordinating the economic actors. They can be the market, the state, networks or associations. There are numerous arrangements and there is variety in each type of co-ordination method. A predominant configuration always exists in each society, for example, the market in the United States and the state in France. Power is distributed in highly varied ways between types of co-ordination methods and within each one, just as personal interests and social obligations are also unequally distributed in each mechanism and between them. It should also be noted that actors are engaged in more than one system of institutional arrangements and it is at this level that an actor can borrow an idea and circulate knowledge on innovations made possible because institutional systems and arrangements are inconsistent and their principles and procedures are interpreted. It is at this level that a society finds the flexibility needed to adjust to new circumstances.

Lastly, it is only at the fifth level that Hollingsworth brings into play the norms, rules, values and conventions which govern the behaviors of actors. The latter provide coherence to a society such that innovations cannot be easily transferred from one society to another. The deeper the institutional level and the more rooted it is in the behaviors of actors, the more difficult it becomes to change it and by extension, the more difficult it becomes to innovate. For example, an organization can introduce new ways of interacting with its users in order to deal with unflattering results or declining performance. These social innovations can attain the level of norms and rules if the organizations of a whole society face the same difficulties and thus require a profound transformation of rules or norms. In order to innovate, a society must be able to restructure the institutional arrangements, which requires that powers be redistributed. Sustainable innovations pass through networks of actors who use their collective power. Although it appears plausible that there cannot be innovation without institutional change, the density of levels nevertheless does not make for a balanced institutional transformation. Other inconsistencies will then appear.

The organizational structure integrates the norms and rules of a society and there is no dichotomy between organization and institution. Organizations are exposed to the same environment in a society. Organizations change and influence the institutional environment as the latter influences the co-ordination methods of organizations; they are evolving jointly. In this respect, societies are different. Some have weak general institutional arrangements such that organizations are the locus of autonomous and flexible action which respond more easily to new knowledge, and are thus highly innovative.

Systems possess this basic function of innovation which tends to spread by itself. Organizations adopt these programs more through mimetism and normative adaptation and less through coercion. Organizations tend to adopt these norms without necessarily identifying them as an adequate response to their problem but tend to conform to what is produced in the environment. At this stage of the process, innovations are legitimized and accepted by the spokespersons of the organization whereas implementation is a phase which must take into account the representations expressed by other members of the organization. By proposing these innovations as solutions to the problems of efficiency, they must also reconstruct the legitimacy so as to harmonize the differentiated logics which govern action and to keep in line with the major institutional principles. Processes are thus activities which harmonize organizations with their environment. Processes are internal to the organization but are also subject to external influences.

To sum up, after a long period of development of social innovations which were designed at the outset to solve a performance problem, their content becomes increasingly standardized and some universal criteria emerge. These relate simultaneously to procedures, processes and rules which govern the organization's internal relations. It is thus relevant to examine organizational actors who are the carriers and not merely the passive receivers of these innovations. They interpret and negotiate their role not according to prescribed rules but in accordance with the meaning they give to it, considering the expectations of others.

Innovation process or building legitimacy

The process relates to local realities and the implementation of actors' practical knowledge. The process consists in comparing the contexts, contents and knowledge that actors have in order to give meaning to the new emerging reality. This is when logics of actions and strategies are deployed, the reality is questioned and an agreement is negotiated through persuasion, discussion and exchange of arguments, but sometimes through ruse, manipulation and use of force. At this point, the institution comes into play as a cognitive system. An innovation process brings to light all the strategies and activities deployed by the actors in order to construct a new relational universe, to oppose it or to maintain the status quo. A process is situated in a diachronic plan. It is important to take account of organizational actors or groups of actors not only because they support or obstruct the innovation but because they are first of all its starting point.

An organization is a collection of world representations and not only an entity characterized by a single representation. The differences between these representations affect the conception of social innovation. The formal structures cannot predict how participants perceive their roles or how their representation will be expressed in the innovation process. This is why it must be seriously considered.

Under these circumstances, an innovation is rooted in the organization only if the actors agree and adjust their world representation. Each group brings to the table its goals and means, the cognitive logic of which guides action. However, action is possible only if the different logics of action are aligned. Social innovation disrupts the stability of alignments which must be re-ordered. Only the actors can negotiate these alignments because they are the only ones who really know the motives and interests of each group within the organization. A change involves moving from one type of institutional practices toward another type (Bacharach, Bamberger & Sonnenstuhl, 1996).

Two aspects of the process are highlighted: (a) the process brings into play actors who have enough autonomy to interpret and negotiate agreements; (b) the innovation process consists of legitimation activities. The transformation activities form a process of negotiation, bargaining or accommodation which accompanies any innovation because groups protect their interests and put forward new ones. Their arguments are based on the concepts of efficiency in order to justify and legitimize their choices. Innovation is a process which thus takes the form of a network in which the actors discuss, debate, fight, accept, reject, adopt or come to terms with the actions taken and the decisions made. The result is a new organizational form which is equivalent to a new state of tension and co-operation that nevertheless provides a degree of stability. According to Strauss (1978), the negotiated order leads to a degree of continuity. However, an agreement prevails as long as it is not disrupted by another change, a lay-off, a drop in the market, new aspirations of users and consumers, a change of government, a new more authoritarian director, collective bargaining process which stumbles over wages, problems related to the recognition of employees' contribution to productivity or a new social policy. In this sense, the agreement is transient and the "negotiated order" is temporary. It is occasionally assessed, often renewed, but it can be altered and, at other times, rejected. Any change in the agreement requires a new negotiation.

An agreement is effective and complies with the meaning given to it by the actors if it is legitimized. Legitimation is the process of justification and explanation, and adds a cognitive validity to the meanings objectified by language, the rudimentary theoretical propositions and explicit theories. An institution starts with a convention built on joint interests but whose agents are vulnerable to defection, renegotiation or 'free riding' (Douglas, 1999). To enjoy the status of an institution, a convention thus requires a parallel cognitive configuration, an analogy which obscures its human origins. This is why the institution appears to be part of the order of the universe and seems to be obvious to those who support its logic. This, then, reinforces the institution's inherent trend toward inertia which limits the flexibility of human action.

Innovation thus requires a system to legitimize the sequences of transformation and to abandon or renounce alternative realities. The former reality must be re-interpreted in light of the system legitimizing the new reality. At first, social innovation introduces values and normative structures such as the ideal of democracy, partnership-based governance or transparency, which contradict other values such as unilateral authority, control and coercion.

Supporters of the neo-liberal ideology legitimize their position not by optimizing the gains that can be achieved by one category of social actors at the expense of another category, but rather as the achievement of greater freedom which is thus accessible to all. For them, competition between individuals is natural since it represents the primacy of the individual over the social groups who hinder personal growth. Similarly, the opening of markets gives access to modernity and the values of consumerism to regions of the world which have been deprived of them. On the other hand, social groups who defend democracy legitimize their position by referring to the primacy of the group over the individual, by sheer force of numbers, by rejecting all decisional authorities higher than the community, and through shared decision making, viewed as the only guarantee of organizational effectiveness against coercive authority and a single power. In their view, it is human nature to act together, to help each other, to develop a collective identity which depends on human solidarity.

These two major principles establishing the legitimacy of some versus others clash, and one of the two will triumph but not without integrating the other's values so as to be accepted as a compromise. In their regulative form, institutions intervene in particular to restrict change. Actors open up to change while defending their reference frameworks, being willing to change in order to make co-operation more effective. As pointed out by Berger and Luckmann (1966), a substantive theory is demonstrated to be pragmatically greater than other theories not by virtue of its intrinsic qualities but by its applicability to the social interests of groups which become their carriers. Similarly, it is not necessarily the one who has the best theory who wins but the one who has the most power and can thus impose his theory on others.

Studies have mainly dealt with the internal characteristics of organizations which explain innovation. How can knowledge, which is a critical resource, be produced? To this end, it is necessary to understand the micro-arrangements at the institutional level of a society. Institutional arrangements like those found in national systems of innovation relate to communications and methods of co-ordination as well as their diversity. This can involve, on the one hand, the transfer or circulation of people from one organization to another through joint projects, joint publications, financial links and a strong link between individuals in alliances and partnerships. On the other hand, this can involve the hierarchy, the market, the state and reciprocity which are methods that are different from the former in terms of co-ordination and connection. Associations and networks dominate the co-ordination methods of the knowledge economy because they cross borders and link up actors of diverse origins despite distance. However, institutions influence the creation of innovation and the development of society.

Innovation thus encounters limits because institutions and organizations evolve together, and actors and institutions are mixed in a process with several components (Nelson, 1993; Freeman, 1995; Lundvall, 2002). To succeed in innovation, the protagonists do not merely follow the rules but break them, get away from them and change their environment in order to gain advantages. Indeed, it is the meta-rules and norms which bring societies in line and provide coherence to the various social groups and arenas.

Conclusion

With social innovation, not only efficiency is promoted but also social capital, social networks, sharing, and the feeling of participating in the development of democracy. Pragmatic demands and social practices including democracy and justice as well as effectiveness and efficiency are at the center of social innovation. This really means transforming society from the bottom-up. How is this consent built, leading to a co-ordination method which is effective in achieving the expected goals, within the meaning given to it by the actors and within the constraints imposed by institutions? Following the stages of a process is to follow the itinerary of legitimization through which the actors negotiate implicitly or explicitly their conditions of support for innovation. In this Chapter, we aimed at showing how organizations can be transformed through a process of innovations. The process is much too often described as a set of voluntary activities rootless to institutional rules, norms or knowledge. Nonetheless, the process of innovation is feasible if former institutional arrangements are shaken and their legitimacy questioned. On the other hand, the organization as the locus of the innovation process becomes the object of innovation since social actors evolved within organizations. These processes can also be useful for any kind of organization such as associations or informal grouping. Those specific processes also aim at urban revitalization and spatial intervention because social activities are produced through the collapse of different organizations in the cities and regions. Despite the differences between forms of organizations, processes of innovation are quite similar and analogies can be easily made.

It is the actors who, through their network, develop intense and complex collective action leading to a change in the social system. Only this collective action can lead to a major transformation. It is the networks of actors who cross several organizations and use their collective power to change the system and the decision-making structures through frequent actions which lead to progressive innovations. The stability of institutions contributes to progressive changes rather than radical transformations. Interactions are mediated by the socially constructed spirit of actors' patterns of perception and representations. Neo-institutionalists attach importance to cognitive structure which results from the adaptation and is a response to the influence of the environment. There are inconsistencies in complex organizations which are better understood as coalitions governed by numerous rationalities and negotiated authority and not by a unified system of co-ordination. These coalitions have open borders and such organizations are therefore better prepared for innovation.

Actors transform the organization to which they belong by deconstructing previous arrangements, adopting new practices which break with the institutional arrangements. A new form of action emerges and encourages those who are not involved in it to change their form of action and imitate or adapt a variation of this form. Thus, co-ordination methods change and, at the level of society, there are also transformations guided by innovations in governance. Those who innovate are those who succeed in transforming their institutional environment.

The three components of institutions - rules, norms and knowledge - are continually present in all social situations but there is always one which dominates, depending on the context, circumstances and the time of the activity. Organizations are subject to the influences of the past and of their environment, external pressures, and the relational, cultural and historical influences which last and act on the structures. Norms and rules are solidly embedded in institutional systems. The broader their application, the more actors integrate them into their action; the more coherent and sustainable they are, the longer their existence.

To thoroughly understand innovation, this neo-institutional perspective presumes a program of studies and research on how institutions are connected with the process of innovation and its diffusion. Longitudinal studies will help to grasp the trend toward isomorphism and mimetism, the methods of building legitimacy and the action of networks in favor of innovations. Comparative studies between different societies as well as the contribution of several disciplines in the social sciences and humanities will provide a better understanding of the inter-influence of values, norms, rules and conventions, as a system which puts limits on the extent of innovations while attributing resources to them.

References

Abell, P., 1995, The New Institutionalism and Rational Choice Theory; in: Scott, R.W. & S. Christensen (eds), *The Institutional Construction of Organizations. International and Longitudinal Studies,* Sage Publ., Thousand Oaks, London and New Delhi, pp. 3-14.

Alter, N., 2003, *L'innovation ordinaire*, PUF, Paris.

Bacharach, S.B., P. Bamberger & W.J. Sonnenstuhl, 1996, *The Organizational Transformation Process: The Micropolitics of Dissonance Reduction and the Alignment of Logics of Action,* Administrative Science Quarterly, 41, pp. 477-506.

Barnett, W.P. & G.R. Carroll, 1995, Modeling Internal Organizational Change, *Annual Review of Sociology*, Vol. 21, pp. 217-236.

Berger, P.L. & T. Luckmann, 1966, *The Social Construction of Reality. A Treatise in the Sociology of Knowledge*, Anchor Books, Doubleday, New York.

Callon, M., 1992, The Dynamic of Techno-Economic Networks; in: Coombs, P. et al. (eds), *Technological Change and Company Strategies*, Academic Press, London, pp. 72-102.

Commons, J.R., 1931, Institutional Economics, *American Economic Review*, Vol. 21, pp. 648-657.

DiMaggio, P.J., 1988, Interest and Agency in Institutional Theory; in: Zucker, L.G. (ed.) *Institutional Patterns and Organizations: Culture and Environment*, Ballinger Publ., Cambridge Mass., pp. 3-21.

Douglas, M., 1999, *Comment pensent les institutions*, La Découverte, Paris.

Durkheim, E., 1995, *Leçons de sociologie, Quadrige*, Presses Universitaires de France, Paris (original edition 1950).

Esping-Andersen, G. (ed.), 2002, *Why We Need a New Welfare State*, Oxford University Press, Oxford.

Freeman, C., 1995, The National System of Innovation. Historical Perspective, *Cambridge Journal of Economics*, Vol. 19, N°. 1, pp.5-24.

Garfinkel, H., 1967, *Studies in Ethnomethodology*, Prentice Hall, Englewood Cliffs, New Jersey.

Hollingsworth, J.R., 2000, Doing Institutional Analysis: Implication for the Study of Innovations, *Review of International Political Economy*, Vol. 7, N°. 4, pp. 595-644.

Laville, J.-L., 2005, *Éléments pour un cadre d'analyse du changement social démocratique*, CRISES seminar, April 2005.
Lawrence, P.R. & J.W. Lorsch, 1967, *Organization and Environment*, Harvard Business School Press, Cambridge.
Lundvall, B.A. (ed.), 2002, *National Systems of Innovation. Towards a Theory of Innovation and Interactive Learning*, Pinter, London and New York.
March, J.G. & H.A. Simon, 1958, *Organizations*, Wiley, New York.
Merton, R.K. ,(1949) 1973, *Social Theory and Social Structure*, Free Press, New York.
Nelson, R., 1993, *National Systems of Innovation: A Comparative Study*, Oxford University Press, Oxford.
North, D.C., 1990, *Institutions, Institutional Change and Economic Performance*, Cambridge University Press, Cambridge.
Pettigrew, A.M., 1985, *The Awakening Giant. Continuity and Change in Imperial Chemical Industries*, Basil Blackwell, Oxford.
Powell, W.W. & P.J. DiMaggio, 1991, *The New Institutionalism in Organizational Analysis*, The University of Chicago Press, Chicago.
Reynaud, J.-D., (1985) 1997, *Les règles du jeu. L'action collective et la régulation sociale*, Armand Colin, Paris.
Schumpeter, J. A., (1931) 1967, *The Theory of Economic Development*, Oxford University Press, Oxford.
Scott, R.W., 2001, *Institutions and Organizations*, Sage Publication, Thousands Oaks.
Scott, R.W. & S. Christensen (eds), 1995, *The Institutional Construction of Organizations. International and Longitudinal Studies*, Sage Publ., Thousand Oaks, London.
Selznick, P., 1996, Institutionalism 'Old' and 'New', *Administrative Science Quarterly*, Vol. 41, pp. 270-277.
Strauss, A., 1978, *Negotiations. Varieties, Processes, and Social Order*, Jossey-Bass, San Francisco.
Van de Ven, A.H. & M.S. Poole, 1995, Methods for Studying Innovation Development in the MIRP; in: Huber, G. P. & A. H. Van de Ven (eds), *Longitudinal Field Research Methods. Studying Processes of Organizational Change,* Sage Publications, Thousand Oaks, pp. 155-185.
Weber, M., 1995, *Économie et société, volume 2 L'organisation et les puissances de la société dans leur rapport avec l'économie*, Plon Agora, Paris (original edition 1957).
Woodward, J., 1965, *Industrial Organization: Theory and Practice*, Oxford University Press, London.

4 The Agile State, an Organizational View on Spatial Development Policy in The Netherlands

Roy G. Mierop

Introduction

The Netherlands is a densely populated country. Therefore spatial planning is an important policy field for the government. Plans traditionally were the key instruments to regulate initiatives regarding the development and renovation of town and countryside. The state today has to act in an environment that is characterized by great and increasing complexity and dynamics. The country is covered with many plans, but the realization of these plans is problematic. In the field of spatial planning the government reacts on this situation by applying the concept of the so-called spatial development strategy. A major obstacle for an effective deployment of this strategy is the circumstance that the governmental organizations involved are not yet adapted to the changed environment they have to operate in. They lack the agility necessary to cope constructively with fast and unexpected changes in their environment.

In this Chapter the spatial development policy, as is intended by the Dutch government, is regarded from the organizational point of view. It is based on the practical experience of the author, in his capacity of organization consultant, and on the research he conducted in the framework of his PhD study. The research project tries to establish the structural, cultural and technological conditions for agile organizations in the public administration of The Netherlands via case studies on the application of spatial development policy on national, regional and local levels.

Spatial policy making in a changed society

Horizontality

In a discussion with a city manager about the issue of interactive policy making the manager sketched the following imaginary situation (Mierop & Bastiaansen, 2002: 11, 12).

> The city is working on the renovation of the center area. As is customary the city's planning department is given the assignment to draw up a plan. Of course participation of the inhabitants is included in the planning process. In several meetings citizens have the opportunity to comment on the draft plans presented by the city. During one of these meetings a controversial part of the center plan is put on the agenda. On behalf of the inhabitants of the area, an action group presents an alternative plan. This plan is professionally underpinned and is presented in a penetrating and compelling way, using state of the art visualization techniques. The city is only able to counter the alternative plan with some vaguely colored felt-tip drawings of the area, to abstract for the citizens to understand. Moreover the cities professionals have no answer on the well-founded alternative plan of the action group. This occurrence causes deep frustration in the planning department. The performance during the participation meeting is experienced as a failure by the civil servants

involved. They were not able to present their plan effectively. More important is that with a jolt they realized that citizens can effectively organize themselves, that they have their own network of contacts and that they are able to mobilize knowledge when needed. The professionals of the planning department up till now unconsciously took it for granted that they always had more knowledge and information at their disposal than citizens did. Suddenly one is aware of the fact that the city probably even has a knowledge backlog and that it is doubtful if the organization is able to gain lost ground in time. What to do?

This situation indeed is imaginary, but in the eyes of the city manager certainly not unrealistic. It is an illustration of the changed, horizontally developed relations that are characteristic for the nowadays society in The Netherlands. Articulate and individualistic citizens no longer automatically recognize the authority of government. Authority has to be earned time and again (Albeda & Etty, 2002).

Societal changes have an impact on spatial planning too. The Council of Housing, Spatial Planning and the Environment (VROM-Raad, 2004) points at the strongly increased maturity of citizens. The conditions for this are created by the increased availability of information and the possibilities one has for participation, lodging objections and appeal. Secondly, there is the increased emancipation of parties on the playing field of spatial planning. This group has grown, it has obtained its own sector positions and the actors have to collaborate more often more considerably. In the third place the positions in the real estate market have changed. Government for a long time already does not have the land in possession that it wants to develop. Institutional investors, real estate developers and developing contractors often have acquired the landownership long before the actual development is at hand. This calls for enhanced process orientation in public sector planning to clearly point out how the government will deal with these real estate positions. In the fourth place there has to be reckoned with the poor subsidy context for spatial policy making. Because of the current overall economical climate and the financial and economic government policy spatial projects are increasingly dependent on private sector funding. It underlines the necessity of collaboration within the public sector and between public and private parties.

Dynamic connectedness

In many policy documents governmental organizations show the awareness of the speed with which changes take place. The Social and Cultural Planning Office (Sociaal en Cultureel Planbureau, 2000) for instance points at the impact of technological developments such as the explosive growth of mobile telephony. In a few years The Netherlands has got more mobile phones than households. Another example is the advance of the personal computer. Between 1995 and 1998 the possession of a pc with modem has tripled and the number of internet connections five folded. It is expected that this growth will continue in the coming years.

With the advancing computerization the importance of territorial boundaries also diminishes (Wetenschappelijke Raad voor het Regeringsbeleid, 1998a). In the field of public administration we see the abolishment of internal borders of the European Union. In the field of economics there is an increasing globalization. Economical relations are not limited to the territory of a state but extend over the whole world. Companies thrive when they operate in networks on regional, national and international level. But citizens also put the network concept in practice. Individuals have access to a fast amount of information files with the help of ICT. They are able to form an opinion on their own on all kind of issues and to rapidly share their opinion with many others. Because of this beliefs can change quickly. Citizens seek connection with each other, but they do this to a larger extent outside the official channels and participation procedures and not under governmental steering. Existing institutions like political parties and labor unions in practice more and more turn out not to be the platforms for connectedness. Citizens establish their own platforms and remove them when they don't experience the added value of it any more. The 'big stories' of long-established institutions prove to draw less and less interested parties. The 'little story' of an individual or a group more often than not is the starting point for a process within which supporters check in and a community comes into being. Citizens can take part in several communities and they form the connection between these communities. This way an archipelago originates consisting out of many centers with a great variety of content, size and life span. The archipelago is not hold together by hierarchy. Functional and dynamic connectedness is the driving force that spurs individual citizens to organize themselves around issues that have their real concern. An example of this is the protest movement that manifests itself during the meetings of the World Trade Conference. Modern society appropriately is referred to as a network society (Castells, 2000). And practice shows that often this concerns horizontal networks that develop without top-down steering and that ignore city limits, provincial limits or country limits and the accompanying hierarchical governmental structures.

Turbulence

In the classic approach of policy making the processes of policy formulation and policy execution are sequentially structured and are organizationally separated. This is a useful approach when there is a high degree of predictability of developments in the policy area and when the extent to which societal change can be effected by government policies is large. In other words, when government can operate under stable societal circumstances and when the behavior of citizens, the way they will respond to government policy, is totally predictable.

In our network society these premises turn out to be less and less tenable. Stability has made room for turbulence. This circumstance can be characterized as: "a state in which the dimensions of space and time, the warp and weft of the fabric we call earthly reality, radically mess up. In space fixed and familiar positions and benchmarks are getting adrift. What we used to place here unexpectedly turns up there and vice versa. Such a state we use to describe with the term 'instability'. Over time the fixed and planned order and progress become adrift. Earlier and later get entangled with all the consequences for the distinction between the short term and the long term. For this situation we use the term 'unpredictability'. The resultant of instability and unpredictability is called 'uncontrollability'" (Zwart, 2001). Under these circumstances it is not possible any more to give a one dimensional and linear relation between cause and consequence. Reality is much more complex and time and again turns out to be more colorful than is the case in the perception of policy makers. Finding the greatest common denominator as policy base more and more is becoming an impossible task for policy makers. Everything seems to be connected to everything and in addition to that everything seems to change color over time. The consequence of this is increasing uncertainty. Not only regarding the feasibility of a policy, but also regarding the question if specified policy measures will have the intended outcome.

As a result of turbulence governmental steering has become more complex, also in the field of spatial planning (VROM-Raad, 2004). The concept of the network society makes it clear that the steering role of government is limited. Imperious steering seldom pays off any more even though the ambitions of spatial policy are not diminished. Still, the pursuit of a sustainable quality of the environment is the central point of focus in the government policy. This intrinsic ambition however has to be substantiated with limited financial means and under the condition of reduction of the burden of rules. Therefore spatial planning has to be renewed. "It is due time to change course when it comes to the arrangement of the spatial environment in our country. Town and country planning as we have known it for more than a century does not work any more in our dynamic society. The plans with a time horizon of ten years or longer, that have been designed from behind the desk, are overtaken by reality ever faster" (Interprovinciaal Overleg, 2001: 7), so the Dutch provinces let know via their umbrella organization Interprovinciaal Overleg (IPO).

New performance requirements for the public sector

The role of government

Increased societal complexity and dynamics pose new performance requirements to the government. The foundation of this lies in the changed views on the role of government. The awareness has come into being that the position of the center of all steering is no longer tenable. The paradigm of pure hierarchical steering is under pressure (Frissen, 2000). Central steering from one singular point has a certain slowness which does not fit in any more with the societal turbulence and with the pace of change. In addition much more actors are participating in public decision making. They have disposal of a lot of knowledge and of the means to realize their goals. This variety hampers government to provide for coherence solely on its own strength.

The still predominantly vertical organizational orientation of the public administration is at odds with the development of horizontal networks. Horizontality strengthens citizens in their belief to be treated as clients by the government and as equal participants in policy formulation and decision making. Also citizens more and more adopt an autonomous attitude because they have adequate inquiring capabilities on many issues of public decision making. Because citizens are able to dispose of much information they are capable themselves to directly oversee the way in which government performs its duties. Under these circumstances horizontal forms of planning, inspection and account are necessary that correlate with the concept of checks and balances (Eenmalige Commissie ICT en Overheid, 2001).

The new beliefs about the role of government are strikingly put to words by 'The Group of 100', a community of concerned citizens from different sections of society, among which the well known soccer coach Johan Cruijff. They state that in an individualizing society the call becomes stronger to shift powers and responsibilities downwards, to city and district councils, companies and social organizations such as environmental and human rights organizations and most of all to citizens themselves. Governments have to search for answers on social issues in partnership. Opportunities for this arise when less regulatory density leaves more room to local authorities for an own interpretation. "Together with 'their' citizens local authorities form a public partnership and are more able to make choices that suit the real needs on the spot, for instance when it concerns schools, safety, social welfare and health care and the design of the public space. Impassioned neighbors who are responsible for each other stand up only when self-determination and self-responsibility can go hand in hand in all day practice, surely when this responsibility is coupled with an 'own' district budget. After all without neighborhood partnership there is no solution for safety, beauty and wholeness of the environment." (De Groep van 100, 2001: 19)

New public management

The need to modernize government is embedded in the international movement of New Public Management. The foundation for this movement was made by Osborne and Gaebler in their talked-about book 'Reinventing Government' (Osborne & Gaebler, 1992) in which the concept of an entrepreneurial government was outlined in ten operational principles (Box 4.1).

> **Box 4.1: Ten operational principles (Osborne & Geabler, 1992)**
>
> Osborne and Gaebler suggest that governments should: 1) steer, not row (or as Mario Cuomo put it, "it is not government's obligation to provide services, but to see that they're provided"); 2) empower communities to solve their own problems rather than simply deliver services; 3) encourage competition rather than monopolies; 4) be driven by missions, rather than rules; 5) be results-oriented by funding outcomes rather than inputs; 6) meet the needs of the customer, not the bureaucracy; 7) concentrate on earning money rather than spending it; 8) invest in preventing problems rather than curing crises; 9) decentralize authority; and 10) solve problems by influencing market forces rather than creating public programs.

A practical application of these principles in American government can be found in the so-called Blair House Papers of the Clinton-Gore administration (Clinton & Gore, 1997). Strengthening the service orientation of government organizations, outside-in thinking and acting and breaking through unnecessary bureaucracy were the central points of focus in their approach of government modernization. Their guidelines for change can be divided in three groups: (1) deliver great service, (2) foster partnership and community solutions and (3) reinvent to get the job done with less. Clinton and Gore expected their civil service organizations to have the ability to collaborate and bundle resources to effectively and efficiently contribute to the approach of societal issues. Illustrative is the plea to remove the barriers between more than 600 federal subsidy programs. The existing compartmentalized, centralized top-down approach turned out to be not flexible enough for government to effectively operate under fast changing circumstances in society over the whole country. Key principles to make the move to result-oriented collaboration and the removal of barriers for effective government action are noted in Box 4.2.

> **Box 4.2: Key principles for result-oriented collaboration (Clinton & Gore, 1997)**
>
> In moving to partnerships that focus on results and remove barriers to effectiveness, the key principles are:
> - Improved accountability: make results the principal measure of success.
> - Program consolidations: merge funding streams in ways that make sense to grantees and customers, such as around common results. If this is not feasible, then streamline and simplify.
> - Administrative simplification: streamline processes, eliminate micromanagement, and reduce wasteful paperwork across programs. Provide one-stop shops and single points of contact.
> - Eliminate barriers: help identify and solve problems, removing barriers to results.
> - Increased flexibility: devolve decision making; set national goals and objectives, with much more flexibility for states and communities to determine how those are achieved.

Different government

The process of modernization in The Netherlands has been set in on all levels of government for quite some time (Mierop & Bastiaansen, 2002). The need for modernization and improvement of the quality of the public sector is explicitly recognized in the coalition agreement of the Cabinet Balkenende II (Kabinet, 2003a). It is perceived as a huge and complex operation aimed at transforming the public administration organization and at changing the culture and behavior of politicians, civil servants and the Dutch citizen. The Dutch Cabinet has laid down its philosophy on modern government in a white paper (Kabinet, 2003b). In the Cabinet's analysis the far-reaching developments in society that took place during the last 50 years were inadequately translated in new roles for citizens and their organizations, the civil society, and for government. Citizens have expectations of the government that can not be lived up to and the government assumes an unrealistic concept of citizenship. As a consequence of this mismatch the legitimacy of much governmental action is under discussion. Therefore it is necessary to modernize government in its relationship with citizens and in the way it operates. A modern government has to exercise restraint when it comes to issuing rules and has to give citizens and their organizations more room. It has to secure public interests and the demands of the constitutional state. It has to perform with high quality where market and civil society are not capable to execute public duties.

The Cabinet points at the connection between the way a government shapes its relation with society and the way in which it is organized. Its view on a modern government organization is elaborated in an action program (Kabinet, 2003c). This ambitious program for change primarily focuses on central government. The intended organizational change is approached along four lines of action: (1) improvement of service for the citizen, (2) regulatory reduction and alteration, (3) redesign of the internal organization of central government and (4) renewal of the relations between central government, the provincial government and local government. The program is comprehensive and covers the organization of the processes of policy formulation, policy implementation and inspection as well as the redesign of secondary work processes. When it comes to policy making the focus of change is on breaking through the compartmentalization. Ministries are still too much oriented inward. Thinking inside out is considered to be a major obstacle for interdepartmental collaboration and for an integrative approach of societal issues that have to be the starting point for collaborative policy making. The connection between separate policy fields must be reinforced. This applies for spatial planning too. Also the effectiveness of public-private partnership has to be increased.

Coherence between policy making and implementation

The government also asks attention for the coherence between policy making and policy implementation. In the past policy these were separated and organized as more or less stand alone processes. This separation is still regarded as necessary but there is a growing awareness of the need to overcome its disadvantages, especially when it concerns the tension between ministerial responsibility and control 'at a distance' on executive public sector organizations. Also the efficiency of implementation activities has to be improved. Measures are found necessary to increase a joint implementation of subsidy arrangements and the connection of ICT networks to enable a smooth exchange of information between the processes of policy formulation and execution.

The Scientific Council for Government Policy (*Wetenschappelijke Raad voor het Regeringsbeleid*) underlines the importance of an appropriate assignment of responsibilities and competences to various actors in society, including government. The Council pleads for tailor-made policy making with respect to the various issues that have to be approached and with respect to the way in which a government faces the actors involved in policy execution. In the analysis of the Council, citizens want clarity about the appropriateness, the distributive aspects and the tenability of government policies. Citizens want to recognize the criteria for good governance in the policy goals (what), in the division of responsibilities and competences (who) and in the quality of service and treatment (how). The dynamics of the environment citizens and government have to operate in, and the increased individualization, compel to be considerate with the differences in action taking capacity that exist within seemingly homogenous groups. Therefore a custom-made approach is necessary. Government has to consider the fact that the behavior of citizens also will be determined by the way a government treats them and by the extent to which stimuli and sanctions connect to their real and essential interest. (Wetenschappelijke Raad voor het Regeringsbeleid, 2005)

New performance requirements

Three essential, new performance requirements for governance can be deduced from the earlier given analysis of the change in beliefs about the role of the government in modern society in The Netherlands (Mierop & Bastiaansen, 2002).

In the first place the ability to collaborate on the basis of added value. Governmental organizations often picture themselves beforehand as the director of the policy making process, also when it comes to interactive policy making processes. This point of view is rooted in the classic belief that government is the central point of steering in policy making processes. It stems from thinking from statutory authority. Claiming a role beforehand however is at odds with the horizontal relations that have emerged in society. A role can only be fulfilled effectively when it is granted by the parties with whom a government collaborates, on the basis of the added value they see in this role.

The added value of a government can stem from its ability to direct social capacity to an issue that has to be dealt with. For instance, taking care that inhabitants are proud again of their district local government lays the foundation for future collaboration on many fields of quality improvement of livability. Added value also can be delivered by building active trust (Van Wijngaarden, 2001) among the parties in collaboration. Parties give evidence of active trust when they not only verbalize it but also, and especially, when they practice it in real action. A government itself sets the example by sticking to the agreements it made. And last but not least, added value also lies in the skill to bring and hold together all relevant parties.

In the second place it comes to delivering made-to-measure. Citizens are used to be serviced tailor-made in many areas. They expect the same demand-oriented treatment from their government too. That requires the capability to deal with various target groups simultaneously and requires adequate scope in policy making to offer a framework for tailor-made solutions. The government has to get a sharp insight in the real needs of various target groups and in their perception of the policy issue at hand. Then the resources it has at its disposal, have to be clustered around the policy issues and the corresponding target groups. Modern government is able to configure its policy instruments and services in arrangements that are focused on the specific needs of various groups. Citizens do have to recognize themselves in government policy. Demand-oriented work means that the width, the intensity and the duration, in short the measure of collaboration, is tuned to the character of the policy problem that has to be dealt with. It applies to collaboration with external parties as well as to collaboration within the government organization. The content of the policy issue determines with whom collaboration is necessary, what the intensity of the collaboration has to be and how the process of collaboration has to be organized.

In the third place a government has to be able to mobilize knowledge with adequate speed. Policy making in the network society is a stirring and knowledge-intensive process. Working outside-in pre-supposes the ability to bundle and focus knowledge in a short span of time on the integrated approach of social problems and to make knowledge accessible for all parties involved. To be decisive, knowledge has to flow freely through the organization to be deployed there where it is needed the most. Knowledge therefore has to be extricated from the policy 'silos'. Modern ICT is an important instrument to enable this. Its potential however cannot be utilized to the full when the government organization is compartmentalized. Modern government therefore constantly tries to break down the barriers between departments and services to attain the sharing of insights, vision and methodologies.

Not only the boundaries inside a government organization must be permeable, it also applies to the boundary between the organization and its environment. Society harbors a vast potential of knowledge. It does not only encompass the professional knowledge of institutes like universities, research organizations and consultancy firms. The experiential knowledge of citizens is just as important for a creative and innovative approach of societal problems. Government has an important task in supporting citizens to explore, to make explicit and to apply their knowledge. For that a change is necessary in the way knowledge is perceived. Often experiential knowledge is appreciated less than professional knowledge and this is an obstacle for effective use. Citizens express their knowledge in their own language that deviates from the jargon of government professionals. Modern government understands and speaks the 'knowledge language' of citizens and therefore it communicates especially in concrete images and not in abstract figurations and texts. Its added value in interactive policy making arises because it knows how to connect the experiential knowledge of citizens with the professional knowledge of specialists.

Spatial development policy

The concept of spatial development policy

The concept of a developmental approach to spatial issues by the government was for the first time explicitly and systematic explored by The Scientific Council for Government Policy. With a thorough analysis the Council substantiated its opinion that the current intrinsic and process-oriented interpretation of spatial planning on national level is not tenable any more in the Dutch society. From the view point of spatial planning the Council defines a network society as "a society in which the social, economic and cultural structures are not determined any more by the shared use of a space, but by the connections between an individual actor (company, person or institute) and places, persons or activities elsewhere" (Wetenschappelijke Raad voor het Regeringsbeleid, 1998b: 94). Important is the observation of the Council that the network society does not so much as produce dullness or uniformity but that it changes spatial coherences. Distance is a less determining factor for the choice of location of companies and citizens. Spatial barriers are conquered by the application of modern technology in the field of communication and transport.

Moreover new spatial coherences manifest themselves, in the opinion of the Council, "fairly unexpected, are often instable and so undermine a national planning approach [...]". Often the coherences stem from "flighty cultural location choice motives that cannot be described in models in advance[...]". Therefore the Council is of the opinion that successful spatial policy requires a 'spatial development strategy' and "that is more than assigning a certain function to specific spatial entities" (Wetenschappelijke Raad voor het Regeringsbeleid, 1998b: p. 95). Such spatial development policies assume a dynamic approach to town and country planning and translates this in new institutional arrangements and intrinsic orientations. Especially in the recognition of the dynamics lies the opportunity to harmonize various and often conflicting interests of the users of space. Key concepts are differentiation and selectivity. In the network society spatial and social dynamics cannot be locked up any more in generic concepts such as urban nodal points, the compact city or compact city regions. Instead the Council pleads for open intrinsic concepts that need a territory-specific elaboration. Essential characteristics of a spatial development strategy are: (1) the emphasis on the meaning of integrative design on regional level, (2) direct coupling of planning to capital expenditure and (3) the need of political goal formulation coupled to checks and balances.

Emphasis on integrative design on regional level

The Netherlands has a tradition in national spatial planning. The benefit is that strategic development projects can be identified and implemented timely. By emphasizing integrative design on regional level, regions get the opportunity to respond to emerging spatial patterns. The girth of regions will have to be geared to this and can vary according to the nature of the spatial challenges. Reorganization of political-administrative boundaries is not necessary. The Council advocates the necessity to organize and facilitate temporary collaborations in order to deal with spatial challenges. An integrative mode of operation is focused on the search for possibilities to accommodate various interests, demands and claims in a region through concrete development designs. It is a form of investigative design.

Direct coupling of planning and capital expenditure

Direct coupling of planning and capital expenditure replaces the classic division of conceptual planning and financing. It reinforces policy effectiveness. The obligation of the government to execute is emphasized. This also has consequences for the governance dimension of spatial planning. Participation does not regard abstract plans any more, but is focused on tangible development initiatives that will increase the commitment of actors and will strengthen the meaning of the discussion. The coupling also works the other way around. Spatial development politics means that capital expenditures with substantial spatial consequences have to be combined with planning.

Coupling of political goal formulation and checks and balances

The spatial arrangement of an area is a democratic matter. Therefore it is emphatically a political move. However, too early coalition forming has to be prevented between public administrators and strong parties in the region. This after all can seriously harm the legitimacy of policy decisions. Politicians have to take the lead with concrete proposals when development initiatives do manifest themselves. After that however, room has to be made to bring in various elaboration alternatives from society into the process of planning. Parallel to this, coalitions can be formed between governmental and societal actors. Spatial development politics implies an open approach to the planning process. That cannot function well without elaboration of new institutional checks and balances. Supervision is necessary to ensure that all relevant stakeholders get the opportunity to participate in the discussion. Various development alternatives have to be included in the assessment. The control on this cannot be placed in the hands of the same body that also participates in planning and decision-making.

Interpretations of the concept

The concept of spatial development strategy was formulated in 1998 and enjoys a substantial interest. Professional specialists and policy makers have since dedicated themselves to further interpretation and elaboration of the concept in view of its application in practice. The process of interpretation is not over yet. Under professionals, attention is especially given to elaboration of the definition. In the opinion of the Council for Housing, Spatial Planning and the Environment the concept of development planning is not new and a radical change from 'admittance policy' to development policy is out of the question. The Council considers both types of spatial planning necessary. Spatial development politics is seen by the Council as a governing style and is defined as: "the entirety of public interventions in the physical domain, planning included, that is directed to the actual realization of spatial quality, in dialogue with interested parties and societal organizations and often in collaboration with market parties" (VROM-Raad, 2004: 26). A government performs the task of securing a careful process and looks after the public interest as much as that is plays the role of negotiator who knows how to commit parties to the realization of the intended result.

The Rathenau Institute considers spatial development planning as a social and cultural assignment for administrators, civil servants, citizens and entrepreneurs (Rathenau Instituut, 2004). The arrangement of the physical environment is considered a political challenge to keep The Netherlands healthy in economic, ecologic and social-cultural sense. In the 21st century this calls for a trend shift in thinking and acting in order to find a new balance between public and private parties. The Institute considers a substantial change of the role of government necessary. A government cannot deal with spatial development challenges solely on its own strength because of the gap between policy and practice, an awaiting organizational culture and a lack of means. Development planning is not only a new mental perspective, it is also another mode of operation. Persons involved need other competences and also a certain social idealism. From this point of view the Institute defines development planning as: "the interactive development of integral and implementation-oriented area arrangements that per definition stem from collaboration, that will lead to public added value and that can count on commitment of parties involved"(Rathenau Instituut, 2004: 11).

The Netherlands Institute for Spatial Research (RPB) adds the aspect of innovation to the concept of spatial development politics. The Institute considers it not sufficient any more to come to feasible projects through compromises reached in the collaboration between public and private parties. It is important to apply smart planning practices and to develop innovative spatial concepts to deal effectively with increasing and often conflicting spatial claims. The Institute even advocates system innovations in spatial planning, to bring about structural changes in society. Spatial development planning is seen as a method to generate transition and is defined as: "an area-oriented policy practice that anticipates the expected societal dynamics, that links the various spatial claims in a new way, that is supported by an active input of parties involved and that pays attention to active implementation." (Ruimtelijk Planbureau, 2004: 6, 7).

At this moment in The Netherlands spatial development politics is put in practice by policy makers on all governmental levels. According to the Ministry of Housing, Spatial Planning and the Environment spatial development planning is characterized by integrated area development (Ministerie van VROM, 2003). Projects are realized on the basis of an integral vision in a joint learning process of complementary parties. These parties pursue a quality leap by financing and implementing a project 'envelope' in which projects are developed coherently and in which balancing of costs and revenues can take place. In the National Spatial Strategy, that was laid down by the Cabinet in 2004, this approach is translated in a spatial policy that focuses more on stimulating developments in stead of putting up restrictions. Central government urgently invites co-authorities, social organizations, citizens and private sector parties to participate in area-oriented and broadly supported regional and local vision development and policy implementation. The governments involved take the position of partner of entrepreneurial citizens and companies. They enhance the dynamics instead of discouraging it by a multitude of rules. The revision of the Spatial Planning Act provides for more room for regional and local initiatives. Policy implementation takes up a central position. In connection with this instruments for land price policy are modernized, and the formation of development corporations (*ontwikkelingsmaatschappijen*) within the central governance.

On local government level the principles of spatial development politics already are being applied over a longer span of time, implicitly or explicitly. Examples are neighborhood development and development programs for large cities. As no other government level, local authorities know the 'stubbornness' of working realization-directed and working in collaboration with citizens and entrepreneurs in practice. Applying spatial development planning in practice shows that the administrative process has to be structured in broad outlines (Vereniging van Nederlandse Gemeenten, 2003). Collaboration with parties involved on the basis of joint ambitions accelerates the process of plan formulation and decision-making. Drawing in private sector parties is often only advisable when it comes to concrete projects and when the period of implementation is calculable.

On provincial level too, spatial development politics is well received (Interprovinciaal Overleg, 2001). In the perception of provincial policy makers spatial development politics require a combination of policy making and the ability to actually execute policy. Provinces have to be able to take the initiative in plan formulation and they must have the means (finance, personnel, knowledge) at their disposal to implement the plan. Therefore the establishment of regional land agencies is being contemplated. Furthermore it is recognized that spatial development politics is of consequence for the internal organization of a province and for the way provinces shape their collaboration relations. Available knowledge and expertise will have to be deployed differently. Civil servants will have to develop new skills and all persons involved, politicians too, will have to go through a learning process. The formation of a distinct task field for spatial development is being considered, that has to be embedded in the provincial organization.

Change of strategy

Although there are various interpretations of the concept of spatial development politics, a change in strategy to reach substantive policy goals can be established. As was noted earlier the Scientific Council for Government Policy has used the expression 'spatial development strategy' for this. In the classic approach to spatial planning the emphasis was put on the deployment of an 'admittance' strategy to realize policy goals. Development initiatives came from citizens and entrepreneurs and were adjusted through a system of do and don't regulations, incorporated in, sometimes sharply outlined, spatial zones. The government considered itself as it were in the role of a gatekeeper who admits desirable initiatives and locks out undesirable initiatives. This role will also stay necessary in the future. However, under the changed societal relations this admittance strategy is not sufficient any more. When in a plan locations are designated as zones for housing, industry or shopping, this does not necessary mean that these functions will be realized there on the desired point in time. Furthermore, changes in spatial requirements and in choice of location can occur rapidly so that the period of tenability of spatial plans is shortened. That's why a government will have to take initiatives itself to stimulate desired spatial developments. This requires a development strategy that explicitly observes the interests and motives of other space needing actors in society. The possibilities and impossibilities of the market for supply and demand of real estate will have to be taken into consideration. This calls for designing and calculating simultaneously in addition to the flexibility that is required to respond to changes, even when these are not foreseen. Regional development thus gets the character of a joint enterprise of all parties involved. From this perspective a regional plan is not any more a spatial plan any more but also a business plan. In such a plan not only the spatial projects that will be realized are specified, but also the contribution each party will make to these projects, how financing is guaranteed and how costs and benefits are shared out. So, one can speak of a joint venture. It will only succeed if all parties, including governments, act on the basis of secured trust, a demand-driven orientation and a great and active situational awareness.

Change of strategy requires change of organization. The current government organization responsible for spatial planning is built for the admittance strategy. That manifests itself in a basic organizational design that is predominantly structured along sector lines with specialized and task-oriented policy units as key building blocks. This organizational design has rendered good services but now in practice proves to be not suitable any more for an effective deployment of the development strategy.

The need for organizational modernization

Spatial development strategy in practice

As was mentioned before the spatial development strategy is applied on all governmental levels. Distinctive examples are the central government policy laid down in the Agenda for a Living Countryside (Ministerie van LNV, 2004), the regional development planning of the Province of Groningen (Provincie Groningen, 2000) and the urban development program Via Breda of the city of Breda (Gemeente Breda, 2004a). The intrinsic challenges for the governments concerned in these cases differ. The approaches they put into practice however show many similarities and are primarily focused on actually bringing about concrete projects. Key characteristics are: (1) situational awareness, (2) program management, (3) relation management and (4) directorship.

Situational awareness

On central government level as well as on provincial and local level attention and efforts are focused on the implementation of concrete plans. Beforehand policy frameworks are determined indeed, but these emphatically contain room for interpretation on the basis of specific situational circumstances. In other words: the logic of the situation is directional for concrete action. For government the action can be of controlling nature but also can involve concrete development initiatives. The process of implementation often takes a long time. Therefore one prepares oneself for situational changes and for the fact that changes that cannot be influenced can have implications for earlier drawn implementation plans and initiatives that were undertaken. This requires flexibility in implementation programming and instruments with which the implications of changes can be calculated quickly. The city of Breda for instance applies the instrument of the so-called 'switchboard'. Regular evaluation is a fixed part of a work process that has the character of the process planning.

Program management

A regional orientation is the crux of the spatial development strategy. This approach has two important starting points. The first starting point is that the boundaries of a region in which concrete initiatives have to be taken are determined by the nature of the development problem that has to be dealt with.

The second starting point is that the specific possibilities of that region are utilized maximally for the spatial development. These starting points require a coherent approach of the various development projects. In practice this is organized through program management or multi-project management. However, in this case it does not concern special, once-only activities that are executed besides the going concern activities of the governmental organization. Working area-oriented has a continuous character. In addition the results of the actions taken have a highly profiling value for the political management. Because of that, putting programs into effect has become a core activity of the government organization and program management has become part of the primary steering capacity. This requires a servicing attitude of formerly autonomous units. They have to learn to think and act in terms of delivering added value in stead of determining their relation with regional development programs on the basis of their authority embedded in rules and regulations.

Relation management

Many actors with various interests are involved in regional development. Their contribution to the implementation of the development policy is vital. The concern for establishing and maintaining trust is a crucial factor for successful collaboration. Collaboration starts with jointly determining the development challenge, the phase of problem articulation, and is continued in the following phase when the contribution to the regional development of each of the parties involved is determined. In the next phase of implementation, collaboration can even take the form of partnership. Good and lasting communication relations therefore are of great importance. In practice we can see that the concern for good relation management is secured organizationally by, among others, the appointment of civil servants as account manager or regional manager.

Directorship

In practice government applies a process-oriented approach in regional development. Bringing together and keeping together all relevant actors and mobilizing the needed knowledge potential are considered to be part of the core duty of government. Often government takes the initiative to this end and posts itself in the role of director of the process of collaboration. This is especially the case in the phase in which the development issue is determined and in the following phase of contribution determination. In the phase of implementation of the regional development plan government fulfils various roles at the same time, ranging from director and principal to participant in collaboration and supervisor of concrete projects. An important instrument to put the role of principal in practice is the performance agreement. To execute the role of director effectively, government needs a certain basis of influence. In this field a shift is taking place from rules and regulations as basis of influence to material assets in the form of landownership. On the level of local government this manifests itself in the transformation of the traditional municipal land and real estate department, with a mainly bookkeeping task, to a strategically acting development company. On the level of central government a joint development department is being established. On provincial level already so-called land banks are in use and the possibilities of establishing provincial development companies are being investigated.

Organizational barriers

In practice there still is a tension between the requirements of the spatial development strategy and the possibilities the internal government organization offers for this method of working. This tension has its origins in a number of organizational barriers.

In the first place it turns out that compartmentalization has become a way of life in all sections of the civil service organization. For instance, when consulting its personnel, Breda's management explicitly recognized the persistent presence of compartmentalization. It was found that a gap exists between verbal and written statements directed against compartmentalization and actual action in practice. There is still a strong inclination to think and act from policy territories. Significant in this respect is the use of the term 'policy competition'.

In the second place the basic design of the existing civil service organization is still generally based on a sector line up. Each sector is responsible for its 'own policy field'. This is embedded in the task description of departments and in the job description of staff members. The sector orientation is enhanced by the system of planning and control. Resource allocation and accountability still are mainly structured along sector lines. The policy territories are clearly recognizable in the budget. Collaboration is stimulated but sector departments have the primary authority over the resources that are assigned to them. Therefore much co-ordination is needed to come to collaboration. Organization-wide spatial development programs are thus confronted with the tension between decisiveness and collaboration with sector departments. Always there is the threat that the program organization will become detached from the standing line organization. Knowledge management and competence management are poorly developed in practice. This seriously hinders a smooth exchange of knowledge and information that is needed for an integrative way of working.

In the third place management en staff members are creative in evasive behavior. 'We already work in the new way' is a much-used argument to avoid change and one is inventive enough to underpin this argument in word and writing. Instead of actively working together in an integral way, in regional development in practice the principle is applied that each sector works integrally and therefore does not have to give up anything regarding its autonomy. Thinking from competences and not from added value still predominates. This way of thinking manifests itself for instance in the reflex to divide integrated societal issues, like regional development, into sub-issues that are formulated in such a way that they match with the competences of existing policy departments.

In the fourth place there is still a lack of connectivity and interoperability in the information infrastructure. The adoption of the 'architecture' concept to coherently organize the acquisition, communication, management and reuse of information is gaining ground, but the situation in many organizations in practice bears the resemblance of an empire of information islands. Each department of agency has its own information systems that are directly related to its field. Connecting information systems across various organizational units still meets obstinate resistance. Exchange of immediately usable information is time consuming, if possible at all. Human interfaces are necessary still to translate data from one department to useful information for other departments. This does not only apply to information for use in primary processes but also for the exchange of management information.

Indications for an emerging organization concept

In many places a process of organizational modernization has started off. This also applies to the examined cases of the Ministry of Agriculture, Nature and Food quality (Ministerie van LNV, 2000), the province of Groningen (Provincie Groningen, 2001) and the city of Breda (Gemeente Breda, 2004b). In all of these cases the main focus of the process of modernization is de-compartmentalization. Organizational change is not initiated purely in consideration of the spatial development strategy, but it does contain the ingredients that enable a smooth deployment of this strategy. The modernization aims at increasing decisiveness by streamlining the processes of decision-making and implementation of decisions taken. Furthermore, program management is enhanced by adequate organizational bedding of strategically important development programs and by shortening the communication lines with the civil service organization's top management and with those who are politically responsible. An important point of interest is also the stimulation of situation-driven collaboration. This concerns for instance the establishment of organization units with liaison functions and the incorporation of methods for impact evaluation of changes in regional development in decision-making on development projects. Possibly the most important ingredient is the overall pursuit of organizational flexibility by, for instance, increasing the interchangeability of personnel, the removal of 'walls' between budget posts and the introduction of basic data registrations for joint use.

When we observe the organizational modernization from a greater distance then the outlines become noticeable of an emerging concept for the design of governmental organizations in the field of spatial planning. Their task is to work on spatially relevant and topical societal problems in a concrete and realization focused way. Moreover, governments choose to actively search for forms of collaboration that are tailored to situational conditions, such as for instance entering into temporary engagements with public and private parties and to work in networks. There is an increasing awareness of the impossibility to get detailed clarity in advance about the roles and tasks government has to fulfill in the dynamic forms of co-operation it participates in.

To operate in this way government organizations must have the ability to move along with the dynamics in their environment. An agile government organization is able to fold itself with adequate speed around emerging societal problems. When necessary it is able to determine new priorities and quickly implement them and it has the capability to deploy strategies, tuned to situational conditions, to realize policy goals. Furthermore agile organizations are capable to implement changes smoothly, without big shocks. The concept of agility is gaining ground in Dutch government. The Minister Dekker of the Ministry of Housing, Spatial Planning and the Environment for instance, on a press conference on September 17, 2004 about the 2005-budget, has characterized her Ministry as an organization that is developing itself "in the direction of a flexible core department. An agile organization focused on collaboration with other ministries and governments, from the European Commission to local authorities." (Dekker, 2004).

Agility: the vital ability

The concept of organizational agility

Agility can be defined as the ability of an organization to respond rapidly and to be focused on unexpected changes in the environment (Meade, 1997). It is this vital ability that makes government organizations less vulnerable for unforeseen societal developments that occur at high speed. This ability enables governments to maneuver themselves in a better position so that they can quickly respond successfully to emerging needs of citizens and to changes in policy programs resulting from shifted political priorities (Eppink, 1978). The concept of agility up till now has been elaborated mainly for industrial organizations. A government organization that pre-eminently has to dispose of a high degree of agility is the military. After all military organizations in modern time have to be able to effectively operate in highly dynamic and complex circumstances. It figures that in this field of government activity the need to develop the concept of agility is most manifest. In a study for the American Ministry of Defense six key dimensions of agility are distinguished (Alberts & Hayes, 2003).

These are:
- Robustness: the ability to maintain effectiveness across a range of tasks, situations, and conditions;
- Resilience: the ability to recover from or adjust to misfortune, damage, or a destabilizing perturbation in the environment;
- Responsiveness: the ability to react to a change in the environment in a timely manner;
- Flexibility: the ability to employ multiple ways to succeed and the capacity to move seamlessly between them;
- Innovation: the ability to do new things and the ability to do old things in new ways; and
- Adaptation: the ability to change work processes and the ability to change the organization.

When we look at the practice of spatial development policy in The Netherlands, as was outlined before, these dimensions seem to be applicable in this field of work too. To be effective in the deployment of its spatial development strategy government must have the ability to change direction in response to unexpected developments, such as the emergence of new building initiatives or the loss of planned projects. Changing direction has the character of plying against the wind. The point is to choose such a position in each emerging situation of change that maximum use can be made of the circumstances in order to stay on policy course. So agility is not the same as opportunism. Just as important is the dexterity to implement changes in the organization quickly and smoothly. New projects will have to be started up quickly and obsolete projects will have to be canceled with the same speed. This requires the free flow of people and means through the organization in order to be deployed there where this is necessary regarding the changed situational circumstances. Government organizations therefore will have to be able to fathom timely the possibilities a new situation offers (the situational logic) and have at their disposal the skill to make use of these possibilities effectively. Skill indicates proficiency, the presence of practical know how to select and actively implement work methods and organizational forms that are situation-tailored. So agility encompasses more than adaptation to change circumstances. The essence is to cleverly use changed circumstances in order to realize intrinsic policy goals. Agility is the key proficiency of a government organization that has adapted itself to the changed societal circumstances. It is the desired result of this adaptation.

Organizational conditions for agility

The existence of the organizational barriers mentioned earlier points out that government organizations in general do not yet have the necessary dexterity and skills for agility at their disposal. The process of modernization focuses on creating the required organizational conditions. Practical experience indicates that with reference to this the following areas of conditional development are of importance: (1) demand-oriented performance, (2) changeability of the organization, (3) culture, (4) leadership and last but not least (5) application of ICT (A.T. Kearney and The London School of Economics, 2003).

Demand-oriented performance

Citizens have become used to a demand-oriented treatment when they turn themselves to private sector companies for products or services. They expect the same treatment from government. The so-called 1-counter principle (Programmabureau Overheidsloket 2000, 1997) is now implemented in most of the municipalities in The Netherlands. With this a demand-oriented work method is being applied that places citizens in the position of customers and that puts the individual needs of a citizen centrally in the offering of government services. In policy making the demand-oriented focus takes shape in the form of interactive work processes (Pröpper & Steenbeek, 1998) with citizens, entrepreneurs, social organizations and other government authorities, ranging from the sharing of information to policy co-production. In the latter case all participants in a policy project are co-responsible for the realization of the policy goals. Performing in a demand-oriented way has major consequences for the civil service organization. The arrangement of the front office is not so much the problem as well as the functioning of the back office. When, for instance, a district bureau succeeds in deploying an integrated approach to a district issue in dialogue with the residents, it is confronted with the municipal line departments that are hardly able to give up their sector and supply-driven work orientation. And how much effort doesn't it take to apply a truly integrative consideration and treatment of large regional development problems within ministries or provincial government organizations? To really perform in a demand-oriented way a government organization has to be able to connect sector activities problem-centered. Co-ordination between individuals and organizational units will have to be based above all on the principles of mutual adjustment and lateral communication. Supply-side thinking will have to be replaced by demand-oriented action. In this approach the specific content of spatial planning issues determines the arrangement of internal and external work processes. This will have to be managed explicitly. For instance by vigorously supporting integrative initiatives taken on the work floor, by giving budget control to organizational units that are lined up for integrated regional development and by embedding these budgets as clearly recognizable en entities in the budget book.

Changeability of the organization

An agile government organization moves along with the dynamics of the environment. It has to be able to change smoothly. Well known is the proverb that an organization has to get used to find itself in a state of permanent change. In these dynamic times change is the only constant factor. This sounds logical. Practice points out however that it is not feasible to be in a state of permanent change. In many places change fatigue has occurred. This certainly is the case in those situations where structure changes happen in rapid succession while a clear vision on the future organization is missing. More then often cynicism arises and the change process stagnates. In practice we see the emergence of another organizational vision. Not change but the changeability or manageability of the organization is the central point of focus here (Volberda, 2004). To be agile a government organization has to be able to free resources from existing activities with adequate speed to deploy them in new activities that stem from changes in the environment. This requires certain management skills together with the organizational quality to timely and actively respond to directional decisions. Government organizations have to be designed in such a way that they are able to absorb changes in their environment. Then it is possible to meet even unexpected developments without the need of substantial structural interventions and major changes in work processes of individuals and units. Changeability is embedded in the business rules, the doctrines and the modus operandi of the organization. In other words: the organizational boundaries are permeable (Ashkenas, Ulrich, Jick & Kerr, 2002). By that an agile organization is able to quickly put together units to approach urgent problems or realize specific goals and to regroup them with the same pace to fulfill new assignments. Discussions about tasks and competences do not fit in. In stead the energy has to be directed to mobilizing all knowledge and instruments the government organization possesses in order to place these resources in the service of the joint ventures that are organized around current societal problems such as the spatial development in certain areas. To this end staff members are organized and equipped in such a way they can be brought together on every desired moment in the right configuration to approach these challenges. In the ideal situation such demand-oriented clusters arise automatically. Staff members then look each other up to jointly work on development issues based on a clear understanding of what goes on in society and of the strategic intention of their organization.

Culture

An agile government organization runs on assertive, flexible and professional staff. Four behavioral aspects are essential to function effectively in an agile organization. In the first place this is responsible entrepreneurship. When it concerns the detection of developments and needs in society and taking initiatives to formulate policy issues an entrepreneurial behavior is expected from staff members. The necessary room to move has to be given to them. But employees are also members of the government organization. They have to be aware that they are considered by citizens the representatives of the government. This poses certain demands on the way they act. When given ample room to move, it may also be expected that employees will always check intended actions with the goals and possibilities of their organization. Staff members determine their own agenda but that agenda must be geared to the strategy of the organization.

In the second place a strong external orientation is necessary. It is essential to know what goes on in society and to understand how citizens perceive and experience certain circumstances and developments. Employees of the civil service organization therefore need to be visibly present in society and need to actively participate in the discussions that are taking place. This not only requires much of their communicative skills and social intelligence. It also requires the ability to timely recognize patterns in the statements of citizens to get a clear sight on what citizens expect of the government and to assess rightly if and how these expectations can be met. In formulating policy assignments the added value of the government contribution has to be made clear. Added value not only has to lie in determining new regulations but can also be achieved by creating room within prevailing policy frameworks or by organizing knowledge that is present in society for an effective approach of spatial development issues.

In the third place operating in an agile organization requires a high degree of mental flexibility of each staff member. Outside-in thinking presupposes that employees can detach themselves from their 'own' policy field and that they make an effort of sharing their knowledge for an integrative approach to societal issues. Old ways of 'silo thinking' and acting will have to be abandoned and employees will have to be willing and able to fulfill various roles when the situation asks for it. Effective collaboration with actors inside and outside the civil service organization also requires the willingness to adapt to their language.

In the fourth place achievement-oriented behavior is needed. Realization, and with that the actual effect or outcome of concrete development initiatives, is the central point of focus. Citizens judge their government on results booked and not on policy intentions. As was mentioned earlier collaboration is also necessary for governments to operate effectively. Therefore attention has to be paid explicitly to delivered performances, and actually realized results as well the way in which development initiatives are approached. Employees of agile governmental organizations consider their work more in terms of the added value that they deliver than as a task that has to be fulfilled. Their behavior is such that they spontaneously inform their environment about the actions that they intend to execute and about the outcome of executed actions. Evaluation of applied work methods, for instance by way of After Action Reviews, enables them to learn from practical experiences.

Leadership

In agile government organizations employees must have room to take initiatives themselves. To support this, executives must not have the urge to want to control everything. It is much more important to stimulate experiments and to direct the energy mainly to facilitating staff members who improve the effectiveness of the organization with their initiatives. Employees perform optimally when they feel really connected to their organization. Executives play an important role in strengthening this solidarity. They have a position that enables them to invite employees to actively participate in improving the organization. And by stimulating the sharing of knowledge through the whole organization they can contribute to the increase of connectedness between departments. Employees are expected to dare to take risks. They are prepared to do this if they are able to trust their organization. Trust grows when employees see that values and norms of the organization really and consequently are applied in the behavior and functioning of executives. Executives have to be able to rely on assignments being executed and that is not a matter of giving detailed instructions followed by meticulous control of the execution. Effective leadership requires a strong people-orientation. Passion is required for a continuing good performance. Employees will do their work with passion when they experience too this passion in the executives. Leadership in an agile organization therefore has a transformational character. A leader tries to influence the thinking and the behavior of staff members by making them enthusiastic for his vision, policy course or plan of action. Leadership is focused on broadening and strengthening the needs of employees and on connecting these needs with the goals of the organization. A transformational leader shows trust in himself and in his co-workers, poses high demands on his own and another person's performance, behaves creative and innovative, formulates goals and tasks in ideological terms and shows strong commitment and conviction.

Application of ICT

Essential in the spatial development strategy is the awareness of the fact that the phase of policy realization will take a long period of time, much longer than the time needed for policy making. During realization a government has to respond to unexpected changes in the spatial situation. Also many actors with their own specific information requirements are involved in the process of policy realization. Agility means the ability to timely adjust in order to continue progression in the direction of the intended policy effects. This requires up to date and adequate information about the realization of policy effects in relation to the results of initiatives taken by various actors. Policy partners therefore have to be able to exchange information smoothly about their activities and progress in the joint area of operation. Because of the fast amount and variety of the data a well-considered application of ICT is indispensable. Key elements of adequate information management for spatial development policy are: (1) a properly organized database management, (2) a high level of interoperability and (3) a flexible technical infrastructure (Association for Federal Information Resources Management, 2003).

Data management must be based on an explicit and operational elaboration of the causal relation between policy goals and desired concrete outcomes. The data warehouse of spatial development policy contains data about policy goals, instruments, task setting of policy partners, activities, accomplished achievements and concrete results. Hereby it is important that data are accepted as correct by all parties involved and are considered the right starting point for assessment of the situation and for further decision-making. So there must be a collective database, built up out of various basic registrations for joint use.

In this vision all policy partners are part of one information network. Important in the arrangement of the network is that each party keeps its own identity. Each party has to be able to point out which contribution it has made to the realization of intended effects. That is an important condition to increase commitment to the development policy and it creates the foundation for collaboration and self steering within the collective policy framework. Each policy partner then has the obligation to place the relevant data that it possesses at the disposal of others in direct communication. The effectiveness of their collaboration is determined to a large extend by the interoperability of the various information systems that the policy partners are using. In order to be able to actually function as information network, the sharing of data between software and hardware configurations of various suppliers has to be made possible.

The ICT-infrastructure of government organizations is established generally in an autonomous way. In practice decisions about the acquisition of ICT-facilities often were taken ad hoc, using that what was available at the moment. Furthermore, the focus was on software and less on the technical infrastructure. The effect of this course of action is maybe best described by the metaphor of freight traffic. Government was focused on the trucks and not on the highways. It is necessary to have good trucks at one's disposal, but without a well-planned system of highways it is not possible to transport the cargo from A to B in an efficient manner, taking account of the needs of customers. Also traffic-jams will occur when the increase of trucks cannot be relieved by fast and timely adjustment of the road system. An agile government therefore has to invest in the build up of a technical infrastructure that has the flexibility and the reliability to accommodate the dynamic and information-intensive process of development-oriented spatial policy making. After all, the essential contribution of ICT lies in the collection, the management, the exchange and the reuse of information. The challenge for an agile government is the application of a coherent approach to data registrations, information systems and technical infrastructure, without ending up in a rigid management of the organizational database (information household). A suitable interpretation of such an approach can be found in the concept of Service-Oriented Architecture (SOA). SOA can be described as an architectural style that provides for a loose coupling between the elements of the information household. Many organizations, governmental too, have a heterogeneous ICT-infrastructure regarding operating systems, system software, applications and computer platforms. The existing infrastructure is suitable for the execution of current business processes. An agile government has to respond alert and quick to changes in the environment which requires the use of new work methods and organizational forms. Adjustment of the ICT-infrastructure will be required in many cases to be able to deliver the new information services that evolve out of new work methods and organizational forms. Considering the large investments in the existing ICT-infrastructure building a completely new infrastructure is seldom an option. An infrastructure configured according to SOA-principles has a somewhat loose structure. Because of this organizations can ad new information services bit by bit or upgrade current information services. It is even possible to render those services via various channels, using existing infrastructure. So investments already made in ICT-infrastructure can be protected.

A few closing remarks

This Chapter started with the reflection of a city manager. The situation he sketched was fictive indeed but in day-to-day reality we experience that it is no fiction. The environment government has to operate in has changed. Increased complexity and dynamics of society require new performance-demands of government. Regarding the concern for the physical environment the Dutch government responds to this by the concept of the spatial development strategy. In practice it turns out that the internal government organization is not yet geared to the new strategy. It lacks the necessary agility. By now a process of organizational modernization is started up. On all levels of government the civil service organization is adjusted and a start has been made with the regulatory simplification. De-compartmentalization and de-regulation are key issues. Adjustment of the civil service organization, alone, however will not be sufficient, because it is only a part of the fabric we call government. Agility bears on the way government as a whole functions. Two aspects deserve special attention: (1) the elaboration of the principle of subsidiary and (2) the functioning and organization of political management.

The principle of subsidiarity regards the division of responsibilities and competences over central government, provincial government and local government. The relation between these governmental levels is determined by law and in practice is generally perceived as indisputable. One of the consequences of this is the occurrence of extensive governmental circuits of consultation when issues are concerned that do cross-governmental boundaries. That is pre-eminently the case with the integrated and area-oriented approach of spatial development problems. The governments involved do react still too much on the basis of their competences and still too little from the added value they can deliver to regional development. This rigid interpretation of the principle of subsidiarity is experienced increasingly as a barrier for decisive government action. Illustrative for this is the emergence of the term 'governmental hustle and bustle'. An unambiguous and broadly supported solution is still missing. There is the willingness though to experiment with new interpretations of subsidiarity, as is the case with the development policy for 'a vital countryside'. When we extrapolate the line that has been started in with the countryside policy, then the image emerges of a government that functions more like a network and less as a system of hierarchical positioned layers. The principle of subsidiary remains but is elaborated more flexibly in the governmental network. So the role and competences of government organizations involved can be tailored to the nature and content of the spatial problem in a region.

The second point of attention concerns the functioning and organization of the Boards of Administrators and the Chambers of Representatives. Now we see the emergence of area-related roles in governing bodies, such as project-ministers in central government, provincial area-executives and district-aldermen in local government. It is a step in the right direction. In current practice these public administrators have a combined portfolio. The responsibility for a region or district is combined with the responsibility for a sector policy field, such as environment, traffic, housing or economic development. In theory this is a useful organization principle but in practice there is a struggle with the tension between the area-related portfolio and the sector policy portfolio. This has to do among others with the political rationality to profile oneself on certain issues and with the need to achieve concrete policy results within the governing period of four years. This tension is maintained by the civil service bureaucracy that is still being guided too much by a sector orientation. Whenever the combined responsibility is applied successfully, this is to a great extend due to good personal relations between individual administrators. Good personal relations are always important but are not sufficient for a durable continuation of spatial development policy. The latter is only possible when the required integrative way of working is adequately safeguarded organizationally on civil service level and on political level.

Spatial development policy is also of consequence for the functioning and organization of the Chambers of Representatives. What has to be the role of Representatives of the people in interactive policy making processes, in which the political management and the civil service organization consult directly the parties involved with regional development and reach agreement with each other about concrete projects? How do Representatives have to interpret their controlling task when the responsibility for policy implementation is laid in the hands of parties outside the own organization? What has to be the role of sector commissions in the assessment of integrated regional development plans? Those are but a few examples of questions that illustrate the search for organizational forms for agile government that do justice to democratic decision making in our modern network society.

Government faces the fundamental challenge to transform itself into an agile organization. Standardized and proven solutions are not available and the resistance to change is extensive in some places. Returning to old and familiar organizational models and methods of governing is no option, if only because society in The Netherlands has changed. There is not just resistance. We see an increase of change agents within the public administration, who dedicate themselves to modernize government. Tenacity and the skill to detect opportunities for organizational change and for actually taking advantage of it, are crucial qualities. The best guarantee to become an agile government occurs when political administrators and civil servants give evidence of agility in their personal way of thinking and doing. Maybe the most important quality to achieve success therefore is a personal attitude that is founded on agility: agility as state of mind.

References

A.T. Kearney and The London School of Economics, 2003, *Improving performance in the public sector*, A.T. Kearney Inc., Chicago.
Albeda, H.D. & W. Etty, 2002, *Richting en rekenschap*, Stichting Rekenschap, www.rekenschap.nl, 2006-04-10.
Alberts, D.S. & R.E. Hayes, 2003, *Power to the edge*, CCRP Publications, www.dodccrp.org, 2006-04-12.
Ashkenas, R., D. Ulrich, T. Jick & S. Kerr, 2002, *The Boundaryless Organization*, John Wiley & Sons, San Francisco.
Association for Federal Information Resources Management, 2003, *Achieving Mission Agility through IT*, AFFIRM, www.affirm.org, 2006-04-05.
Castells, M., 2000, *The Rise of the Network Society*, Blackwell Publishing, Oxford.
Clinton, B. & A. Gore, 1997, *Blair House Papers*, National Performance Review, http://govinfo.library.unt.edu, 2005-01-07.
De Groep van 100, 2003, *De publieke zaak in de 21ste eeuw*, Stichting De Publieke Zaak i.o, Amsterdam.
Dekker, S.M., 2004, *Begrotingsspeech Dekker: Ruimte bieden aan ontwikkelkracht, persconferentie begroting 2005 Nieuwspoort*, 17 september 2004.
Eenmalige Commissie ICT en Overheid, 2001, *Burger en overheid in de informatiesamenleving*, Ministerie van Binnenlandse Zaken en Koninkrijksrelaties, Den Haag.
Eppink, D.J., 1978, *Managing the Unforeseen. A Study of Flexibility*, PhD Thesis, Administratief Centrum, Ermelo.
Frissen, P., 2000, *Sturing en publiek domein*, Wiardi Beckman Stichting, Amsterdam.
Gemeente Breda, 2004a, *Via Breda. Structuurvisie en uitwerking*, Gemeente Breda, Breda.
Gemeente Breda, 2004b, *Gemeenschappelijk sturen op samenwerking*, Gemeente Breda, Breda.
Interprovinciaal Overleg, 2001, *Van ordenen naar ontwikkelen*, Interprovinciaal Overleg, Den Haag.
Kabinet, 2003a, *Meedoen, meer werk, minder regels*, Hoofdlijnenakkoord voor het Kabinet CDA, VVD, D66.
Kabinet, 2003b, *Kabinetsvisie 'Andere Overheid'*, Kabinet, Den Haag.
Kabinet, 2003c, *Actieprogramma 'Andere Overheid'*, Kabinet, Den Haag.
Meade, L.M., 1997, *A Methodology for the Formulation of Agile Critical Business Processes*, PhD Thesis, University of Texas, Dallas.
Mierop, R. & C. Bastiaansen, 2002, *De Actieve Overheid*, Lemma BV, Utrecht.
Ministerie van LNV, 2000, *Impuls voor vernieuwing. Organisatieontwikkeling bij LNV*, Ministerie van LNV, Den Haag.
Ministerie van LNV, 2004, *Agenda voor een Vitaal Platteland*, Ministerie van LNV, Den Haag.
Ministerie van VROM, 2003, *Best practices ontwikkelingsplanologie*, Ministerie van VROM, Den Haag.
Osborne, D., & T. Gaebler, 1992, *Reinventing Government*, Penguin Books USA Inc., New York.
Programmabureau Overheidsloket 2000, 1997, *Handboek Van vraagpatroon naar loket*, Programmabureau Overheidsloket 2000, Den Haag.
Pröpper, I.M.A.M., & D.A. Steenbeek, 1998, *Interactieve beleidsvoering*, Bestuurskunde, Vol. 7, nr. 7, pp. 292-301.
Provincie Groningen, 2000, *Provinciaal Omgevingsplan*, Provincie Groningen, Groningen.
Provincie Groningen, 2001, *Samen werken. Veranderagenda Provincie Groningen*, Provincie Groningen, Groningen.
Rathenau Instituut, 2004, *Ontwikkelingsplanologie als sociaal-culturele opgave*, Rathenau Instituut, Den Haag.
Ruimtelijk Planbureau, 2004, *Ontwikkelingsplanologie, Lessen uit en voor de praktijk*, Ruimtelijk Planbureau, Den Haag.
Sociaal en Cultureel Planbureau, 2000, *Digitalisering van de leefwereld*, Sociaal en Cultureel Planbureau, Den Haag.
Van Wijngaarden, B., 2001, *Strategische samenwerkingsverbanden in organisatienetwerken*, www.managementsite.net/scripts/artikelen.
Vereniging van Nederlandse Gemeenten, 2003, *Ontwikkelingsplanologie. Noties uit de gemeentelijke praktijk*, Vereniging van Nederlandse Gemeenten, Den Haag.

Volberda, H.W., 2004, *De flexibele onderneming*, Kluwer, Deventer.
VROM-Raad, 2004, *Gereedschap voor ruimtelijke ontwikkelingspolitiek*, VROM-Raad, Den Haag.
Wetenschappelijke Raad voor het Regeringsbeleid, 1998a, *Staat zonder land*, Sdu, Den Haag.
Wetenschappelijke Raad voor het Regeringsbeleid, 1998b, *Ruimtelijke ontwikkelingspolitiek*, Sdu, Den Haag.
Wetenschappelijke Raad voor het Regeringsbeleid, 2005, *Transactie als bestuurlijke vernieuwing*, Amsterdam University Press, Amsterdam.
Zwart, C.J., 2001, *De overheid is geen geluksfabriek*, Raad voor Verkeer en Waterstaat, Den Haag.

5 Combating Poverty in Europe and the Third World: Social Innovation in Motion

Pasquale De Muro, Abdelillah Hamdouch, Stuart Cameron and Frank Moulaert

Introduction

This Chapter focuses on the comparative social innovation content of governance structures set up to fight social exclusion in Europe and the Developing World. To this purpose results from various research projects, both theoretical and empirical, are brought together. The analytical perspective (second Section) has been drawn from research on social innovation done by Frank Moulaert and his team since 1990 (Moulaert, 2005; Moulaert, Martinelli & Swyngedouw 2005; Moulaert, Martinelle, Swyngedouw & Gonzalez, 2005; Hillier, Moulaert & Nussbaumer, 2004; Moulaert, 2002; Moulaert, Delvainquière & Delladetsima, 1997; Moulaert, Delladetsima, Delvainquière, Demazière & Leontidou, 1994;), and theories of *empowerment* and *capabilities* as used by A. Sen and J. Friedmann in their analysis of the struggle against poverty (De Muro, 2005) and underdevelopment. Elements from these analyses are used to provide lessons on the dynamics and agency of the governance networks of combat-poverty initiatives in Europe and the Developing World.

In addition, two bodies of empirical results on network dynamics have been mobilized. The first one covers the governance of international co-operation networks of non-governmental organizations (NGOs) and Development Assistance Associations, located in the Rome metropolitan area but operating in Africa, Asia and Latin America (Rhi-Sausi, Coletti, Conato & Rufini, 2004; Osservatorio Romano Azioni Contro la Povertà, 2005; De Muro, Hamdouch, Cameron & Moulaert, 2007). The second one concerns network initiatives to combat social exclusion in large European cities, as analyzed in EC research projects co-ordinated by *Institut Fédératif de Recherche sur les Économies et les Sociétés Industrielles – Centre National de la Recherche Scientifique*, Lille (France) and School of Architecture Planning and Landscape/Global Urban Research Unit, Newcastle (United Kingdom) (see special issue of Urban Studies in October 2005).

The third Section examines and compares the reality of the networks of NGOs combating poverty in the developing world and mainly located in Rome. How are these networks organized? What are the positive and negative catalysts of their dynamics? How do they position themselves vis-à-vis the powers curtailing their development agendas? And how does the articulation of the different spatial scales to which the networks belong work out?

The fourth Section then investigates social relations and governance within and across organizations fighting socio-cultural, economic and political exclusion in deprived neighborhoods of European cities. It focuses on the role of organizational culture, the formation of group and community identities, the integration of objectives and agendas of different partners, the positioning vis-à-vis economic and political power relations and the articulation of spatial scales within the network geographies.

Dimensions of Social Innovation \ Disciplinary Approaches	Aim of the Initiative	Change in the organization of the initiative	Role of the « special » agents: leadership, creative individuals	Role of « path dependency » and of the structural constraints.	How to overcome the tensions between normativity and reality?
Management and organizational science	Improve the coherence of an organization in order to achieve its objectives (financial profits, ethical work, ecological products).	Build a space for the exchange of information and ideas. "Horizontalize" the decision-making and communication systems.	The innovative actors in the organization are empowered within the organization.	Awareness of path dependency in relation to the business culture and its organization.	Tangibility of objectives. Regularization of the relationships between the organizational elites and the rest of the organization. Learning dynamics.
Relationships between economy, society and environment (including social responsibility)	Integrate the social and ecologic aims within the mainstreams agendas of businesses.	Stress on the human relations dimension of work. Quality of work and social relations.		Tension between the mainstream and the ethical entrepreneurship (represented by the tension between professional organizations).	Interfaces between business and society Ethical forums.
Art and creativity sciences	Social innovation.	Cognitive processes open to all ideas: Communication between individuals. The role of the relationships and inter-personal activities.	Particular attention attributed to individually created initiatives.	Historical inspiration for contemporary social innovation (grand examples, practical experiences).	The role of information and its assimilation by the creative community. The discovery of constraints and solutions. Revision and interactive refinement of the proposed solutions.
Territorial Approach (Integrated Area Development)	Satisfaction of human needs…	… in accordance to changes in the governance relations.	Increased focus in the role of the community and its social agents.	Substantial importance of the historical reproduction of institutional capital.	Through multi-level governance and the creation of networks of co-operation between community agents.
"Another world is possible"	Alternative economy and sustainable development.	Participatory democracy and direct action.	Importance of charismatic and status quo challenging leaders.	Awareness of the structural over-determination of the capitalist led globalization.	Through collective mobilization.

Illustration 5.1: Dimensions of social innovation in relation to disciplinary approaches (Source: authors)

Social innovation: A multi-dimensional concept

The social innovation concept has played a significant role in a variety of pre-paradigmatic, intra-disciplinary and multi-disciplinary debates (Moulaert & Nussbaumer, 2005; Hillier, Moulaert & Nussbaumer, 2004). Both Max Weber (1922, in 1978) and Emile Durkheim (1909, in 1970; 1893, in 1984) have stressed the intrinsically social nature of human progress; Weber compared social inventions with technical inventions, while the 'Godfather' of technological innovation Joseph Schumpeter was the first to stress social innovation as a necessary condition for the efficacy of technological innovation (Schumpeter, 1932; 1942). Moreover, he recognized the multi-dimensionality of the logic of development, with the social as one of the most predominant dimensions.

In contemporary social sciences, the concept of social innovation has become increasingly important.[1] Illustration 5.1 summarizes features of four readings of social innovation in four different disciplines or thematic foci that have worked with approaches based on social innovation: management science (Damanpour, 1991), ethical and sustainable entrepreneurship (Moulaert & Ailenei, 2005), sciences of arts and creativity (Mumford, 2002) and urban geography and sociology addressing problems of area-based development (Integrated Area Development; Moulaert, 2002; Laville & Delfau, 2000; Favreau & Lévesque, 1999). Illustration 5.1 considers a fifth line, a reading that is linked to the need to make social innovation tangible. Processes of social innovation respond to mechanisms of alienation – one of the main consequences of social exclusion – that should be overcome, and to gaps in socio-political institutions and the non-satisfaction of human needs. These processes are path-dependent: the path-dependency of a social innovation initiative always takes into account the historical trajectory, the territorial and institutional setting, the availability of human and financial resources, institutional capital, etc. Some consequences of this contextualization are immediate:
- The specific nature of each innovation strategy;
- The 'realist' mobilization of resources;
- The influence of historical heritage, which often means a return to an idea or a practice of 'the old days', rather than a 'new' idea;
- The translation of norms of innovation according to the possibilities to overcome the constraints.

Networking social capital

The impact of many social innovation initiatives depends significantly on the synergies created between social capitals. That is why in the sequel of this Chapter we focus on the transformation of social relations (or social capital) and its governance – always with the objective of achieving the satisfaction of human needs. We address social capital by analyzing networks of social innovation and their dynamics. Briefly speaking, a social network can be defined and identified using seven dimensions: its raison d'être, the behavior of the individual and collective agents that constitute it, the type of communication between them, the interaction of the network with its environment, the creation of its own institutions and identity, as well as the power relations that reproduce the network (Moulaert & Cabaret, 2006). The empirical domains, which we address here, are networks to combat social exclusion in urban Europe and in developing countries, especially Africa. The nature of the network elements will vary according to the case and its context, but in general we will examine our case studies following a common grid as detailed in Illustration 5.2.

To theorize the links between the different features of the network, various theories can be utilized. However, for our purpose, social innovation theories, taking into account power relations, institutional dynamics and creative strategies as a way out of social exclusion, will lead the way (for surveys see Moulaert, Martinelli & Swyngedouw, 2005; Moulaert, Martinelli, Swyngedouw & Gonzalez, 2005). The implementation of development agendas and strategies to overcome exclusion is (among others) a function of the social efficacy of networks, i.e. the social coherence of individual and collective ambitions as they take shape in communication between network agents, the procedures of decision-making, the institutionalization of social interaction and of the behavioral rules (Hamdouch, 2005), as well as the empowerment within and across networks.

Features of the network	Dimensions of social innovation	Empowerment/Incapacitation
Raison d'être or purpose of network	Satisfaction of human needs	(Process of) definition of human needs
Behaviour of agents	Role of 'leading agents'. Integration of all network members	Identify the means permitting each network member to discover his(her) agency logic within the network –Self-empowerment
Type of communication	Modes of communication providing access to communication and decision-making for all members	Exchange of opinions on the priorities of development and needs to be satisfied, the decision making systems, relations of co-operation and of democratic control
Interaction with the environment	Networking with other networks (variety of spatial scales and institutional environments)	Mobilization over shared development agendas. Develop countervailing power and increase visibility of social movements supported by connected networks
Creation of institutions within and for the network	Legitimize and socialize procedures for communication, decision making and democratic control. Institutionalization of leading agents (Associations, NGO, Development Agencies)	Co-ordination procedures based on speaking up (*prise de parole*), initiative taking, mutual adjustment, partcipation, individual and collective learning, experimenting
Creation of identy	Pursue unity between the development view of the network, its ambitions and perenniality	A shared identity can be a key factor of empowerment
Role of power relations	The network as an agent of reproduction and consolidation of social change forces	Inter-network co-operation as a vector of more efficient social movements

Illustration 5.2: Social Network and Social Innovation: a combined analytical grid (Source: authors and Moulaert & Cabaret, 2006)

Networking for Human Development: the case of 'Rome – World'

A dynamic institutional context

Rome has a long-standing tradition – a cultural legacy – in solidarity initiatives and groups, rooted in its catholic and socialist popular cultures. In the last decades, the city has also shown a lively civil society, engaged not only on local social and political issues (social exclusion, homeless, environment, housing, etc.) but also increasingly at the international level, especially in poor countries and regions of Africa, Asia and Latin America (Rhi-Sausi, Coletti, Conato & Rufini, 2004).

Since the 1990s, in Italy the crisis of the national state caused by the increasing pressure of global economic forces and local political interests brought about a change in the model of Italian international development co-operation. As with welfare policy, national and international co-operation policies have been downsized together with a partial 'delegation', on one side to the EU and, on the other side to local governments (regions, provinces, municipalities). The reduction of development aid has resulted in Italy becoming the industrialized country with the lowest share of national public aid as a proportion of Gross Domestic Product, after the USA.

In this critical context, civil society organizations (CSOs) found a new space and momentum to expand their international activities. This expansion was facilitated and led by the rise of global social movements since the mid-1990s, and by the crisis of traditional top-down (inter)governmental co-operation policies.

In the same period, a coalition of progressive parties has held, and still retains, the government of the city of Rome. The municipal government benefited from the administrative decentralization to municipalities that the central government started off in the 1990s; decentralization gave more autonomy and new functions to local governments, especially for welfare policies, but also for international co-operation. Furthermore, the city's governing coalition – being also an expression of catholic and socialist cultures – created a friendly political environment for Roman CSOs, by increasing the occasions for dialogue and close co-operation with them. In the last five years, the Mayor – a charismatic leader with a large popular consensus – also decided to boost the foreign policy of Rome by taking a number of political initiatives at the global scale in the field of development co-operation 'between world cities' (e.g. the 'Glocal Forum', a network of 100 cities with over 500,000 inhabitants), with a special attention to Africa.

In this favorable institutional environment, the Roman fabric of CSOs, community-based organizations, NGOs, grassroots movements and associations was consolidated and began to demand new forms of collaboration with local government on international co-operation: moving from 'information' sharing and reciprocal 'consultation' to 'partnership' (deciding and acting together) and 'delegation' (supporting independent community initiatives).

Developing institutions for decentralized co-operation

To communicate with the municipal government, the diverse and numerous Roman organizations started an informal process of co-ordination and discussion: a civic movement was born that put 'friendly' political pressure on the municipality. In October 2002, the city council in a deliberation formally recognized that "the collaboration and the support of associations, organizations and social forces working in the city in the international co-operation sector are essential for Rome" (Consiglio Comunale di Roma, 2002:1). Besides municipal government representatives, the members of the Committee can be representatives of any Roman CSO (not only NGOs), and private and public enterprises that are engaged in international development co-operation. The Committee is also open to trade unions, universities and research centers, United Nations organizations, and others.

Main objectives of the Committee are "to have recurring meetings to set up a regular exchange between the municipality and the [Roman] forces of civil society that are active in the international co-operation sector, in order to determine and to plan, also over the long term, initiatives and activities, promoted by different actors working in the sector, with the purpose of co-ordinating them as well" (Consiglio Comunale di Roma, 2002:1). In March 2003 the Committee started to work. One of its first decisions was to establish four thematic boards: 1. Peace and international solidarity; 2. Combat poverty and MDGs (United Nations Millennium Development Goals); 3. Intercultural and development education; 4. Sustainable development. The Committee created also a restricted (elected) 'Commission' that should co-ordinate the Committee and act as an interface with the municipality. In fact, the steering Commission includes many leaders of the civic society, and thus expresses the political leadership of the Committee.

The creation of the Committee has been generally considered – both by municipality and associations, in Rome and elsewhere – a success, and a milestone in the field of decentralized co-operation in Italy. Its open and democratic nature has attracted a large number and variety of Roman organizations. At the beginning of 2006 there were more that 150 member organizations. In fact, almost all the largest and most representative Roman CSOs active at the international level are affiliated to the Committee, but so too are many small associations and neighborhood associations, each with one representative.

Fighting poverty and deprivation

The field where Roman decentralized co-operation seems most effective and widespread is the fight against global poverty. The board of 'Combat Poverty' includes more than sixty organizations, and twenty-two of these have planned and started a common project, with twin objectives. The first is to meet the original spirit of decentralized co-operation: building bridges between local communities in the North and local communities in the South. More precisely, the aim is to look for (or support the creation of) local coalitions of CSOs in the South and to establish a peer-to-peer collaboration and partnership for fighting poverty. In other words, the first objective is to build a glocal network against poverty. The second objective is to consolidate and enhance the collective action against poverty of Roman CSOs. There are, in fact, already dozens of Roman organizations engaged in a wide range of projects against poverty (on education, training, health, sanitation, water, food security, microcredit, etc.) around the world, but almost all the projects have been independently designed and implemented by single organizations. If, on one side, this guarantees a certain degree of autonomy, on the other side it produces an excessive dispersion of energy and means and lack of co-ordination, and it prevents the building of synergies. As a result, a large number of (too) small projects against poverty can be observed, that lack critical mass and have a minor impact.

The common project of the Combat Poverty board has received 50 percent of its funding from the municipality; the other 50 percent have been provided from internal resources of the organizations. In the first stage of the project, in order to build a base of common knowledge and awareness and to encourage the circulation of information, a survey was conducted among all the organizations of the Committee that have projects against poverty (Osservatorio Romano Azioni Contro la Povertà, 2005). The survey discovered about 700 projects of Roman CSOs around the world, with an overall budget of more than 114 million Euro. The results of the survey have been discussed in a public conference. The second stage of the project should take place in various African countries, where the board aims to meet local CSOs and support them to build 'twin' committees in order to discuss and implement together future common projects against poverty.

Limitations and constraints

Since its foundation, the Committee has been very pro-active and has discussed, planned and organized a large number of initiatives for international development and co-operation. One interesting feature of the Committee is that, besides working on decentralized co-operation, it is itself very decentralized; in fact, the four thematic boards work autonomously and each one has its own agenda.

Still, the Committee suffers some significant drawbacks, such as:
- An excessive fragmentation of small initiatives and projects, that limits their effectiveness. The capacity to build a 'critical mass' is still limited;
- A confrontation with local government about the overall municipal budget for international co-operation and the criteria for its allocation;
- An internal confrontation between organizations that are more supportive of the municipal international strategy and others that are more politically autonomous;
- The prevalence of collective initiatives and projects carried out in Rome (e.g. cultural events,

educational activities, conferences, research) rather than abroad;
- An insufficient and inadequate communication system within the Committee and between the citizens and the Committee. The Committee, for instance, still has no website and mailing list, no press office, no newsletter; printed information materials are produced only occasionally. As a consequence the flow of information is irregular and ineffective;
- The presence of a minority of free-riding organizations which are just out there seeking some municipal funds.

Most of those limitations derive from three factors. The first is time: the Committee has been working for just three years. Given the large number of organizations and their heterogeneity, the Committee is still young: the rules of the game, the conventions and the routines are not yet entrenched and shared. The second factor is path-dependence: the organizations (especially NGOs) have been working for a long time within a specific institutional framework (national and corporate) and a given development co-operation model (vertical and top-down). In the last years, the framework and the model have changed, but the behavioral inertia of several NGOs makes the required adjustments difficult and slow. But path-dependence is also connected to the third factor: an obsolete or inadequate educational and professional background of many CSOs staff and leaders.

An innovative informal network

In spite of the aforementioned limitations and constraints, a strong informal network has been established in Rome in the field of decentralized international co-operation. The network has a non-hierarchical structure, it is growing and branching out and shows some relevant social innovative features:
- It has re-launched a debate within the Roman civil society about the role of the city in international co-operation and about new models of territorial (decentralized) co-operation with the global South. New occasions of open public discussion have been organized, and traditional approaches to development have been challenged. Participation of associations has been enhanced and facilitated;
- It has created a new 'collective agent' (the Committee) that has become since 2003 an institutional and political reference for the municipal government; since then, international co-operation policies are no longer only a (local) governmental but also a local governance matter;
- The network partners share a basic set of values: a human-rights-based approach to development with a strong emphasis on basic needs and common goods such as water, a total rejection of war; a critique of the intergovernmental approach (especially of World Bank, International Monetary Fund and World Trade Organisation) to co-operation and development, and a trust in local-to-local (or community-to-community) co-operation between North and South;
- A strong capacity to catalyze and mobilize human and financial resources available in the Roman territory and to channel them into projects and initiatives at a local and international scale.

In sum, through the laborious construction and functioning of the network, an accumulation of social capital can be observed. The question now is about the dynamics of scale: how global will be the benefits of this local resource? Will the network be capable of becoming a glocal force?

Innovation in social relations to combat social exclusion in European cities

As with the case of the organizations of international co-operation located in Rome, the analysis of European urban experiences concentrates on the transformation of social relations among agents (individual, collective) involved in the struggle against social exclusion as well as on innovation in governance of these relations. Two research projects for the European Commission have served as an empirical basis for this analysis: The role of local development to fight social exclusion (EC, Social Policy; see Moulaert, 2002) and SINGOCOM ('Social Innovation, Governance and Community Building; FP5, SERD-2000-0028; see Moulaert, Martinelli & Swyngedouw, 2005, final report; Moulaert, Martinelli, Swyngedouw & Gonzalez, 2005), with the main emphasis given to the second of these research projects.

The sixteen detailed case studies of SINGOCOM were organized in 10 cities in 6 European countries. The majority of these cases were located in urban neighborhoods with problems related to economic development, integration of people into the labor market and socio-political participation.

Social Innovation Initiatives and their territorial settings

A distinction can be made between: (1) neighborhood centered initiatives; (2) neighborhood initiatives with a wider intra-urban/regional spread effect; (3) 'neighborhood-located wider impact' initiatives; and (4) city-wide initiatives. Illustration 5.3 provisionally classifies the initiatives from this point of view. The spatial reach considered here only takes into account the impact of the initiative as such and not the 'parallel' learning and communication dynamics in which most of these projects are involved. For example, many of the projects are involved in pan-European networking and exchange of experience, either within formal European arrangements (e.g. URBAN) or through spontaneous affinity search (as is the case for CityMined, BuurtOntwikkelingsMaatschappij BOM (neighborhood development organization), Antwerp, Leoncavallo, Associazione Quartieri Spagnoli, Olinda).

Territorial Reach	Initiatives
Neighborhood centred initiatives	Butetown History and Arts Center, Naples AQS, Naples Piazzamoci, Brussels LimiteLimite, Roubaix Ass. Alentour
Neighborhood initiatives with a wider intra-urban/regional spread effect	Rhondda Arts Factory, Newcastle New Deal, BOM Antwerp, Berlin Quartiersagentur Marzahn, Vienna LA21 (District 9), Vienna Local Area Management
'Neighborhood-located wider impact' initiatives	Newcastle Ouseburn, Milan Leoncavallo, Milan Olinda, Berlin Kommunales Forum Wedding
City-wide initiatives	Brussels CityMined

Illustration 5.3: Territorial reaches of the Socially Innovative Initiatives (Source: authors)

The distinction between neighborhood focus and wider-spatial-scale targeting is scientifically and politically significant, and the research shows that a combination of scales, especially for partnering and resource mobilization, strengthens the chance of positive outcomes in social innovation initiatives.

Contrary to the neo-liberal adagio that targeting deprived neighborhoods is a strategy based on a 'negative choice', some of the most successful strategies (BOM Antwerp, AQS Naples) show that such a neighborhood focus can work very well if mobilization of resources and governance of partners are established at complementary spatial (institutional) levels. This does not mean that all locally-inspired social innovation strategies should target neighborhoods; the metropolitan or urban scale – the city as a whole – is the appropriate level when a better integration of inter-area co-operation and an improved integration of urban governance scales are pursued.

Innovation in social relations and governance: the role of empowerment

The analysis of the dynamics of social innovation has been done by use of the ALMOLIN model (Alternative Model for Local Innovation). This model establishes a relationship between on the one hand the alienation of human needs (and those of their communities of belonging) which is expressed according to different forms of social exclusion, and on the other hand the resistance of human beings against social exclusion. This resistance takes on a variety of forms, which are often combined: protest through political and social organization (including discursive strategies), definition of strategies to bypass the alienation and the non-satisfaction of needs, in particular by establishing initiatives to satisfy human needs and to create (or reinforce) social relations facilitating the realization of such initiatives (elements of governance and political empowerment).

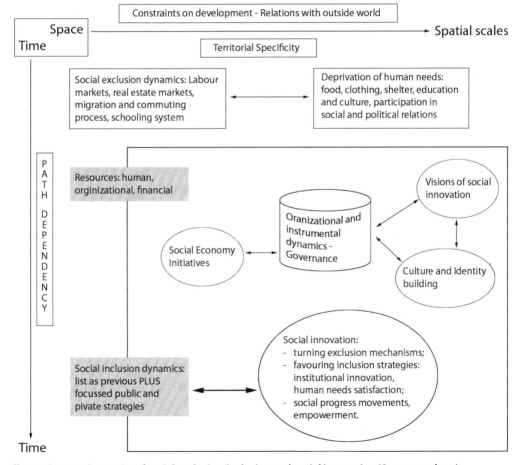

Illustration 5.4: Dynamics of social exclusion/inclusion and social innovation (Source: authors)

The ALMOLIN model is presented in a schematic way in Illustration 5.4. Its lower part represents what we could call 'the factory of social innovation', the essential features of which are explained in Moulaert, Martinelli, Swyngedouw and Gonzalez (2005).

The most significant conclusion of this research on the social relations within SINGOCOM is that these initiatives and organizations of local development have become key markers of the current urban landscape, and that many of them have asserted themselves as important leverages for galvanizing socially-inclusive urban redevelopment processes. Analyzing the sixteen cases with respect to the dynamics of 'factories of social innovation', we identified three significant features that are common to all initiatives: a) type of origin of the initiative; b) the processes linking the problems of exclusion they seek to resolve, the forces that guide them (including motivations) and their network organization in articulation with state and market; c) their scalar effect (spatial scales and their articulation).

a The origin

While all projects are clearly articulated within the state/market/civil society triangle, the most creative and innovative in terms of generating new forms of delivery, attending to new needs, and experimenting with innovative institutional or organizational arrangements, are those that originate from within civil society. Those initiated by the state – usually the local state – tend to be less successful and are generally seen as instruments to re-establishing fading governmental legitimacy.

b The process

While all initiatives have to and do interact with both market and the state, the nature of the institutional embedding of this arrangement is of central importance in shaping its innovative dynamics. To the extent that civil society initiatives become 'captured' by the state, their innovative dynamics are generally weakened and become part of the bureaucratic apparatus. Governments in fact have the tendency to 'cherry-pick' from civil society initiatives those that are seen to be successful. Their incorporation, however, often saps their innovative energies. Some of the initiatives are fully aware of this dialectic between integration and autonomy and try to maintain a fine balance between co-operation (with market and state) on the one hand and oppositional tactics on the other. The latter, in turn, pre-empt full incorporation while generating a continuous innovative dynamic as the relationships between both state and market need to be revisited continuously.

c The scalar effect

While the projects are decidedly local and in some cases even place-specific, there is an emergent trend to engage in 'scalar' politics. This refers to the articulation of the local initiatives with processes, institutions, and social capacities that operate at other spatial levels or scales. To the extent projects are successful in doing so, their effects are longer lasting, while transcending the particular place-specificity engenders the potential for broader political-economic transformations. Of course, such scalar politics are decidedly janus-faced as the new institutional arrangements that accompany such trans-scalar networks are not necessarily as inclusive or participatory as is often portrayed (Swyngedouw, 2005).

In sum (see Illustration 5.5), the selection of case-study projects suggests that significant creative energies are mobilized in urban re-development through such civil society initiatives. In fact, these processes that often target the 'truly' disadvantaged have become vital for mediating the pervasive mechanisms of social exclusion and economic hardship that have characterized contemporary urban change. It is ironic, therefore, that these initiatives have not gained the academic and policy attention that they deserve compared with the more spectacular, although not necessarily more significant, strategies of urban re-development through large scale top-down renovation mega-projects (Moulaert, Rodriguez & Swyngedouw, 2003).

Yet, stimulating and fostering socially-innovative projects has become a vital and necessary component of urban social change. The policy framework that might permit the unleashing of even greater socially innovative dynamics across Europe's cities and in connection with cities in other continents is the next stage of this work.

Initiative	Innovative vision	Innovative delivery	Innovative institutional organization	Innovative process	Innovative Scalar Effect
Newcastle NDC	The concept of the community leadership of regeneration	The delivery of holistic regeneration Capacity building across a wide range of distinct communities	Experimentation built into project development and appraisal	Attempts to link bottom-up and top-down style initiatives	Attempts to 'mainstream' innovative activities at wider geographical scales
Ouseburn Trust Newcastle	'Brokerage' role between community and government – Bridging 'structural holes'	New facilities	Widened 'cracks' in the mainstream local state form Network form	Enlarging policy domain	Articulating gap between place qualities and local government
Olinda Milan	Creation of subjects capable of 'agency'	Increasing socio-political capabilities	Integration of assistance and work insertion	Legitimize new practices and social claims Construction of shared interest Setting new standards	Mobilization of resources from a wide array
Leoncavallo Milan	Needs satisfaction based on reciprocity	Increasing socio-political capabilities Satisfaction of human needs outside market relations	Tresholding lowering procedures Centrality of spatial dimension and availability of 'free' space	Legitimize new practices and social claims Construction of shared interest Provision of space and visibility	Wider mobilization around social, cultural, and political issues. Resource for collective action
CityMin(e)d Brussels	Mobilization of unlikely partners from different geographical scales and from a heterogeneous social composition	Fostering networks that enhances self-efficacy	Fuzzy network arrangements	Non-territorial focus and autonomous-project driven. Mobilising 'vacant' or vaguely defined socio-spatial settings	Target strategically a micro geographic scale in order to have a positive impact on the development at another, often larger, scale

Chapter 5: Combating Poverty in Europe and the Third World: Social Innovation in Motion

Limite Limite Brussels	The creation of a 'third' space between different groups in friction and to transform the hegemonic urban regime	Broadening the capability sets of the participants	Heterogeneous and unusual alliance formation in network organization	Mobilising 'vacant' institutional and geographical spaces	Local network organization in order to effectuate changes at higher institutional level
Local Agenda 21 Vienna	Opening up democratic space	Providing mediating platform Free space for experimentation	Modernized institutional arrangements	Emergence of a new power field.	Some effectuation in breaking open higher level institutional gridlock
Local Area Management Vienna	Relatively limited – re-establishing existing power fields	Poor	Modernized institutional arrangements	Poor – Restricted and confirming existing power relations	Problematic involvement of EU scale (accountability rules – limited innovation
Quartieri Spagnoli Napels	Focus on citizenship rights	Associative delivery Creation of local capacity and social capital formation		Catalyst of Resources	Wide national and international recognition
Piazziamoci Naples	Participation and counter-institutional power	Oppositional engagement resulting in capacity building and creation of expertise		Process of interaction more important than outcome	Confrontational dynamics – creativity of protest
Alentour Roubaix (Lille)	Alentour arose in the context of public renewal policy – civil society counterpart to public initiative. Empowerment of weakest social groups	Delivery of food, social, maintenance and cultural services to the 'truly' disadvantaged. Particular focus on weakest social group	Alentour worked with all social actors in the neighborhood	Initial attempt at innovative networked organization, but ultimately largely incorporated within the local state	None
Wales – all initiatives	Access to and engagement with facilities and opportunities for personal development, enjoyment and self-representation	Reaches non-traditional groups and involves them in open, activist, and empowering manner.	Open organizational structure	Extension of horizons, altering 'views'	While articulating with higher scale levels (municipality, EU), autonomous direction maintained and innovative relations developed
Kommunales Forum Wedding Berlin	Introducing new ideas in the field of action around area based civil society action for local quality of life	Welfare provision delivery	Partnership approach	Information and education based process to increase local public participation	Project worked through to the Berlin city-wide level as well as to other policy domains
Quartiers Agentur Marzahn NordWest Berlin	Establishing institutional links between immigrant and host society	The building of access organizations	Intercultural mediator between different social-ethnic groups	Social capacity building	Set-up by city government

Illustration 5.5 The Socially Innovative Character of the Projects (Source: authors)

Conclusion

The analyses and experiences presented in this Chapter clearly show the relevance of the social innovation approach as a conceptual and operational framework for the study of the strategies against poverty in developing countries as well as in large European cities. The combination of the analysis of governance dimensions with the characterization of the dynamics underlying the emergence and the spatial-institutional structuring of social networks devoted to the combat against poverty and social exclusion provides a useful, unified 'lens' through which various strategies and experiences can be interpreted.

This integrated approach also stresses the variety and richness of the social innovation dimensions in all initiatives against poverty and social exclusion deployed by civil society and non governmental organizations in different social, institutional and spatial contexts.

Finally, this approach suggests that the various local experiences and cases could be mobilized in order to promote a cross-learning basis, both at the intra-organizational and inter-organizational levels, as well as across geo-continental cultures. Through this experience-sharing and knowledge-pooling dynamics, one could learn cumulatively about 'feasible' context-sensitive social innovation strategies. It also sheds light on which pitfalls, errors and risks social innovation actors must face, and on how these difficulties and inhibiting factors could be avoided or managed.

References

Consiglio Comunale di Roma, 2002, Istituzione del Comitato Cittadino per la cooperazione decentrata, *Deliberazione Consiliare*, N° 144, 17 October.

Damanpour, F., 1991, Organizational Innovation: A Meta-analysis of the Effects of Determinants and Moderations, *Academy of Management Journal*, Vol. 34, pp. 555-590.

De Muro, P., 2005, La lotta alla povertà: dalle visioni alle azioni; in: Osservatorio Romano Azioni Contro la Povertà (ed.), *Roma e la povertà nel mondo. Indagine sulle azioni della società civile*, Sinnos, Roma.

De Muro, P., A. Hamdouch, S. Cameron & F. Moulaert, 2007, Organisations de la société civile et gouvernance de la lutte contre la pauvreté dans le Tiers-Monde, *Mondes en Développement*, Numéro spécial sur "Les organisations de la société civile", M. Labie (ed.), forthcoming in October 2007.

Durkheim, E., (1909) 1970, *La Science sociale et l'action*, Presses Universitaires de France, Paris.

Durkheim, E., (1893) 1984, *The Division of Labor in Society*, The Free Press, New York.

Favreau, L. & B. Lévesque, 1999, Développement Economique Communautaire. Economie Sociale et Intervention, Presses Universitaires du Québec, Sainte-Foye, Québec.

Hamdouch, A., 2004, Innovation, article Corpus, *Encyclopædia Universalis*, Version 10, p. 14.
http://www.universalis.fr/corpus2.php?napp=&nref=C040051

Hamdouch, A., 2005, Emergence et légitimité des institutions, co-ordination économique et nature de la rationalité des agents, *Innovation: The European Journal of Social Science Research*, Vol 18, N° 2, June, pp. 227-259.

Hamdouch, A. & F. Moulaert, 2006, Knowledge Infrastructure, Innovation Dynamics, and Knowledge Creation/Diffusion/Accumulation Processes: A Comparative Institutional Perspective, *Innovation: The European Journal of Social Science Research*, Special Issue "The Knowledge Infrastructure: Analysis, Institutional Dynamics and Policy issues", F. Moulaert and A. Hamdouch (eds), Vol. 19, N° 1, March, pp. 25-50.

Hillier, J., F. Moulaert & J. Nussbaumer, 2004, "Trois essais sur le rôle de l'innovation sociale dans le développement terrorial", *Géographie, Economie, Société*, Vol. 6, N° 2, pp. 129-152.

Laville, J.-L. & G. Delfau, 2000, *Aux sources de l'économie solidaire*, Editions Thierry Quinqueton, Daumont.

Moulaert, F., 2002, *Globalisation and Integrated Area Development in European Cities*, Oxford University Press, Oxford.

Moulaert, F. (ed.), 2005, *Urban Studies,* Special Issue, Vol. 42, N° 11.

Moulaert, F. & O. Ailenei, 2005, Social economy, économie solidaire and third sector: history, practice and analysis, *Urban Studies*, Vol. 42, N° 11, pp. 2037-2053.

Moulaert, F. & K. Cabaret, 2006, Planning, Networks and Power Relations: is Democratic Planning under Capitalism Possible?, *Planning Theory*, Vol. 5, N° 1, pp. 51-70.

Moulaert, F., P. Delladetsima, J.-C. Delvainquière, Ch. Demazière & L. Leontidou, 1994, Local Development Strategies; in: *Economically Disintegrated Areas: A Pro-Active Strategy against Poverty in the European Community*, Reports for the EC, DG Research, IFRESI-CNRS, Lille.

Moulaert, F., J.C. Delvainquière & P. Delladetsima, 1997, Rapports sociaux dans le développement local. Le rôle des mouvements sociaux; In: Klein J.-L. (ed.), *Au-delà du néolibéralisme: quel rôle pour les mouvements sociaux?*, Presses de l'Université du Québec, Sainte-Foy, Québec.

Moulaert, F. & A. Hamdouch, 2006, New Views of Innovation Systems: Agents, Rationales, Networks and Spatial Scales in the Knowledge Infrastructure, *Innovation: The European Journal of Social Science Research*, Special Issue "The Knowledge Infrastructure: Analysis, Institutional Dynamics and Policy Issues", F. Moulaert & A. Hamdouch (eds), Vol. 19, N° 1, March, pp. 11-24.

Moulaert, F., F. Martinelli & E. Swyngedouw, 2005, S*ocial Innovation and Governance in Local Communities*, SINGOCOM, Final Report to the European Commission, FP 5, IFRESI, Lille.

Moulaert, F., F. Martinelli, E. Swyngedouw & S. González, 2005, Towards Alternative Model(s) of Local Innovation, *Urban Studies*, Vol. 42, N° 11, October, pp. 1969-1990.

Moulaert F. & J. Nussbaumer, 2005, The Social Region. Beyond the Territorial Dynamics of the Learning Economy, *European Urban and Regional Studies*, Vol. 12, N° 1, pp. 45-64.

Moulaert, F., A. Rodriguez & E. Swyngedouw (eds), 2003, *The Globalized City: Economic Restructuring and Social Polarization in European Cities*, Oxford University Press, Oxford.

Mumford, M.D., 2002, Social Innovation: Ten Cases from Benjamin Franklin, *Creativity Research Journal*, Vol. 14, N° 2, pp. 253-266.

Osservatorio Romano Azioni Contro la Povertà (ed.), 2005, *Roma e la povertà nel mondo. Indagine sulle azioni della società civile*, Rapporto 2005, Sinnos, Roma.

Rhi-Sausi, J. L., R. Coletti, D. Conato & G. Rufini, 2004, *La città di Roma nella cooperazione e nella solidarietà internazionale. Esperienze e prospettive*, CeSPI – Comune di Roma.

Schumpeter, J. A., 1932, *Entwicklung, unpublished paper*, translated by C. Becker and T. Knudsen, October 2002 (see: www.schumpeter.info).

Schumpeter, J. A., 1942, *Capitalism, Socialism and Democracy*, Allan and Unwin, London.

Swyngedouw, E., 2005, Governance Innovation and the Citizen: The Janus Face of Governance-beyond-the-State, *Urban Studies*, Vol. 42, N° 11, pp. 1991-2006.

Weber, M., (1922) 1978, *Economy and Society: An Outline of Interpretive Sociology* (Edited by G. Roth and C. Wittich), 2 Vols., University of California Press, Berkeley.

Note

1. State of the art literature surveys on innovation can be found in Hamdouch (2004), Hamdouch and Moulaert (2006) and Moulaert and Hamdouch (2006).

Part II

Cases

6 Local Development as Social Innovation: the Case of Montreal[1]

Juan-Luis Klein, Jean-Marc Fontan and Diane-Gabrielle Tremblay

Introduction

Local economic development presents itself in diverse forms. These forms often correspond to local systems formed by a concentration of businesses structured into diversified networks and effectively integrated into the global market. These local business networks represent the links in an 'archipelago economy' that is both globalized and localized (Amin & Thrift, 1992; Veltz, 1996; Benko & Lipietz, 2000; Braczyk, Cooke & Heidenreich, 1998; Fontan, Klein & Tremblay, 2005). Studies about local economic development have shown three important findings (Pecqueur, 1989; Tremblay & Fontan, 1994; Joyal, 2002; Stöhr, 2003; Amin, Cameron & Hudson, 2002). First, the emergence of relevant cases of local development depends on the capacity of economic, political and institutional actors to associate their expertise and resources. Secondly, such an association is closely related to the capacity of these socio-economic actors to innovate and learn, both individually and collectively. Thirdly, the variety and combination of local development initiatives constitute conditions allowing local areas to adapt to the strategic and productive flexibility required by the nature of interspatial competition in the context of the global economy. These findings are essential components of a strategy of development based on local initiative (Arocena, 2001; Klein, 2005).

The concept of local economic development and its use as a guiding strategy for developing marginalized areas (Bryant & Cofsky, 2004) is not endorsed enthusiastically by all. Some authors have doubts about the impact or the relevance of local development initiatives. They consider that communities undergoing severe economic crises are too devitalized and lack the capitalistic vigor to assume the responsibility for their development (Polese, 1996; De Mattos, 1999; Amin, 2005). Also, the impact of local development may appear as a grain of sand in a global context shaped by the broad currents of globalization (Polese & Shearmur, 2002). Moreover, Amin (2005), after analyzing the New Labor third way policy in the UK, concludes that socio-economic and entrepreneurship programs based on the social capital and the force of the community are in fact justifications for rethinking development policy in a liberal way and accepting the existence of a second-class citizenship for an important portion of the population.

These criticisms are well founded, particularly when they are applied to top-down strategies based on neoliberal policies. But another perspective is possible when local strategies of development are designed by local actors themselves, especially when these strategies are elaborated by social actors and are based in social economy objectives (Lévesque, Bourque & Forgues, 2001; Moulaert & Nussbaumer, 2005). We put forward the idea that such a point of view may bring us to see local development as a type of social action that belongs to the social movements approach. Seen in this perspective, social initiatives in local spaces represent a specific type of collective action. As a response to marginalization, social actors implement concrete productive or economic reconversion projects in order to compensate for the lack of capitalistic resources in their territory and to improve local residents' quality of life. We will describe two Montreal cases that show how local collective actions have assumed a strong leadership in shaping the directions taken in the reconversion of two industrial districts of Montreal where brownfield sites dominated as a consequence of the Fordist crisis which occurred in the 1980s. These cases are the Lachine Canal Zone in the South-West district and the Angus Shops in the Rosemont district.

These two cases are comparable in several ways. First, the two cases have a great symbolic value, in that they involve the remnants of Canada's cradle of industrialization. Secondly, these cases are the two largest industrial development sites in the city of Montreal. Thirdly, both these projects fall within a voluntary reconversion strategy preceded by and embedded in social mobilizations that both demanded that the productive and industrial function of the neighborhoods concerned be preserved. In short, these two cases can be seen as two laboratories where Montreal's socio-economic actors innovate and have been able to test out different means for sparking socio-economic growth. These cases also represent laboratories for researchers, in allowing them to analyze the effects of social mobilization on local development and the conditions required for this development to occur for the benefit of local populations and not at their expense. In both cases, the local community developed representative social organizations in order to guide the development. By describing the two cases we will be able to show that social movements have a structuring effect, especially in terms of strengthening local identities and developing strategic objectives, but that this effect remains weak and its position a fragile one if these social movements are unable to assume and maintain a leadership role in planning and implementing the projects that result from the development process.

Our analysis is presented in four parts. First, we will introduce our conceptual framework which is inspired by the theory of social movements, especially by the resource mobilization approach. This conceptual framework will allow us to put the role of social mobilizations triggered by a local community seeking to preserve its existing assets back into the theoretical context of the revitalization of social movements. Secondly, we will briefly outline issues and problems specific to the Montreal metropolitan region, particularly the situation of old industrial areas currently undergoing restructuring. This is the type of area in which the two experiences studied are taking place. Thirdly, we will describe these two experiences. And finally, we will shed some light on the innovative dimension of the social movements' implication in local development.

Local community development: a new sphere for collective action

The economic crisis in old industrial areas in aging industrial cities was a relatively widespread process in North America since the 1980s and the 1990s. This crisis resulted from a series of factors linked to production, transportation and consumption. These factors are associated with globalization, as 'city-regions' are taking shape in a context of 'metropolitanization' and new forms of interspatial competition (Borja & Castells, 1997; Scott, 2001; Sassen, 2002, Klein & Tardif, 2006). Globalization is occurring alongside a process of political, social and economic fragmentation. This has been termed the 'archipelago economy' (Veltz, 1996), or even the 'archipelago society' (Viard, 1994), which is redefining the role played by political and social actors at every level of governance (local, regional, national and international).

The crisis in old industrial areas has triggered economic devitalization in the communities that lived in them, but it also triggered a process of social revitalization as community actors mobilized to preserve their existing assets. The mobilizations have thus played a beneficial role in decision-making regarding the location of economic activities. The analysis of this aspect, which is in our view a crucial one, leads to the recognition of a type of social movements that are rooted in local communities (Klein, Tremblay & Dionne, 1997). Our viewpoint is based on the paradigm of 'collective action' and 'resource mobilization', a perspective developed by authors such as Tilly (1984), Tarrow (1994) and Melucci (1992). Based on the work of these authors, we define a social movement as a series of collective actions in which social actors mobilize resources in order to exert pressure on different spheres of power.

Social movements and collective action

The emergence of a socio-economic mobilization is generally linked to the emergence of an economic crisis. Through the combination of diverse elements, individuals' reactions under the strong leadership of a few leaders lead to forming a social group centered on a goal aimed at ending this process of marginalization and fragmentation. These individuals recognize that their lack of access to decision-making is a blockage and this gradually leads the group to adopt a collective leadership that is able to organize a contestation of the established power structure. The strength of a collective action is linked to the contesting group's organizational capacity, and the resonance the cause pursued achieves among the general public. The public dissemination of a social cause helps a collective action to emerge and crystallize, which transforms the contestation into a structured social movement, with clearly-defined opponents, agents, organizations and goals.

Based on the work of Tilly (1984), it can be said that social movements develop in parallel to overall developments in society, which are expressed by a repertoire of collective actions that is structured in the context of the development of modernity, and that is now expanding in accordance with an ever-more-present 'information and global society' (Castells, 1997; Castells, 2002). The modernization and globalization of societies is generating a very diverse range of social movements. Some social movements evolve from an attitude of confrontation and protest against the state and private business to an attitude of promotion of the local in the face of the dominant actors: in the face of the 'Polity' and its members, as Tilly would say. They are embedded at the local scale, even when they 'jump scales', from local to national and to global, in there fight for equity as well as for being recognized as different (Swyngedouw, 1997). Doing so, they produce a sense of group belonging by creating a sense of local community belonging (Melucci, 1993).

From collective action to the mobilization of local resources

Collective actions assign a different meaning to local spaces and local economic development than those given to them by the institutions of power, especially when they denounce the distance between the logic of production and the logic of social reproduction imposed by globalization (Melucci, 1992). Due to economic restructuring (industrial relocation, demographic devitalization, gentrification), the centrality of certain repertoires of collective action has been rendered obsolete. For example, strikes were among the tools used by the labor movement and represented a dominant repertoire of action during the entire Fordist period. Strikes are still an effective tool for unions, but they cannot always use them. When companies in an old industrial area close one after another, strikes are no longer possible because the site of confrontation disappears (Fontan & Klein, 2000; Klein & Fontan, 2003). Social actors must then innovate, that means discover, test out and put in practice new repertoires of actions, such as social and economic partnerships.

So we assume that, in rural as well as in urban areas, collective actions of social movements have enlarged their repertoire of action, according to the issues at stake. In doing so, they add to the strategy of denunciation of inequalities and pressure for better conditions for the exercise of democracy: a new strategy based on the combination of contest and partnership in order to preserve community assets in terms of services and jobs. The scale of these collective actions has also changed, moving more toward demands at the local level, as shown by social movements' involvement in local economic development corporations in Montreal (Tremblay & Fontan, 1994; Morin, Latendresse & Parazelli, 1994; Joyal, 2002) and contributing to the localization and the re-scaling of public power (Swyngedouw, 1997; Brenner, 2003).

New spheres of collective action thus emerge in underprivileged areas, including the struggle to strengthen citizenship, the struggle to reintegrate the most disadvantaged into the job market, the struggle for equity in terms of public investments, and the struggle against the relocation of production activities or public institutions. All of these demands are directly related to the viability of local communities as places in which to live and work.

A key question, however, is whether local development is limited to what can be done locally by local actors. This question is at the heart of the debate on local development, as pointed out by Amin (2005). When we attempt to answer this question, the perspective of resource mobilization is useful. Firstly, we have to specify that, in our understanding, resources obviously refer to financial resources, but also to the local community's institutional thickness (participation of leaders, potential for local support and the organizational capacities of the performers of collective actions); thus it means resources that are present within a local community. We refer to these resources as the socio-territorial capital of a local community. Secondly, although we agree with arguments that assign to the community a central role in local development, we believe that restricting development to its endogenous resources would be a limited understanding of the action of a local movement for redevelopment. The danger of this viewpoint lies in the fact that the various supra-local levels of power see it as an opportunity to abandon their responsibilities vis-à-vis local community development problems and to hold these communities accountable for the crisis situation they find themselves in, as Amin (2005) denounced. When central governments initiate local development policies that make communities accountable without giving them the necessary resources and powers to implement solutions, this is not a positive contribution to solving local problems. And this is in fact a prevalent trend today.

However, collective actions aimed at local development are occurring in a context where local actors are not isolating themselves in a local and strictly endogenous vision of development. The examination of a variety of collective actions designed by civil society shows that local development does not necessarily mean turning in on oneself (Fontan, Klein & Lévesque, 2003). Social actors in local communities are in fact demanding more than a simple appropriation of abandoned resources and relinquished responsibilities. They are demanding full participation in the management of society by calling for the state and decision makers to change their attitudes and behaviors toward marginalized communities and territories or those in the process of being marginalized. Local development carries a strong political demand for fuller citizenship and greater democracy. This can be seen by looking at social movements in Montreal, especially the two cases we will examine in this Chapter.

Territorial tensions in Montreal's reconversion

Various writings and evidence show that, after a lengthy crisis, like most of North America's first industrial centers, the Montreal metropolitan region is in the process of reconversion to the new knowledge-based economy (Fontan, Klein & Tremblay, 2005; Klein, Manzagol, Tremblay & Rousseau, 2005; Tremblay & Rolland, 2003). The representatives of the business community and of the main private and government institutions shifted toward the development of high technology businesses. One of the elements which sparked the adoption of this strategy was the task force created by the federal government in 1985 and chaired by Laurent Picard, a well-known figure in the university community. Based on the deliberations of its sixteen institutional leaders from Montreal, the task force produced what is known as the *Picard Report*, which became a reference on Montreal's economic reconversion for both public and private practitioners. The report contains a strategy that encourages private leadership, internationalization and the development of high-technology sectors (telecommunications, aerospace, biopharmaceuticals, information technologies and microelectronics). These objectives were to be implemented at the agglomeration level and were expected to result in planning operations at the metropolitan level (Tremblay & Van Schendel, 2004).

The transition to this new economy occurred quite naturally in some suburbs, which successfully developed 'technopolitan' strategies, as they specialized in high-value-added and high-tech sectors such as aeronautics, aerospace, pharmaceuticals and multimedia (Klein, Tremblay & Fontan, 2003; Tremblay, Klein, Fontan & Rousseau, 2003; Tremblay & Rousseau, 2005). However, the inner cities, especially the city's first industrial areas on the periphery of the Central Business District, were hard hit by the effects of this change. This has resulted in specific problems and issues in these areas. The industrial function that once characterized them was gradually relocated elsewhere, with severe effects on them. Begun in the 1950s and intensifying in the 1970s, the relocation of the industrial sector from these areas triggered all the problems associated with social and urban destructuring. Residents in these neighborhoods experienced major economic and social problems: unemployment, low incomes and population loss.

Recognition of these problems inspired a dual reaction from Montreal's social actors. On the one hand, the problems required a new kind of response. It was no longer a question of reducing poverty by increasing workers' wages, but instead of doing this by creating new jobs and facilitating access to these jobs for unemployed people. On the other hand, it was difficult for the actors to work toward the socio-economic redevelopment of their districts by using traditional collective actions such as demonstrations, strikes, roadblocks, etc. They turned to actions that emphasize local actors working in synergy, for example, by using collaboration and partnerships. The sphere of the struggles and the methods used were adapted to the crisis situation facing residents in these areas. While in the past, such mobilization was often limited to putting pressure on the public actor or on management, community development experiences now rely not only on these pressures, but also increasingly on collective or social entrepreneurship to drive innovative initiatives. Underlying these experiences is a desire to prevent job losses and the devitalization of the community.

The strategy proposed by the associational community was elaborated by organizations rooted in what we referred to earlier as the marginalized districts, that is, those put in a difficult position by industrial redeployment. These districts mobilized around the community leaders to defend their assets and undertake development strategies that are adapted to new economic conditions, and respect the interests of the local population. The main results of this mobilization can be seen in what is described by the actors as a 'community economic development' strategy and in the creation of organizations of Montreal's Community Economic Development Corporations (CEDCs) devoted to the application of this intervention strategy (Fontan, 1991; Hamel, 1991).

The central goal of the CEDCs is to promote the partnership between the actors in their districts. Their aim is to get actors to work together and to implement partnership-based development projects, which allows actors to make contact with each other and to identify common goals. The second main goal of the CEDCs is to support local entrepreneurship in order to help create local jobs. Finally, the third goal is to enhance the employability of the jobless, that is, to provide individuals with the skills needed to re-enter a job market undergoing intense restructuring. The districts or boroughs constitute the space in which the CEDCs act. In this way, the existence of boroughs as intermediary public spaces allows the potential of local territories as a framework for collective action rooted in social movements to be realized. This constitutes an important change in community action, one that has been the subject of numerous debates even within the Montreal social movement.

The second type of strategy originating in social movements is the strategy resulting from union action. Since the early 1980s, unions have adopted a strategy that has re-oriented their action and transformed them into important development actors. In reaction to globalization and industrial redeployment, the unions have focused their action on the fight for jobs by creating investment funds and tools to prevent plant closures.

A good example of this strategy is the creation of funds for the purpose of fighting business closures and investing in job creation. The first and largest fund of this type was the *Fonds de solidarité* (Solidarity Fund), created in 1983 by the *Fédération des travailleurs et travailleuses du Québec* (FTQ, Quebec Federation of Labor) with the explicit goal of creating jobs. The FTQ fund has about 500,000 shareholders and assets of nearly five billion Canadian dollars. This then prompted Quebec's second-largest labor confederation, the *Confédération des syndicats nationaux* (CSN, Confederation of National Trade Unions), to create a retirement fund in 1996, a fund called Fondaction, with goals similar to those of the FTQ fund, but more oriented toward venture capital investment in social economy enterprises. Fondaction has a quarter of a billion dollars and counts nearly 50,000 shareholders.

Again, from the perspective of the fight for jobs, the unions have established forms of action that seek to anticipate crisis in firms before they arise and to suggest changes that could help prevent the crisis. This is true, for example, of the FTQ organization, *Urgence-Emploi*, and of the CSN's employment watch project, the *Projet de veille pour l'emploi*. These services support the efforts of local unions to prevent massive layoffs. They develop, jointly with management and government organizations, recovery plans for firms having difficulties, thus suggesting a determination on the part of the unions to participate in business governance.

The creation of CEDCs by the community associational movement and the establishment of union tools and services devoted to supporting the creation or consolidation of jobs and to preventing business closures are among the actions carried out by the Montreal social movement to make the fight for jobs one of the strategic orientations of Montreal's reconversion. In so doing, both the unions with their significant financial assets and the community organizations with their potential for social mobilization have become actors recognized by both government authorities and the business community. Moreover, this focus on employment provides direction to the otherwise uneven actions of Montreal actors as a whole.

The Canal Lachine Zone and the Angus Technopole: two significant cases of social local development

The two examples we will look at show the potential and limitations of the collective actions of social movements in the area of local economic development. The first example is the South-West CDEC action to revitalize the Lachine Canal zone which began in the 1980s. The second case is the Angus Technopole. This Technopole was developed and implemented by the *Société de développement Angus* (SDA) in the Rosemont area. The Technopole and the SDA both emerged from the *Corporation de développement économique communautaire* (CDEC) in the Rosemont-Petite-Patrie district. They stem directly from the economic action of the Montreal urban social movement to revitalize old industrial areas.

Rosemont and the South-West are respectively both important pericentral districts. These two cases are part of a process which highlights, at times the conflict, and at times the collaboration, between social actors and local economic actors, private enterprise, the city, and government institutions.

The case of the Canal Lachine Zone: partnership-based governance of an economic space

The territory of the Canal Lachine Zone includes the former municipalities of Lachine, LaSalle and Verdun, all of which became boroughs of the new City of Montreal on January 1, 2002. It also includes the southwest district of the former City of Montreal, which is itself made up of six districts that belong to the oldest population areas of Montreal Island. Thanks to the Lachine Canal, Southwestern Montreal became a bastion of industrialization in Canada. Several steel and manufacturing plants were set up on its banks starting in the first half of the 19th century. These enterprises employed thousands of workers who lived close to their place of work.

When the Lachine Canal was closed to shipping in the 1960s, Southwestern Montreal entered a long period of economic decline. One by one, the plants either closed or laid off a very great number of workers. As a result of a drop in the birth rate and the population exodus to more affluent neighborhoods in the suburbs, the population began to decline. Public investment mainly took the form of welfare transfers: social assistance or employment assistance. Private investment decreased. Investors, put off by the territory's less attractive image, either fled or bypassed it.

In the late 1960s, under the leadership of social actors, often clergy members, the population was mobilized and reacted to the socio-economic deterioration of their territory. Between 1965 and 1980, many important initiatives were undertaken by Montreal community groups - citizens' committees, community clinic and pharmacy, legal aid clinic, day care centers, housing committees, food banks and community newspapers.

In 1984, community groups in Pointe-Saint-Charles, one of the Lachine Canal neighborhoods broke new ground by creating an organization dedicated to the economic development of their territory. - the *Programme économique de Pointe-Saint-Charles* (PEP). This was Montreal's first CEDC (there are twelve today). In 1988, faced with the continuing collapse of the territory's economy, local actors came together to form the *Comité pour la relance de l'économie et de l'emploi du Sud-Ouest de Montréal* (CREESOM), which developed an action plan whose central proposal was to extend PEP's mission to the entire district. In 1989, PEP became the *Regroupement pour la relance économique et sociale du Sud-Ouest* (RESO). Less than three years later (1992), the CEDC *Transaction pour l'emploi* was created in the territories of LaSalle and Lachine. Its mission was similar to that of RESO, that is, to create and retain jobs, to develop basic and occupational training, as well as to favor employment insertion and partnership of community actors to revitalize the local economy. The initiatives of these two organizations, which quickly became key resources in the region, were responsible for the creation of collective strategies for revitalizing firms, particularly through local alliances for employment. These strategies were implemented in close co-operation with the unions. RESO can be seen as an example of a CEDC. RESO has taken on the challenge of reconversion through a concrete intervention. When plant closures multiplied, when poverty was spiraling upwards and when there were no resources to attract firms, RESO showed that it was possible to change this trend, improve the employment situation within existing businesses, achieve social insertion and training of the jobless, attract firms, revitalize the existing infrastructure, and create jobs and wealth. Thus, there was a shift from reactive, confrontational action to pro-active entrepreneurial action. Since their creation, the CEDCs have maintained a key role in promoting collaboration (*concertation*) at the local level and local development. The Quebec government's decision to make RESO a Local Development Centre gives recognition to this role[2].

The Angus Technopole: a case of resource mobilization for industrial development

Located on a site of nearly 500,000 m² and implanted in 1904, the Angus Shops were the first Fordist plant in Montreal. It was specialized in the manufacture of locomotives and rail-cars for the railway industry, so that they represented an important milestone in the industrialization of Montreal and Canada as a whole. The shops' production declined over the years. From a maker of locomotives and rail-cars, they became a repair and maintenance facility, and of the six thousand jobs required to ensure production in the postwar years, there were barely more than a thousand left at the time of their final closure in 1992.

The Angus Shops were part of the CP (Canadian Pacific Railway) industrial corridor, one of the largest concentrations of manufacturing plants in Montreal where more than 30,000 people worked until the early 1990s. The closing of the Angus Shops represented the end of the decline of the CP's activities in Montreal and of the gradual dismantling of the various rail networks. Although the line is still used and several of the industries along it are still operating, many facilities such as the switching yards, repair shops and branch lines are no longer in use. A number of actors are involved in conversion of the disused lands. The most important are the CP, the company that owns the site, and the *Société de développement Angus* (SDA), created by the CDEC Rosemont-Petite-Patrie. In addition to these actors, there are the City of Montreal, which controls land use through zoning regulations, the federal and provincial governments, which have financial resources and programs applicable to conversion of the site, and Fondaction, the fund created by the CSN (Confederation of National Trade Unions) which is a SDA's financial partner.

From the start, the site conversion set the community, represented by the CDEC, against the owner of the property, that is, the CP. On the one hand, the CP wanted to develop a huge residential complex. On the other hand, the CDEC was promoting an industrial revitalization project aimed at creating jobs for local residents. In 1992, the CDEC made redevelopment of the Angus site its main priority, which resulted in it setting up a working committee which in 1995 became an independent organization, the SDA. Although connected to the CDEC, this organization is autonomous and has its own board of directors, whose members include local community representatives as well as powerful financial partners.

The Angus Technopole project is the outcome of a lengthy process that began with the conflict between the local community and the CP. The conflict exploded as soon as the facilities were shut down, when the CP wanted to have the zoning regulations changed in order to convert the site to residential and commercial use. The CDEC mobilized local actors and residents against this project. Without the residents' consent, this change was impossible, especially since the City of Montreal favored, in its master plan, strengthening the industrial vocation of this sector. Due to community opposition, the CP was thus unable to carry out its residential project.

After an intense round of negotiations, the two main actors modified their respective projects and reached a compromise. The site was divided into two parts. the CP ceded the western portion of the property to the SDA, that is, some 250,000 m². In return, the SDA and the community agreed not to dispute the zoning change required for CP to develop its residential project on the other part of the site. As these two projects were being launched, that is, the industrial project and the residential project, the SDA and the CP continued their negotiations until a final agreement was signed in 1998, when the SDA then proceeded to acquire a first section of the property. The site development work was begun, and should continue for about ten years. The total cost of the work has been estimated at $250 million.

The first phase of the work involved converting some of the existing facilities into an industrial mall, which was done in 2000. After that, a second building was erected in 2001, two others in 2002, another one, which is specialized on social economy businesses, in 2004, and a new one in 2005. In 2006, more than 30 companies, for more than 800 jobs, operating in various sectors were implanted in the 6 buildings that composed the technopole.

It is important to mention that the question of land ownership was crucial to development of the Angus project and in terms of the SDA being able to maintain its leadership in the project. Because it owns the property, the SDA holds two important cards in negotiations with its financial partners. On the one hand, it owns an asset evaluated at nearly $15 million of CAD (Canadian Dollars), allowing it to establish itself as a powerful partner. And, on the other hand, it is the project manager and is therefore in relation with the city hall, the two levels of government and the financial partners, especially Fondaction, having built its legitimacy as a representative of the local community.

The strategy adopted by the Angus project developers aims at making the most of the asset represented by the social and organizational density of the community (density of relations) in order to counteract the tendency of industrial firms to locate in the suburbs. The SDA has thus adopted a proactive strategy, supported by strong leadership from local socio-economic organizations. In concrete terms, in the neighborhood where the project is located, this leadership is bringing a number of organizations and mechanisms into play representing both residents and the business community in order to develop resources (fiscal advantages obtained from the provincial government for example) and attract firms. From this point of view, it can be said that the SDA has chosen to develop the site by attempting to reproduce business location factors generally associated with the new economy. It proposes services that foster innovation and synergy around a collective learning process. It tries to set up the conditions to establish co-operative networks, on the one hand between companies, and on the other hand between companies and community socio-economic organizations, whether from inside or outside the area (universities, training centers, unions, research centers). To achieve this, the SDA counts on institutional support from main leaders from the Montreal business and social community.

The development of a project seeking to attract businesses associated with the new economy into a devitalized community such as Rosemont raises the question of the human resources. What can be done to ensure that the local workforce and thus the local community benefit from the infrastructures set up and the businesses established? To gain an overall profile of the neighborhood's workforce and its training needs, the CDEC set up a working group called the *Comité de Relance Angus* (Angus Revitalization Committee). This committee was set up in the context of an agreement between the federal and provincial governments targeting labor force retraining. Made up of representatives from various socio-economic sectors (academic institutions, private companies, government institutions, financial institutions, community organizations and trade unions), this committee, which operated from 1995 to 1997, was mandated to identify basic, occupational and professional skills in the local community as well as training deficiencies, which led to the development of a strategic plan aimed at socio-economic integration of social strata that had been excluded from the labor market.

One of the committee's recommendations was to set up companies to assist in reintegrating the labor market. The SDA thus invested in two such initiatives. The first was the *Centre intégré de formation en environnement et recyclage d'ordinateurs* (CIFER) (Integrated Environmental Training and Computer Recycling Center). This company's workers acquire expertise in computer assembly. The second was the launching of the *Atelier de recyclage de bois* Angus (Angus Wood Recycling Shop), which recycles wood salvaged from the old CP facilities and buildings. The skills the workers gain in both cases should open doors for them in the regular job market, including with companies located in the Angus Technopole. In addition, with the support of the Quebec government, to encourage the hiring of the local workforce, the SDA developed a preliminary job-training program for people willing to acquire the skills required to meet the needs of companies wishing to locate on the site.

The Angus Technopole is the outcome of a typically community-based collective action, but which is not strictly limited to the local community. The project is in fact redefining the meaning of 'local', in that it has prompted solidarity from the Rosemont community, but also support from many organizations from outside the neighborhood (*Université du Québec à Montréal*, SNC-Lavalin, Fondaction, *Investissement Québec*, PricewaterhouseCoopers, *École Polytechnique*, etc.). The SDA has brought all the organizations involved to forge a broad partnership that mobilizes resources that are far more extensive than those of the neighborhood actors. Its structuring effect is being felt in the neighborhood around the project, but goes beyond this, in that it has succeeded in linking up actors from various backgrounds. Its impact is obviously being felt primarily at the neighborhood level, but also at the level of the city of Montreal, primarily on the level of the entire former CP industrial corridor. Moreover, it is interesting to note that the companies that have already located on the site, companies which, it should be stressed, have not only come from the local community, have embraced the social aspect of the project while creating productive and organizational linkages. This is proven by the fact that these companies agreed to invest strongly in training their workforce, as the SDA had hoped, which is a very different attitude from the attitude traditionally shown by Quebec firms. This contributes to supporting our thesis of a blend of the community and the business dimensions of the project, in a 'third generation' type of community initiative. The Angus Technopole is neither an exclusively social and endogenous based project nor an exclusively business oriented one, but a project that merges both two dimensions.

Local initiative as social innovation

The previous two cases show how employment is a rallying point for actors and has an effect on the type of development that is implemented. The public actor, the private actor and the civil actor each have a role in partnership-based experiences. In this context, the interventions of the civil actor can help to attract investments and develop entrepreneurship in conditions that are profitable for both the local community and outside private capital. The objectives of these experiences are to mobilize market resources, non-market government resources and non-monetary resources from citizens. The industrial reconversion initiatives springing from civil society come from within the social economy. These initiatives are by definition part of the third sector. Nonetheless, the successful or ongoing reconversions have encouraged the creation not only of social enterprises but also of private firms, without excluding public sector initiatives. In experimenting with strategies that balance economic and social development, will these reconversion initiatives lead to or result in bridges being built between the various types of firms and organizations, which would reflect the development of a 'plural economy'?

In Montreal, the involvement of the civil actor is contributing to the redefinition of the concept of 'economic reconversion' by broadening the understanding that public and private actors currently have of the types of activities to be reconverted as well as modalities and results to be gained from such projects of reconversion (Fontan, Klein & Tremblay, 2005). This opens other avenues for tomorrow's economy which will undoubtedly be based more and more on relations and knowledge (Borja & Castells, 1997; Tremblay & Rolland, 2003). Seen from this angle, economic reconversion can innovate in fostering high technology activities as well as in the development of culture and services that improve the quality of life of citizens (Hillier, Moulaert, & Nussbaumer, 2004). In addition, the knowledge developed through the initiatives of civil society has the advantage of combining already well-proven sectoral development strategies with innovative strategies for supporting entrepreneurship.

Thus, although the new economy is propelling us into the field of technological innovations, these innovations are also intimately related to social innovations (Klein & Harrisson, 2006). On this level, the reconversion initiatives put in action by civil society in Montreal are particularly innovative because they construct new relations between the development actors, that is, public, private and civil actors. These bridges make it possible to envisage a plural form of governance and economy that is likely to be responsive to the needs expressed by the population, including those of territories facing difficulties, while at the same time being compatible with the elites' aspirations for growth.

Conclusion

Social mobilization contributes to the development of projects that can extend well beyond the boundaries of local communities and that can have structuring effects on the entire metropolitan economy. It is in fact the metropolitan regional economy development task that is being targeted by bottom-up collective action. The resources that mobilization has succeeded in bringing into play are not only local, and it is here that its main contribution to development lies. It is when the mobilization of local actors is able to bring into play resources from inside and outside the community, resources both private and public, individual and collective, that the developmental dynamics triggered put the urban spaces concerned into a state of synchronism, as well as tension, with the global economy.

However, all locally-defined strategies, even with the participation of organizations representing the local community, do not necessarily translate into concrete projects that benefit the actors rooted in the community. Social organizations must be involved in the redevelopment process, which is in implementing the projects, and must retain an important role in the leadership guiding these projects. The capacity to withstand economic devitalization and create projects is not enough. There must be more. There must be economic involvement by the social organizations, which raises the challenge of the mobilization of financial resources and of how these resources are targeted by social movements.

This Chapter aimed to look at the question of local economic development from a new angle, that is, in light of the dynamics of resource mobilization. Indeed, the innovation process does not lie in the origin of the resources mobilized but rather in the social dynamic that makes possible the mobilization of a range of resources for the benefit of a local community. From this perspective, local development as a bottom-up strategy of action does not concern only the local spaces where new projects are carried out, and it is not limited to local actors. Local development should instead be seen as a process launched by local actors who mobilize public and private actors of various kinds and, especially, the effects of which extend beyond the boundaries of the local. This point of view sees the local not only as a group of citizens in a limited territory, but also and especially, as a wide range of actors and actions, whose unity is forged as the mobilizations take place, and at a political and economic level where the actors negotiate their integration into wider dynamics. Local development has then to be seen as a laboratory where different types of actors use their power and their social relations to innovate for the benefit of a local community. While much research previously stressed the local and close proximity dimension of the source of innovation and of local development, our two cases highlight the fact that the mobilization goes beyond the local dimension and local resources. This is an important insight which leads to questioning some of the research and normative prescriptions which highlight the importance of the local but neglect its embeddedness in a larger environment.

References

Amin, A., 2005, *Economy and Society*, Vol. 34, N° 4, pp. 612-633.
Amin, A, A. Cameron & R. Hudson, 2002, *Placing the Social Economy*, Routledge, London.
Amin, A. & N. Thrift, 1992, Neo-Marshallian Nodes in Global Networks, *International Journal of Urban and Regional Research*, Vol. 16, N° 4, pp. 571-587.
Arocena, J., 2001, *El desarrollo local: un desafío contemporáneo*, Taurus, Montevideo.
Benko, G. & A. Lipietz (eds), 2000, *La richesse des régions*, Presses Universitaires de France, Paris.
Borja, J. & M. Castells, 1997, *Local & Global: Management of Cities in the Information Age*, Earthscan Publications, London.
Braczyk, H. J., P. Cooke & M. Heidenreich (eds), 1998, *Régional Innovation Systems*, UCL Press, London.
Brenner, N., 2003, 'Glocalization' as a state spatial strategy: urban entrepreneurialism and the new politics of uneven development in western Europe; in: Peck, Jamie & Henry Yeung (eds), *Remaking the Global Economy: Economic-Geographical Perspectives*, Sage Publications, Thousand Oaks, London, pp. 197-215.
Bryant, C. & S. Cofsky, 2004, *Politiques publiques en développement économique local: comparaison internationale des approches, des programmes et des outils*, Economic Development Canada (www.geog.umontreal.ca/Dev_durable/rapports.htm).
Castells, M., 1997, The Information Age: Economy, Society and Culture, Volume II, *The Power of Identity*, Blackwell Publishers, Oxford.
Castells, M., 2002, *La galaxie Internet*, Paris, Fayard.
De Mattos, C., 1999, Teorías del desarrollo endógeno: lectura desde los territorios de la periferia, *Estudios Avançados*, Vol. 13, N° 36, pp. 183-207.
Fontan, J.-M., 1991, *Les corporations de développement économique communautaire montréalaises. Du développement économique communautaire au développement local de l'économie*, unpublished doctoral thesis in sociology, Université de Montréal, Montréal.
Fontan, J.-M. & J.-L. Klein, 2000, Mouvement syndical et mobilisation pour l'emploi: renouvellement des enjeux et des modalités d'action, *Politique et société*, Vol. 19, N° 1, pp. 79-102.

Fontan, J.-M., J.-L. Klein & B. Lévesque, 2003, *Reconversion économique et développement territorial*, Presses de l'Université du Québec, Sainte-Foy, Québec.

Fontan, J.-M., J.-L. Klein & D.-G. Tremblay, 2005, *Innovation socioterritoriale et reconversion économique. Le cas de Montréal*, L'Harmattan, Paris.

Hamel, P., 1991, *Action collective et démocratie locale. Les mouvements urbains Montréalais*, Presses de l'Université de Montréal, Montréal.

Hillier, J., F. Moulaert & J. Nussbaumer, 2004, Trois essais sur le rôle de l'innovation sociale dans le développement territorial, *Géographie, Économie, Société*, Vol. 6, N° 2, pp. 129-152.

Joyal, A., 2002, *Le développement local. Comment stimuler l'économie des régions en difficulté*, Éditions de l'IQRC, Québec.

Klein, J.-L., 2005, Iniciativa local y desarrollo, *Revista latinoamericana de estudios urbanos y regionales EURE*, Vol. XXXI, N° 94, pp. 25-39.

Klein, J.-L. & J.-M. Fontan, 2003, Syndicats et communautés dans la gouvernance locale, *Recherches Sociographiques*, Vol. XLIV, N° 2, pp. 239-266.

Klein, J.-L & D. Harrisson (eds.), 2006, *L'innovation sociale*, Presses de l'Université du Québec, Sainte-Foy, Québec.

Klein, J.-L., C. Manzagol, D.-G. Tremblay & S. Rousseau, 2005, Les interrelations université–industrie à Montréal dans la reconversion à l'économie du savoir; in: Guillaume, R. (ed.), *Les systèmes productifs au Québec et dans le Sud-Ouest français*, L'Harmattan, Paris, pp. 31-54.

Klein, J.-L. & C. Tardif (eds), 2006, *Entre réseaux et systèmes: les nouveaux espaces régionaux*, GRIDEQ, Rimouski (Can.).

Klein, J,-L., P.-A. Tremblay, & H. Dionne (eds), 1997, *Au delà du néolibéralisme: quel rôle pour les mouvements sociaux?*, Presses de l'Université du Québec, Sainte-Foy, Québec.

Klein, J.-L., D.-G. Tremblay & J.-M. Fontan, 2003, Systèmes locaux et réseaux productifs dans la reconversion économique: le cas de Montréal, *Géographie Économie Société*, Vol. 5, N° 1, pp. 59-75.

Lévesque, B., G. L. Bourque & E. Forgues, 2001, *La nouvelle économie sociale*, Desclée de Brouwer, Paris.

Melucci, A., 1992, Liberation or Meaning? Social Movements, Culture and Democracy, *Development and Change*, Vol. 3, N° 3, pp. 43-77.

Melucci, A., 1993, Vie quotidienne, besoins individuels et action volontaire, *Sociologie et sociétés*, Vol. XXV, N° 1, pp. 189-198.

Morin, R., A. Latendresse & M. Parazelli, 1994, *Les corporations de développement économique communautaire en milieu urbain : l'expérience montréalaise*, Collection: Études, matériaux et documents, 5, Département d'Études urbaines et touristiques, Université du Québec à Montréal, Montréal.

Moulaert, F. & J. Nussbaumer, 2005, Defining the Social Economy and Its Governance at the Neighbourhood Level: A Methodological Reflection, *Urban Studies*, Vol. 42, N° 11, pp. 2071-2088.

Pecqueur, B., 1989, *Le développement économique local*, Syros, Paris.

Polese, M., 1996, Le développement local, revu et corrigé: récit d'une douce illusion dangereuse; in: Côté, S., J.-L. Klein & M.-U. Proulx (eds), *Le Québec des régions: vers quel développement?*, GRIDEQ, Rimouski (Can.), pp. 321-335.

Polese M. & R. Shearmur, 2002, *La périphérie face à l'économie du savoir : la dynamique spatiale de l'économie canadienne et l'avenir des régions non métroplitaines du Québec et des Provinces de l'Atlantique*, INRS-UCS et ICRD, Montréal et Moncton.

Sassen, S. (ed.), 2002, *Global Networks, Linked Cities*, Routledge, London.

Scott, A.J. (ed.), 2001, *Global City-Regions. Trends, Theory, Policy*, Oxford University Press, Oxford.

Stöhr, W., 2003, Development from Below: Vingt ans plus tard; in Fontan, J.-M., J.-L. Klein & B. Lévesque (eds), *Reconversion économique et développement territorial: le rôle de la société civile*, Presses de l'Université du Québec, Québec, pp. 119-143.

Swyngedouw, E., 1997, Neither Global Nor Local: 'Glocalization' and the Politics of Scale; in: Cox, K.R. (ed.), *Spaces of Globalization: Reasserting the Power of the Local*, Guilford, New York, pp. 137-166.

Tarrow, S., 1994, *Power in Movement. Social Movements, Collective Action and Politics*, Cambridge University Press, Cambridge.

Tilly, C., 1984, Social Movements and National Politics; in: Bright, C. & S. Harding (eds), *Statemaking and Social Movements*, University of Michigan Press, Ann Arbor, pp. 297-317.

Tremblay, D.-G. & J.-M. Fontan, 1994, *Le développement économique local: la théorie, les pratiques, les expérience*, Presses de l'université du Québec, Québec.

Tremblay, D.-G., J.-L. Klein, J.-M. Fontan & S. Rousseau, 2003, Proximité territoriale et innovation: une enquête sur la région de Montréal, *Revue d'Économie Régionale et Urbaine*, N° 5, pp. 835-852.

Tremblay, D.-G. & D. Rolland (eds), 2003, *La nouvelle économie: où? Quoi? Comment?*, Presses de l'Université du Québec, Collection d'économie politique, Québec.

Tremblay, D.-G. & S. Rousseau, 2005, Le secteur du multimédia à Montréal peut-il être considéré comme un milieu innovateur?, *Géographie, Economie et société*, Vol. 7, N° 1, pp. 37-56.

Tremblay, D.-G. & V. Van Schendel, 2004, *Économie du Québec*, Ed. St-Martin, Montréal.

Veltz, P., 1996, *Mondialisation, villes et territoires*, Presses Universitaires de France, Paris.

Viard, J., 1994, *La société archipel ou les territoires du village global*, Éditions de l'aube, Paris.

Notes

1 This Chapter is an updated and revised synthesis of two papers published previously. The first one is titled 'Collective action in local development: the case of Angus technopole in Montreal' (*Canadian Journal of Urban Research*, 2004, Volume 13, Issue 2, pp. 317-336.) The second one is titled 'The Fight for Jobs and Economic Governance: the Montreal Model' (in: Booth, Ph. & B. Jouve (eds), *Metropolitan Democraties. Transformations of the State and Urban Policy in Canada, France and Great Britain*, 2005, Ashgate Publishing, Hampshire, pp.133-146.)

2 Local Development Centers were created and funded by the provincial government to give local initiatives a support. They were composed by local civil society representatives.

7 Social Innovation, Spatial Transformation and Sustainable Communities: Liverpool and the 'Eldonians'

Peter Roberts

Introduction

Few cities in the United Kingdom in recent decades have faced as many intense restructuring challenges as Liverpool. During the 1970s, 1980s and early 1990s the final collapse of the port-based economy took place; the gradual erosion of employment in the port itself, in port-related manufacturing activities and in shipbuilding and ship repairing finally came to an end, leaving only a small number of jobs in what was once the dominant economic sector. The economic collapse of the traditional economy of Liverpool, and Merseyside more generally, is well-documented and is not rehearsed at length herein. However, the very particular nature and structural characteristics of the evolution of the economy of Merseyside provides a classic demonstration of the intense social, economic, cultural and environmental interactions which have shaped the growth and eventual decline of so many traditional industrial regions and cities.

Such interactions yield much more than the parameters within which an economy evolves. Rather, the intense and all-embracing nature of the interactions has been instrumental in shaping the social relations, urban form, educational opportunities, environmental conditions, health and welfare facilities, and the very physical fabric of towns and cities. The outcome of the various processes of evolution is manifest in both the physical and cultural landscape of a place. In the case of Liverpool, the consequence of this classic evolutionary process was the creation of a unique city; a once proud world city, described by Lane (1997:1) as the 'western gateway to the world', and a city which was created to serve as the physical transport interface between the new economy of Industrial Revolution Britain and the international sources of raw materials and international markets upon which the new economy depended. Put simply, Liverpool, together with the other urban centers of Merseyside, were products of global, as much as local or national processes of evolution. As a consequence, when the traditional economy of the region collapsed, the very rationale of the city itself was threatened. Although the most dramatic account of the collapse of a traditional port-based economy in the UK was based on an analysis of Clydeside (Checkland, 1976), the 'upas tree' model used to illustrate the consequences of the decline of a dominant industry could equally be applied to Merseyside. High direct, indirect and consumption multipliers have parallels in the intensity and complexity of social relations and in the form and functioning of the communities and neighborhoods of the city.

Matching the international nature of the economy, the social structure of Merseyside reflects the range and complexity of the international links that were fostered by the growth of the port. Migrants entered Merseyside for two main reasons. Firstly, Liverpool was the 'western gateway' of Europe and successive waves of European emigrants passed through the port on their way to North America and other destinations. However, not all of these migrants took final passage and some remained in Liverpool, thereby contributing to the rich ethnic and cultural mix which added both people and diverse traditions to the city. A second source of cultural and ethic diversity was associated with the shipping industry upon which the port was based; migrants initially journeyed to Liverpool as crew members, but many later settled in the city and some were joined by their families. These patterns of migration established Liverpool as a multicultural city over a century earlier than was the norm in Britain. The resulting ethnic and cultural diversity remains evident in the city and region, and has recently been celebrated in various ways, including a community-based urban design scheme known as 'Threshold to the Ends of the Earth', which reflects the various origins, cultures and contributions of the many migrant groups (Jeffrey & Roberts, 2005)

A further note of context is necessary at this point in order to set the scene for what follows. This relates to the highly contested nature of politics and community management in a city such as Liverpool. Accepting that an inevitable consequence of ethnic and cultural diversity, coupled with rapid economic and population growth, is the creation of a multi-layered social and political structure, it is hardly surprising that many of the communities and neighborhoods of the city reflect the origins and values of those who reside in them. Whilst not as deep or intense as the traditionally fractured community structures which were evident in Northern Ireland or Clydeside – an intensity which has thankfully been reduced in recent years – the communities and neighborhoods of Liverpool, and of adjacent urban areas such as Birkenhead, Wallasey and Bootle, also reflected the various ethnic, religious and cultural traditions of the population. The very strength of these ties of kinship and community came to represent an important asset when the economy of the Merseyside region declined. Kinship is relatively easy to define, whilst ideas such as community and neighborhood have frequently proved more elusive or difficult to isolate. As Meegan and Mitchell observe (2001:2176), in relation to the operation of urban economic policies in Liverpool and Merseyside, although the terms neighborhood and community remain contested concepts, there is a need for policies "which can provide the social resources and process to help produce [...] viable and coping communities by facilitating associational activity". This policy agenda would appear to represent not only an important element of community capacity, but also provides an essential means of ensuring that such capacity is maintained and strengthened over time.

The following Sections of this Chapter consider various dimensions of social innovation in the design and operation of urban regeneration and sustainable communities policy through the case of one city – Liverpool - and one neighborhood and community within the city – the Eldonian Village. In order better to understand the significance of the Eldonian experiment, the discussion of the case is guided by an analysis and assessment of the wider characteristics of regeneration and sustainable communities policy and practice; the analysis and assessment provides the criteria which are used to determine the progress of the Eldonian Village. A final Section of the Chapter offers some observations and conclusions which are intended as lessons and examples of good practice that may be applicable elsewhere, although these lessons should be seen as offering guidance rather than providing a fixed template which can be applied to other communities irrespective of the particular history and characteristics displayed in an individual place. This final Section also offers some general reflections on the direction of travel of sustainable communities policy in the UK, including the question of how best to introduce and maintain appropriate governance arrangements and methods for ensuing social and community cohesion.

Sustainable communities and regeneration policy and practice

The intention in providing this Section of the Chapter is to establish a baseline of policy and practice against which the performance and achievement of individual neighborhood actions can be assessed. Although there are many particular factors which determine the extent to which an individual neighborhood initiative is able to deal with the range of difficulties which beset inner urban areas, there is considerable evidence of the presence of certain generic or fundamental characteristics which would appear to represent the basic elements involved in successful placemaking and neighborhood management. Although it would be to exaggerate to suggest that such elements are ubiquitous, it is apparent that the basic requirements for a successful place are both enduring and capable of replication (Roberts, 2005). The latter point is important, because identifying the characteristics of successful placemaking is of little point in the absence of a conscious attempt to communicate the lessons of best practice. As a footnote, it is also the case that the lessons of poor practice can offer valuable insights into the weakness inherent in some aspects of theory, practice and community politics; this is an observation illustrated by the experience of the Third European Poverty Programme in Liverpool (Moore, 1997) and by cases elsewhere.

There is a growing body of evidence which can be used to establish the characteristics of good and best practice, and this evidence can be employed in order to help to define the fundamental criteria that allow both the content and process of sustainable communities and regeneration practice to be evaluated. At this juncture it is important to note the essential difference between the twin policies: sustainable communities and regeneration. The latter policy area developed during the 1970s in the UK and has evolved through a series of elaborations: early regeneration policy chiefly concentrated on economic regeneration and on land and property (or physical) matters, whilst later versions of regeneration policy and practice have increasingly incorporated an explicit social and environmental dimension. Throughout this pattern of policy evolution in terms of the content of regeneration, a parallel pattern of process innovation has taken place. Process innovation has seen the emphasis shift from what has been typified as business-led regeneration investment, to a new emphasis on the role of community-led regeneration which places social inclusion and cohesion at the center of the process. Reflecting on the findings of some 1960's area regeneration research projects, the Joseph Rowntree Foundation (2000) has identified five key conclusions that would appear to represent some of the features of best practice:
- the need for excellent analysis and a comprehensive understanding of urban disadvantage, including social exclusion;
- the importance of developing and managing innovative partnerships;
- the essential nature of neighborhood empowerment, including excellence in governance;
- The vital role performed by strategy at city-wide and regional levels; such strategies allow local and neighborhood action to be planned and implemented in an ordered and supported manner;
- The desirability of developing national policy support which can be used to set a context for individual actions.

This Section of the Chapter returns later to these attempts to evaluate practice.

The second policy area referred to in this Section – sustainable communities policy and practice – goes beyond regeneration in two senses. First, it is concerned with both new and old places. Second, it represents an explicit attempt to relate the sustainable development paradigm to place and placemaking. The first of these characteristics is most important. Given that regeneration activity is concerned with dealing with the problems encountered in places that have experienced some form of market failure, be it environmental, social, economic or physical in nature, then it is both inappropriate and somewhat illogical to refer to the creation and management of new places by using the same term. What sustainable communities policy and practice seeks to do is, first, to apply a comprehensive set of theoretical and practical principles to the creation and management of new places in order to ensure that they are established correctly and well-maintained over the longer-term. The second aspect of the sustainable communities approach is through its retrospective application to the various processes of regeneration: in effect this implies that regeneration can be considered as a sub-set of the sustainable communities approach and that the act of regeneration aims to bring a failing place up to the standard of successful places. This is an important distinction because it implies that regeneration itself is not sufficient; rather, having regenerated, it is essential to maintain momentum and to continue to manage the place in question as a sustainable community.

This introduces the second distinguishing feature of sustainable communities policy and practice, this is the essential concern with place and placemaking. This focus on space and place can be seen as a means of capturing and mobilizing the fundamental characteristics of a successful place as defined through the application of the spatial dimension of the concept of sustainable development (Roberts, 2003). Although various attempts have been made to express the spatial consequences of sustainable development, such as the European Spatial Development Perspective (Council of Ministers Responsible for Spatial Planning, 1999:10) notion of a "triangle of objectives: a balanced and sustainable development", the role of individual places in developing sustainable development has generally remained somewhat hazy. In part this is a consequence of the difficulties encountered in attempting to 'ground' spatiality in terms of the specific conditions of place, but it also reflects the problems which are experienced in attempting to translate national or international policy priorities into locally-relevant practice. However, recognizing that some past attempts to establish new communities have failed due in part to the fact that they only provided buildings rather than offering a comprehensive range of sustainable community features, it is now generally been accepted that the 'one-size-fits-all approach', which has failed to emphasize sufficiently the importance of place, is unlikely to be able fully to deliver the requirements of sustainable development at the level of an individual community. As a consequence of this analysis, national governments have increasingly recognized the validity of research which points to the importance of allowing individuals to be "socialized into an appreciation of who they are and what is expected of them" (Johnston, 1991:256).

So the sustainable communities approach has now achieved a level of recognition and application which reflects the realization – evident in both the academic and practice literature – that either a restricted in scope or constrained in time approach to the resolution of deep-rooted neighborhood and community challenges is unlikely to bring about positive and lasting change. Further recognition of this conclusion led to the publication of the Sustainable Communities Plan (Office of the Deputy Prime Minister, 2003) and the accompanying five year plan for implementation (Office of the Deputy Prime Minister, 2005a). In addition, and in recognition of the skills and knowledge required to support the move to the adoption of the sustainable communities approach, in 2004 the UK Government published the results of a review exercise: The Egan Review: Skills for Sustainable Communities (Office of the Deputy Prime Minister, 2004). Taken together these documents spell-out the desirable attributes of a sustainable community and the accompanying skills agenda. The sustainable communities principles and skills agenda were given further recognition at European level in December 2005 through the adoption of the Bristol Accord (Office of the Deputy Prime Minister, 2005b). This document represents a commitment by the EU member states to work toward the adoption of the sustainable communities approach.

Bringing together the sustainable communities approach and the long-term experience of regeneration provides a basis for the development of performance criteria that can be used to evaluate the success or otherwise of individual sustainable communities and regeneration programs. These criteria can also be of assistance in the formulation of policy and practice guidance, including operational guidance at the local or neighborhood level. However, in assessing the performance of existing programs or formulating new policy measures, it is also important to identify examples of good or best practice. There are three reasons for promoting the identification and evaluation of practice examples: firstly, such cases provide a means of testing and calibrating the validation of performance criteria, secondly, examples provide illustrations that can be used to demonstrate methods of working and the merits of good practice to other organizations and individuals, and, thirdly, case studies offer a means of establishing the knowledge required by those seeking to either gain the skills necessary to work in the sustainable communities field or to practice those skills in relation to the opportunities associated with individual programs. The third of the above noted points is of particular importance and is emphasized in the EU-wide research and knowledge exchange program which has been established following the Bristol Accord (ODPM, 2005b): in short, there is a growing acceptance of the need to identify, evaluate and disseminate the lessons of good and best practice in order both to reduce the time taken for successful innovations to be generally adopted as representing normal practice, and to minimize the unnecessary duplication of negative practice experiments. The aim of minimizing duplication can be justified as a means of accelerating the adoption of successful practice and thereby reducing the number of instances where the 'wheel is reinvented'; this aim also offers potential for cost and human resource savings and the avoidance of policies and methods of working that have failed elsewhere.

A number of researchers have examined the characteristics of regeneration, especially at neighborhood level, and are in general agreement as to what constitutes successful practice (Joseph Rowntree Foundation, 2000; Meegan & Mitchell, 2001; Burwood & Roberts, 2002). As is demonstrated below, these characteristics are also broadly in accord with the fundamental requirements of the sustainable communities approach. Key elements of successful regeneration include:
- the presence of an overall vision and strategy that can be used to ensure full engagement in the process of regeneration and which can guide the various processes of engagement;
- the need to establish a broad-based and lasting partnership upon which governance, leadership and collaborative arrangements can be based;
- the importance of using the partnership as a means of empowering a neighborhood – this is an essential requirement if actions are to be sustained;
- the need to build community capacity in order to allow empowerment to establish deep roots and in order to ensure that sufficient skilled persons are available;
- the importance of creating social (or 'soft') infrastructure in a neighborhood – this includes the establishment of both community organizations and the full range of social and welfare facilities, including health, education and cultural provision;
- the need to establish appropriate economic (or 'hard') infrastructure, including transport, communications and utility services;
- the desirability of creating new and additional economic activities in order to widen and strengthen the range of employment opportunities available, and the importance of ensuring that local

people can gain access to employment through the provision of direct guidance, training and intermediate support;
- the need to ensure that all development is delivered at a high standard and that environmental resources are well-managed and used to best effect;
- the desirability of providing adequate housing built to high standards and the importance of repopulating central urban areas;
- the need to monitor, evaluate and review strategy and the implementation of programs at regular intervals in order to ensure both their efficiency and effectiveness.

These characteristics of practice have contributed to the emergence of the sustainable communities model both through the direct demonstration of what works and why, and through the isolation of the skills required to ensure the effective delivery of policy. As noted above, regeneration is now regarded as a sub-set of the sustainable communities approach and can be defined as the retrospective application of the sustainable communities model to a place which has experienced problems. Informed by the established characteristics of the practice of regeneration in the UK and elsewhere, the sustainable communities model can be summarized as having eight basic component parts which are brought together and delivered through an essential ninth component concerned with placemaking. In one sense this model reflects the best practice of regeneration, but it also represents the traditional goal of planning, as represented in the Garden City paradigm developed and implemented by Ebenezer Howard in the 1890s. The Garden City (or social city) model shares many characteristics with the modern sustainable communities approach and this offers a degree of confidence that the approach is both theoretically valid and capable of replication (Roberts, 2005); this is especially the case in relation to the social relations and governance aspects of communities.

The eight basic components of the sustainable communities model reflect the objective of creating "places where people want to live, now and in the future" (ODPM, 2005a:56) and embody the principles of sustainable development. They:
- balance and integrate the social, environmental components of a community, in accord with accepted interpretations of how this can be achieved;
- meet the needs of the current and future generations – this reflects intra-generational and inter-generational requirements;
- respect the needs of other communities.

Put in simple terms, the sustainable communities approach can be seen as an important means of delivering the sustainable development agenda to places and people. This explicit consideration of the often neglected spatial dimension of sustainable development is of particular importance in relation to the social justice element of the debate. In particular, the interplay of spatial and social justice concerns, which can be seen to be manifest in many deprived communities, has led to the presence of factors which make it difficult to deal with deprivation in isolation from spatial exclusion (Roberts, 2003). Whilst the creation of a sustainable community seeks to remove or reduce these elements of exclusion, the individual community cannot always successfully address such matters in the absence of appropriate policy measures and instruments at a higher level in the spatial hierarchy. Thus, for example, whilst it is evident that spatial and social exclusion can be exacerbated by the continuing absence of adequate public transport, it is equally the case that the absence of adequate pathways for obtaining advanced skills and higher education can effectively exclude the residents of a disadvantaged community from mainstream economic activities.

Reflecting the explicit and implicit objectives of the sustainable communities approach, the reality is that all of the eight basic components are essential elements for creating a sustainable community. The absence of any of the basic components will undermine the achievement of the overall objectives and this suggests that the components should not be regarded as optional 'dishes' on the placemaking 'menu'. Rather, the presence of all eight components as a total package is a necessary precondition for successful placemaking. The eight basic components will be 'blended' by the ninth placemaking component in different ways in order to reflect diverse local circumstances, but all sustainable communities should be:

- active, inclusive and safe – they should be inclusive, offer a sense of community identity and belonging, be tolerant, offer respect, be friendly and co-operative, and provide opportunities for culture, leisure and sport;
- well run – they should enjoy representative and accountable governance with strategic and visionary leadership, strong and effective partnerships, effective engagement with the community, a strong and inclusive voluntary and community sector, and a sense of civic values and responsibility;
- environmentally sensitive – they should actively seek to minimize climate change, protect the environment, minimize waste, make efficient use of natural resources, protect bio-diversity, minimize negative environmental impact, and create cleaner, safer, greener neighborhoods;
- well designed and built – they offer a sense of place, user-friendly green spaces, a sufficient range of affordable and accessible housing, excellent buildings, appropriate layout, density and design, buildings and public spaces which promote health and which are safe, accessible jobs and services by public transport, walking and cycling;
- well connected – sustainable communities offer transport facilities that reduce dependence on cars, facilities for safe walking and cycling, appropriate local parking, available telecommunications, and good access to regional, national and international networks;
- thriving – they feature a wide range of jobs and training opportunities, sufficient land and buildings to support economic activity, dynamic job and business creation, a strong business community, and economically viable and attractive town centers;
- well served – they have good schools, colleges and universities and opportunities for lifelong learning, high quality local health, social and family services, a good range of affordable public, community, voluntary and private services, and service providers who think and act long-term and beyond their own immediate boundaries;
- fair for everyone – they recognize the rights and responsibilities of individuals, respect the rights and aspirations of others also to be sustainable, and have due regard to the needs of future generations in current decisions and actions.

In addition to the eight basic components noted above, it is also essential to recognize and ensure that a ninth component – placemaking – is in evidence and that the skills of placemaking are made available to all partners and actors. Placemaking can be defined as the various process of planning, implementing and managing the full range of activities that are evident in a community and these activities reflect the contents of the eight basic components noted above; the art and science of placemaking can also be described as integrated spatial planning, implementation and management. In the absence of effective and lasting placemaking, individual improvements to the condition of a community are unlikely to prove worthwhile or to survive over the long-term.

All of the above observations suggest that the process of sustainable community creation, including the regeneration of failed places, should be established as a comprehensive package of measures which is implemented through an appropriate integrated placemaking vision and strategy. Partial or unco-ordinated actions are unlikely to be able to deliver an enduring and socially inclusive community. As such, the sustainable communities operational components, which closely match the characteristics of successful regeneration, appear to offer appropriate criteria for assessing the performance of the case study which is presented in the following Section of this Chapter.

The Eldonian Village

As noted in the introduction to this Chapter, the inner areas of Merseyside, and of Liverpool in particular, have long been regarded as amongst the most difficult and challenging neighborhoods in the UK in terms of the social deprivation, poor environment and economic difficulties which are experienced. One such community is the Vauxhall area, a part of inner Liverpool which has experienced severe difficulties since the 1950s, with such problems set within the general context of an entire inner city in decline (Shelter, 1972). Even through the Vauxhall area was initially less challenged than some of the inner Liverpool communities, the fortunes of the area were dependant on a fragile economic base. When key elements of the traditional local economy went into steep decline from the late 1970s onwards, with the final collapse of the port as a major employer and the loss of jobs in a number of port-based manufacturing establishments, especially the Tate and Lyle sugar refinery which eventually closed in 1981, the local level of unemployment and the incidence of economic and social distress increased rapidly. Coupled with the economic problems encountered in the neighborhood, the Vauxhall area was also subject to a number of other pressures, including blight and some clearance of tenements and other unfit housing brought about by road building proposals and housing policies. As Leeming (2005:62) has observed, the perception at the time was that "The decline of the docks, dock-related activities and population meant that there was no need for high density housing in the inner city area, so the plan was to demolish the tenements and move the people into peripheral municipal estates". So the rationale for the intended upheaval and dispersal of the communities in the Vauxhall area was the classic combination of the erosion of the economic base of the area coupled with physical malaise, social disadvantage and a poor general environment. In this case, as in many other inner areas, this mix of negatives was exacerbated by the policy objectives of the local authority, which identified the need for new road building, the consequences of the construction of the second Mersey Tunnel, and other area 'improvements'.

The proposal for the clearance and redevelopment of part of the Vauxhall area – centered around Eldon Street – was met with firm local opposition. A similar pattern of opposition was growing in the inner area communities of many towns and cities as the wisdom of comprehensive redevelopment was increasingly questioned by community development workers and authors such as Norman Dennis. In his work in Sunderland, Dennis (1970) had challenged the very assumptions on which the policy was based and the method of survey sometimes used: a brief site visit conducted from a moving vehicle. Irrespective of the growing evidence of the failure of comprehensive redevelopment to meet the needs of the residents of inner urban areas – Meller (1997:93) describes how the policy failed to recognize the "real need for this disruption" and that "its economic and social consequence was barely considered" – the policy continued, but with rapidly diminishing support. In Liverpool, comprehensive redevelopment policy was further undermined by the accelerating collapse of the local economy which, for example, meant that inner area road schemes were no longer required on the scale originally planned and that local residents were increasingly workless. Continuing with comprehensive redevelopment was, therefore, no longer an appropriate method for dealing with the problems of the inner areas, indeed, decanting the population of the inner area communities "uprooting long-standing communities" with "no attempt to retain those communities on the new estates" (Leeming, 2005:62), increasingly made little sense. By the late 1970s the situation in Liverpool had deteriorated further, with the city council now proposing (at the same time as it was considering a new round of clearances in the Vauxhall area) the demolition of some of the residential tower blocks built during the 1950s. These tower blocks had been built as replacement accommodation for the population displaced by an earlier round of comprehensive redevelopment and, as was the case in other cities in the UK and North America, they had deteriorated soon after they were built (Meller, 1997).

At the center of the debate on the future of the communities in the Vauxhall area, were matters related to a number of the dominant concerns of the urban sociological discourse of the 1950s, 60s and 70s. Pahl (1975) noted that planners and associated professionals were increasingly blamed for many of the problems of the inner cities, often much to their surprise. An insight into this critical debate is offered by Meller's observation that the people in these inner area communities had often been excluded from discussions about the redevelopment of the area in which they lived, or had lived, and that little consideration had been given to how their lives were being affected by planning and other decisions. Although such people had been excluded from many of these earlier discussions, "now they were finding a voice" (Meller, 1997:94). In the case of the Vauxhall area, and especially the neighborhood around Eldon Street, as noted earlier these matters came to a climax during the late 1970s when the local authority proposed a further round of demolitions of tenement housing blocks. One of the consequences of the proposed demolitions was that the residents would be moved to peripheral municipal estates, many of which (as noted above) had already become problem areas, but these relocations would not be organized on a community basis. Rather than transferring a community as a whole to a new location on a peripheral estate or new town, the intention was to perpetuate the already discredited policy of moving people as individuals, thereby fracturing family, friendship and community ties (Leeming, 2005)

Bringing these various strands together, the residents of the Eldon Street area insisted that they did not want to move away from their neighborhood and that they did not want to see the destruction of their community. Put into the words of the submission made by The Eldonian organization for a World Habitat Award, "Twenty five years ago a group of people were told by the City leaders that their houses were to be demolished and they would be scattered across the City to make way for industrial redevelopment. They said no" (The Eldonians, 2003:1). Saying 'no' was the first step in a remarkable transformation which demonstrates many of the key characteristics of social innovation and community determination.

Combined with the threat of demolition of the tenement housing, as noted earlier, the local economy had suffered further decline with the loss of jobs on the docks and at major employers such as the Tate and Lyle sugar refinery and the British American Tobacco factory. Unemployment in the Vauxhall area increased from 16 percent in 1971 to 41 percent in 1991, population loss continued and a pattern of social and environmental deprivation became deeply etched into the urban fabric (Meegan & Mitchell, 2001). However, despite the severity of the combined social, economic and physical problems, the residents in the Eldon Street area negotiated an agreement with the Liberal Party who controlled the local authority which would allow them to stay in the area. The package was complicated: the residents of one of the tenement blocks - Portland Gardens - would be re-housed in temporary accommodation, the block would be demolished and replaced by new build housing paid for by the city council, when the houses were built they would be bought from the council and managed by the Portland Gardens Housing Co-operative, and then the original residents would move into the new houses. By planning the replacement of housing in this way a cost saving would be achieved because Value Added Tax was not levied on council house building (Leeming, 2005). The initial model was designed as a rolling program of housing renewal, which would gradually improve the total housing stock in the area.

Just as this program was beginning, the economic situation deteriorated further with the final closure of the Tate and Lyle sugar refinery. At the same time the political situation was changing with the election of a Conservative Party central government. The new government decided to alter the system that provided central government funding for local authorities – the Rate Support Grant (RSG) and to cap any increase in local taxes. The adjustment of the RSG system allocated finance on the basis of expenditure in previous years, and because the Liberal administration in Liverpool had used the local authority reserves to avoid the need to increase local taxes, the RSG allocated to Liverpool was reduced (Leeming, 2005). Thus a city in rapid decline, which needed additional public investment in order to prevent further economic malaise, population loss and social distress, suffered a major reduction in central government financial support and was unable to replace this lost income by increasing the local tax rate. The deteriorating political situation in Liverpool resulted in the growth of extreme left-wing groups, including Militant Tendency. In 1983 the Labour Party came to power, with the left-wing directing much policy and its implementation. The emergence of the new administration resulted in a protracted period of confrontation between the Eldonians and the city council; this confrontation was a consequence of the incoming administration's view that the city council should retain control of houses built for co-operatives. The Portland Gardens replacement scheme was one of the blocks of new housing taken back into municipal control, so ending the initial attempt of the Eldonians to redevelop their community in situ (Meegan & Mitchell, 2001; Leeming, 2005). Furthermore, the city council announced that it intended to discontinue the program of replacing unfit tenement blocks within an individual community.

In this situation of direct conflict with the city council, it became apparent to the Eldonians that they needed to seek an alternative pathway to achieve their objective. Their next move was to attempt to acquire the site of the former Tate and Lyle sugar refinery, obtain planning permission, clear the contaminated site and redevelop it for housing. Having secured some £6.7 million in grant support and loans to remediate and develop the site, the Eldonian housing co-operative required planning permission to develop the former industrial site for housing use. This was refused by the city council, thereby precipitating a further round of conflict, which eventually resulted in a successful appeal against the refusal of planning permission. However, the most significant change in the fortunes of the Eldonians came about after the intervention of central government. In the early 1980s the Conservative administration introduced a new policy vehicle for the delivery of urban regeneration – the Urban Development Corporation (UDC). The first two UDC's were designated for Merseyside (the Merseyside Development Corporation, or MDC) and the London Docklands. By including an area of land within a UDC boundary, the Development Corporation was able to grant planning permission and provide other forms of support. In 1988 the boundary of the MDC was extended to include the Tate and Lyle site (Meegan & Mitchell, 2001) and this allowed the planned housing development to proceed.

By 1990 the site had been cleared, remediated and 145 new houses had been built (The Eldonians, 2003). The initial phase of housing development was designed with the active involvement of the potential tenants, and this level of community engagement has continued since. At the same time as this initial development took place, the Eldonian housing co-operative was reconstituted as the Eldonian Community – based Housing Association (ECBHA), an organization registered with the central government Housing Corporation as a social landlord. The new ECBHA was controlled directly by the community. Further organizational development saw the introduction of a range of other initiatives, including a number of what can best be described as community welfare facilities and community business.

Key to the extension of the Eldonian portfolio was the establishment of a suitable organizational structure. In simple terms the organizational model incorporates a community trust, which is fully representative of the local community and which has over 600 members, as the overarching body (see Illustration 7.1). The trust is a charity, which in the UK allows it certain tax and other advantages, and it is locally-based with very clear social aims and objectives. The ECBHA is positioned within the organizational structure alongside another body known as the Eldonian Group Ltd, this body has a broader economic and social development remit and is concerned with the provision and management of a range of individual enterprises and facilities, including both physical activities, such as the community sports hall, and other 'soft' services, such as a training scheme for neighborhood wardens (The Eldonians, 2003).

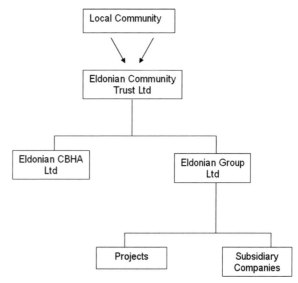

Illustration 7.1 – The Eldonian Organisation

The considerable range and variety of activities established by the Eldonians illustrates the power of community determination and social action when developed in partnership and applied through clear leadership. This partnership and leadership approach is evident in a number of examples of social innovation, above and beyond the extent of community control which is demonstrated in Illustration 7.1. In specific terms, the evolving Eldonian Village portfolio currently comprises, amongst other initiatives, the following elements:
- Eldonian House - a residential care home for the elderly;
- Robert Lynch House – an extra-care facility;
- Eldonwoods Day Nursery – a 50-place nursery for children aged from three months to five years;
- Elaine Norris Sports Center – offers a range of sports and leisure facilities;
- Eldonian Village Hall – a meeting place, pub and social venue;
- Eldonian Neighborhood Wardens – a warden training, employment and safety service.

In total the Eldonians directly employ over 90 staff, operate eight community businesses and social enterprises, have created jobs for over 250 people, have provided over 400 affordable homes, have an asset base of over £50 million, have stimulated over £100 million of private investment, have an annual turnover of over £2 million, have transformed the physical environment of the area and, most importantly, have stabilized social relations in an area which was subject to considerable pressure for change. In short, and in the words of the nomination for the World Habitat Award given to the Eldonians in 2004, the Eldonian project demonstrates "how local communities can bring about significant and lasting improvements, not only to their housing but also to many other aspects of their lives" (Diacon, 2004:5).

However, the social innovation initially stimulated by a threat to this inner area community in the late 1970s has yielded other benefits. Building on their experience within the Eldonian Village and the specific advisory and management services provided to other communities and organizations, the Eldonians have launched a 'Beyond the Boundaries' program. This is a program of direct collaboration, support and good practice dissemination that extends to the adjacent area of Vauxhall and beyond, including other parts of Liverpool, Merseyside and North West England. The program includes a further extension of the Eldonian social enterprise service, involvement in providing a master plan for the Vauxhall area and developing over 2,000 houses, establishing a retail complex, extending the neighborhood warden scheme, and creating a range of training and employment support services.

Whilst it is a relatively easy matter to outline and trace the development of the Eldonian experiment, it is much more difficult to evaluate and assess the overall impact and outcomes of the project. A number of attempts have been made to identify the key features of the Eldonian experiment as an example of effective and sustainable social innovation. The Eldonian Group has commissioned a social audit process that reports on specific elements of the work program (The Eldonian Group, 2003), whilst other assessments, including the assessment undertaken as part of the process of judging the World Habitat Award given to the Eldonians in 2004 (Building and Social Housing Foundation, 2004), have provided insights into the general performance of the Eldonian program. Academic evaluations have been provided by a number of researchers, including Leeming (2005:67) who concluded that the Eldonians " are now considered by many – including Liverpool City Council – to be a best practice model of successful sustainable urban development" and by Meegan and Mitchell (2001:2186) who observe that " the Eldonian Village and associated housing developments have created a distinctive community" and that " the social interaction within the [Eldonian] group, set in the context of opposition from within and support from without the wider city, provided the behavior and interaction that mark out community". These observations point to the strengths of the Eldonian program, strengths which the Eldonians themselves isolate as:
- community ownership – local people are in control of decision-making;
- design and good practice – collective responsibility for design, layout and quality of life;
- innovation and business enterprise – an emphasis on the economic realities and a commercial approach;
- partnership – utilizing professionals and key stakeholders to create strong, sustainable and dynamic partnerships;
- leadership – strong leader and shared goals to unite the community and enable it to take control of its own destiny (Building and Social Housing Foundation, 2004).

Returning to the characteristics of a sustainable community and successful regeneration which were presented in the second Section of this Chapter, it is evident that the Eldonians have established social, physical, environmental, economic and governance structures which reflect both the characteristics of established good practice and their aspirations for future policy and its delivery. In more specific terms:

- active, inclusive and safe – the Eldonian Village offers a range of social opportunities and the management of the neighborhood reflects the views of the community itself;
- well run – the Eldonian Village is well-managed and enjoys transparent governance and representation which is accountable to all members of the community;
- environmentally sensitive – a once derelict and contaminated site has been reclaimed, the Leeds – Liverpool Canal, which runs through the site, has been improved, and the area is generally clean, safe and green;
- well designed and built – the housing located within the Village has been built to reflect the desires of the members of the community and is well-maintained and well-managed;
- well connected - the Village is close to the city center and is linked by a regular bus service; other site services, and facilities have been provided or improved by the Eldonians;
- thriving – in the context of the challenges faced by the regional economy this is an example of an improving local economy with community business providing a range of employment opportunities;
- well served - the Eldonians have provided a range of services, including education, training, health, sports and cultural facilities, they acknowledge the need to enhance retail facilities and a number of other services in the area;
- fair for everyone – members of the community are involved in most aspects of decision-making and implementation, the members of the community are keen to promote both inter– and intra- generational equity, and the residents have a real desire to share their facilities, successes and support with other communities located beyond the boundaries of the Village.

Whilst not suggesting that the Eldonian Village is perfect or fully meets all of the sustainable community aspirations, it is evident that much has been achieved, chiefly through social innovation, community solidarity, the presence of a clear sense of vision and purpose, and the adoption of a highly professional approach to the management of all aspects of the Village. The Eldonians themselves recognize that there is a need to remain vigilant and that there are still many tasks to be undertaken both within the Eldonian Village and more generally. Some observers have criticized aspects of the Village itself and the Eldonians as an organization. For example, parts of the Village are fenced-off from the surrounding area, but access to the Village is unrestricted and it cannot be described as a gated community. Others have criticized the relatively unadventurous design of some of the housing units, but these are the houses that local people wanted; and the layout has been used by the Merseyside Police as a model of how to provide neighborhood security. Despite such criticisms, the general consensus is that the Eldonian Village represents a model of best practice and that it offers a practical example of how to retrofit the sustainable community approach to a failing neighborhood.

The importance of the Eldonian Village goes far beyond its physical manifestation. It is a statement of what is possible and how a community can best proceed to develop a human environment suited to its needs. The presence of such a place at the heart of the Vauxhall area of Liverpool provides an important message about the potential of people to transform places.

Lessons from Inner Liverpool

Social innovation and community solidarity are the twin foundations upon which the Eldonian experiment was built. These qualities were evident in the early days of the initiative and they have endured and matured during the last two decades. As was the case in the early 1980s, the Eldonian organization has created and retained a genuine sense of local self-determination, and a high level of democratic accountability continues to be evident. The features of strong and resilient communities are difficult to replicate quickly in other neighborhoods, but it would appear that many straightforward lessons can be identified and applied elsewhere.

An essential requirement for successful social innovation through spatial transformation is the presence or introduction of a shared identity, and this the Eldonians were able to establish at an early point in time. Although the case study community was assisted in this task by the presence of a faith-based local community, the Eldonian organization is not an exclusive group and the sense of community present in the area would appear to transcend the pre-existing social relationships which were based upon the local church, Our Lady of Eldon Street. Whilst many members of the local community have much in common, it is evident that there are many different 'voices' within the Eldonian community and the sense of common purpose which is evident in the area is more a reflection of the attachment that local people have for 'their' place, rather than a statement of a closed or restricted social mindset. This quality of place, together with the sense of belonging which accompanies it, is a fundamental requirement for creating a platform of social stability from which community innovation can proceed. The determination of the community at the outset that it should not be 'swept away' (Coxon, 2005:5) provided the foundation for further action.

Allied to the above qualities of a shared identity and a sense of belonging to a place, the Eldonians have been able to adapt and shape their neighborhood through the establishment of a collective strategic vision, on the one hand, and the direct application of a high degree of pragmatic maneuvering, on the other hand. Whilst the capability for political maneuvering and opportunism which the Eldonians developed and implemented might appear to be based on insubstantial foundations, in reality, the tactics of political and organizational positioning were dictated by clearly thought-out and well-developed strategic objectives. To paraphrase a former resident of Liverpool, John Lennon: how do you know where you are going, if you don't know which way you are facing? The Eldonians had a clear sense of their intended eventual destiny at the outset of their journey, even if the precise line of route was not yet fully determined.

Strategic vision and a sense of purpose are, however, of little benefit to a community in the absence of reality and confidence. Another Liverpool characteristic, which is amply demonstrated by the case of the Eldonian Village, is a sense of determination and a confidence which reflects the belief that the cause for which you are fighting is correct. Although some might criticize the Eldonians for their willingness to accept support from the Conservative government's MDC, in reality this was the only meaningful source of direct assistance available to them at that time. However, prior to the extension of the MDC boundary the Eldonians had already demonstrated considerable confidence and a real determination to fight for their community. These qualities represent the outcome of a long process of community formation, some elements of which have their roots in the establishment of the original immigrant communities of Liverpool. The partnership structures which result from such an 'organic' process of community creation are likely to be more enduring than the relatively transitory partnership groupings of professionals and formal organizations which are frequently evident in the operation of many 'normal' short-term regeneration projects. Such 'organic' partnerships are also by their very nature subject to considerable democratic control and accountability; as such they represent an embedded form of community democracy and operational accountability, which transcends any arrangement imposed from outside.

Although community-based 'organic' partnerships provide firm foundations for social innovation, it can be difficult to exercise leadership or guidance in such situations. However, once established and successful, the leadership function necessary for the guidance and management of a community-based initiative can be easier to exercise. A common problem encountered in such situations is that of establishing progression and succession arrangements; introducing new leaders and managers can be difficult, as can moving from collective informal decision-making to a more structured business model. The Eldonians case demonstrates the benefits that are associated with making the transition from informal to formal structures, and also reflects the boost in capability and confidence which results. Given the distrust of certain professionals which existed in the communities of the Vauxhall area of Liverpool, it is no surprise that the Eldonians decided to draw upon local sources of expertise and capability, including the employment of professionals from the local area and the training of local people to undertake professional functions.

An additional characteristic evident in the operation of the Eldonian initiative, and one which is of immense value to other communities, is the emphasis placed by the Eldonians on sharing the lessons of both positive and negative experience. The 'Beyond the Boundaries' project aims to provide both assistance to other communities elsewhere and a platform for the future development of the Eldonian Village. However, the assistance offered by the Eldonians does not stop at providing direct help to other communities in the Vauxhall area. The Eldonians have assisted many other communities to realize their potential. Such schemes of assistance include projects elsewhere in Merseyside, in the North West Region of England and at other national and international locations. Whilst the aspiration of supporting the enhancement of community capability globally may appear to be overambitious and to reflect certain inherent contradictions, the Eldonians do have much to offer neighborhoods elsewhere. In the same way that Jacobs (1961) demonstrated that communities could successfully oppose comprehensive redevelopment, and there is little doubt that this revelation provided inspiration to many thousands of communities in North America and Europe, the Eldonian Village offers a practical demonstration of the power of social innovation and community action when it is clearly constructed and well-led.

Finally, it is important to reflect on the ways in which the lessons from the Eldonian Village and other community-based initiatives have influenced the direction of travel of sustainable communities and regeneration policy in the UK. First, the very substance of sustainable communities policy can be seen to encapsulate the lessons from the experience of the Eldonians and other communities in the UK (Burwood & Roberts, 2002). This experience has demonstrated that social inclusion and community solidarity are essential requirements for lasting policy action, but it also warns that the fragmented implementation of individual elements of policy is unlikely to bring about the comprehensive transformation of a community which is necessary to ensure its long-term survival. Second, one of the other essential requirements for successful social action is the provision of excellent accountability and governance arrangements; this is a quality that is evident in the Eldonians and a number of other community initiatives and it has now been recognized as a fundamental necessity by the recently published Local Government White Paper: Strong and Prosperous Communities (Department for Communities and Local Government, 2006). Third, an essential additional quality, also recognized in the White Paper, is the need to promote community engagement in, and 'ownership' of, the programs that shape the future of a neighborhood. This is a quality that the Eldonian Village demonstrates at the highest level.

Considered within the context of the general shift toward a greater emphasis upon the comprehensive planning and management of community interventions which has been evident in UK urban policy over the past decade, the Eldonian 'experiment' has remained at the leading edge of practice. As noted earlier, this innovative approach to social and community development has been recognized through both national and international awards for best practice and has provided a practical model which has been replicated elsewhere. One final lesson that can be gleaned from the experience of the Eldonian Village, is the importance of providing sufficient time for an initiative to become established and embedded (Leeming, 2005). The Eldonian Village has taken some twenty years to mature, and this is four times as long as the average lifespan of a community or neighborhood project. What this suggests is that far more attention than is currently the case needs to be devoted to providing continuity and to ensuring that effective progression and succession arrangements are put in place at the start of the process of community building. Inspiration and confidence are essential factors in establishing an initiative, but clarity of vision, determination and long-term succession planning are the factors which would appear to provide the staying power that allows social, economic and physical innovation to be transformed into enduring social and community cohesion.

References

Building and Social Housing Foundation, 2004, *World Habitat Awards,* Building and Social Housing Foundation, Coalville (UK).
Burwood, S. & P. Roberts, 2002, *Learning from Experience*, British Urban Regeneration Association, London.
Checkland ,S., 1976, *The Upas Tree*, University of Glasgow Press, Glasgow.
Council of Ministers Responsible for Spatial Planning, 1999, *European Spatial Development Perspective*, Office for Official Publications of the European Communities, Luxembourg.
Coxon, A., 2005, Razing Questions, *Housing Today*, Vol. 425, p. 5.
Dennis, N., 1970, *People and Planning: The Sociology of Housing in Sunderland,* Faber, London.
Department for Communities and Local Government, 2006, *Local Government White Paper: Strong and Prosperous Communities*, The Stationery Office, London.
Diacon, D., 2004, The World Habitat Awards; in: Building and Social Housing Foundation, *World Habitat Awards,* Building and Social Housing Foundation, Coalville (UK).
Jacobs, J., 1961, *The Death and Life of Great American Cities,* Vintage Books, New York.
Jeffrey, P. & P. Roberts, 2005, *Intelligence Report 1: Lessons from the Exemplar Programme 2005,* RENEW, Liverpool.
Johnston, R., 1991, *A Question of Place*, Blackwell, Oxford.
Joseph Rowntree Foundation, 2000, *Key Steps to Sustainable Area Regeneration*, Joseph Rowntree Foundation, York.
Lane, T., 1997, *Liverpool City of the Sea*, Liverpool University Press, Liverpool.
Leeming, K., 2005, Sustainable Urban Development: A Case Study of The Eldonians in Liverpool; in: Shakur, T. (ed), *Cities in Transition,* Open House Press, Altrincham.
Meegan, R. & A. Mitchell, 2001, It's Not Community Round Here, Its Neighbourhood: Neighbourhood Change and Cohesion in Urban Regeneration Policies, *Urban Studies*, Vol. 38, pp. 2167-2194.
Meller, H., 1997, *Towns, Plans and Society in Modern Britain*, Cambridge University Press, Cambridge.
Moore, R., 1997, Poverty and Partnership in the Third European Poverty Programme: The Liverpool Case; in: Jewson N. & S. Macgregor (eds), *Transforming Cities,* Routledge, London.
Office of the Deputy Prime Minister, 2003, *The Sustainable Communities Plan,* Office of the Deputy Prime Minister, London.
Office of the Deputy Prime Minister, 2004, *The Egan Review: Skills for Sustainable Communities*, Office of the Deputy Prime Minister, London.
Office of the Deputy Prime Minister, 2005a, *Sustainable Communities: People, Places and Prosperity,* Office of the Deputy Prime Minister, London.
Office of the Deputy Prime Minister, 2005b, *The Bristol Accord,* Office of the Deputy Prime Minister, London.
Pahl, R., 1975, *Whose City and Other Critical Essays on Urban Sociology and Planning*, Penguin Books, Harmondsworth (UK).

Roberts, P., 2003, Sustainable Development and Social Justice: Spatial Priorities and Mechanisms for Delivery, *Sociological Inquiry*, Vol. 73, pp. 228-244.

Roberts, P., 2005, Establishing Skills for Tomorrow, *Town and Country Planning*, Vol. 74, pp. 296-297.

Shelter, 1972, *Reprieve for Slums*, Shelter, London.

The Eldonian Group, 2003, *Social Audit Report*, The Eldonian Group, Liverpool.

The Eldonians, 2003, *Eldonian Village UK – Submission for Building and Social Housing Foundation World Habitat Awards 2003*, The Eldonians, Liverpool.

8 Bottom-up in Gouda East: Design Atelier R&M Activity Center

Edward D. Hulsbergen

Introduction

Bottom-up activities to improve living conditions in a degrading neighborhood occur by definition in existing districts, and as such are closely linked to urban renewal and regeneration. The last decades show an increasing attention to 'urban problem areas', on many levels, from the European to the municipal scale. The multidimensional character of the urban tasks and the need for integrated approaches to sectors, actors, disciplines and scales are more or less accepted in policy and science (Roberts & Sykes, 2004), at least verbally. In The Netherlands (not unlike in other EU-countries), the discussion about so-called problem areas always is a mix of 'one sided' opinions. Either the built up environment and the housing stock composition in terms of housing typology and (low) rent and prices gets the blame or the 'one sided' population composition in terms of (low) income and (many) migrants. Much is expected from improved 'social cohesion' on the one hand and on the other better conditions for 'market forces' (see e.g. *Dossier 56 wijken aanpak*, http://www.vrom.nl; for a critical comment, see *De locale integratie agenda* by VNG, http://www.vng.nl).

The general opinions about what 'the problem' is in the (relatively) poor urban districts, and what to do about it, reflect the many disciplines and interests, are often well-meant, and are mainly top-down. In this Chapter the spotlight is on a bottom-up initiative in the middle sized town of Gouda in The Netherlands. Though it concerns a specific location and therefore unique in its form, the problems encountered are common enough to have relevance for other districts. In The Netherlands there are many voluntary organizations, also in decaying districts. Information sources are: *Habitat Platform*, the Dutch foundation to implement the World Habitat Agenda which organizes a data bank of initiatives which are seen as valuable instruments (http://www.instrumentenwijzer.nl), *Kei Stedelijke Vernieuwing* and Kei Kennisbank (urban renewal and knowledge bank; http://www.kei-centrum.nl), the Habiforum test beds (http://www.habiforum.nl), *Onze Buurt Aan Zet* (OBAZ, the move is with our neighborhood, http://www.onzebuurtaanzet.nl), and the *Stichting Eigenwijks*, a foundation of co-operating residents in Slotervaart, Amsterdam (http://www.steunpuntwonen.nl/eigenwijks/).

The R&M Activity Center in Gouda Oost (district East) is a locally based initiative, run by volunteers. The project started in 1997, was formalized in 2000, and at the end of 2005 it was on the crossroad of disappearing or taking a new shape which occured.[1] Active in this bottom-up neighborhood initiative, I cannot remember a single moment that we thought we were 'innovative'. Aiming to make it work, we made use of everything and everyone we could imagine. What we tried to get done was based on the ideas we had, on people who wanted to work in our direction, on instruments which seemed useful, on contacts that might help. The continuity of the project relied heavily if not totally on the presence of a full time volunteer Rachid Tighadouini, who wanted to get young unemployed residents off the street. The prizes that R&M won were always related to selected activities. We were, more than once, amazed that people judged our project to be some kind of social innovation, but this was of course always in comparison with the activities of other organizations.

Innovation is relative. A popular expression states that 'there is nothing new under the sun', indicating that newness is basically a matter of distance. Social innovation with its complex societal context might even be hardier to recognize than any other form of innovation. Given that the greater part of science and policy is a matter of recombining existing knowledge, methods and applications, and that innovation in these fields is rare, how true must this be for bottom-up projects by residents? With one's feet in the neighborhood there is hardly or no time to consciously recombining theory and instruments. Thinking and acting strategically will depend greatly on practical intuition, on perseverance and probably on much luck in preventing disasters. Surviving is the main priority, and to survive one keeps a close eye on what is useful.

Context Gouda

The municipality of Gouda is situated in the central part of the province of *Zuid Holland* (South Holland, The Netherlands), about 20 kilometers from Rotterdam, 30 from The Hague and 35 from Utrecht (Illustration 8.1). The settlement dates back to more than eight centuries ago, with 1272 as year of 'city rights'. Famous buildings like the St. Janskerk (St. John's; 1755 m2 of stained-glass windows), the Town Hall (late gothic), the Weigh-house (with its large white relief representing the act of weighing cheese), and the fronts along the canals in the city center are so many tokens of its rich history of the fifteenth, sixteenth and seventeenth century. Industrial remains of the nineteenth (pipes, yarn, candles) and the first half of the twentieth century (pottery, rope, candles, cigars) can still be observed, as well as its past as market place, harbor and cross-road for water transport.

The present economic vehicles seem to be: automation services (*automatiseringsdiensten*: 2075 working persons; 262 businesses); business administration (*zakelijk beheer*: 1609; 1184); engineering offices (*ingenieursbureaus*: 1995; 165); health and welfare (*gezondheid en welzijn*: 1977; 92); infrastructure (*infrastructuur*: 1877; 47) and other building industry (*andersoortige bouwbedrijvigheid*: 1527; 375); retail non-food (*detailhandel* non-food: 1570; 387); and wholesale trade (*groothandel*: 1464; 374). (Source: data on working persons and businesses, per 1st January 2005, Chamber of Commerce of the Rotterdam Region).[2] This economic basis is somewhat specific in the Rotterdam Region, but in line with the economic base in The Netherlands as a whole.

In the municipality's economic vision (Gemeente Gouda, 2005a) economic data are limited to the number of businesses (2600), employment (36.500) and unemployment (1.600; 4.4 percent). The economic decline is admitted, but not specified. The emphasis for the future is on a broad economic spectrum, with ambitions focused on regional mobility and accessibility, a good climate for businesses, mainly offices, employment, retail and leisure, culture and tourism, education, and diversification of the housing stock. In the Spatial Structure Plan (*Ruimtelijke Structuurvisie*, Gemeente Gouda, 2005b) the present economic situation is only verbally mentioned. It is acknowledged that the position of the city is 'under pressure', and that Gouda is developing from a self-supporting regional center to one of the centers in the social-economic region Midden-Holland. Also here a clearly underpinned point of departure is missing. The municipal's urban policy and its implementation is basically top-down. The focus is mainly on the central city, and some (new) investment areas in the outskirts (Westergouwe), while the other districts have a subordinate position.

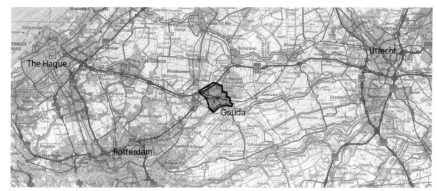
Illustration 8.1: Gouda in the region

Illustration 8.2: Position of Gouda-East

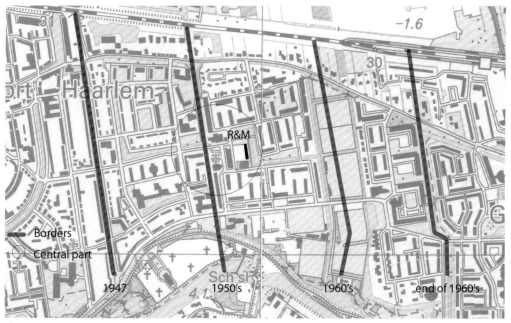
Illustration 8.3: Expanding borders of Gouda: the growth of East
(Maps in 8.1, 8.2 and 8.3 Courtesy by Topografische Dienst Kadaster)

Nowadays the territory of the municipality comprises about 1.811 hectares. The population size is 71.764 per 1st of January 2005 (Gemeente Gouda, 2005c). According to the population census data there are 14.927 residents of allochthon origin.[3] Of Moroccan origin are 6100 residents, for a great part living in the districts Gouda Oost (30 percent of the district's population of 5.563) and Korte Akkeren (population: 9.917; on the western side of the city). Both these districts are to be regenerated in the next decade.[4]

The regeneration policy and its implementation are divided into two separated tracks: the so-called *wijkaanpak* (neighborhood approach), which is about social and welfare aspects, and the *wijkontwikkeling* (neighborhood development), about physical, spatial-functional, economic, and management aspects, including a number of participative activities by residents and entrepreneurs focused at these sectors.[5]

The preparation and implementation of the regeneration is a considerable investment in the existing city, financially (including work force) by the municipality and housing corporations, as well as socially by residents, local entrepreneurs and institutions. Therefore, it is remarkable, that districts like East play no explicit role in the city's spatial and other plans. Obviously these areas are seen by the authorities as problems to be treated; not as opportunities to use, exploit, and expand.

Gouda East

Gouda East was planned and built during the years 1950-70. There are about 1.600 dwellings, a few from the first half of the century twentieth century, and only a hundred dwellings were built after 1970. The built up environment consists mainly of middle high-rise blocks and a number of (semi) detached houses. For decades, East was the end of the city, on the edge of very wet polder land. As the district was never designed as a whole, but was developed in zones - with nowadays perceivable frontlines of the fiftieth, mid-sixtieth and end-sixtieth – the road infrastructure is a knitting, and as such a structural problem. (Illustration 8.2 and 8.3)

The district has already for decades to contend with the usual problems, so characteristic for (early) post war urban extensions in The Netherlands, but also elsewhere in Europe: aging and neglect of buildings and public spaces, the disappearance of all kinds of amenities, population changes with growing vulnerability and deprivation, and unemployment. Many dwellings are relatively cheap, the average property values and the average income are among the lowest in Gouda (Gemeente Gouda, 2000).

The situation worsened with the building of another district east of East in the 1990's, called Goverwelle. This new district not only drained East functionally when the amenities started leaving, but also the traffic to and from Goverwelle had and still has to go through East. In the municipal's vision these (infra)structural problems do not exist (Gemeente Gouda, 2005d), that is that the traffic and noise problems are supposed to be dealt with by limiting the speed and by making some adaptations to the roads.

Gouda East is nowadays a so-called *herstructureringwijk*, literally: district under reconstruction (Stuurgroep Wijkontwikkeling Gouda, 2000). The term *herstructurering* (restructuring) in The Netherlands has two meanings, depending on the discipline: in the field of social housing its meaning is the increase of dwelling types attractive to residents with moderate and higher incomes, which is also the main idea in national policy documents (e.g. Ministerie van VROM, 2000; see also Houterman & Hulsbergen, 2005a). In the field of urbanism (urban planning and design) the term refers to the improvement of the urban structure, not only housing typology, but mainly infrastructure and mobility, amenities, etc, in relation to use; in short improving the spatial, functional and user networks (Houterman & Hulsbergen, 2005b).

The policy in Gouda seems to try to avoid the pitfalls of both separate approaches by organizing small projects in various fields (participation, information, physical renewal, businesses), which in combination should create a livable and sustainable district. An *Adviesgroep* (advisory group) with residents from local organizations advises the *Stuurgroep Wijkontwikkeling* (steering group district development; a co-operation between housing corporations and municipality). In the years 2004 and 2005 many municipal documents were produced regarding plans and (phases of) implementation. At present, the municipality focuses on the (spatial and functional) regeneration of the central area.

R&M Activity Center

R&M is a residents' volunteers organization aimed at improving the living conditions in Gouda East, in addition to the formal (professional) organizations. It was initiated in 1997 by two residents, whose names stand for R&M: Rachid Tighadouini (in those days) a local baker with a shop in the district center and Melchior Verstegen, a retired economist who as a full time volunteer worked for the district for years. They cared about the lack of perspectives, in particular for young Moroccan residents, and wanted to stop the increasing environmental decay and marginalization caused by growing unemployment and low incomes, and the reduction of social ties by the growing ethnic and cultural diversity in East. In 1997 the main problem was to find a location for activities. Finally, the Activity Center got space in a former school building in the middle of the district (Illustration 8.3), which was empty and without any function at the time. The municipality, as the owner of this 'Anne Frank building', subsidized the rent, heating costs and a number of activities, in the form of a modest lumpsump.[6] The preparations in the building were made during summer 1998; the actual project started officially in September 1998. The

---

Box 8.1: Aspects of interest in the R&M-project (2000 – 2004):

- The initiative is combined Moroccan/Dutch.
- Moroccans run the project daily, seven days a week
- The users are mainly Moroccan youth, and there is a (class) room in use by elder Moroccans.
- The volunteers are both from Moroccan and Dutch origin.
- The aim is to work with the young people, to give them a place, to improve their understanding of the Dutch society, the situation of Moroccans in The Netherlands, in order to improve their perspectives and (employment) opportunities. The project is meant as an element to improve the livability (among this the reduction of damage and crime) in the neighborhoods and district, for all residents.
- The project is supported by the neighborhood organization, the local police, various private and privatized parties, and the municipality. It is not linked to the local mosque or church.
- The project adds a new function in the marginalized and marginal functioning central part of the district.

main conclusions of the first-year evaluation (September 1998 - September 1999) were satisfying and hopeful. There was a demand for new activities, and volunteers for new activities were available. In July 2000, after some years of discussion with the municipal and professional welfare organizations, the *Stichting* (foundation) *R&M Gouda Oost* started officially, as a corporate body positioned between the municipality and the activity center (See Box 8.1).

Between 2000 and 2004 many activities were organized for different age groups: leisure activities as well as those geared toward education and employment, and the introduction of flat wardens and environmental reporters. The project consisted of a number of sub-projects concerning social activities for different groups, language courses and other lessons, sustaining residents in their search for work, help to understand Dutch society and bureaucracy, safety, and so on. (Box 8.2)

Box 8.2: R&M agenda 2000 – 2004:

Daily activities:
- Drop in, clubhouse and reception of the youth (16-25 years) and adults
- Consulting hours, support and information on questions about education, work, healthcare, neighborhood

Weekly activities:
- Language lessons (Arabic, Dutch)
- School homework help and supervision
- Scouting
- Sport and swimming
- Music (djembe) group
- Movie

Occasionally:
- Discussions and debates about subjects that affect the neighborhood (local questions, municipal policies, events somewhere else raising questions, etc.)
- Reception of interested groups, institutions and media, political parties; local and from elsewhere
- Festivities (of importance for groups of residents, e.g. at the end of the Ramadan)
- Excursions
- Employment market

Projects:
- Flat wardens, in co-operation with one of the social housing corporations
- Environmental reporters, to report on garbage
- Surveillances on New Year's eves (1998 – 2002), to prevent damage ('vandalism')
- Odd-job service (2000-2001), to gain experience with this kind of service to the neighborhood

One of the project's original intentions in the long run was to contribute to the spatial and economic regeneration of the district. However, this never had the approval of the municipality. Already in 1997, even in June 1999 the authorities proposed to embed the project in the urban welfare organization. This gave rise to growing tensions between the (local) initiators of the project and the (urban and regional) welfare institution (which also acted as the representative of the municipality). The R&M-initiators were opposed to this embedding, for the initiative was a result of neglect of problems in East; they stressed its local character. Finally, in November 1999, the municipality decided on the one hand to continue its support and on the other to study the possibilities for an independent status (foundation). Medio 2000, the project had succeeded in continuing and in strengthening its position in the neighborhood. The negative response and fears that were expressed by a number of Dutch residents in the first half-year had changed into critical approval. So far it had survived the conflicts and division in the Moroccan population. Surrounded by the uncertainties of the restructuring of the area, for that moment it was an example of what could be done.

At the end of 2003, the municipal's social policy changed, and with that the financial support to R&M. In March 2004 the board decided to dissolve the foundation per 30th of April 2004 ('Queen's day' in The Netherlands), but to keep the activity center open and activities going as far as was financially possible. In 2005 the relations between the center and the municipality improved, and financial support continued, this support being about as much as the rent and heating of the building. Though there was always some support for R&M in the Municipal Council, the initiative also had met much distrust. A new Alderman succeeded in shaping acceptable relations between R&M and the involved municipality services.

During 2005 a number of residents worked on establishing a neighborhood association as a corporate body. The association formulated two main targets: Gouda East clean, whole and safe; solidarity between the residents in East. The strategy: to obtain a broad base in all residents groups, activities directed to social cohesion and personal development (work, health, upbringing children), activities with volunteers for all residents groups on demand, recognizable work plan, concrete services (courses, activities) and result (more safety, health, labor participation), dialogue with involved parties, businesses and organizations, transparent organization and actions, and diversifying the means of existence of the association. So far, R&M has been managed by volunteers among the residents, but this could very well change as a consequence of the municipal's changing social policy: the financing of short term projects without emphasis on long term continuity.

Design Atelier 2003

Although the majority of initiatives and projects has been successful, R&M has never become an explicit participant in the restructuring plans for the neighborhood. For some activities use has been made of the center's space and organizational capacity, but R&M has so far not been explicitly seen as a strategic asset for the neighborhood (Houterman & Hulsbergen, 2005c). The context of the R&M-project changed with the municipal decision to restructure' Gouda Oost', adopting a so-called 'active neighborhood approach' to improve the living conditions. In this situation, in the end of 2002, R&M developed the idea to organize residents in a design atelier, to contribute to the district's regeneration at hand. This design atelier was developed and implemented in co-operation with FORUM, a nationally working institute for multicultural development, to stimulate residents' empowerment, participation and knowledge development (http://www.forum.nl), one of their spearheads being so-called *woonateliers* (residential workshops; Phagoe, 2005). The neighborhood development approach of R&M was combined with the FORUM's multicultural approach.

In this paragraph the aims, concept, method and results are shortly described.

Aims

The general aims of the Design Atelier Gouda East were:
- To bring together, for a limited period, residents of migrant and autochthon origin;
- To discuss and study their wishes and needs with respect to the living environment, the adaptation and regeneration of the neighborhood, and the social contacts between residents; and
- To give the results a form, which could be presented to other residents, the municipality and the (social) housing corporations.

Three organizations were relevant:
- The local residents' initiative R&M Activity center;
- The nationally oriented organization FORUM; and
- The municipality's department *Wijkontwikkeling* (district development).

Each organization had its specific aims.
- R&M, who organized the meetings, wanted to make three statements. The first, to show that thinking and working on a possible future of the central part of the district is a true form of residents' participation. The second, to demonstrate that rather simple spatial-functional adaptations of the existing environment could lead to surprising improvements on the short term. The third, to raise again several equivocated dilemmas in the regeneration of the district.
- FORUM supported financially and professionally the atelier as one of the institution's experiments in participation, bringing together residents from different origins, and for a limited period to discuss housing wishes and needs, and to design possible solutions.
- The municipality's district development organization supported it as a local residents' initiative, was available to act as informant during workshop sessions, and in the end helped and financed the publication; it also worked as a link to the *Stuurgroep Wijkontwikkeling Gouda Oost en Korte Akkeren* (Steering group district development Gouda Oost en Korte Akkeren, a co-operation of the municipality and housing corporations).

Concept

The concept of the atelier was simple: involve residents in contemplating and (re)designing the central part of the district. The central part was the chosen location of study and design, as the municipality saw (and still does see) this location as a major issue in the regeneration of the district as a whole (the municipality did not see the integrated improvement of the present functional-spatial structure of the district as a major task).

The Steering Group expressed the wish to take the *Structuurvisie* (structure plan) *Gouda Oost* as point of departure for the atelier (Stuurgroep Wijkontwikkeling Gouda, 2000). From municipal side the prevention of 'unnecessary expectations' regarding the possible implementation of the atelier result was stressed. Both wishes were discussed in the atelier; it was decided to accept the focus on the central part, however without further restrictions. Participants were invited to share their personal experiences in the district and city, as well as their ideas about future perspectives and expected constraints. The creation of a safe environment was also part of the concept, as well as the use and strengthening of existing knowledge and skills.

In these matters there were differences between R&M and FORUM, corresponding to their initial aims, which gave rise to interesting discussions in the preparation of the actual design atelier. However, the co-operation proved fruitful in the combination of emphasis on the spatial, functional and social characteristics on the one hand and on the other emphasis on the possibilities to generalize the approach and results to situations elsewhere.

Method

The method comprised several steps and activities during twelve collective sessions in the auditorium of R&M, and a number of activities by small groups and individuals:
- Start: during the first meeting the proposed atelier tasks were discussed, and participants were invited to contribute to the proposal and come forward with suggestions for the week to come; as home work the participants had to make pictures of characteristic and valuable spaces and places, and pictures of situations in need of improvements
- Next sessions: lectures of professionals from FORUM and Steering Group, followed by discussion; design activities
- Design sessions, and report.

In total, and in varying compositions per meeting and design session, 27 autochthon and allochthon residents participated in the design atelier. They stimulated each other to give an impulse to the renewal of their neighborhood from a residents' perspective. During the atelier sessions many ideas and possibilities were expressed, and proposals put forward. Firstly, on the neighborhood level, especially the infrastructure, attainableness and recreational routes, which were not only discussed but also drawn on maps; secondly, on the level of the proposed center. The input for the conceptualization of a new central area were the expressed needs of the residents and cases from elsewhere, presented and explained by a professional architect from FORUM.

The report was organized by R&M. The general introductory chapter was written by a member of FORUM, the other chapters and drawings were produced by residents. The (full color) publication was supported by municipal (wo)manpower and financing. (Stichting R&M Gouda Oost i.s.m. FORUM (Utrecht) en Stuurgroep Wijkontwikkeling Gouda, 2003)

Results

The results consisted of (1) a program, (2) the identification of dilemmas with respect to the spatial-functional regeneration of the district, and (3) maps and architectural drawings of possible spatial interventions. Emile Gerbrands, architect and one of the participating residents in the atelier, gave form to the ideas that came up (Illustrations 8.4 and 8.5).

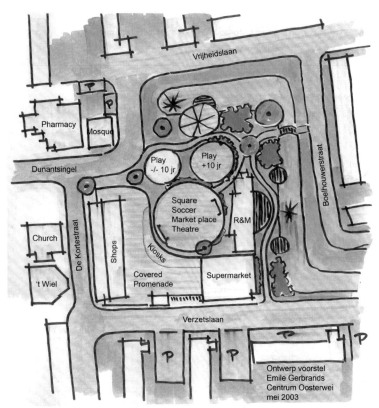

Illustration 8.4: Design proposal center Gouda East (Courtesy of Emile Gerbrands)

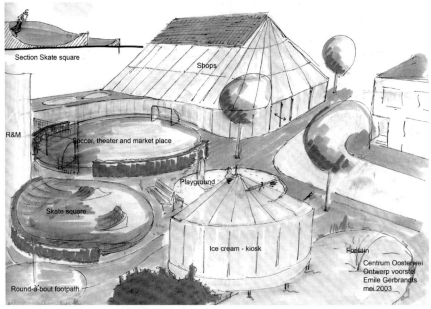

Illustration 8.5: Sketch possible future center Gouda East (Courtesy of Emile Gerbrands)

Program

The program started with the motto: a district where living, recreation and sleeping are good. The points of departure were:
- Start with a proposal to improve the district that needs limited financial means; show that the district can benefit from concrete bottom-up activities;
- Make use of existing elements: the square and the street, the empty school, sports and shop buildings, un(der)used spaces in flats in the center and elsewhere in the district;
- Focus on low threshold activities and entrepreneurship; and
- Give space to idealistic residents.

Identified problems to be dealt with, were:
- Uses: annoyances of hanging about in the streets, noise at night, drugs dealing, driving and parking behavior;
- Safety: pavement, green and water; sagging, dirt, maintenance of trees and shrubs; and
- Attractiveness: buildings, fronts and shops.

Program subjects:
- Connections
    - extern to the center of Gouda and to the central railway station
    - intern to the amenities and activities and to the local railway station Goverwelle
- Amenities
    - daily general and special necessities of life (vegetables, meat, fish)
    - medical care (general practitioner, dentist, physiotherapist, drug store)
    - household articles, clothing, bikes
    - post office, bank, police office, mother center, hair dresser
    - meeting places: snack bar, café, gift and souvenir shop, sitting accommodations
    - social cultural: local center, religious meeting places, 'R&M'
- Businesses
    - kiosks near the apartment buildings, employment agency
    - repair businesses for clothing, bikes and apparatus
    - spaces for starting businesses
- Parking
    - on the street and in parking buildings
- Events
    - exotic market
    - cosy excitement
- Objects of interest
- Dwellings.

Points of attention:
- Communication to the residents and potential investors and entrepreneurs
- Space for active residents.

District dilemmas:
- The road infrastructure was never designed on the scale of the district, but was knitted on in each building phase. The result was and is a problematic system, hardly able to efficiently support the

local traffic movements of bicycles and cars, car-parking in the neighborhood, and unable to cope with the through-traffic which burdens East since the building of Goverwelle in the 1990's.
- All spaces in the district have a 'function' (housing, traffic, water/green, sports, etc.). Space for transformation therefore depends on the priorities of those who have the power to make decisions. It is an open question if these priorities are based on local interests or are rooted in perceived urban or regional necessities, with East being a pawn instead of an urban relevant district. The demolishment of cheap housing is a lasting threat (even if the general policy of the housing corporation is to prevent this).
- The limited seize of the central area cannot provide space for all local needs. A main question was how to deal with the interests of vulnerable and deprived residents, and the needs for 'green' recreation like meeting in the open air and picnicking, a wish of specific groups of residents.
- A fourth dilemma concerned the support of households and users, in the near and more distant future, which should be sufficient to keep the center lively, paying and attractive. East always had a low priority in the municipality, with a final blow in the 1990's when the local amenities were largely replaced to the shopping center in the newly built Goverwelle. Also the present municipality's priority to investments in a new urban extension in the western part of the city (Westergouwe) is not reassuring.

The situation beginning 2006

In the first half of 2005 several studies about the central part of East were taken together from an urbanism point of view (Bet, 2005). In this document attention was paid to the work and proposals of the R&M-atelier, apart from studies by the municipality and advisory offices focused on, for example, the expected population and needs for amenities and businesses. As a conclusion in this 2005-document two development models for further exploration of the possibilities were proposed. In fact these two models gave also rise to deepening the discussion about the spatial consequences of interventions, about costs, but also about the effects on the living conditions of specific groups of residents. A curious fact is that the municipality favored another model than the residents in the Advisory Group. Meanwhile, also a document appeared with so-called neighborhood action points for the next two years (Gemeente Gouda, 2005e: 31-35).

In December 2005 there was a municipal initiative to organize another design atelier as part of the residents' participation. This was postponed, as only a few residents responded. [7] The initiative was rescheduled in February and March in 2006, in the form of a three-evenings atelier, mentored by a professional organization specialized in 'participation' (Início, Rotterdam), supervised by an urbanist and a social geographer. The participants were residents, mainly of autochthon origin. The first evening was focused on 'desired image quality' in the central area of green and water, buildings, art objects and spatial forms. The second evening concentrated on 'functionality', the desires and ideas of amenities and what activity should be made possible in the center, including dilemmas and priorities. During the third evening conclusions and recommendations were discussed and formulated or drawn on maps, partly in reaction to design sketches made by two professional urban designers. Interesting is that these sketches, unexpectedly, showed the intention to solve some structural problems in the district's infrastructure. At the end of March a formal evening was organized by the municipality about the 'participation' so far. The R&M-atelier 2003 results were memorized, as well as the outcomes of the two 'partnering conferences' in 2005. Also the improved design sketches which would form the bases for the contacts with residents and potentially interested parties were introduced and explained.

Finally the results of the three workshop evenings were presented and in printed form offered to the Alderman present and rest of the participants (Geljon & Zoeteman, 2006).

Conclusions and recommendations

R&M is an interesting bottom-up initiative and activity. But is R&M innovative? The initiative has started as 'complementarily' to the existing formal, professional institutions. A recent example is the 'mother center'. The R&M-concept of a women's center for the neighborhood dates back to 2000. The try outs did not work out well, mainly because the women's activities were not totally spatially separated from all kinds of other activities (for young and older males). Meanwhile in the formal district's center 't Wiel, more attention was given to activities for women. However in the course of 2005, 'R' found out that a number of Moroccan women did not participate and stayed home. So a new concept was developed for a women's activity, with four women residents in 2003. Finally in 2005 this was proposed as a project in the context of neighborhood development. An empty (school) location was available and the project was sustained by the municipality (neighborhood development).

Already in the running start there were protests from the district's social center 't Wiel (owned by the welfare institution, which runs the activities there). The regional supplement of a national paper beginning December told: 'No two women centers'. The situation is complex; also within the district there are opposing groups, which see the R&M bottom-up initiatives as a threat. Despite this, due to the persistence of R&M and a (female) civil servant, the women's initiative did progress.

For municipal policy, a local initiative like R&M is sometimes convenient to get things done or moving; it can be used as external push and therefore be tolerated. But it does not easily fit in the usual procedures and an organization like R&M is therefore rarely seen as a partner.

R&M's innovative strength might have been its practical flexibility in developing new concepts and doing things in a complementary way, even if the institutional actors behave as if no complementary action is necessary. Institutions always will say that their activities are sufficient. And, if its acknowledged that their activities are not sufficient, they will state that they know what should be done, and are only waiting for public or private financing to allow them to do a better job.

The R&M-approach is the small and difficult road of 'volunteering', with little financial costs, to stay relatively independent of institutional, political and other vested interests. It uses this independency to do what formal institutions will not or cannot do, find too complex or nonsensical.

In 2000 a number of 'tips' were formulated by request of Habitat Platform, The Hague (Hulsbergen & Vellinga, 2001). The following seem still relevant:

Tips to the active residents:
- Don't let yourselves be framed.
- Have the courage to be active. Formal rules are meant to accomplish something, not to hinder.
- Organize, look for people to talk about subjects of your interest.
- State what you want, and how. Look for implementation possibilities.
- Accept that every actor in the neighborhood renewal has own interests, and will communicate these openly or not.

- Make a work plan with time schedule. Time schedules are important for not losing the notion of time, and that time flies. Schedules are not dogmatic instruments.
- Make use of the services of other parties, but always keep in mind that these must facilitate you, unless reciprocity is profitable to your interests.
- Seek to understand the debate between the municipality and other actors. If useful to your course, try to connect.
- Communicate in the district, explain what you have in mind, and show responsibility about commitment, investment and result.
- Accept that initiatives might fail, your own initiative as well as the initiative of someone else.
- Every experience is (also) an opportunity for learning. Make ideas work.

Tips to the (local) government
- Don't assume that the aims and means of residents fit in the present municipal frame.
- Be clear about the official dividing-lines between civil services or departments.
- Solve difficulties in the formal decision process and competitive responsibilities between municipal services; don't avoid these. Change procedures that do not lead to satisfactory results with residents.
- Take into account, that residents might be totally in the dark with regard to official procedures; or (justly) show no understanding.
- Be aware that a neighborhood's first function is to the benefit the residents; a neighborhood is not a peony in the urban vision; neighborhood and city are complementary in function.
- Clarify the municipal ambition and desired development directions. Residents can eventually hook on.
- Let active residents decide about the design of the living environment. Regard residents as (potential) investors in their neighborhood. Behave supportive and leave room for initiative. Adopt a neighborhood initiative.
- Draw up a vision which leaves space for active residents. Make plans flexible and include possibilities to financially and materially sustain neighborhood self-organizations.
- Be attentive to active residents; contact and visit them. See this as your own responsibility; don't just delegate this to the private sector as a short-term project.
- Be very thoughtful about the free time residents invest in their neighborhood.
- To get entangled in (own) regulations is undesirable for any actor.
- For the neighborhood economy: create conditions for (local) entrepreneurship. Provide space for starting businesses; but also cheap starters' capital, professional mentoring, starting with business administration and the management of business line networks. Give space to local experiments.

Finally

Scientific and policy viewpoints are strongly influenced by disciplinary and sectoral divisions, based on "the premise that particular aspects of human activity can be isolated for separate (…) individual professional treatment" (Moser, 1997). R&M certainly had to cope with (not to say: suffered) from this phenomenon. As the activities of the center ranged from daily social activities, to looking after neighborhood-interests and, cultural and sport activities, in a municipally owned building, R&M had to deal with four different municipal services. Complicating was and still is that the Mayor and Aldermen decided to limit formal contacts to the Alderman responsible for 'social services', a department that seems to prefer to deal with the formal institutions. Moreover, the present policy is focused on a 'project approach' (of a limited time span) and 'competition' between organizations. As such this would not be a problem, but in this competition R&M is 'measured' against the rules for professional institutions, without having the same financial rights in budgeting projects. As R&M is one of a kind in Gouda, it does not get a status that could fit in. The situation improved in 2007.

If R&M is worth to be mentioned as innovative, the designation 'innovation' to this local volunteers project might be the enduring look for opportunities to keep activities going; as long as is possible.

References

Bet, E., 2005, *Centrum Gouda Oost, Definitiefase, Definitie van de opgave voor de herontwikkeling van het centrum van Gouda Oost*, Projectbureau Wijkontwikkeling Gouda Oost, Den Haag en Gouda.

Geljon, M. & H. Zoeteman, 2006, *Werkatelier Centrumontwikkeling Gouda Oost. Drie avonden, acht hoofdzaken*, In opdracht van de gemeente Gouda, Projectbureau Wijkontwikkeling, Início, Rotterdam.

Gemeente Gouda, 2000, *Woonruimte statistiek per 1-1-2000*, Dienst Informatisering en Statistiek, Gemeente Gouda, Gouda.

Gemeente Gouda, 2005a, *Economische Visie Gouda 2005-2010*, Gemeente Gouda, Gouda.

Gemeente Gouda, 2005b, *Ruimtelijke Structuurvisie Gouda 2005-2030*, Gemeente Gouda, Gouda.

Gemeente Gouda, 2005c, *Bevolking en grondgebied per 1 januari 2005*, Statistische publicatie, Afdeling Informatisering en Statistiek, Gemeente Gouda, Gouda.

Gemeente Gouda, 2005d, *Mobiliteitsvisie Gouda, variatie in verkeer en vervoer*, Sector Stadswerken, Afdeling Ruimtelijk beleid, Gemeente Gouda, Gouda.

Gemeente Gouda, 2005e, *Wijkactiepunten 2006-2007, startdocument oktober 2005*, Afdeling Wijkaanpak, Gemeente Gouda, Gouda.

Houterman, R. & E. D. Hulsbergen, 2005a, Slopen geen optie: liberalisering van de volkshuisvesting en regeneratie van hoogbouwwijken in Praag, *VHV-bulletin*, Vol. 32, nr.2, pp.18-22.

Houterman, R. & E. D. Hulsbergen, 2005b, Tweede kans voor 'de stad van de toekomst', *Atlantis*, Vol.16, nr.3, pp.7-12.

Houterman, R. & E. D. Hulsbergen, 2005c, Neighbourhood Initiatives: Time for Bottom-Up; In: Hulsbergen, E.D., I.T. Klaasen & I. Kriens (eds), 2005, *Shifting Sense in Spatial Planning*, Series Design/Science/Planning, Techne Press, Amsterdam, pp. 331-340.

Hulsbergen, E.D. & B.M.K. Vellinga, 2001, *Buurtvernieuwing door actief burgerschap. R&M Gouda Oost als casus en instrument*, Stichting Habitat Platform Den Haag i.s.m. Faculteit Bouwkunde TU Delft, Den Haag.

Ministerie van VROM, 2000, *Nota 'Mensen, Wensen, Wonen'*, Ministerie van Volkshuisvesting, Ruimtelijke Ordening en Milieu, Den Haag.

Moser, C., 1997, Urban Social Policy and Poverty Reduction; In: Burgess, R., M. Carmona & T. Kolstee (eds), *The Challenge of Sustainable Cities*, Zed Books, Londen, pp.44-61.

Phagoe, J., 2005, *Handreiking Woonateliers*, FORUM, Instituut voor Multiculturele Ontwikkeling, Utrecht.

Roberts, P. & H. Sykes, 2004, *Urban Regeneration A Handbook*, Sage Publ., London.

Stichting R&M Gouda Oost i.s.m. FORUM (Utrecht) en Stuurgroep Wijkontwikkeling Gouda, 2003, *Atelier 'Centrum voor Oost', Toelichting en Presentatie Bewonersatelier Gouda Oosterwei*, Gouda.

Stuurgroep Wijkontwikkeling Gouda, 2000, *Gastvrij Gouda Oost. Samen werken aan een visie. Wijkontwikkelingsplan Gouda Oost*, Gouda.

Websites (March 2007)

http://www.habiforum.nl
http://www.instrumentenwijzer.nl
http://www.kei-centrum.nl
http://www.onzebuurtaanzet.nl
http://www.steunpuntwonen.nl/eigenwijks/
http://www.vng.nl

Notes

1. The author of this chapter, resident and volunteer in East, was deeply involved in this process of formalization, participated in the board of the Foundation R&M, and nowadays is a member of the Vereniging (Association) R&M Gouda Oost. For a description of the developments until 2000, see Hulsbergen & Vellinga, (2001), this publication was supported by the foundation Habitat Platform in The Hague, the Dutch institution in the frame of World Habitat (abolished in 2007).

2. The data bases (city, region, country) were placed at the disposal of the author by a staff member of the Chamber of Commerce, after his request for an overview of Gouda's economic position. As this was not available, it was decided to send the 2005-data. The present overview is the responsibility of the author.

3. Allochtoon (allochthon) is the term used in The Netherlands to identify residents from foreign origin, and as such to distinguish them from autochthons. The CBS-definition (National Census Office) is also applied in Gouda. Allochtoon: all persons with at least one parent born abroad. Allochthons born abroad are labeled 'first generation'; those born in The Netherlands 'second generation'. Allochthons of the first generation are subdivided in 'western' and 'non-western' (Turkey, Africa, Latin America; and Asia except Japan and Indonesia, based on their social-economic position in The Netherlands) (Gemeente Gouda, 2005c:9).

4. The population size 'Gouda Oost' is a reconstruction by the author, based on the 2005 statistical data. In the 2005-data Gouda Oost does not exist any more. An eastern neighborhood of the district East (called Oud-Goverwelle, with a new name Sportbuurt) is statistically added to the district Goverwelle, and the other three neighborhoods are statistically added to the district Kort Haarlem. Remarkable is, that Oost still exists in the local renewal planning. This phenomenon sometimes confuse the discussions.

5. The term 'regeneration' is used here, as the municipality's expressed aim is to have a multi-sector, multi-actor and multi-scale approach. Whether the actual process will qualify up to the standards of regeneration (i.e. beyond mere renewal) is an open question. For definition and fundamental discussion about regeneration, see Roberts & Sykes, 2004.

6. In fact R&M was and still is a very cheap center compared to the existing formal institutions, as volunteer work is what keeps it going.

7. In my view caused by: the limitations in the task, only a few meetings planned, unclear professional urbanistic or architectural support; lack of detailed information to the residents, and the presentation as a 'participation' rather than a 'design' activity.

9 Urban Development and Self-help Activities in León, Nicaragua

Jan Bredenoord, in co-operation with Desiree van de Ven and Patricia Ardiles

Introduction

For several years, the Municipality of León in Nicaragua has been successfully striving to achieve sustainable urban and rural development. Part of this success is due to a socially-oriented land policy, which stimulates individual self-help housing and social housing projects. This land policy is implemented through the León South East Plots Program 1998-2008 of the Municipality of León, which delivers an average of 500 plots per year to low-income households[1]. The plots are sold for the individual construction of houses by the families themselves or by construction workers. Additionally, non-governmental organizations (NGOs) also build and sell plots with dwellings to low-income households. These two activities provide hundreds of households with new possibilities for the improvement of their socio-economic situation. Presently, the building of neighborhoods is the most important issue, together with the planning of infrastructure and basic urban services, such as schools, health services and sports facilities. At the same time, the municipality takes care of tasks related to public policy, such as the elaboration of future visions and zoning plans and the co-ordination with local actors.

The ongoing participation of inhabitants and entrepreneurs, with their skills of self-help construction and self-organization, is considered essential, and is in agreement with the desired future urban development of León. In most cases, the self-help construction process appears spontaneously because low-income households do not have any other alternative in the housing market. Therefore, the municipality has incorporated self-help processes within local policies and urban planning strategies. This helps local NGOs and local government to support the creation of small associations.

Because the development of León's economy faces many difficulties, local government is keen to initiate a new strategy for economic development. Besides, in the above-mentioned León South East (LSE) Plots Program for housing, high priority will be given to economic development involving all interested parties and potential participants. Eventually, this should lead to a renewed Plots Program, with the objective to develop land for economic activities. In this scheme, branches of local businesses or associations can play an important role. This Chapter presents the significance of self-help construction and self-organization processes as part of local development strategies and the battle against urban poverty. The working philosophy is based on strengthening local potentials in order to benefit all: individuals and households, as well as housing and job associations. In this vision, the municipality's main role is providing technical and organizational knowledge, and bringing local actors together.

The development process in León since 1990[2]

Initially the Municipality of León focused on the realization of housing projects on a small scale. Before 2000 the support of Nicaragua's central government was very limited. However, León was successful in obtaining assistance from international city links with Hamburg (Germany), Zaragoza (Spain) and Utrecht (The Netherlands).[3] An example of this was the William Fonseca housing project built in the early nineties; a small-scale development which could not satisfy the large demand for dwellings from the growing population in the whole city.

Due to growing demand, low-income households were illegally settling at the outskirts of the city by building slums; a process which produced conflicts with existing communities. Between 1988 and 1995, the municipality purchased land to avoid these problems, and simply divided it into plots for self-help housing activities. In many cases, the plots were given to households for free, and as a result the exploitation of these simple land developments was problematic. In some cases, the absence of plans for infrastructure and other facilities led to difficult negotiations with water and electricity companies.

The method of urban development described above did not lead to the structural improvement of the living and work conditions of the local population. During the preparation of a new integrated urban policy, together with a corresponding strategy for its execution, it became clear that two elements would be important:
- Developing an integrated vision for the whole urban and rural area of the municipality, as a framework for social and economic development (the provision of space and infrastructure for all desired activities)
- Searching for and involving local initiatives and entrepreneurship as building blocks for the execution of the local (municipal) policy.

Since 1995 the municipality has been working with these two elements to develop the city and the adjacent rural area in an integrated manner. The municipality is assisting inhabitants and entrepreneurs with the aim that these actors could create chances for themselves. But this assistance is quite limited, as a result of the weak financial situation of municipalities in Nicaragua. However, giving responsibilities to inhabitants and entrepreneurs to make small achievements is the only way possible to provide perspectives and a sense of worth to households. This new approach gives them small-scale perspectives through a step-by-step method in a middle to long term program. However, across the entire municipality the impact can be larger, in view of the potential large number of beneficiaries.

The core business of local government in housing policy is based on the earlier mentioned León South East Plots Program. Expanding this socially oriented policy toward specific economic goals implies the development of local communities, as well as the creation of their corresponding economic space. Improving the position of small local enterprises is one of the main goals to improve local productive conditions and to generate local employment. Although there are some hopeful developments in León, the successful achievement of the economic goals must be considered a long-term task (Illustration 9.1).

Socio-economic profile and opportunities

Population, income and work

The second largest city of Nicaragua, León is located 90 km north of Managua, approximately half of the way toward the border with Honduras. The area of the municipality is 862 km2, of which only 3 percent is urban land. The estimated population was 210.000 in 2004, of which 165.000 were living in the urban area (Municipality of León & Cooperación Española, 1999). The municipality expects an average annual rate of growth of 3 percent. The average number of residents per dwelling is between 5 and 6. The economic situation is very difficult, as expressed by income indicators: 41 percent of the local population earns less than US $ 85 on a monthly basis; 26 percent between US $ 85 and 170; and 25 percent more than US $ 170; while 8 percent claimed to have no income at all (López, 2000). The main economic sectors include carpentry, leather and furniture manufacturing, food preparation (bread, milk, fruits, etc.), personal and professional services and transport. Most of the industrial production is closely related to the goods produced in the rural area.

A study of the labor market (Municipality of León, 2005) showed that in 2004, 51 percent of the potentially economic active population was officially unemployed, a total of 53.085 inhabitants (25.480 men and 27.605 women). However, around 50 percent of the 'officially' unemployed are developing economic activities in personal services and small trade, which are not officially registered. In the whole León region, cattle breeding, fishing and shrimp-culture are potential economic activities, while in the urban area tourism, furniture manufacturing and the processing of milk, leather, fruits, vegetables and nuts are the activities with the highest potential.

Illustration 9.1: The City of León with the expansion plan South East (I, II and III) (Courtesy of Municipality of León ©)

Decentralization of governmental tasks

In 2003, the national government of Nicaragua elaborated a progressive national economic development plan (Government of Nicaragua, 2003), which is based on the promotion and utilization of regional potential. The idea is to invest in major specializations in regions offering the best potential, and especially in those that have good co-operation between the government and private businesses. It is a challenge for each region to develop its own potential in close co-operation with regional and local stakeholders.

For the national housing policy, developed since 2005, the government invited the regions and main municipalities to establish collaborations with NGOs and the private sector. Although the National Development Plan and the housing policy (Government of Nicaragua, 2005) do not imply a direct transference of competences and means to regions and municipalities, they can be both seen as a first step. It is expected that more steps will be taken in the future to decentralize governmental tasks to the lower levels of governance. This might be also the case in relation to policies concerning the welfare of communities and education. It is presently not very clear which governmental tasks will be transferred to regions and municipalities.

Municipal planning in León

Since 1995, the Municipality of León has been very successful in implementing integrated planning policies for the municipality as a whole. The Strategic Municipal Development Plan (Municipality of León, 2004) is the most recent example. The latest Urban Economic Development Plan (Municipality of León, 2005) recommends focusing on production-chains: from raw products/materials to final products; for example from cattle to meat products and from leather to shoes. On the other hand, in León there is demand for new industrial areas with modern facilities. The municipal strategy to promote industrial production aims at supporting entrepreneurs and promoting new employment. For this goal, the municipality is trying to bring economic actors together in order to gather sufficient financial means to provide new industrial spaces for the establishment of new companies or the expansion of existing ones.

In order to develop a professional municipal housing policy, the municipality of León is preparing new housing policy documents (*Diagnóstico* and *Documento municipal de política de vivienda*) in co-operation with a program supported by the Association of Netherlands Municipalities – Nicaragua. This program provides technical and organizational assistance for 15 municipalities in co-operation with the central government and the national association of housing NGOs. Main results are to be expected in the year 2007.

Sustainable development and participation

Physical planning in León is based on the concept of sustainable development. The Local Agenda 21 (United Nations, 1992) is based on the assumption that future development must be supported on three pillars: economy, community and environment. Following Agenda 21, León has formulated its own sustainability definition with corresponding criteria.

Under the present circumstances it is important to improve the municipal organization in León in order to promote local housing construction and economic development. The self-help activities of individuals and entrepreneurs should be supported in every possible way. Therefore, the participation of individuals, communal and commercial organizations in the main local planning processes, as well as the definition of priorities, has been implemented. As an example, the municipality initiated a process of participation for organizations of residents and entrepreneurs, associations, welfare institutions and NGOs, for the municipal budgeting (*Presupuesto participativo*) decision-making process.

Municipal management in León functions at two levels: (1) city/municipality and (2) neighborhood/urban project. At the first level there is co-ordination between the municipality and private 'actors' such as organizations of citizens and entrepreneurs, co-operatives, welfare organizations and (other) NGOs, which together form the Municipal Development Committee (*Comité de Desarrollo Municipal*, CDM). The execution of the guidelines of municipal policy and the determination of priorities are their main tasks. At the second neighborhood level, it is also important to co-ordinate co-operation between all actors, where several participants should invest in area-focused projects. The local NGOs play a very important role in the LSE Plots Program, since they are building housing projects within LSE areas on a relatively large scale (Illustration 9.2 and Illustration 9.3).

Illustration 9.2: Housing project with prefabricated elements in León South East (Photo: Jan Bredenoord)

Illustration 9.3: Organized housing in León South East (Photo: Desiree van de Ven)

About housing in León South East

Housing policy of the municipality

In 2005, the municipality of León started implementing a local housing policy, which was later given a high priority in view of the development of the national housing strategy in 2006. In general, housing is seen as a private matter. The municipality has to assign land for housing developments and to elaborate zoning plans for new urban areas, like the one in León South East (LSE). The municipality also provides building permits and performs building control; the traditional public tasks of local governments.

With its active land policy, the LSE Plots Program provides an essential impulse for access to housing by certain social groups. In fact the LSE Program forms part of the local housing policy for lower and middle income groups. But most construction activities are done by households, NGOs and small contractors.

Several NGOs have been very successful in obtaining subsidies for housing projects in LSE for low-income households. In order to obtain subsidies from national government the municipality will develop its housing policy. The hopeful contacts with governmental institutions like FOSOVI (*Fondo Social de Vivienda*) and INVUR (*Instituto Nicaragüense de Vivienda Urbana y Rural*) provide new perspectives. An important aspect of municipal housing policy is the foreseen establishment of a bank for building materials in León (in 2006), considered an important instrument to assist households with the self-help housing process.

The León South East Plots Program

The LSE Plots Program provides plots for the construction of houses with the accompanying official land titles. When a household is able to obtain property for the construction of a house, it gets at the same time a perspective for the future, because it will be able to start a small business or other economic activity. Some households can purchase the plot by paying it off in one term, but in most cases a payment arrangement is authorized by the LSE-project. When the plot is completely paid, the household gets the legal property title. The LSE Plots Program has already developed and sold 2500 plots (by the end of 2005). Some plots were bought by NGOs for the construction of houses for low-income and middle-class households. The prices of the plots are between US $ 450 and 1500. Their area varies between 150 m2 and 250 m2. The cheaper ones have streets without pavements, while the most expensive areas the streets have a hard surface and footpaths are provided.

About self-help housing

Self-help housing construction activities are generally undertaken by households or by individuals with the help of household members and friends. The first phase is in most cases the pioneer-phase, in which they usually do not use professional help. The households often build simple accommodations with cheap materials like poles, cardboard, plastic and old zinc sheets. This first dwelling, often constructed in the backyard, is only a temporary shelter to be used while the household is gradually building the house at the front of the plot. When a household has a regular income it is able to buy building materials gradually.

But there are many technical problems during construction: in León houses must be earthquake resistant, but in most cases the households do not know how to build them in this way. Technical assistance should be available, but this is not the case at present. The most difficult parts of the construction of the house – the foundations, the construction of pillars and the construction of roofs – should be the work of professionals, but the households generally ask relatives and friends to help in order to limit the costs, although many households have members with some experience in construction. Sometimes, a household hires professional carpenters and other construction workers for special tasks. Some households do not want to go to a bank or a NGO for construction loans, because they do not want to make financial commitments.

Housing rojects by NGOs

Several NGOs have implemented successful housing projects in LSE. Part of this success is a result of the subsidies that they obtained from the central government, through INVUR. In some cases the houses are being sold to households for very low prices because of subsidies or private donations. In other cases the prices of the houses are reduced because of the help of volunteers in the construction. Households may contribute with their own labor in order to reduce the costs of the house.

The cost that the household eventually pays is generally given in the form of a loan with the character of a credit arrangement or a mortgage. The quality of the houses varies: it may be small and built with simple materials; in this case it is generally a starting unit to be enlarged through the years. In other cases they are complete houses with durable materials at obviously higher prices. The use of prefabricated elements is very common, but the quality of the houses in question is lower than the average.

Several NGOs are working in LSE in housing construction, including Caritas, Fundapadele, Habitat for Humanity and Ceprodel. Other NGOs are expected to work in the future. A Mexican company, Arnecom, is realizing a housing program in LSE for its own workers and the UNAN University will do the same for its academic staff and other workers (Illustration 9.4). Each of these NGOs has its own policy and criteria related to their different target groups. The main differences relate to the quality of the houses, their prices and the donations. The municipality is trying to co-ordinate these policies within the framework of municipal housing policy.

Community development

Since the eighties in Nicaragua an organization has existed, known as *Movimiento Comunal*, based on the organizational structure of the Sandinist Party FSLN. In every neighborhood they assist with the establishment of a committee of residents and the election of its members. These neighborhood committees organize activities for health care and capacity building, among others, and have communication with the local municipality, water and electricity companies and local NGOs (Illustration 9.5).

Central government strives to establish more independent neighborhood organizations, not connected with a particular political party. In León they deal with two independent neighborhood organizations and a co-ordinating one. For urban development goals there is a co-ordinating organization known as ACOPOE (*Asociación Comunitaria Los Poetos*) which has the followings tasks:

Illustration 9.4: Housing project realized by Arnecom (Photo: Jan Bredenoord)

Illustration 9.5: Neighborhood meeting with the municipality in León South East (Photo: Desiree van de Ven)

- Management of the community center;
- Providing information to the residents and the identification of their problems;
- Communication with the municipality and other organizations;
- Organization of public health campaigns and cultural and sports activities;
- Organization of courses and training for residents.

Other possible future tasks are:
- The formation of a public safety team (in co-operation with the police);
- The formation of a maintenance team (concerning waste; in co-operation with the municipality).

The neighborhood committees are autonomous, but good co-operation with the municipality is always an advantage, a process which requires a co-operative approach on both sides and a municipal budget assignation for its implementation.

Most residents of León South East are very interested in developing the neighborhood environment, including the street pavement, public illumination and green areas in streets and playgrounds. The municipality is trying to involve the residents in such initiatives and has appointed a social worker to promote community development and neighborhood activities. As a result of this, an association of residents with legal character has been established, uniting existing neighborhoods with new ones in the Neighborhood of the Poets (Illustration 9.6).

The maintenance of public spaces and facilities is a basic municipal task, but its execution can be contracted out to resident organizations or local companies, and this could bring work to the neighborhood, giving impulse to community development. Other possibilities for community development are the establishment of small associations for specific tasks, such as the construction of a small group of houses or workshops.

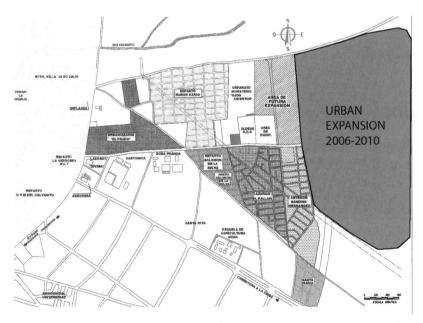

Illustration 9.6: Neighborhood of the Poets in LSE (Courtesy of Municipality of León ©)

Self-help and the role of associations

Self-help (housing) concepts are essential for improving the circumstances for living and working in these contexts. Self-help can include the activities of individuals, households and associations. Within the frame of associations it is easier to get loans and to organize training programs. Therefore the stimulation of associations is always a good strategy.

Self-help housing processes are worldwide phenomena and may appear in very different ways, depending on the culture, building methods, local materials, family bonds and local leadership. In Nicaragua, family bonds are important, but there is also a large number of single mothers. Because the construction of houses requires specific knowledge, self-help housing is not a solution that applies to all. When there are strong family bonds and the help of friends is possible, self-help activities can be very successful. In other cases the support of NGOs is desirable, since they can offer possibilities for loans, technical assistance and training programs.

When there is professional support for self-help activities, residents can develop technical knowledge in construction and eventually maintain their houses properly and expand them gradually. These activities normally make them proud of their houses. Mutual construction of houses is being stimulated by the NGOs Habitat for Humanity and Ceprodel; a process which greatly lowers the cost of a house. Even single mothers are involved in this type of co-operation, which also involves their household members and friends.

The building materials bank in León

The planned building materials bank in León will provide a new credit facility for low income households for the construction of dwellings by a step-by-step method. The households do not get money but building materials, and the value of the materials determines the amount of the loan. The building materials bank will also supervise the construction and the technical quality of the house. The municipality of Utrecht did a pre-investment study for the establishment of this bank. The municipality of León prepared the business plan and successfully applied for subsidy at INVUR. Partly due to this subsidy the building materials bank is established in 2006. The bank will function as a revolving fund, in the same way as the Plots Program.

Housing by associations and NGOs

The establishment of associations of residents for housing purposes has been done by NGOs on a small scale. The municipality could benefit from reliable associations, for example, by offering profitable contracts with the building materials bank, which highlights the importance of working in groups. Housing activities promoted by Associations and NGOs give various credit facilities. Until now one can find four different possible ways to obtain credits for the construction of houses.

Housing by Ceprodel credits

The NGO Ceprodel has been working to establish an association of 45 households in LSE, with the goal of promoting housing and economic activities among its members. Their philosophy is based on the model *Barrio Cooperativo*, a successful 30 years-old experience in Uruguay. Ceprodel will give organizational and technical expertise to the households and at the same time will provide corresponding loans. Ceprodel obtained by the end of 2006 an international loan from the Bank of the

Municipalities in The Netherlands (*Bank Nederlandse Gemeenten*) of EUR 300.000 for the construction of new houses and private house improvement. The housing associations working in the Municipality of Utrecht will guarantee this loan.

Housing by Habitat and Caritas credits

A second initiative is the one of Habitat for Humanity, an international organization working in Nicaragua since 1984, which has different offices in the country including one in León. They are constructing minimal houses through a method based on working in small groups. The houses have a floor space of 36 - 42 m2, and their total costs are approximately US $ 3.000. The households pay approximately US $ 25 per month, over 10 – 15 years, but without interest. They also use a revolving fund for the loans, so the money can be used again and again. Caritas Nicaragua is offering comparable credits for families. Ceprodel, Habitat and Caritas all use the philosophy of creating sustainable communities, in a social and economic way.

Housing by Fundapadele donations

The local NGO Fundapadele (*Fundacion para el desarrollo de León*) is constructing a large amount of simple houses for very low income groups in León South East and is mainly donating these houses to the families and they involve the labor of the benefited families with the construction. Donations are possible as a result of obtained subsidies from INVUR-FOSOVI and other private donors

Housing by Corporate Programs

The earlier mentioned corporation Arnecom realized a vast housing program for their employees near the location of León South East. They realized the program with profitable credit facilities for the families.

Participants in urban land development

For efficient processes of participative land developments, it is important to know who are the actors/participants and what are their interests, in order to stipulate the rules of the game and to bring all forces together. Land development can be an *urbanización* for housing or a land development for the establishment of (new) businesses. Small businesses in León are above all family businesses. A family business can provide continuity, but this is not always a guarantee of success. It is important to assist these businesses when the directions of these companies are being strongly supported by their employees.

Land development for housing (*Urbanizaciones*) in LSE

There are three models of land development for housing purposes:
- The municipality purchases the land, divides it into plots and sells these to households from the municipal target groups. This is the main practice of the LSE Plots Program.
- A private person or land developer purchases the land, divides it into plots and sells these to households, by mutual agreement with the municipality. However, this way requires an agreement of co-operation.
- A private person purchases land and develops it without consulting the municipality.

Since the two last mentioned possibilities could be present in the near future, the municipality should try to combine these actions with municipal planning and gear all activities to one another. A disadvantage of municipal housing policy is the exclusive focus on target groups on the one hand, and the requirement of establishing a closed form of land exploitation within the LSE Plots Program, on the other hand.

When private parties are involved in land development (with or without building dwellings) they evidently try to deal within the free housing market, which results in houses or land for middle and higher income groups. However, the demand for expensive plots is very limited, while the demand for cheap plots and houses is huge. Nevertheless, the involvement of private parties in the total housing production in León will grow and the municipality should be prepared to deal with this process. Eventually all private developers will ask the municipality for help for the development of technical infrastructure and public facilities.

Land developments cannot be realized without the involvement of the companies for public facilities like the water company and the electricity company. In Nicaragua one cannot expect companies to provide the necessary facilities immediately, because there is a structural lack of financial means. In the existing land development schemes in LSE, additional investment was provided by the European Union, which was executed with the help of the UNDP (United Nations Development Program) in Nicaragua. Within this framework, the LSE Plots Program acted as a motor of development for all the infrastructural measures. With such an urban program it became possible to ensure the adequate steering of urban growth.

Land development for economic activities

Bringing together the different actors for the development of a new industrial area is an essential challenge for the municipality. In León this is very difficult because the actors are not aware of the crucial investment needs. As a consequence there was no common land development for economic activities in past decades. However, the new spatial possibilities made possible by the León South East expansion plan could create new prospects for the combined interests of the different parties. The LSE expansion plan can be very favorable because of:
- The excellent possibilities for connecting the location with the main road to Managua and the relatively short distance to the existing city;
- The advantage of the common infrastructure; for new neighborhoods and for economic land development in LSE;
- The LSE-project is remote from the area that is often affected by the discharge of ash from the volcano Cerro Negro.

The possible ways of land development for industrial activities and businesses are:
- The municipality purchases land and develops it to sell the plots to companies and co-operatives. The financial risks for the municipality are high and this could only be done with the help of the national government.
- A private developer or NGO purchases land and develops it to sell the plots to companies or co-operatives. This activity can be expected only when there is a possibility of making profit.
- A public-private company is established for this goal with the participation of the municipality, central government, infrastructure companies, associations of entrepreneurs and co-operatives.

The last mentioned possibility is the best one, but there is no experience with such a complex partnership in León. Nevertheless, such a partnership would appear to be necessary and possible with the help of the state through the National Development Plan. The municipality will probably take the initiative for this, without taking unnecessary risks at the start of the process by following a step-by-step method which includes:

1. Bringing the participants together and elaborating a first agreement of co-operation (intention to participate);
2. Developing a physical plan for the establishment of the professional branches with higher potential in a combined location in LSE, with the corresponding infrastructure and environmental protection measures;
3. Calculating the probable expenses (the purchase of the land, the deployment of infrastructure) and incomes (by selling the plots);
4. Making a definitive agreement of co-operation, and fixing the contributions of the different participants in the exploitation and the formal start of the partnership project;
5. Commonly requesting subsidies from the state and foreign donor agencies;
6. Executing land development.

Carrying out these steps can be foreseen during 2007, but there are some limitations. The main problem has a political character, while the absence of local commitment is another discouraging aspect. But the local and regional potentials are very promising and may represent the start of a new perspective.

Developing local knowledge

The municipal role in housing and planning has gradually changed from an executing role to a policy making and facilitating one. Strengthening local government can be done with concrete project support, as it is done with the LSE Plots Program for Housing. The stimulation of self-help housing and other self-help activities, together with the promotion of public-private partnerships, is a fundamental activity of the municipality. The present land policy for housing and the future public-private land policy must be explored in order to stimulate the local and regional economy. The management of participative land developments can be improved by training the managers of local government. Training of private actors and associations with public-private developing processes is also important, in order to improve their business management and their abilities to co-operate with private as well as public partners.

Knowledge development in municipal organizations

The training of municipal managers should be directed at the two earlier mentioned levels of planning and execution: (1) city/region and (2) neighborhood/project. At city level training should include the development of an integrated vision for the future. Given such a vision, the different municipal sectors can receive adequate steering, while priorities can be determined and projects and investments at the neighborhood or project level can be legalized. Therefore, knowledge development within the municipal organization is crucial for the achievement of the main goals of urban planning.

Knowledge development of inhabitants, entrepreneurs and associations

An adequate positioning of self-help concepts in urban planning implies the need for the training and education of households, groups and associations. This is the case with people willing to work in the construction of houses and houses with a workshop. People working in self-help housing and getting professional training simultaneously can improve their position in the labor market, especially in the construction sector (Illustration 9.7). The sector of professional education could offer an intelligent match in this process.

Furthermore, the management of small businesses and associations can be improved with adequate training; they can be assisted to improve their product and marketing, as well as with the introduction of modern managerial skills. People willing to start a small trade need to follow courses in bookkeeping and business administration. Local professional education could play a role in this process. *The Escuela Taller* (technical school) in León is offering courses for construction skills. The technical school La Salle stimulates innovative technical designs of students, which can also be used in the field of self-help housing. The local school for tourism is training young people to improve tourist services in hotels, restaurants and recreational facilities.

Illustration 9.7: Young people at work, constructing a community center in León South East (Photo: Desiree van de Ven)

Final recommendations

Looking back at the hopeful results of the LSE Plots Program, it becomes clear that the continuation of this program is necessary in order to develop the city in a proper way, providing new perspectives to households and entrepreneurs, while using their social and economic potentials.

LSE Plots Program and civil society

The LSE Plots Program has been the developing motor of the South East expansion of the city of León. It stimulates inhabitants, entrepreneurs, companies and NGOs to contribute to the construction of houses and the development of new communities. As a result of the mentioned program, illegal land occupations are no longer common. After 2008, the Plots Program (1998-2008) may act as an independent program, benefiting from the revolving fund and international experiences with city-links.

Establishing good co-operation between all parties and groups within the LSE *urbanizaciones* is a main goal of urban management. Social development processes are still going on in the LSE neighborhoods and urban management authorities are willing to facilitate bottom-up community development in these areas. The social and economic potentials of the growing LSE communities are increasingly visible.

Public-private partnership for economic projects

The existing Plots Program for housing has offered a positive development model during past years, under circumstances in which the local authorities were able to purchase land for land developments. However, the present circumstances are changing, since private landowners are not always willing to sell land to the municipality, a fact which implies a major change in the involvement of landowners and developers. There is also a trend toward higher prices for the purchase of land for urban development. Public-private partnerships for land development, with purposes of both housing and economic development, are considered indispensable in view of the increased legal difficulties of land expropriation for these goals.

Public-private partnerships are even more important in order to develop land for exclusively economic activities, since it demands larger investments for the purchase of land and the development of infrastructure. This means that a vast area must be reserved and equipped within the LSE district. This process requires a close co-operation between the interested parties and all participants must be involved from the initial phase onwards. New forms of co-operation require good urban management on different levels. Associations may form a very important factor in economic development in León and therefore they must be stimulated by all possible means. This Chapter has presented a model for the participation of the several actors in process of urban development of León and for the step-by-step method.

Knowledge development and social emancipation

Municipal management in León has been developing at the two levels described above. The *Comité de Desarrollo Municipal*, which functions at the highest municipal level, is very significant for the integration of the interests of local communities, working associations and businesses. The improvement of the municipal organization to work in a more professional manner is considered crucial. The social emancipation of inhabitants, small entrepreneurs and other population groups through knowledge development is closely connected with the actual needs and can bring social and economic emancipation closer.

Final Analysis

After presenting the main features of the recent activities and processes of urban development in León, the overall conclusion is that existing self-help and self-organization activities have great importance in city life, and that the LSE development program can be considered effective in achieving its goals. Economic development, however, does not have strong foundations and concrete results are presently lacking. The municipal government should try to bring all actors together for the development of new industrial and business areas, for which LSE offers good spatial potential. Nevertheless, it becomes clear that there is not a firm enough foundation for a strong and endogenous process of economic development. The challenge for the municipality is to make a break-through in this bottleneck bringing all participants together to initiate an area-focused economic project using all combined efforts.

References

Bontebal, M. & P. van Lindert, 2006, *Development Matters; Decentralised International Cooperation: North-South Municipal Partnerships*, Faculty of Geosciences, Utrecht University (Neth.).
Bredenoord, J., 2005, *Urban Development Strategies in León Nicaragua*, Dutch University Press, Amsterdam.
Government of Nicaragua, 2003, *Plan Nacional de Desarrollo*, Managua.
Government of Nicaragua, 2005, *Plan Nacional de Vivienda*, Managua.
López, E., 2000, *Análisis de proyectos de vivienda urbana 1980-2000 en el municipio de León*, FLACSO, Costa Rica and León, Nicaragua.
Municipality of León, 2004, *Plan Estratégico de Desarrollo Municipal* (PEDM), León.
Municipality of León, 2005, *Plan Económico de Desarrollo Urbano (PEDU)*, León.
Municipality of León & Cooperación Española, 1999, *Plan Estratégico de León*, León.
United Nations, 1992, *The Local agenda 21*, Rio de Janeiro.

Notes

1   The 'León South East Plots Programme 1998-2008 of the Municipality of León' is the English designation by the author of a series of (informal) documents, like project proposals and annual reports, all in Spanish some in Dutch, all well-known through the Municipality of León, and in The Netherlands through the Municipality of Utrecht and the Association of Netherlands Municipalities (VNG, in The Hague). See for more information: http//:www.utrecht.nl/international and http//:www.alcadiadeleon.gob.ni.

2   For a description of the urban development process of León since 1990, Bredenoord (2005).

3   The city to city co-operation Utrecht-León has been described by Bontebal and Van Lindert (2006: 301-314). The León South East Programme was nominated in 2005 for the Euro Cities Award as a good example for North-South city to city co-operation.

10 Battling the Digital Divide from the Bottom-up in Lima, Peru

Ana María Fernández-Maldonado

Introduction

Thousands of commercial cybercafés - the so-called *cabinas públicas de Internet* - have emerged since 1998 in cities and villages in Peru, without any support from the state, non-governmental organizations (NGOs) or private firms. *Cabinas* have been the fruit of local economic and cultural practices in combination with the availability of networks due to the modernization and extension of the telecommunications infrastructures. Habitually used by adolescents and young adults, *cabinas* have produced the democratization of access to computers and Internet in Peruvian cities. Thanks to them, many people from the lower-income groups of society are benefiting from cheap and widespread access to Information and Communication Technology (ICT) connectivity. Despite the restrictions of poverty and low levels of telephone penetration, Peru ranks among the leading countries in Latin America in terms of the percentage of Internet users. In December 2005 there were more than 33 thousand *cabinas* providing Internet service in Peru (OSIPTEL, 2007). In March 2007, 42.11 percent of Peruvian households had at least one member who connected to Internet in *cabinas,* while only 4.64 percent of households had home Internet (INEI, 2007).

The objective of this Chapter is to describe the peculiar features of the emergence of *cabinas* in Peru's capital city, Lima, illustrating their potential to battle the digital divide. To understand this situation one has to be aware of the urban dynamics operating in Peruvian cities, in this case in Lima. The Chapter begins with a brief description of the urban and socio-cultural setting of Lima, followed by an analysis of the recent transformations in the field of telecommunications in the next Section. The focus of the third Section is the use of Internet in Lima and how it affects the different population groups, with special emphasis on the youth and low-income residents. The fourth and last Section discusses the social innovative character of these developments.

Main features of urban development in Lima

Since its Spanish foundation in 1535 until the first decades of the twentieth century, the capital of Peru grew at a very stable and slow pace. Since the 1940s, a demographic transition process began to affect Peru, producing a drastic reduction in mortality and accelerating population growth. An immense migration stream coming from rural areas in the Andes headed to Lima. Since the migrants were unable to find a place in the job market, informal settlements – called in Peru *barriadas* – began to form in the hills at the periphery of the city since 1958.

During the last fifty years, Lima's main way of urban development has been the *barriadas*, which can be considered as the fruit of the indifference of the state for social concerns on the one hand, and the initiative of the population to find an own solution to their main needs, on the other. This has been interpreted as an 'implicit agreement' between the state and the poor, which is functioning in Lima since the emergence of peripheral *barriadas* in the late 1950s. In this pragmatic arrangement, the state does not spend its few resources in providing the habitat for the poor, and can address its investments to more productive ends. In return, the poor are given land titles and a free hand to build their habitat at their own pace and taste.

As a result of five decades of urban *laissez-faire*, the poor have a great deal of experience in informal entrepreneurship. They have not done it so bad; regarding housing, *barriadas* have produced a positive regard in the eyes of their own residents and urban researchers: Lima is known in the urban literature as the city of *barriadas*. They have been praised by the level of organization of the residents to build their neighborhoods and the individual effort to gradually build their own dwellings. *Barriadas* inspired John F. Turner and W. Mangin (1968) for a pragmatic approach – the so-called self-help – to housing for the poor.

Informal economic activities, widely present in Lima, have also inspired a new economic paradigm, a second 'pragmatic' approach, this time for economic development. In this approach, the capacities of the poor for generating new urban jobs and improve their own livability have been highlighted. The informal sector has been advocated by Hernando de Soto as the 'Other Path' - referring to the Shining Path - for local economic growth (De Soto, 1986).

Informal entrepreneurship has also taken the lead in a vital urban sector as public transportation.[1] In 1990, public transportation was left completely in the hands of 'the free market', without any regulation. Since then, Lima is the only Latin American capital city that does not have an organized system for public transportation. As public transportation is not profitable enough for formal businesses, the informal sector has taken over this task, in such a way that urban chaos and congestion have increased. This seems to be the fate of Lima: due to the lack of government initiative, only the informal sector seems able to provide some of the services residents need at affordable prices.

In the 1990s the informal sector entered into the ICT business with relative success and now has an important role. Retailing in ICT-related products, renting computers and peripherals, and providing informal computing services were part of the initial trade. Offering more affordable prices, the informal sector currently provides ICT hardware, software and services to a good percentage of institutions and businesses of the formal sector of the economy, as well as individual users.

In July 1990, and after a decade of great political instability and deep economic crisis, the government applied a 'shock therapy' to stabilize and restructure the economy. Processes of privatization and deregulation were launched and the largest public enterprises were sold, mainly to foreign corporations. These structural changes had profound spatial and functional effects in the city. The traditional local commercial, financial and real-estate groups have been weakened and replaced by foreign firms and economic groups, which have pumped huge capital into new projects, in an order of magnitude that has no equivalent in the history of Lima, with the exception of the 1920s (Ludeña, 2001). The main changes in Lima's functioning affected four main groups of urban activities: information-intensive functions, industrial functions, cultural and entertainment functions, and commercial functions (Chion, 2002).

In Lima's new urban context, telecommunications and 'advanced' economic sectors have become important new urban agents. New nodes and centralities have emerged in different points of the city while the Central Business District has moved from its original location in the city center to San

Isidro, a high income area well-connected with the city center. Shopping malls, private complexes and recreational facilities for the higher income groups have been recently built taking the form of 'islands of modernity' close to road infrastructures. These consumption and entertainment centers have not been limited to the districts of modern Lima, but also been built in popular peripheral districts, in a trend that suggests the desire of the masses to participate as consumers in the 'global way of life'.

The 'new Lima' is more complex and contradictory than ever before. The dichotomy between the formal/informal or rich/poor sides of the city that became so evident during the 1980s is, by far, inadequate to describe Lima's multiple contradictions. Ludeña (2001:17) describes the changes as a "contradictory process of democratization and social exclusion in the use and development of the urban space." Lima presents exceptional features that are not easily seen elsewhere. The elite have not moved from their traditional quarters and Lima has not developed 'fortified enclaves', while an important share of the new urban facilities has been located outside the traditional prestigious locations to attend the demand of the 'new' consumers living in peripheral *barriadas*. It is in this context that the telecommunications revolution has affected the city, where a real Internet boom has been experienced in an incredibly short period. "Lima emerges in the year 2000 plagued with cabinas públicas, cybercafés and cybershops" (El Comercio y Apoyo, 2002: 214).

The privatized telecommunications sector

Internet service provision is a segment of the telecommunications sector which emerged and became commercial during the 1990s. In most Latin American countries the role of the state in this sector is limited to the regulation to promote free competition. In Peru, the two state-owned telephone companies were sold to Telefónica de España in 1994, which agreed to invest to expand and improve the networks with the condition of a period of five years of 'restricted competition'. When the two companies were joined together, Telefónica became the largest company in the country, the one with the greater assets and higher revenues.

The modernization and expansion of the networks that followed the privatization resulted in a sharp increase of fixed monthly access charges. Telephonic diffusion and service quality has greatly improved since then, because the contract with Telefónica obliges this firm to modernize the networks and to provide the service to any household that asks for it inside the city. However, after three years of large growth right after the privatization, fixed lines showed very little increase due to the high monthly charges. Since December 2005, the penetration of fixed telephony in households of Lima has decreased 7.52 percent (INEI, 2007). In March 2007, the rate of teledensity for fixed telephony in Peru was 8.76 (OSIPTEL, 2007) which represents less than half of teledensity rates in the largest countries of the region. Only Cuba, Haiti, Honduras and Nicaragua have lower rates. On the other hand, mobile telephony shows a sustained growth and has greatly contributed to the increase of the total teledensity. In March 2007, there were 35.67 mobile telephones per hundred inhabitants in Peru (OSIPTEL, 2007). [2]

Despite the huge technical improvements, the telecommunication sector is characterized by low levels of competition and the strong domination of Telefónica in most segments, and especially in the basic services. The regulatory frame and the regulatory body for telecommunications (OSIPTEL) have been ineffective in promoting competition, for several reasons. On the one hand, the decision to sell the two telephone companies to one firm, which eventually grouped the two original companies in one, was not wise for the sake of competition. Additionally, Telefónica International increased its participation in Telefónica del Peru from 35 percent to 97.1 percent by means of an aggressive financial operation (the so-called *operación Verónica*) to buy Telefónica shares in the New York and Lima stock markets, executed in 2000 (Rozas, 2003).

On the other hand, as in other countries where Telefónica has bought the former monopolies, the firm has taken advantage of its initial monopolist position to diversify its operations into new business ICT-related areas. This has promoted "a process of entrepreneurial concentration – by means of fusions, acquisitions and strategic alliances – without precedent, given its magnitude and nature" (Rozas, 2003:92) in the region, which is highly visible in Peru. The Telefónica group has in Peru twenty one enterprises, including commercial services, publicity, editorial services, digital services, data services, technical services, global communications, financial services, message services, international backbone service (Emergia), and call centers (Atento). In all of them Telefónica had a 100 percent participation, with the exception of Telefónica del Peru and Telefónica Data Peru, with 97.1 percent of participation (Rozas, 2003).

The presence and dominance of the Telefónica group in Peru is higher than in other countries of the region. As owner of the basic networks, Telefónica evidently has a firm control of fixed telephony, with 98.95 percent of the market. In mobile telephony, traditionally a sector with higher levels of competition, Telefónica operated 56.9 percent of the 9.8 million subscriptions in March 2007. Besides basic services and mobile services, this firm also dominates other important segments: public telephony (90.1 percent in March 2006), Internet service provision in *cabinas públicas* (60 percent of the market in December 2002); renting of local, national and international backbone circuits [3] (85.2 percent, 87.41 percent and 57.74 percent, respectively, in June 2003); and cable TV (94.8 percent of the market in June 2005) (OSIPTEL, 2007). Furthermore, Telefónica dominates another highly competitive sector, Internet service provision.

Even if Internet connectivity, basic telephony and Asymmetric Digital Subscriber Line (ADSL) broadband services are available in the whole city, effective access is constrained by the high prices of telecommunications services, the most expensive of Latin America. With such prices, it is no surprise that Peruvian teledensity is still one of the lowest in Latin America. Therefore, the privatization of the telecommunication networks in Lima has improved the service and the diffusion compared to the previous levels, but produced a virtual monopoly of Telefónica, even in those sectors that are traditionally subject to higher levels of competition such as mobile telephony and Internet provision.

The dominance of Telefónica is translated in a policy of monthly charges that perpetuates the traditional socio-economic polarization circumstances of the city, favoring the richer groups and penalizing the poor, which have to opt for out-of-the-home schemes to get telecommunication services. Torero, Schroth and Pascó-Font (2003) analyzed the impact of the new telecommunications on the welfare of urban consumers, elucidating how the new structure of tariffs with high fixed monthly charges has favoured those users with high consumption habits, in other words, the more affluent groups. For middle-income households, the monthly payment of the telephone charges is generally a monthly worry. Disaggregating access figures by socio-economic level, poor users (low and very-low income sectors) are worse-off, particularly the very-low income sector, for whom access is more difficult to reach than before privatization. Since people in the bottom two socio-economic categories make up the majority of Lima's inhabitants, public dissatisfaction with the telephone charges does not seem so paradoxical.

Main features of Internet use in Lima.

Since home telephone and Internet connection is so expensive, eight out of ten Peruvian Internet users go regularly to *cabinas* to connect to the Internet (INEI, 2007), paying an average of US$ 0.35 for one hour of Internet connection, which decreases to US$ 0.25 in lower income areas. According to an estimation of OSIPTEL, there were more than six thousand *cabinas* in Lima in 2005 (San Román, 2005) and 33 thousand in Peru in December 2005 (OSIPTEL, 2007). Illustration 10.1 showing the main places of Internet access (not exclusive) for users in Metropolitan Lima in 2004, reveals where Internet users access the net. As a comparison,[4] Illustration 10.1 also shows the main places of connection to Internet in Lima and in Mexican cities in 2004.

	Lima	Mexican cities
Cabinas / cybercafés	88 percent of users	37 percent of users
Home	14 percent	78 percent
Workplace	12 percent	62 percent
School / University	10 percent	26 percent
Relative or friend's home	7 percent	14 percent

Illustration 10.1: Places of connection to Internet in Lima and in Mexican cities in 2004 (Source: Apoyo, 2004; AMIPCI, 2005)

Internet use out-of-the-home is, however, more difficult to measure than Internet use at home and work. The best way to get a good picture of the total use of Internet - in the case that most people use collective facilities to access the net - is through home surveys. The National Institute of Statistics (INEI) carries out home surveys[5] every three months, with the purpose of monitoring the use of ICTs and Internet use at home and outside-the-home. According to the last survey (March 2007) 21.37 percent of Peruvians older than 6 years old connects to the Internet in *cabinas*, while in Metropolitan Lima, the proportion rises to 29.76 percent. On the other hand, the proportion of households with home Internet connection in the whole country is 4.64 percent, while in Lima it is 10.82 percent (INEI, 2007). Illustration 10.2 shows the difference between the proportion of home connections and total Internet use according to socio-economic sector among the population from 8 to 70 years old in 2004.

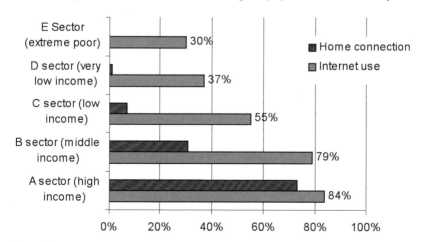

Illustration 10.2: Internet use and home connection according to socio-economic sectors in Metropolitan Lima in 2004 (Source: Apoyo, 2004).

The proportion of Internet users in 2004 showed in Illustration 10.2 also reveals high levels of use in low- and very low-income sectors, in proportions that are remarkably higher than in other cities of the developing world. A high level of use in the low-income sectors is precisely the strength of the Peruvian experience, a process that would be unthinkable without the proliferation of Internet *cabinas*. They constitute a social innovative process established by informal entrepreneurs and geared toward the local (deprived) groups. Thanks to their sustained growth, most of the growth of Internet use during the last years comes from the most vulnerable sectors, as shown in Illustration 10.3 for the 2003-2004 period.

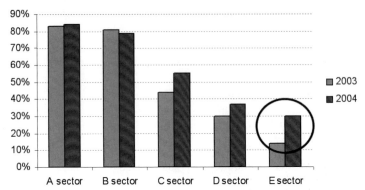

Illustration 10.3: Growth of Internet use according to socio-economic sectors in Metropolitan Lima, 2003-2004 (Source: Apoyo, 2004)

An important feature of Internet use in Peru is that it is mainly an affair of the youth, as Illustration 10.4 shows. The figure also indicates that digital differences in Peru are a matter of age but not of gender. The greater presence of women using Internet in *cabinas* is especially seen in the 12-18 year old and the 19-24 year old groups. They coincide with the groups that attend the secondary school and university, respectively.

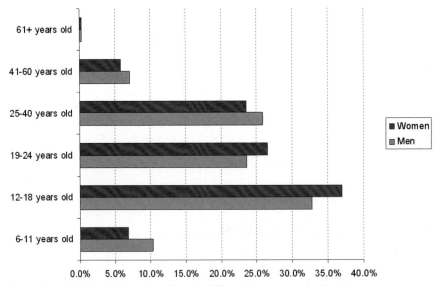

Illustration 10.4: Internet use in *cabinas* in different age groups in Peru in 2007 (Source: INEI, 2007)

In Lima, the youth of the users is also striking, as Illustration 10.5 shows, but the average levels of penetration are higher than in the whole country. Studies on Internet use in Lima have found that children of higher income households begin to use computers at the age of 5 or 6 since they generally have home connection, or of 9 or 10 in *cabinas*, when they do not have it (Quiroz, 2004). The generational gap is clearer in households of lower income sectors, in which the children and teenagers are the ones who have the most advanced skills to use electronic communication and to surf the Net. A simple visit to the *cabinas* will be useful to acknowledge the young age of most of the users.

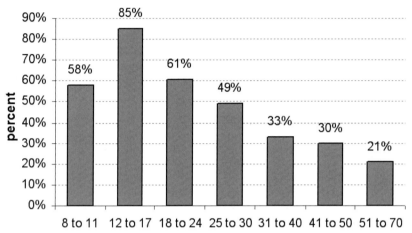

Illustration 10.5: Internet use in different age groups in Metropolitan Lima in 2004 (Source: Apoyo, 2004)

The main uses of Internet are evidently very much related to the young age of the users: communications, education and entertainment. *Cabinas* are clearly geared to students and there is a clear increase of concentration of *cabinas* close to educational institutions. Children and youth are fascinated with the Internet, due to its multifunctional use and its symbolic value. Computers and the Internet are considered by people as modern and therefore highly valuable. Studies about Internet use in youth in Lima (Quiroz, 2004; Colona, 2003) have identified that Internet is widely considered a medium for individual progress in the difficult and competitive world of today. Due to this notion, parents and educators of all sectors encourage the use of computers. The high affinity of the general population with the new technologies seems to have been promoted by the widespread aspirations regarding education as a tool for upward mobility.

The effect of the presence of *cabinas* is visible in the Peruvian society. *Cabinas* have become a familiar urban facility at neighborhood level. Users, especially the youth and those from popular low-income sectors, say that Internet use is effectively improving their daily lives. The use of computers and Internet by school and university students has become common. Teachers express the opinion that the use of computers by students is improving the quality of education. Peruvians have changed their recreation habits and since 2002 the visit to the *cabina* has become the main recreation activity. In addition, Peruvians have much better communication with their relatives abroad than before, which has increased the level of remittances to the country. At city level, *cabinas* offer a series of urban services that have been systematically denied to poor neighborhoods. The services provided by libraries, post offices, recreation facilities, study places, youth centers, training centers, and other similar facilities that have been always lacking in informal neighborhoods are now offered online in the *cabinas*. Despite of the importance of this topic for the decrease of vulnerability or deprivation at neighborhood level, no studies have been done yet (Fernández-Maldonado, 2004).

Cabinas are mostly informal businesses and as such they are not registered in public institutions, and do not pay taxes regularly (only local taxes). They are generally family businesses established without high investments, which do not get enough profits to 'formalize' the business. Their monthly income is usually only enough to pay the costs and provide the family income. Due to the little economic accumulation, they do not generally provide the best quality services. Evidently, collective access is fine for young people without great responsibilities, but it is not the best technical environment for sophisticated or specialized uses. Although there are some *cabinas* with more specialized equipment and possibilities, most users simply go to the nearest *cabina* not far from home. The place of access determines the limits of Internet use, and in the case of Lima's *cabinas*, their thresholds are very low. If we take into consideration the recent telecommunication trends at global level in developed countries, we can see that most of them (very high-speed broadband, WiFi, mobile Internet, etc.) are not applicable for those who access the Internet in collective places. This informal initiative for Internet access of people without home connection is, therefore, an uncomplicated answer to the current demand.

Recently, public and private institutions have understood the fundamental importance of the *cabinas* as providers of ICT connectivity and are beginning to implement different programs to use them as a bridge between citizens and government or institutions. Different networks of *cabinas* are currently promoting e-government activities, payment of taxes and fines, and facilitating the use of Internet by Small and Medium Enterprises (SMEs). *Cabinas* have become a topic of high interest for the general population. Peruvians are proud of the *cabinas*, which they consider a national product.[6]

The diffusion of Internet to the masses has not been a matter of great government concerns. Despite that the International Telecommunications Union has presented Peru as a good practice example in terms of telecommunication policies, the view from the inside out is that the Peruvian state has done surprisingly little to promote universal access to ICTs. The only exception is FITEL, a fund for rural connectivity established with the Telecommunications Law in 1994, which is in fact a tax from 1 percent of telecommunications revenues. On the other hand, the different public administrations have not done much to promote technological innovation, the generation of local knowledge, or, more importantly, to develop a vision to guide Peru's transition to the Information Society.

Internet and youth in Lima

Surveys and simple observations in *cabinas* in Lima have been useful to document and give to a good general picture of how much Internet use in Lima is dominated by young users. The mainstream Internet culture in Lima is very much a youth culture, but also a popular culture, since in absolute numbers most users belong to popular sectors. To better understand its background it is relevant to provide a picture of the circumstances of today's youth, guided by the interpretation of distinguished thinkers of Latin American cultural studies.

Demographic processes have made Lima a city with high proportion of young people. The period of explosive urbanization has already been passed and the natural growth rate has decreased along with fertility rates.[7] As a result of these changes, the share of young people in the working age has increased markedly, but not the jobs. If in the 1980s it was difficult to find a formal job for young people, it is now even more difficult than before. The second of third generation of migrants is now urban and educated, but still cannot find an adequate place in the job market so they see their future opportunities as dim.

Their virtual exclusion from regular and formal work has great effects in all other aspects of their daily life. Most of these trends are not exclusive of Peru or Lima, but are common to other Latin American realities. However, since Peru's economic and employment troubles have been deeper, the resulting trends have been more dramatic and affected the whole society. In all the processes mentioned here, with the exception of social and political violence, computers and Internet play an important role.

1. Emigration to the US, and in lesser extent to Europe or other countries in the region (Venezuela, Argentina, Chile and Brazil), has been one of the ways out to fight unemployment and the lack of economic opportunities, not only in low-income sectors, but also in the middle-income sectors. Surveys have given worrying high percentages of the will to emigrate among youth groups.[8] Despite the great difficulties to get a visa, there are approximately two and a half million Peruvians abroad, approximately 10 percent of the total population of the country. 43 percent of residents of Lima declares to have a close relative living abroad (Universidad de Lima, 2005). Most of them are young people who emigrated during the 1990s. It is estimated that one in five households living in informal settlements of Lima receive foreign remittances.[9] Communication with close relatives living abroad is actually an important reason for older adults to learn how to use the Internet. In the meantime, the younger members of the family are in charge of the indirect online communication.

2. Increased education and training to better compete in the employment market has been another frequent strategy of the youth. It is now not enough to complete a university study to find a proper job in Lima. Due to the large demand for formal employment, post-graduate and specialization studies are now considered indispensable. People with higher resources are increasingly following post-graduate studies to increase their chances to get the few well-paid jobs. Since the 1990s, there is a flourishing business sector providing education and training to young people of all sectors of society. Not only very expensive private universities have proliferated, but also thousands of 'technical' institutes (of doubtful quality) that provide (short) evening courses for those who cannot afford expensive studies. From the latter, computing courses are the most popular, since computing skills are regarded as essential for getting a job. It is within this business sector that provides services to students that the first *cabinas* emerged in the late 1980s, when they only offered computers to rent.

All this is supported by the belief that education is the best investment for upward mobility. There is also a clear relationship between the use of new technologies, educational values, and aspirations of progress, in which computers and the Internet are seen as a way toward modernity. In most surveys conducted since the rise of the Internet in Lima users mention school and academic motives as important motives to use the Internet (Fernández-Maldonado, 2004). A slight decrease in Internet use is measured during months with (summer and mid-winter) holiday periods, which suggests the use of Internet by youth for educational purposes (INEI, 2007).

3. The retreat of youngsters into blasé and individualistic attitudes, and a striking indifference toward political participation are also related processes. In Lima this can be linked to internal circumstances: today's youth was raised in the middle of political violence and witnessed the failure of the state to impose the rule of law during almost a decade. However, this is also a Latin American trend. In *Consumers and Citizens*, García Canclini (1995) has lucidly explained why these processes arise: the exercise of citizenship rights has been displaced from political participation to consumption practices, something which is especially valid for young people. He adds that (young) people perceive that some aspects of citizenship, as where do I belong or who represents my interests, are better answered in the private consumption of commodities and mass media, than within

the abstract rules of democracy or participation in political parties or unions. The re-structuring of the public sphere originated by the new role of electronic media partly explains these huge transformations.

The new consumption practices that replace the traditional citizenship practices are satisfied through mass and communication media rather than through the *material* consumption of commodities, due to the economic troubles of great part of urban residents. There is an increase of the gap between material aspirations and consumption possibilities, which is evident in the case of Lima, where the proportion of television sets per inhabitant during the dramatic 1980s increased up to 95 percent of households. If almost all people, poor and rich, currently have access to television broadcasting, this means that there is a wide access to symbolic consumption. The combination of higher symbolic consumption and less material consumption that is present in low-income groups is obviously highly frustrating for the youth and may end up in explosions of violence.

Hopenhayn (2004) has enumerated several contradictions of being young in Latin America. Today's youth has a higher access to information than before and less to power, a higher access to education and less to employment, it has more skills for living an autonomous life but fewer possibilities to materialize it. "Urban youth from popular sectors suffers this gap with increased strength: they have, in average, three more years of education than their parents and therefore more potential productivity; they have socialized with the media cultural industry since they were children; but they experience three or four times higher unemployment than the older generations, they are stigmatized by the society as possible delinquent, they do not achieve economic or housing autonomy and their expectations grow with the same intensity than their frustrations." (Hopenhayn, 2003:301).

4 The lack of economic prospects of the youth has also resulted in the increase of crime and in processes of political violence, which were clearly seen in Peru during the period of deep economic recession of the Peruvian economy. Youth is more easily associated with violent attitudes and political insurgence than the rest of population groups, while at the same time it is the main victim of acts of violence. The features of youth-related violence have been so perturbing that they have become an important topic in the local social sciences during the 1990s. Processes of social violence as by the *barras bravas* (groups of hooligans) or urban gangs have received attention, but it was political violence, which increased to unforeseen limits, that constituted the main societal worry.

Huge frustrations resulting from the clash between aspirations toward a certain quality of life and daily realities in Peru's (young, educated and impoverishing) population is considered also as one of the factors that produced the emergence of insurgence movements that led to the most intense, extensive and prolonged internal armed conflict in Peru's history, according to the Truth and Reconciliation Commission (2003). The conflict, which affected Peru since the early 1980s, escalated until Lima became the main scene of the political struggle, between 1989 and 1992. While the Shining Path consolidated a significant presence within youth groups of popular sectors in Lima during this period, a huge wave of terrorist acts, some of them of extreme violence and cruelty, traumatized the population. Shining Path's cadres and main followers were young university or school students of Andean origin, frustrated in their aspirations for upward mobility (Truth and Reconciliation Commission, 2003).

5 Finally, another response to the youth troubles is the huge empathy of young people with the technological culture. Thanks to their great affinity with the new technologies, the Internet provides the (low-income) youth with easy communication and entertainment along with the feeling of being part of the global culture. The eagerness of today's youth to consume global flows has a wide

scope and begins with the incredible amount of information they get from television flows, up to the skills they rapidly and easily get in their relation with electronic networks and equipment.[10] The adoption of the new technologies is considered a matter of status, as surveys of young people in Lima reveal (Quiroz, 2004; Colona, 2003). ICTs are widely considered as positive, both materially and symbolically.

Martín Barbero (2002:5) has pointed out that this technological empathy is the fruit of a new sensitivity, which has cognitive and expressive elements that differ from the traditional culture, and whose subjects exist in base of their connection/disconnection to electronic devices. He also explains the transformations of the youth's sensitivity through the deep reorganization of traditional socialization patterns of young people. Parents are not any more the models of behavior; the school is not any more the only legitimate place to get access to knowledge; nor is the book the organizing center of culture. He adds that the 'cultural mix-up' of today's youth better expresses the struggles of our change of age, rather than the works of art or the intellectual discourses (Martín Barbero, 2002:4)

It is quite remarkable that the same group, young - university or school - students of Andean origin, who in the 1980s and early 1990s resorted to political violence as an expression of their personal and collective frustrations and hopelessness, are now opting for the connection to global networks as a way out of these same frustrations. For the youth the Internet represents a direct way to connect to 'modernity', to virtually participate in the more advanced part of the world, which for them has more to offer than real life in a mega city of the Third World. In other words, Internet is seen as a huge window to the world which can open new possibilities for them. Unlike broadcasting media, Internet provides real possibilities to interact at global level. Currently, this is more a possibility than a reality, but the fact that this new resource is available does provide people with hope for future personal success. While providing entertainment, information and cheap communication, Internet is providing hope for the future, especially for the youth.

Significance of Internet use in low-income groups

Evidently, the broad availability of Internet access is not in itself a positive condition, but the familiarity with ICTs that this is bringing to the general public and especially children and youth, opens up many possibilities for future. There are no depth-in studies of the consequences of Internet use in the lives of users in Peru. Most surveys establish that users, especially the youth and people from lower-income sectors, express that Internet use is effectively improving their daily lives. It is clear, however, that the effects of the broad access to computers and the Internet have not yet been remarkable for the improvement of the local economy, but they are significant regarding social and cultural aspects.

In her survey on Internet users in 2002 Colona (2003) included specific questions about the meaning of Internet. The answers revealed that (young) users think that accessing the Internet they are partly appropriating a 'global lifestyle', synonymous with progress and modernity. Similar strong links between Internet and modernity were also clearly expressed when she interviewed *cabineros* (administrators of *cabinas*). Colona also identified that for some users Internet represents a space of freedom, a source of endless information, which provide opportunities to intervene globally and in this way it empowers them. These results constitute no surprise, since most people in Peru have the notion that using computers is a modern and forward-looking attitude.

Two very clear profiles of Internet users come forward from the surveys and observations of Internet use in Lima. For the elite and upper-middle class, the new technologies have rapidly become part of their work, school and daily life. These are experienced and sophisticated users of all ages, who have enthusiastically and rapidly embraced ICTs, Internet and electronic devices as a means for improving the comfort, security and autonomy of their everyday life, using them for rapid communication, information, entertainment, co-ordination, security and the individual management of their activities in space and time. Internet use in these groups shows similar features as those observed in countries of the North.

For lower-income users Internet use is quite different, starting with the lack of a home connection. Low-income users are less sophisticated, and their experience with Internet is more recent and less frequent, since their scarce income limits Internet use. Access to the global networks, however, constitutes a crucial asset for improving their standard of living, since computers and Internet provide a series of basic services and functions that are generally lacking in the informal neighborhoods, as post offices, libraries, recreation facilities, study places, youth centers, information centers, among others.

The introduction of Internet in everyday life, then, has more significance for the vulnerable and deprived than for the affluent groups. If for the affluent the Internet is a technological innovation that is complementing or gradually replacing existing telecommunication media, such as telegraph, traditional mail, fax, and local or long-distance telephone, for vulnerable groups access to the Internet makes a big difference. It provides means for communication for people who previously could not contact who were distant from them, because of the absence, scarcity, inefficiency, or non-affordability of traditional communication services. In this way Internet opens up a new world that was previously out of reach. More than making telecommunication easier, Internet is making telecommunication and information *possible* for vulnerable and deprived groups.

Internet and its applications- chat, instant messaging and email communication - are gradually transforming the way low-income people, and especially the youth, get in contact and socialize. A recent study on Internet and youth in Lima (Quiroz, 2004) has identified that it is precisely the low-income youth, who is more inclined to be in online contact with people from different social circles and distant places, while the children of the elite are less eager to have online contact with outsiders. They are reproducing the exclusionary trends of high-income groups that are collectively expressed in the proliferation of gated and private neighborhoods.

Thanks to the common language there is also a more intense online exchange at Latin American level, which is placing young users closer to each other and promoting relationships among them. Trans-cultural flows allowed by global electronic communication, as the apparently unproductive online chat, are slowly, but surely influencing identity building, opinions and beliefs, especially in youth groups, the most frequent consumers of cultural goods. Online chat, participation in transnational communities, consumption of both global and local cultural flows by Internet, radio and television, etc., are promoting the transcendence of locally-grounded identities and habits.

On the other hand, since an important part of online content is produced by global entertainment firms and commercial conglomerates interested in the permanence of the *status quo*, Internet flows are also supporting and promoting conventional views and a commercial and superficial culture. As many Internet researchers have noted, all these novel processes and trends are almost impossible to quantify and measure with precision. It is obvious that Internet use is so recent, especially in the case of people belonging to lower income sectors, that its (sweet or sour) fruits will become clear when this generation turns into adulthood.

Concluding remarks: *Cabinas* as an example of social innovation

The experience of Internet use in Lima shows that an important part of the development of ICTs, its diffusion to the masses, takes place under the three features that characterize Lima's current urban situation: the lack of leadership and indifference of the government toward the social needs of the most vulnerable and deprived population groups, the economic dominance of large (foreign) corporations and the initiative of the lower-income groups to find an 'informal' solution to their needs. This sort of bottom-up initiatives has not been uncommon in Lima, since the explosive growth of *barriadas* during the 1960s and 1970s. Local entrepreneurs have established different types of informal businesses according to the local needs. In these times of global communication, they have managed to give an answer to the demand for communications of low-income groups, which is generally neglected in view of the few revenues it brings. These informal businesses are slowly but gradually contributing to social development in different ways.

(a) *Cabinas* are providing online services to sub-standard neighborhoods. When ICT networks are available in informal settlements and neighborhoods, they are providing urban services that have been absent in these areas. *Cabinas* have become the postal service, telephone system, entertainment and information centers, and the libraries of the digital age. Even if these new services are provided in a different form from traditional urban services – online - they do make a great difference in the lives of low-income users.

(b) The increased online communication between people and their relatives abroad is helping to reverse poverty trends. Money flows from international migrants to their relatives in Peru have increased greatly during the latest years, in a process that has been related to increased communication between people. Many Peruvians of low-income sectors are receiving money from relatives working abroad. In this way, digital communication is having a direct positive effect on the livelihood of poor households.

(c) Processes related to Internet use in *cabinas* are helping counterattacking the urban trends toward polarization and social exclusion in different aspects of urban life. In the case of telecommunications services, the high charges for home telecommunication services are producing a clear division between those who can afford them and those who cannot, but on the other hand, *cabinas* are helping to provide collective access in deprived neighborhoods. The figure repeats itself regarding education. One the one hand, there is an increased polarization between private and public schools/universities. The latter are deeply affected by the lack of resources and cannot offer computer and Internet services in their own premises. However, most students visit *cabinas* for educational and training purposes.

Similarly, the cultural and economic gap between social sectors is increasing and producing local social conflicts, while the Internet is opening a window to the world for the youth. Online communication is not only increasing transnational money flows, but also communication and information flows. These are making bridges between cultures and promoting the liberalization of views and opinions. Stronger information and communication flows, however, are also intensifying social tensions by increasing the awareness of injustice, inequality and exclusion.

All these significant processes give evidence that *cabinas* are fulfilling an important role in urban life in Lima, and especially in the lives of vulnerable groups. *Cabinas* are not only battling the digital divide at local level, but more importantly, they are gradually and indirectly supporting the shift toward a more balanced type of urban development. Therefore, a serious and systematic effort to organize and support the development of *cabinas* should be considered a high priority. Whenever possible, promotion of access should not be restricted to access to infrastructures, but also to improving ICT literacy and advanced skills of all groups of people. Special attention should be given to promoting the use of ICTs for economic goals by the youth. It is also important to measure and document the role of digital services in the strategies to overcome deprivation and vulnerability of households. Finally, the path toward the information society requires a common vision and an organized effort from the side of the State; not only focused on digital access and literacy, but essentially to improve the level of Peruvian education system, which is considered among the most deficient in the Latin American region.

References

AMIPCI (Asociación Mexicana de Internet), 2005, *Habits of Internet Users in Mexico, 2004. Executive Summary*. Available at: http://www.e-mexico.gob.mx/ (June 2005).

Apoyo, 2004, *Usos y actitudes hacia Internet*, Apoyo, Lima.

Avellaneda, P., 2005, *El futuro del transporte colectivo en Lima Metropolitana: ¿hacia la cohesión o la fragmentación social?*, Presentation at the III RIDEAL Seminar 'Transformaciones metropolitanas en Europa y América Latina: ¿hacia un modelo único?', Toulouse (France).

Chion, M., 2002, Dimensión metropolitana de la globalización: Lima a fines del siglo XX, *EURE* (Santiago) Vol.28, No. 85, pp.77-87.

Colona, C., 2003, *Las Cabinas Públicas de Internet en Lima: Procesos de comunicación y formas de incorporación de la tecnología a la vida cotidiana*, Unpublished Research Report, Pontificia Universidad Católica del Perú, Lima.

De Soto, H., 1986, *El otro Sendero*, Instituto Libertad y Democracia, Lima.

El Comercio y Apoyo, 2002, *Anuario 2000-2001*, Empresa editora El Comercio, Lima.

Fernández-Maldonado, A.M., 2004, *ICT-related transformations in Latin American metropolises*, PhD Thesis, Series Design / Science / Planning, Delft University Press / Techne Press, Delft / Amsterdam.

García Canclini, N., 1995, *Consumidores y ciudadanos. Conflictos multiculturales de la globalización*, Grijalbo, México.

Hopenhayn, M., 2003, Conjeturas sobre la cultura virtual. Una perspectiva general y algunas consideraciones desde América Latina, in: Calderón, F. (ed.), *¿Es sostenible la globalización en América Latina? Debates con Manuel Castells*, Vol. II, PNUD, Fondo de Cultura Económica, Santiago de Chile, pp.279-308.

Hopenhayn, M., 2004, *La reconstrucción de lo juvenil: entre postergados y estigmatizados*. Paper for the 2004 Meeting of the Latin American Studies Association, Las Vegas, Nevada, October 7-9.

IADB/FAO, 2003, *Information and Communications Technologies in Support of South American Competitiveness and Integration. Action plan. Executive Summary*, Inter.-American Development Bank, December, Available at: http://www.iadb.org/regions/re3/pdf/IIRSA0204.pdf (July 2007)

INEI, 2007, *Las Tecnologías de Información y Comunicación en los Hogares*. Enero-Marzo 2007, Informe Técnico, N° 02, Junio 2007. INEI, Lima. Available at: http://www.inei.gob.pe/web/BoletinFlotantePrincipal.asp?file=6982.pdf (July 2007)

Ludeña, W., 2001, *Lima: Poder, centro y centralidad. Del centro liberal al centro neo-liberal*. Paper for the workshop 'Las transformaciones de centralidad y la metodología de su investigación', Buenos Aires, Noviembre 26-27.

Martín Barbero, J., 2002, Jóvenes: comunicación e identidad, *Pensar Ibero América. Revista de Cultura*. Año 0, Febrero, Available at: http://www.oei.es/pensariberoamerica/ric00a03.htm (July 2003)

OSIPTEL, 2007, *Información estadística de telecomunicaciones*, Available at: http://www.osiptel.gob.pe/Index.ASP?T=P&P=2635 (July 2007)

Quiroz, M.T., 2004, *Juventud e Internet*, Fondo de Desarrollo Editorial, Universidad de Lima, Lima.

Rozas, P., 2003, *Gestión pública, regulación e internacionalización de las telecomunicaciones: el caso de Telefónica S.A.*, Serie Gestión Pública, CEPAL, ILPES, Santiago de Chile.

San Román, E., 2005, Personal interview with E. San Román, president of OSIPTEL.

Torero, M., E. Schroth & A. Pascó-Font, 2003, The Impact of Telecommunications Privatization in Peru on the Welfare of Urban Consumers, *Economía,* Vol. 4, N° 1, pp. 123-127

Truth and Reconciliation Commission, 2003, *Final Report of the Truth and Reconciliation Commission,* Available at: http://www.cverdad.org.pe/ingles/ifinal/index.php (May 2004).

Turner, J.F. & W. Mangin, 1968, *The Barriada Movement, Progressive Architecture,* Vol. 49, pp. 154-162.

Universidad de Lima, 2005, *Barómetro social: peruanos en el exterior. Lima Metropolitana y Callao,* Estudio 289, Noviembre, Lima.

Notes

1. Avellaneda (2005) has recently evaluated public transportation in Lima, drawing remarkable conclusions. He claims that despite its bad local image, public transportation in Lima is very efficient and economical for the users. His argument is that the network of public transportation is cheap and has a high coverage. Furthermore, this system costs the State nothing.

2. Despite the much larger mobile teledensity than fixed teledensity, a different balance between mobile phones and fixed lines appears when they are measured at household level. 27.22 percent of Peruvian households have mobile phones while 25.64 percent have fixed telephony. In Lima this is 61.11 percent versus 54.16 percent, respectively (INEI, 2007). This suggests that mobile phones are concentrated in homes which already have fixed phones, in the higher- and middle-income sectors.

3. An example of the benefits of Telefónica's dominant position: the rent of a E1 link inside Peru's national territory (with Telefónica) costs approximately double of what the same type of link between Lima and the US cost through one of the three submarine cable operators (IADB/FAO, 2003).

4. The figures of this comparison should not be taken literally, but only as an indication of the general trends, due to differences between the surveys. For example, samples in Lima are taken with home questionnaires, while those in Mexican cities were collected with online questionnaires.

5. These surveys are called the ENAHO (*Encuesta Nacional de Hogares,* National Household Surveys).

6. The notion that *cabinas* are a national product comes from the Red Científica Peruana (RCP), the first Internet service provider in Peru, which opened the first one in 1996 and spread the idea that *cabinas* were an original initiative of the RCP.

7. According to the INEI (http://www.inei.gob.pe) the average annual growth rate in Peru has dramatically decreased from 1.7 percent in the 1995-2000 period to less than 1.5 percent in the 2000-2005 period. Fertility rate (the average number of children per woman) has also decreased greatly, from 3.7 percent in 1993 to 2.7 percent in 2005.

8. A survey among residents of Lima showed that 52 percent of them would like to emigrate to other countries. The proportion rises to 61 percent in the group of those between 18 to 27 years old. Obviously, the poorest groups are more eager to emigrate (Universidad de Lima, 2005).

9. In 2002, Peruvians abroad sent 1.26 billion dollars to relatives in Peru, an amount which represented 8.5 percent of the total export revenues during that year.

10. Examination of the content of the most visited webpages in Latin America show that there is a close link between television flows and Internet flows.

11 The URBAN Initiative or the EU as Social Innovator?

Paul Drewe

Introduction

The European Union does not have a specific mandate in urban policy. It does, however, engage in urban matters. This is not too surprising as a large majority of the EU population lives in cities. So-called 'Community Initiatives' within the EU Structural Funds are launched in search of new approaches to urban problems, to improve the effectiveness of urban policy. Networks of co-operation are to be set up. Good or even best practice experience is to be exchanged between cities (in principle, this also holds for bad or worst practice). The most important initiative, focusing on urban matters, is URBAN, two editions of which have been launched: URBAN I in the period 1994-1999 and URBAN II covering the years 2000-2006. Both initiatives only deal with 15 EU-member states (Illustration 11.1). An *ex post* evaluation of URBAN I has been published in 2003 and a mid-term review for URBAN II in 2002. Recommendations have been made for the period *post* 2006 which are also addressing the ten new members.

The URBAN rationale

Urban problems are 'officially' spelled out as follows: "Poor living conditions aggravate individual problems and distress. In turn, social malaise and the lack of economic opportunity make the individual hostile to his/her environment. This vicious circle is today the cause of conflicts and imbalances, particular evident in the areas where the problems are most acute"[1]. This explains the focus on neighborhoods in cities or small pockets of extreme deprivation. Urban deprivation is considered as multi-faceted, i.e. as having a social, environmental and economic dimension, requiring an integrated approach. The three dimensions are similar to the triangle of objectives introduced in 1999, constituting the notion of a balanced and sustainable development (European Commission, 1999).

The vicious circle mentioned above is to be broken 'by re-valorizing the individual through his/her habitat and not in spite of it'. Or put differently, urban deprivation is to be tackled by an area approach, by targeting a well-defined area of small size. Well-defined means geographically identifiable such as an administrative unit. Moreover, each target neighborhood should be integrated into the rest of the city instead of treating it as an isolated unit. The individuals affected by severe deprivation are not to be treated as passive objects of interventions. The URBAN rationale envisages citizen participation in the development and implementation of Initiative programs. The problem of urban deprivation is supposed to be solved 'at grass root level'.
The keywords of the URBAN rationale are: multidimensional deprivation, integrated area approach, and citizen participation. As a Community Initiative, URBAN is committed to social innovation in urban revitalization.

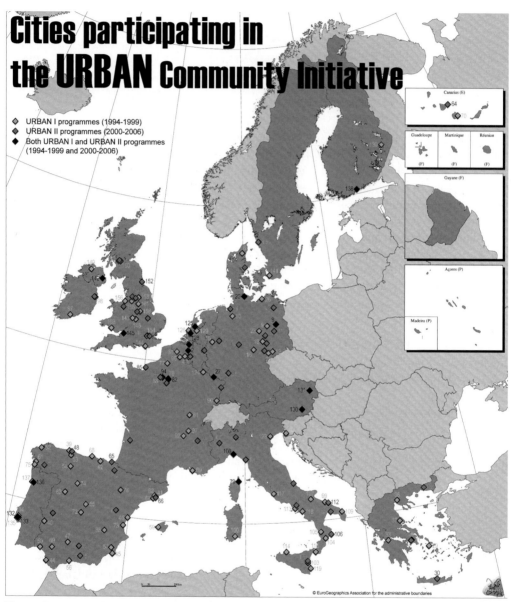

Illustration 11.1 Participating cities in URBAN I and URBAN II (Source: European Commission, Directorate-General Regional Policy, 2007)

URBAN I: the programs

A total of 118 programs has been selected[2] with 900 million euros funding allocated and a total investment of 1800 million. The programs target nearly 3 million inhabitants. Before evaluating the results of URBAN I, one needs to describe some basic facts. The keywords mentioned above can serve as a guideline. Given the area-based focus the kind of area selected is of vital importance as it decides on the degree of multiple deprivation tackled by the programs. The 'troubled urban areas' selected for URBAN are found in different parts of European cities: at the periphery, in inner cities, and in historic city centers. There are also some mixed cases. The areas are located in large as well as medium-sized cities, even in some small cities. Illustration 11.2 refers.

Areas were required to have the following socio-economic characteristics: high level of unemployment, decayed urban fabric, bad housing conditions, and lack of social amenities. "In general, the EC's criteria led to the selection of the most disadvantaged districts. The average unemployment rate in the program areas was over 20 percent, and in some districts as high as 40 percent. The program areas included high concentrations of immigrants and ethnic minority groups, representing up to 70

Type of neighbourhood	Number	%
Peripheral urban area: Those districts on the edge of urban area's, typically including social housing estates that date from the 1960s and 1970s	45	38%
Inner city: The core of the city, typically characterized by abandoned industrial buildings, dilapidated housing and a neglected environment	38	32%
Historic city center: A city centre characterized by historic architecture and the potential to develop cultural heritage	23	19%
Mixed: Areas that combine a variety of the above characteristics	14	12%
Total	120	100%

Type of city	Number	%
Large city (>250.000 inhabitants)	52	43%
Medium city (100.00-250.000)	51	43%
Small city (<100.000)	17	14%
Total	120	100%

Overlap with Objective 1 or 2	Number	%
Objective 1 [regions lagging behind in development]	68	57%
Objective 2 [regions in need of restructuring]	31	26%
Other	21	17%
Total	120	100%

Illustration 11.2: URBAN I program area characteristics (Source: GHK, 2003:9)

percent of the target population of program areas" (GHK, 2003; vi). The funds were allocated mainly to physical and environmental regeneration; entrepreneurship and employment; and social inclusion (in decreasing order of importance). There are however considerable differences across member states (as well as areas) (see Illustration 11.3). Transport and ICT were not considered important issues in the period 1994-1999.

Moreover, different implementation or integration strategies have been adopted in different types of areas and different sizes of cities (Illustration 11.4):
- 'a broad integrated approach' (mostly integrated physical infrastructure works with actions to support SMSEs, training, social inclusion measures and environmental improvements);
- 'integrated approach with a specific focus' (more explicit social focus, emphasis on economic aspects or on physical/environmental issues);
- 'flagship approach' ('a limited number of visible or flagship projects as a means of generating general interest in the program and creating an atmosphere of change and renewal');
- 'community focused approach' (a strong focus on local community groups, aiming to integrate community groups, voluntary groups and residents' associations into the design, management and implementation of the program and its projects).

Member state	Physical and environmental regeneration	Entrepeneur-ship and employment	Social inclusion	Transport	ICT	Technical assistance	Other
BE	43%	40%	14%	0%	1%	3%	0%
DK	10%	27%	21%	0%	5%	5%	32%
DE	23%	49%	19%	0%	0%	4%	4%
GR	40%	42%	12%	2%	1%	2%	1%
ES	45%	23%	30%	0%	0%	3%	0%
FR	14%	51%	29%	0%	0%	5%	1%
IE	38%	41%	14%	0%	2%	5%	0%
IT	62%	18%	14%	3%	2%	1%	2%
LU	43%	30%	27%	0%	0%	0%	0%
NL	27%	52%	12%	0%	0%	2%	7%
AT	50%	36%	12%	0%	0%	3%	0%
PT	27%	20%	46%	0%	0%	7%	0%
FI	47%	22%	19%	0%	5%	6%	0%
SE	18%	33%	26%	0%	6%	6%	11%
UK	22%	31%	36%	1%	2%	7%	0%
EU15	38%	32%	23%	1%	1%	4%	2%

Illustration 11.3: Allocation of funds URBAN I by URBAN II category (actual expenditure) (Source: GHK, 2003: 92)

This brings us to citizen participation. This feature is most clearly present in the community-focused approach to implementation, which has been adopted in all of the 19 UK programs as shown in Illustration 11.4. The role played by the local community in the process depends on the type of management structure, which, in turn, is linked to the existing administrative structure in the area, existing practices, traditions and experiences.

URBAN II: the programs

URBAN II comprises 70 programs, to which the EU has contributed 700 million euros (the total investment amounts to 1580 million euros). These programs cover a population of some 2.2 million. As shown by Illustration 11.5 the URBAN II program areas cover inner cities (the city center or the inner ring of dense, mostly 19th century housing); the periphery and suburban neighborhoods; entire (small) cities; and a mix of inner city and peripheral neighborhoods (in decreasing order of importance).

In an attempt to create more transparent criteria for the selection of areas or sites, nine criteria have been proposed (Commission of the European Communities, 2002:11):
- High long-term unemployment
- Low rate of economic activity
- High level of poverty and exclusion
- The need for structural adjustment due to economic and social difficulties
- High proportion of immigrants, ethnic minorities and refugees
- Low level of education, major gaps in terms of qualifications and high rate of pupil failure
- High level of criminality and delinquency
- Unstable demographic development
- Particularly poor environmental condition.

To be eligible for URBAN II, an area had to fulfill at least three of the nine criteria to qualify as a severe case of multiple deprivation.

Here are some highlights: average unemployment rate of 17 percent; a proportion of immigrants, ethnic minorities and refugees of nearly 14 percent; a reported crime rate of over 100 offences per year per 1000 inhabitants; green spaces of some 10.5 percent of the total surface area. The funds were allocated to physical and environmental regeneration, entrepreneurship and employment, social inclusion, transport, and Information and Communication Technologies (ICT) (in decreasing order of importance). Note that the same definition of expenditure categories had been applied to URBAN I (Illustration 11.2). Once again the proportion of spending regarding these categories varies from country to country and from area to area. Take for example the newcomer of spending devoted to ICT. Overall, only 4 percent of the funds available have been allocated for ICT as against e.g. 26 percent in Bruxelles-Capitale or 30 percent in Milano. However, in addition, ICT is often an essential component of training programs. Unlike URBAN I, no information is available on implementation or integration strategies.

Member State		BE	DK	DE	GR	ES	FR	IE	IT	LU	NL	AT	PT	FI	SE	UK
Broad integrated approach	56	0	0	6	2	30	9	2	2	0	2	1	1	0	1	0
Integrated approach with a specific focus	33	5	0	7	3	0	4	0	9	0	2	1	2	0	0	0
"Flagship" approach	13	0	1	0	2	0	0	0	4	1	0	0	3	1	1	0
Community focused approach	23	0	0	0	0	0	0	1	1	0	0	0	0	2	0	19
Total	125	5	1	13	7	30	13	3	16	1	4	2	6	3	2	19

Illustration 11.4: Type of strategy adopted by all URBAN I and 5 UPP[3] programs by member state (Source: GHK, 2003: 19)

Type of City	Number	%	Population	%
Inner city	31	44%	994.000	46%
Peripheral	27	39%	810.000	38%
Whole city	8	11%	239.000	11%
Mixed (inner and peripheral)	4	6%	113.00	5%

Type of City	Number	%	Population	%
Large city (>250.00 inhab.)	27	39%	874.000	41%
Medium city	31	44%	945.000	44%
Small city (<50.00)	12	17%	337.000	16%

Type of City	Number	%	Population	%
Objective 1: regions lagging behind in development	21	30%	575.000	27%
Objective 1 phasing out	6	9%	134.000	6%
Total objective 1	**27**	**39%**	**709.000**	**33%**
Objective 2: regions in need of restructuring	12	17%	355.000	16%
Objective 2 phasing out	1	1%	33.000	2%
Partially objective 2	6	9%	186.000	9%
Total objective 2	**19**	**27%**	**573.000**	**27%**
Outside objectives 1 and 2	24	34%	874.000	41%

Illustration 11.5: URBAN II areas by type (Source: Commission of the European Communities, 2002:30)

URBAN I: the *ex post* evaluation

The *ex post* evaluation of URBAN I has been split up in a number of tasks. Some of them were carried out for a sample of programs only (see Illustration 11.6).

This is just to highlight the outcome of the evaluation. The so-called 'Community value added' of URBAN I will be dealt with later when it comes to assess the role of the EU as social innovator. As far as the overall effective of URBAN I is concerned, it suffices to report that of the 56 sampled programs 72 percent were judged to have been 'very successful' or 'mostly successful'. Effectiveness is assessed in terms of EU objectives as well as member-state specific success criteria. In addition, national evaluators have identified (main) factors supporting or hindering success. Major supporting factors identified have been:
- combining URBAN with existing regeneration programs;
- selection and combination of projects;
- active participation of the local community in aspects of the implementation and management of the program.

Lack of the latter has been an important factor hindering success together with:
- lack of private sector support;
- difficulties in understanding EC documents and procedures by those involved in the program.

In over 80 percent of the programs the most important domains impacted by URBAN are: the physical environment, improved socio-economic conditions and social capital (according to the national evaluators' assessment).

For an overview by member-state see Illustration 11.7.

Physical improvements range from neighborhood improvements to renovations/conversions of individual buildings or construction of new infrastructure. Improved socio-economic conditions refer to job creation, job training, support to new businesses and increase in social services. Social capital impacts are less tangible as they relate to changing the image of an area, improving the feeling of safety or an increased sense of community. Only in a few cases are non-physical impacts rated higher than physical impacts, notably in Amsterdam (The Netherlands) and in some British cities.

Apart from the top-three impacts, a number of less important ones has been cited. These are in decreasing order:
- institutional impacts (a paradigm shift from government-led to community-led regeneration; multidimensional rather than singular focus; from exclusionary to co-operative);
- city strategies (an integrated approach to urban revitalization as in the strategies already existing in the UK and in The Netherlands);
- city structure and functionality (impact on the overall structure and function of the target area)
- spread of positive impacts on neighboring areas;
- regional development (contribution to overall development of the region);
- displacement of urban problems such as poverty, drugs and prostitution to neighboring areas (e.g. in Antwerp, Belgium);
- resistance from local community against changes of the neighborhood because of increased rents or commercialization (for example in Antwerp and Brussels in Belgium).

The selection of programme areas	20 URBAN programmes
The strategies adopted and implemented	118 URBAN programmes and 5 UPPs
Effectiveness	56 URBAN programmes and 2 UPPs
Management and implementation systems	35 URBAN programmes and 2 UPPs
Impact	118 URBAN programmes and 5 UPPs
Community value added	118 URBAN programmes and 5 UPPs
Conclusions and lessons	118 URBAN programmes and 5 UPPs

Ilustration 11.6: Sample of programs for each evaluation task (Source: GHK, 2003: 2)

		BE	DK	DE	GR	ES	FR	IE	IT	LU	NL	AT	PT	FI	SE	UK
Physical environment	113	1st	1st	1st	1st	1st	1st	1st	1st	1st	4th	1st	1st	1st	1st	3rd
Improvements in socio-economic conditions	107	2nd		2nd	1st	1st	2nd		3rd		1st	1st	4th	3rd	5th	2nd
Social capital impacts	102	4th	1st	3rd	1st	1st	4th	1st	4th	1st	5th	1st	3rd	3rd	5th	1st
Institutional impacts	63		1st	5th	7th	4th	5th	1st	2nd		1st		8th	3rd	1st	3rd
City strategies	58		1st	5th	1st	4th	3rd	4th	4th		6th		1st	1st	1st	5th
City structure and functionality	45		1st	4th	1st	4th	6th		4th		1st	1st	5th	3rd	5th	7th
Spread of positive impacts on neighbouring areas	24			8th		5th	7th	4th	8th	1st	6th			5th	7th	1st	5th
Regional development	10			7th	6th			4th								
Displacement of urban problems to neighbouring areas (i.e. Poverty, drugs, prostitution)	9	4th		9th			8th		9th			6th	5th	5th		
Resistance from local community against changes to the neighborhood (I.e. increased rents, commercialization)	8	2nd		9th			9th		7th					8th		

Illustration 11.7: Impacts of the URBAN I and 5 UPP programs, in rank order by member-state (Source: GHK, 2003: 56[4])

Another line of evaluation has been a perception survey, i.e. small-scale street surveys of residents and non-residents held in 35 URBAN target areas. Respondents were asked whether they have perceived that the area in question has changed over the previous ten years and whether the changes could be attributed to URBAN or to other factors. The methodological limits of the chosen approach make that the street surveys at best have gauged the awareness of the URBAN Community Initiative.

To conclude the highlights of the evaluation results, a comment on the chosen methodology seems in order. The evaluation draws heavily on the opinions of the evaluators, national and others, leave alone the opinions obtained from the respondents of street surveys. This kind of evaluation somehow falls short as far as the measurement of tangible benefits to the target area and population are concerned, except for some selected quotations. The chosen approach differs from the state-of-the-art which emphasizes tangible output and outcome measures. The usual *ex post* evaluation framework also includes monitoring, and the framework for undertaking a SWOT analysis (see Moore & Spires, 2000). By the way, if the tangible output is properly monitored, this also facilitates the evaluation task.

The EU, a social innovator?

Community Initiatives such as URBAN are launched in search of innovative approaches to urban problems. This is a rather complex matter as there are three, sometimes four levels of decision-making involved: local (and sometimes regional) authorities, national governments and the EU. Unlike the Community Initiative itself, the question of innovativeness must be tackled bottom-up. If multiple deprivation has not been reduced by an integrated approach involving the deprived citizens, then it is of no use to pursue the argument. According to the evaluators, URBAN I made a difference to quality of life. Whether the approach was really new, depends on existing policies in member countries. At the outset, most member countries did not have national urban policies. There are five major exceptions to this, to wit Denmark, France, Ireland, The Netherlands and the UK (Germany has an urban policy at the regional level). The other countries, at the outset, had mainly physical planning policies with sometimes locally-initiated programs but more often than not falling short of an integrated approach to urban issues.

Local (regional) authorities and the EU can be seen as the most important facilitators of innovations in the case of a successful implementation of URBAN without a specific EU mandate in urban policy. This is in line with the principle of subsidiarity advocating that decisions are taken at the lowest appropriate or competent level. This principle is usually applied to the relation between the EU and its member-states, but equally holds within countries for national governments versus local (regional) authorities and, ideally, even for the relation between local authorities and citizens. Whether citizen participation really made a difference, can only be judged per area. Note that the evaluators consider the active participation of the local community in URBAN I as a factor supporting success in some cases whereas the lack of active participation, in other cases, is seen as a factor hindering the success of URBAN. Hence the 'success story' of citizen participation has to be taken with a pinch of salt.

If the EU has successfully facilitated innovations, then it would qualify as a 'social innovator'. This issue is related to the so-called 'Community value added' of URBAN which depends on:
- the relation of URBAN I to the existing national programs and policies;
- additionality and leverage;
- transnational co-operation and learning;
- consciousness of EU economic, cohesion and social inclusion policies;
- lessons from URBAN I for URBAN II;
- subsidiarity, proportionality and partnership principles;
- community value added and transaction costs.

The relation of URBAN I to the existing national programs and policies has already been dealt with above. Countries without 'a tradition of tackling neighborhood disadvantage through past and current programs of area-based initiatives', testify to a higher degree of additionality and leverage meaning that additional resources have been deployed including direct and indirect private sector leverage. Direct private sector leverage represents 6.6 percent of total funding. Leverage also includes underused assets that have benefited in the past from public investment, assets put to use in URBAN. As to transnational co-operation and learning, this has been assessed by the evaluators as 'modest', what the program managers being far too busy on delivering the program. The influence on the raising of consciousness of relevant EU policies has been greatest at the local level. The newer the experience, the greater the influence. Lessons from URBAN I for URBAN II relate to procedures, transnational activities and the range of eligible interventions. The latter can be illustrated by the introduction of ICT (with modest results by the way, as mentioned earlier).

The EU initiative has not replaced national levels in the case of existing national urban policies. Does subsidiarity not call for stimulating those national policies where they do not exist? This lesson could have been drawn from URBAN I for URBAN II. On the other hand, to achieve subsidiarity rather appears to be a problem within member countries at the expense of key actors 'close to the ground' and, in particular those for whom the programs are implemented. Citizen participation was probably best catered to by a community focused approach to implementation as practiced in the UK.

Proportionality raises the question of whether a EU intervention such as URBAN is commensurate with the magnitude of the targeted multiple deprivation in Europe. Spending 1.6 billion euros, targeting 5.2 million inhabitants in 188 (actually 190) urban areas (URBAN I & URBAN II) is just tackling the top of the iceberg. At best, the total effort has helped to raise consciousness of the urgency of tackling social exclusion. The innovative aspect of the URBAN Initiative with regard to partnership is that for the first time cities were charged with implementing and delivering a EU program. Actual partnership, however, also depends on the degree of subsidiarity practiced by nation states. It is estimated that on average about 6 percent of the total cost of the initiative has been spent on management and technical assistance. It is impossible to estimate the share of transaction costs, i.e. costs stemming from the regulations and the guidance of the Community Initiative.

Concluding one can say that the EU as a facilitator of innovations has not scored positively on all aspects, but it has made a difference in countries without an explicit national urban policy (also with regard to additionality and leverage). Among the positive aspects are the introduction of partnership, and after all the consciousness of social inclusion policies seems to have been raised.

Outlook for the *post* 2006 period

The evaluators make a case for an urban dimension to the Structural Funds after 2006. Compared to URBAN, however, this dimension is broadened. It is about 'urban renaissance' and competitiveness. Moreover, future area-based interventions require a combination of local, wider urban and regional strategies. One has to differentiate between EU 15-URBAN projects and those of the new member countries. The root causes of urban problems are different: the consequences of market forces, areas improving or degrading, and suburbanization as well as counter urbanization in the former case – urbanization and growth pressures due to central planning in the latter case.

Another question is what is going to happen to the 188 URBAN areas after 2006. Have six or sometimes twelve years been enough to solve the problems of multiple deprivation? Has URBAN pumped the prime? Or did projects simply stop when the EU funding ended? As URBAN has hardly been commensurate with the magnitude of multiple deprivation in EU 15-cities, what are the prospects for 'needy' cities – or the rest of the iceberg – in the *post* 2006 period (in France alone there are 300 *cités* with 1.2 million dwellings, not all them 'troubled', however)? In addition, the new members are facing 'new' urban problems: industrial decline and restructuring; a mismatch of housing demand and supply; a degraded urban environment (brownfield sites), increasing car ownership and declining public transport systems.

Can the EU in the years to come really ensure proportionality with regard to urban problems in 25 member-states? Can national governments cover the deficit? So far only five countries have a national urban policy. In the case that such a policy exists (or is stimulated by the EU), member states could take over the director's role of the EU in URBAN-type policies. It would probably suffice that funding for urban policies in the Structural Funds interventions is earmarked at the European level. This would also strengthen subsidiarity provided member countries, too, apply this principle in dealing with local (regional) authorities and, ideally, with citizens in the targeted areas (for subsidiarity: Drewe, 2006).

France and the UK – two approaches to URBAN

The 'riots' or 'revolts' in the French *cités* in 2005 are the reason for this Section. There were URBAN programs for Clichy-sous-Bois and Aulnay-sous-Bois, among others. When the President of the European Commission promised another 50 million euros for the French URBAN programs, it became known that 100 million euros of already committed funds had not yet been spent. Reason enough for taking a closer look at the evaluation results? But why compare France to Britain? Because of the difference in implementation strategies: in all of the 19 British programs a so-called community focused approach has been applied, against non in the 13 French programs, the majority of which adopted a 'broad integrated approach' (Illustration 11.4). Let us recall: the British approach is marked by a strong focus on local community groups, aiming to integrate community groups, voluntary groups and residents' associations into the design, management and implementation of the program and its projects. In Illustration 11.8 a comparison is made with regard to factors hindering and supporting the success of the URBAN programs and with respect to their impacts (according to the evaluators). Only the most important items are listed.

The French programs have suffered from operational problems such as a weak integrated approach and weak leadership, and – unlike the UK – from a stronger lack of private sector support and co-operation. Whether the latter has been compensated for, by a leveraging of other existing regeneration programs or a better combination of URBAN with existing regeneration programs in France, is unknown. On the operational side, the UK performed better with regard to early capacity building (although the UK also experienced major operational problems). Surprisingly the UK scores 1st on lack of participation of the local community, but also 3rd on active community participation as a success factor. It seems that the community focused approach has not been successful everywhere (for example not in Glasgow North or Hackney Tower).

As far as the impacts of the URBAN programs are concerned, one notes two major differences between France and the UK. In France impacts concentrate on the physical environment whereas in the UK social capital impacts dominate. This could be a significant fact combined with the allocation of funds to social inclusion (Illustration 11.3). Britain shows only a slightly higher percentage than France. But if France has experienced more serious operational problems this could mean that it has been less efficient. Social inclusion covers actions on minorities, refugees, immigrants, equal opportunities, youth inclusion, safety, public health, fight against crime and drugs. The mid-term review of URBAN II provides relevant additional information, Illustration 11.9 refers (based on Commission, 2002:35 and 37).

Most important hindering factors	FR	UK
- Lack of private sector support and co-operation	1st	6th
- Lack of participation of the local community in aspects of the management and implementation of the program		1st
- Difficulties in understanding of European Commission documents and procedures by those involved in program	1st	1st
- Delays in program decision making and implementation		1st
- Complicated funding process and administration		1st
- A weak integrated approach and partnership	1st	
- Weak leadership in the day to day management and overall implementation of the program	1st	
- Failure to forward funding by the local managing authorities		1st
- Selection and combination of programs	1st	
Most important success factors		
- The combination of URBAN with existing regeneration programs	1st	3rd
- The selection and combination of projects	3rd	6th
- Active participation of the local community in aspects of the management and implementation of the program	5th	3rd
- The establishment of an integrated approach with strong partnership	5th	3rd
- Leveraging other existing regeneration programs as a source for match funding	1st	
- Timeliness of program decision making and implementation		1st
- The establishment of capacity building processes from the start of the program	5th	1st
Major impacts		
- Physical environment	1st	3rd
- Improvements in socio-economic conditions	2nd	2nd
- Social capital impacts	4th	1st
- Institutional impacts	4th	3rd
- City strategies	3rd	5th

Illustration 11.8: Most important hindering factors, success factors and impacts: France and UK (Source: GHK, 2003, table 4.4, p. 31 and table 4.5, p. 32; and table 10.6, p.56)

	FR	UK
Unemployment rate	24 (21)	11
Immigrants as a % of total population	13 (31)	9
Proportion of spending devoted to:		
- physical & environmental regeneration	41 (58)	30
- entrepreneurship & employment	22 (18)	28
- social inclusion	21 (9)	33

Illustration 11.9: Summary data from URBAN II, selected indicators, between brackets: Clichy-Montfermeil (Source: Commission of the European Communities, 2002)

The target groups differ. There are more unemployed and immigrants in France than in the UK. Despite of this France favors physical and environmental regeneration at the expense of both social inclusion and entrepreneurship and employment. The overall picture of the UK programs is that of a more balanced spending pattern.

Epilogue

Perhaps the most important result of URBAN is that it has raised the consciousness of the urgency of tackling social exclusion. 'Riots' can be more effective in this respect but they are less durable once they stop being the news of the day. The EU, after all, had put social inclusion on its agenda before 1994. The impact of URBAN may leave to be desired, but its rationale or philosophy still holds: multidimensional deprivation, integrated approach, and citizen participation. The 'urban divide' still is a matter of vulnerability and deprivation (Hulsbergen, 2005). Given the deficient proportionality of URBAN, the urban policy needs to be continued after 2006 although the role of the European Union needs to be revisited as far as the respective roles of the EU and of national governments are concerned, in line with the principle of subsidiarity. Where national efforts fall short, European support could be intensified. Much of what has been put forward in the preceding Sections is based on evaluations commissioned by the European Commission. Maybe the Commission in future should not only want to prove Community value added, but also become more interested in bad-practice experiences. The evaluators, employed by the Commission, should be encouraged to investigate bad practice, too. One is left with the feeling that the evaluators, maybe 'straight jacketed' by the methodology prescribed by the European Commission, lack the discernment and understanding with which to penetrate the heart and essence of the problem as in the case of the French cites. *Ex post* evaluation should be clearly linked to monitoring and early warning. Or one should at least listen carefully to the rappers...

References

Commission of the European Communities, 2002, *The programming of the Structural Funds 2000-2006, an initial assessment of the Urban Initiative*, Brussels.
Drewe, P., 2006, Quo Vadis European Union? Uncertainties Ask for Scenarios, In: Kukliński, A. & B. Skuza (eds), 2006, *Turning Points in the Transformation of the Global Scene,* Oficyna Wydawnicza 'Rewasz', The Polish Association for the Club of Rome, Warsaw, pp. 87 - 96.
European Commission, 1999, *European Spatial Development Perspective*, Brussels.
European Commission, Directorate-Generale Regional Policy, 2007,
http://ec.europa.eu/regional_policy/urban2/pdf/URBAN12_a3_final_3c.pdf, 25th of june 2007.
GHK, 2003, *Ex-post evaluation Urban Community Initiative (1994-1999)*, Brussels & London.
Hulsbergen, E.D., 2005, Vulnerability and Deprivation, in Hulsbergen, E.D., I.T. Klaasen & I. Kriens (eds), *Shifting Sense in Spatial Planning: Looking Back to the Future,* Series Design / Science / Planning, Techne Press, Amsterdam, pp. 45-56.
Moore, B. & R. Spires, 2000, Monitoring and Evaluation, in Roberts P. & H. Sykes eds, *Urban Regeneration, A Handbook*, SAGE, London, pp. 203-227.

Notes

1. Introduction to the URBAN I Community Initiative 1994-1999 (from the official website).
2. Although there were originally 118 programs, the total number is 120 as the Dublin and Brussels programs have been split into two distinct programs.
3. UPP stands for Urban Pilot Projects, a predecessor of URBAN.
4. Underlined ranking indicates equal ranking among several factors. The UPPs included in the *ex post* evaluation of URBAN I are Alexandroupolis, Bilbao, Falun, Helsinki and Leipzig.

Abbreviations Chapter 12

Abbreviation	French	English
ANAH	Agence Nationale pour l'Amélioration de l'Habitat	National Agency for the Improvement of the Habitat
ANRU	Agence Nationale de Renouvellement Urbain	National Agency for Urban Renewal
CDC	Caisse des Depôts et Consignations	(French) Financial Institution
DR	Direction Régionale	Regional Office
FRU	Fonds Renouvellement Urbain	Urban Renewal Funds
GIP	Groupement d'Intérêt Public	Public Interest Group
GPV	Grand Projet de Ville	Large Urban Projects
HLM	Habitations à Loyer Modéré	Public Housing Units
OLS	Organisme de logement social	Social Housing Organisation
ORU	Opérations de Renouvellement Urbain	Urban Renewal Operations
PNRU	Programme National de Renouvellement Urbain	National Urban Renewal Programme
PPUs	Prêts Projets Urbains	Urban Project Loans
PRU	Programme de Renouvellement Urbain	Urban Renewal program
PRUs	Prêts Renouvellement Urbain	Urban Renewal Loans
SEM	Société d'Economie Mixte	Mixed Economy Enterprise

12 The Urban Renewal Program of Caisse des Dépôts et Consignations: Innovative Action to Regenerate French Towns and Cities

Pierre Narring

Introduction

Caisse des dépôts et consignations (CDC) is a state-owned financial institution created in 1816 by Parliament in order to distinguish between the various functions of the depositary state. The primary missions entrusted to it at that time were (1) to preserve the funds deposited with the legal professions and compulsory deposits, (2) to receive voluntary deposits from other public institutions and private depositors, and (3) to administer the first organized provident fund – the retirement savings funds of public servants (Thiveaud, 1991).

These missions have been characterized by the CDC's independence from the state such that the deposited and consigned funds cannot be diverted from public interest. As stated by Thiveaud, "extreme safety rules were required to maintain public trust" (1991: 43, translation), in particular to preserve the confidence of citizens. This is why the CDC has had great autonomy in managing these funds, under Parliament's surveillance and control.

The deposited and consigned funds, whose origin has diversified over the years, have always been managed in view of profitability, which rapidly gave the CDC considerable financial power (Trichet, 1991). Today, these funds are invested in the financial markets in order to generate dividends, the earnings of which are divided into three equal shares:
- one third is paid to the state as participation in the public-interest effort, in the same way as any other private sector company;
- one third is retained by the CDC as its own funds for savings and development;
- one third is redistributed as part of the CDC's public-interest missions.

It is in this sense that the CDC, as an institution, can be considered a social innovation because not only does it not 'cost' society anything (quite the reverse is true, since it pays an annual dividend to the state), it provides public-interest services through its historical missions of managing deposits and consignments, and also contributes to fostering, alongside the state, economic and social development in France, in particular through targeted actions such as its Urban Renewal Program (*Programme de Renouvellement Urbain*, PRU).

Indeed, through its financial power, the CDC has gradually become a key actor in numerous public structures which take action to foster urban regeneration, in particular local communities (the CDC acted as a loan provider to communities from 1966 to 1993), low-income housing organizations (*Habitations à Loyer Modéré*, HLM)), mixed enterprises and regional funding organizations.

While the state has been pursuing a predominantly social 'Policy for the City' (rehabilitation of low-income housing units) since the early 1990s, the CDC observed in 1997 that without reclaiming and developing economic functions, the improvement of low-income housing is not enough to regenerate an urban area. Also, at the same time, a public report (Sueur, 1998) suggested the need for a more comprehensive approach to the city policy, via a concept of urban and social mix. The idea is that urban development cannot be based uniquely on social measures for problem neighborhoods but rather on urban renewal which involves a capacity for investing in large real estate projects with an economic and social mission.

Thus, in 1998 the CDC launched its PRU which became one of the main components of the National Urban Renewal Program (*Programme National de Renouvellement Urbain*, PNRU) created by the French government in December 1999. The first part of this Chapter therefore aims to show how, faced with the challenge represented by urban regeneration in France and the need for a new approach, the CDC has sought to develop innovative action. Based on the PRU's results, the second part attempts to determine in what way this program has constituted a triggering effect for comprehensive urban regeneration projects. Lastly, the third part deals with the impacts of the PRU by assessing the CDC's capacity for innovation in the field of urban planning.

The PRU, action toward urban regeneration: characteristics and achievements

The decision to have the CDC implement an urban renewal program flowed from the medium and long-term track record of the previous programs carried out by the CDC and other interventions of the Policy for the City.

The evaluations of these programs showed that the CDC had learnt to co-operate with the actors involved in the Policy for the City, in particular the local communities, and to contribute to the creation of local partnerships based on the projects. Through this co-operation, the CDC teams were able to develop skills in the area of economic and financial engineering, feasibility studies and project management. Thus, they came out of their role as simple fund providers, getting involved in projects alongside communities and social sponsors, and gradually made themselves known as key partners in this field.

These evaluations also provided the CDC with orientations in defining its future interventions:
- intervening directly to support a project in order to provoke a greater leverage effect than just delegating a budget to a public actor;
- not spreading thin, i.e. allocating limited funds to a great number of operations, but on the contrary, concentrating on commitments to a few projects deemed to be priority projects, in order to provoke significant leverage effects;
- being able to propose to the actors involved in the Policy for the City an entire series of financial interventions and technical support which correspond to all the phases of a project and the numerous expectations of partners;
- decentralizing interventions in order to come up with specific, appropriate solutions for each project and being present on the site;
- contributing to the creation or consolidation of partnerships and to co-operation between the various actors working for the renewal of a neighborhood or site.

Characteristics of the CDC's Urban Renewal Program

Goals of the PRU

The main goal defined for the PRU was operational in nature. It involved contributing to the setting up and funding of 100 projects based on a new approach to urban renewal. This first goal was accompanied by a challenge for the CDC which involved adapting its tools and methods of intervention to this objective. The establishment of an evaluation process as soon as the PRU was launched helped to clarify the strategic goals, namely:
- to couple public intervention with private intervention in order to contribute to the economic revival of some territories;
- to help local communities find innovative solutions to their problems, thereby reinforcing the social usefulness of the CDC's action;
- to support state intervention in this field by reinforcing the CDC's role as a public institution with a specific and clearly identified mission.

Targets of the PRU

Under the agreement between the state and the CDC, signed in 1998, the projects selected by the PRU were to be located in neighborhoods defined as a priority in terms of achieving a better urban and social mix, that is:
- social housing neighborhoods requiring extensive changes, to be restructured;
- older neighborhoods in city-centers and run down urban sectors to be requalified;
- sensitive urban territories.

These projects, moreover, were to aim at the following three goals:
- upgrading of services and development of appropriate urban management;
- redevelopment of run down or fragile areas;
- diversification or better distribution of the supply of housing and economic activities.

Lastly, a project can be selected only if it meets the following criteria:
- firstly, it cannot be undertaken by the market because of its low profitability in the short and medium terms even though long-term profitability can be obtained;
- secondly, it must be clearly defined and included in a coherent overall strategy for the city or the city region;
- it must demonstrate a capacity for completion within the prescribed cost and time limits, which implies that a rigorous project monitoring methodology has been put in place;
- it must be undertaken in partnership and consultation with the various actors involved (including the residents), and must be strongly supported by local political authorities.

It is required that the selected projects be subject to *ex ante*, *in itinere* and *ex post* evaluations.

The CDC's means and methods of intervention

In financial terms, the PRU has been able to mobilize two types of funds:
- The CDC's own funds, up to €45.73 million for 1999, then €457 million over the next four years based on a credit note on a third of the dividends owed to the state (total of €502.73 million over five years, or approximately €100 million per year), used for:
  - funding actions in engineering and project management (pre-operational and operational studies, appraisals, assistance with financing package, and assistance with operation) contributing to the definition and operationalization of projects;
  - investing in the operations; this opportunity for CDC investment represents a clean break with previous periods.

- The savings funds managed by the CDC, essentially Urban Project Loans (*Prêts Projets Urbains*, PPUs) and Urban Renewal Loans (*Prêts Renouvellement Urbain*, PRUs) with a three-year budget of €1.5 billion for each of the loans, extended subsequently.

In addition to these financial means, new tools have been defined to allow the partners involved in a project to finalize the financing package or encourage the actors (owners of housing units or investors, for example) to embark on the project. These are guarantee funds which allow the stakeholders to obtain capital for their project, insurance for owners of the renovated housing units, a public subsidy prefunding mechanism and a system of delegated management of European funds.

Procedures for PRU implementation and follow up

The PRU is structured around local projects, and each project may contain several investment operations. Based on this approach, the CDC's regional teams (*Directions Regionales*, DRs)[1] have been responsible for identifying on their territory urban renewal projects which correspond to the goals and criteria of the PRU. By the end of 1998, they had thus identified 300 projects, each being considered to be either operational (likely to produce results within three years) or emergent. The DRs are then responsible for relations with the partners of each project, since the town or city (or the city region) has been clearly identified as the political motor and carrier of the project. Based on the issues addressed by the project and the difficulties encountered while setting it up, the DRs suggest to the partners appropriate means of intervention by the CDC. The decisions to intervene in engineering or loans can be made directly by the DRs. However, the decisions to invest with its own funds remain the prerogative of the CDC head office as does the choice of tools mobilized, based on suggestions by the DRs.

Achievements of the CDC's Urban Renewal Program

PRU's financial achievements

Out of the €502.73 million of its own funds budgeted over 5 years by the PRU, €433.60 million, or 86.25 percent, were committed by the end of 2003. Out of the savings funds, the PPUs generated €1.84 billion worth of loans and the PRUs generated €2.25 billion worth of loans over the entire period of the PRU. Out of the €433.60 million committed, €61.9 million were devoted to engineering expenditures (14.27 percent), €281.5 million were devoted to investments (64.92 percent) and the rest was used for loan subsidies.

Quantitative achievements of the PRU

By the end of 2003, the PRU had generated 155 investment operations throughout France, with 75 percent of amounts invested being concentrated in 6 regions (Bourgogne, Ile de France, Midi-Pyrénées, Nord-Pas de Calais, Provences-Alpes-Côte d'Azur and Rhône-Alpes) while, conversely, 6 regions (Auvergne, Basse-Normandie, Corse, Limousin, Lorraine and Poitou-Charentes) did not draw any investment operations. The exact number of projects could not be determined because of the perimeter of investment operations but must logically be close to the set goal of 100 urban renewal projects.

To arrive at these 155 investment operations, 1687 engineering operations were needed. At the national level, these operations (146) were devoted to the production of funding and methodology tools to facilitate the networking of regional teams. At the regional level, the engineering credits mostly gave rise to actions being funded jointly with the local communities which ensured the political management of the project.

Qualitative achievements of the PRU

The PRU's achievements can be divided into three major types of operation: commercial real estate (such as offices, industries, shopping centers, cinemas, hospitals and clinics), private older housing and social housing. There has been a fairly wide variety of types of operation, resulting from opportunities which have come up and which have allowed PRU leaders to translate into action and thus prove the strong hypothesis that it is worthwhile to mobilize private investment in urban renewal projects and to intervene in order to put problem neighborhoods back 'on the market'. The implemented operations have also reflected requests made to the CDC by the mayors and have thus represented the PRU's response to a need which emerged from the local level.

The PRU has also been an experiment in searching for co-investors. It should be noted that partnership with the *Caisses d'épargne* has been steady and that the partners have been varied but limited in number at the national level (mainly related to shopping centers) whereas at the local level, they have been more numerous and varied.

The PRU has led to innovative reflection on the real estate market of problem neighborhoods and on the need to link public intervention in urban planning and private investment, particularly in relation to the accessibility of property for the private sector, which is not only a question of price but also of physical development (consolidation needed, accessibility to be improved, and parking to be reorganized).

Investments have generally been made by the CDC from a long-term perspective with often uncertain immediate profitability. The investment management phase (by definition beyond the PRU) is decisive because it is then that the product is adjusted and management is adapted to a market that is better known since it has already been tested.

Results of the PRU: a triggering effect on the comprehensive urban regeneration project

The *ex post* evaluation of the PRU, conducted between January and May 2005, was based on a study of 10 operations or projects that were representative of the CDC's action in the following 10 French towns and cities: Arcueil, Bordeaux, Clichy, Creil, Perpignan, Reims, Roubaix, Saint-Etienne, Toulouse and Vaux-en-Velin.

Results regarding investments in commercial real estate…

…related to the goal of 'putting the neighborhood back on the market'

Regarding the investments made and in most of the cases studied (Roubaix, Reims, St Etienne, Arcueil, Toulouse, and even Clichy), it can be observed that the neighborhood (or site) was not completely 'out of the market' but mainly 'out of investors'. Such an observation would be rash if these neighborhoods were systematically cut off from the urban space as is sometimes the case of highly isolated or highly stigmatized neighborhoods in terms of security. In fact, it is often noted that these neighborhoods can be developed 'within the space of the city or the city region' and that their situation has advantages and can be attractive for activities which do not necessarily work 'in the neighborhood market' (the private clinics center in St Etienne, the Impression Directe company in Roubaix, the Alstom office building in Arcueil, etc.).

The key issue is access to real estate, i.e. liberating it or consolidating it first and then putting it back up for sale at a 'market price'. From this viewpoint, both examples of Roubaix and St Etienne clearly illustrate that the basic problem is that property is not accessible on the market, not only because of the price but also for physical reasons. The property may be held by the public system, which is often the case in spaces surrounding high-rise estates, and needs to be freed through a new development project. An other possibility is, that the property is stuck in a fragmented plot or a community of owners in such a way, that it is never put on the market as entities re-usable by the private sector. The exception is when the private sector acts as a developer, in which case the consolidation cost is out of proportion (this is the problem of investing in older neighborhoods).

As soon as these conditions are present, the production or service activities take place at economic and urban levels which most of the time transcend the neighborhood. This moreover leads to the de specialization of the neighborhood in terms of urban functions as well as in spatial and social terms (the neighborhood is used by people who work in it and not by those who live in it).

However, this reasoning is not entirely right for shopping centers which operate only in the local market and whose success strongly depends on:
- the extent of the marketable expenditures of those living in the neighborhood;
- the customer catchment area which is all the more restricted when the neighborhood cannot be or is less used (for reasons of safety or an urban divide);
- very fierce competition in terms of distribution with other shopping centers nearby or accessible by car, thereby causing the local shopping center to lose a noticeable share of its market.

It is clear that the profitability of businesses which set up in the local shopping center has a direct impact on real estate investment itself (since the rents are wholly or partly indexed to the sales figure). This investment, therefore, is not only physically established in the neighborhood but is also economically dependent on the income status of those living in the neighborhood and the neighboring commercial infrastructure.

To conclude, the issue of putting the neighborhood back on the market must be understood in two ways:
- The return of real estate investors linked to property that is attractive in a latent way. Public action consists in recycling the property by developing it and adapting it physically and financially to businesses whose sales figure does not mainly depend on the neighborhood. Businesses which are thus attracted to the neighborhood, when the opportunity arises and comes to fruition, transform the urban functions of the neighborhood, put the latter back in the 'common right' of the operation of the town or city and get it out of its specialization (social housing neighborhood inhabited by vulnerable and destitute populations).
- The return of real estate investors linked to the neighborhood's commercial market. Public action in urban renewal consists firstly in developing the neighborhood, reducing the urban divide and improving the accessibility and safety of public space. (It is observed in Reims that this type of action can lead to a growth in the neighborhood's customer catchment area). Secondly, public action can direct the diversification of the living environment on offer and/or the housing supply (reduction of the concentration of social housing, new supply of private housing units) resulting in

a greater mix of income levels and types of consumption. (This is currently the philosophy of the National Urban Renewal Program (PNRU) but the cases studied in which this type of intervention can be relevant (St Etienne and Reims, unlike the case of Clichy) are not yet proven because the demolition/reconstruction operations are under way and the effects cannot yet be measured). However, final success will also depend on another level, that of the neighboring commercial and service infrastructure in the town or city or the city region and competition between local services and the forms of mass distribution which are highly attractive even for populations in problem neighborhoods (it is understandable that the CDC was induced to support studies on commercial infrastructure such as in Reims in order to encourage the City to influence the creation of this infrastructure in a way that does not put neighborhoods undergoing urban renewal at a disadvantage).

This differentiation of the notion of putting the neighborhood back on the market thus gives rise to the need to distinguish between two types of commercial real estate investment in urban renewal projects…
- that which will accommodate secondary or tertiary production activities whose economy does not depend on the economy of the neighborhood (clinics, cinemas, offices, business hotels, etc.);
- that which will accommodate local service activities which depend on the economy of the neighborhood itself (such as local shopping centers);

…and to put the notion of 'black zone' into perspective…
The 'black zone' is often a zone where there is no supply of property. Property which is recycled and developed properly for businesses which seek to set up a new establishment in the town or city, can be enough to turn a black zone into an attractive zone. This is all the more so when the business depends less on its immediate social environment and the issues of accessibility and safety are not considered to be very important.[2] The notion of 'black zone' or 'grey zone' which is a great concern for promoters who operate in a relatively social manner, is not necessarily pertinent and the cases studied show that this notion is relative and varies according to the type of real estate investment and the type of activity accommodated.

…related to the CDC's mission as a 'pioneer investor'

As regards investment in the cases studied, the CDC has often positioned itself explicitly as 'the pioneer investor', the first leading the others along. Moreover, as often stated by the directors of the companies established in the area and the elected officials, 'the CDC's presence has paved the way for us to come along as investors'.

The CDC, with the PRU, has not adopted a follow-the-leader attitude but, rather, is proactive as soon as it is called on to intervene. The cases studied show that the CDC does not encourage real estate investment projects suggested on the basis of nothing (based on products or a development strategy which are not connected to local realities). Rather, it seizes the opportunity to intervene and will help make a project more feasible at the request of the local level (the mayor and the actors in partnership with the urban renewal project).

In general, its intervention speeds up the setting up stage of the operation and encourages other actors to join in (St Etienne, Roubaix, Reims, Creil, Arcueil, among others), although it is not always the first actor that the local authorities think of (see the case of Toulouse). And yet its presence is a 'trigger' (The CDC's presence gives credibility to the operation and assurance to other investors, and reveals the potential of the site) because of:

- Its thorough knowledge of the field, projects and actors based on its participation in the local governance of urban renewal, and its continuous, long-standing observation of local communities and cities, which provides it with information that helps to better identify risks and potentials, the credibility of projects, real support from public authorities, and subsidies that can be mobilized.
- The fact that it leans on the state and its public-interest missions (the PRU is contractualized by the state), which gives it resources that comply with the principle of long-term profitability. It can more easily obtain guarantees from local communities for the loans associated with the operation (which is the case for the PPUs and PRUs).
- Its mix of resources for loans (in particular enriched loans) alongside its own funds which gives the CDC a strong position in capital structure (it is noted that the share of CDC loans can reach 50 percent of the borrowed funds mobilized by the project).
- In some cases (Reims, Roubaix and Arcueil), its capacity for associating with a Mixed Economy Enterprise (*Société d'Economie Mixte*, SEM) having the advantages of being locally rooted and linked with the community (which presides over the SEM). This association allows the CDC to evaluate 'from inside' the development operations and their credibility, and provides it with a partner for carrying and managing the investment. In fact, associating with an SEM is not always a guarantee of operational control since some SEMs are not necessarily adapted to the job of carrying and operating commercial real estate (Clichy), or else are not adapted at all (the development SEM which carries the real estate and lease of the 'Casino' in Vaux en Velin).
- In many others cases (Toulouse, for example), its capacity for associating with private professionals (private promoters/operators of commercial real estate) who provide the CDC with a degree of professionalism.

…related to the effects on the comprehensive urban renewal project

The combination of investment in commercial real estate in association with the public and private sectors and the economic approach to the projects produces several triggering effects on urban renewal:

- An effect which reveals the potential of property in problem neighborhoods within the space of the town or city or urban area: the unlocking of the 'property lock' and the demonstrated investment operation leads to a re-opening of the neighborhood onto the town or city, the return to normality, a break with the prejudices of the residents and actors in the town or city (which in turn have an impact on the value of the residential address and thus lead to the diversification of housing);
- A triggering or facilitating effect on the comprehensive urban project in many of the cases studied where there was a real desire for a comprehensive urban renewal project. For example, in Roubaix, the mayor's intention was clear but it was the success of the establishment of the Grand Rue shopping center which led to the success of the cinema project because the image and reality of the city-center had changed. In Reims, the Hippodrome shopping center provided a solution to a problem that no HLM organizations or the City could solve. Private investment refutes the preconceived ideas about the image of the neighborhood (Roubaix), erases the marks of recent history which may have been dramatic (Creil), contributes to functional de specialization and opens up the scope for the urban renewal project by giving meaning to the demolition-reconstruction project of the new National Agency for Urban Renewal (*Agence Nationale de Renouvellement Urbain*, ANRU) (south-eastern district of St Etienne).
- The effect of 'proving' the pertinence of public and private partnership, the advantage of the presence of the private sector in spaces highly marked by public ownership and management of the exclusive niche of 'social housing', thus an effect of opening up to private partnership and mobilizing new actors, possibilities which were unlikely in the past.

...related to the innovations linked to the CDC's action

The PRU does not seem to have implemented highly innovative solutions related to financial or technical engineering (but rather 'standard' tools such as interest, partners' advances, participatory loans and guaranteed loans). Instead, the innovation has been in the assembling of the operational and financial conditions for boosting investment:
- an attitude of voluntary action: the conviction that the economy and private actors are important for urban renewal and a proactive approach to seizing opportunities and responding to requests;
- a capacity for considering long-term risks, beyond the standards and customs of the usual promoters and economic actors;
- an approach based on unity with the local level: knowing the interlocutors, appraising urban projects, identifying opportunities, market niches, the market and local demand;
- a mix of significant financial means.

Results related to private older housing

Under this theme, four sample sites lent themselves to an evaluation: Roubaix (the oldest), Perpignan, St Etienne and Bordeaux.

Operations which are beginning to yield results (Roubaix/Tourcoing and Bordeaux)

The issue of private older housing is central to the urban renewal project of medium-sized and large cities which have a historic urban center (whether a historical city within the usual meaning of the term such as Bordeaux or an industrial city such as Roubaix/Tourcoing). The specific characteristics of each of the two markets are certainly important for identifying the problems and clearly defining the leverages for action specific to each of the cases. However, the comparison of the Bordeaux site with the Roubaix/Tourcoing site shows that the issue converges, that is, how to redefine the terms of private interventions by implementing instruments of public power (to facilitate or constrain) and achieve the goal of urban renewal of neighborhoods under the right conditions of social mix (Roubaix) or functional mix and housing supply (Bordeaux).

In the case of Roubaix as well as of Bordeaux, the setting up phase was long and complex. The PRU supported the process by funding diagnostic or strategy/market studies through financial tools and especially by giving advice to the elected officials and assisting the operator to get set up and develop the frameworks necessary for intervention. In both cases, the CDC maintained close relations with the city and a *Société d'Economie Mixte* (SEM) near the city. Results have now been achieved in Roubaix after a three-year experimental period: more requalifying work (tripling the average amount of work per housing unit), the number of rehabilitated housing units multiplied by sevenfold within a very limited time frame.

The same is true of Bordeaux with a shorter time span of one and a half years and a mechanism which is not fully in place (in particular the pre-funding of subsidies). In both of these cases, private intervention is a key issue for the mechanism:
- In Bordeaux because one of the problems is pressure from the market and investors whose action is not easily compatible with preserving a degree of mix in the housing supply and in the diversification of urban functions.
- In Roubaix, because the private intervention, while less obvious, is an essential leverage due to the extent of the housing problem in the city. This intervention concerns both owner-occupiers (70 percent of housing units) and 'new homeowners'[3] and investors (who are the only ones who can

renew the rental housing supply and prevent purchases by landlords who sell or rent out housing spaces to needy persons for unreasonable profit).

The key issue is to facilitate and guide private intervention with the help of regulatory, fiscal and financial tools of public intervention. This in order to engage in a 'virtuous' path toward the physical requalification of the housing stock, the diversification of supply and the social mix of households who can gain access to housing in these neighborhoods.

The interventions to which the PRU has contributed have begun to yield results on a full scale related to older housing:
- Through engineering, the PRU helped to bring out, in full scale, an operational method of requalifying physical structures, recycling real estate, diversifying products that are launched and thus the housing supply (in terms of the level of rents and types of housing units).
- At the same time, PRU engineering contributed to structuring (in two out of four cases) adapted engineering and brought out the figure of the 'single operator' for the entire operation.
- The PRU reinforced the processes associating the public sector with the private sector, linking regulatory constraints with fiscal incentives, and striving to take into account the mechanisms of the local market and the economic operation of real estate investment.
- The PRU developed adapted financial products ('advance fund' and loans for the poorest households).

New financial products and support for the emergence of the urban renewal operator in private housing (relying on the SEM network) have proven to be the two main keys to success in the entire operation. The CDC gained the role of leading partner even though it has not been directly involved in the day-to-day operation (for example, according to its DR, the CDC, which has been invited to all steering committees, has intervened only in order to complete the mechanism which usually operates without it, once the setting up stage is complete).

Operations whose results are still uncertain (St Etienne, Perpignan)

The PRU's intervention and contribution to support the will for renewal at the local level, which were very positively illustrated by the Roubaix and Bordeaux operations, must be compared with the two examples of St Etienne and Perpignan which illustrate the most difficult obstacles to overcome.

St Etienne is the example of a municipality which hesitated to embark on the path of rehabilitating private housing because, in this city, the idea of older neighborhoods being strategic for urban renewal was new. The CDC, through the PRU and within the Public Interest Group (*Groupement d'Intérêt Public*, GIP) which it helped to establish, has largely contributed to the emergence of the older neighborhoods project and exchanges of experience, allowing St Etienne to find out about and meet with actors from other cities engaged in this mechanism (including Roubaix). However, the CDC has been less involved in the operational implementation of solutions:
- in the financial mechanism that it left to other local operators;
- in the emergence of a 'reference operator'[4] which is nevertheless a condition for success of this type of operation.

Today, the operation has got underway behind schedule and with a degree of timidity (housing block test cases). The issue involved is the threshold effect below which it is unlikely that market forces and the effect of urban renewal by the private sector will come into play. There is a temptation to entrust the rehabilitation of buildings to HLM operators. However, in addition to not knowing whether the latter can rally around such a goal which brings into play know-how that considerably differs from their own, the effect of restoring the dynamics of the market would not be activated. The CDC is following in the background a file *(dossier)* that is managed by the GIP and the SEM in the department (but with financial products which were not put in place by the CDC since the DR was not convinced of the pertinence of the CDC's involvement).

The case of Perpignan is different. The DR has a strong presence there but the weakness of services and local operators has not fostered the emergence of a strong operator which would save time in achieving full operational development (the operation is barely underway today). The CDC's DR is highly involved in setting up the financial support mechanisms in Perpignan (it will directly manage the advance fund scheme). However, it cannot push the local organization and therefore the economic dimension of the urban renewal driving force might well fall far behind the social or procedural approach.

The CDC's role at the national level and the development of an 'older housing product'

It is now clear that the CDC, through the PRU's action in the older neighborhoods, has replaced the action of the state and has opened a path toward urban renewal which goes beyond the sole issue of the rehabilitation of social housing neighborhoods. It anticipated a question that elected officials are now asking the state (which is having problems deciding on a doctrine related to the field).

At the national level, the CDC's action has been twofold:
- disseminating the setting up and professionalizing of many project teams, which are then connected with one another at the end of the PRU period;
- following up the issue of older housing with the state while suggesting the implementation of new actions to improve housing.

The CDC thus plays the role of mediator/developer, at the center of a set of actors which unites three large groups:
- the elected officials of towns and cities confronted with the issue of the role of older neighborhoods in urban renewal and in particular the requalification of the supply of housing units and the related social mix;
- the operators which, as for the pioneers, are fully developing their know-how, and as for the newcomers, are in search of this know-how and learning;
- the central and local administrations.

This role has been acquired in the PRU at an operational and local level (and the practical effects are visible in the field) and is being extended to the national level with the debate on the urban renewal of older neighborhoods with the state. In a prospective way, this debate will have far-reaching repercussions at the local level with the establishment of delegations to manage state aids to housing. It is clear that the operational nature of intervention in older neighborhoods and the leverage represented by private housing in the development of a local policy on housing and diversification of supply will particularly influence the balance of the means allocated to the various housing stocks.

The effects observed for private housing as a whole

The effects of the PRU's intervention in the field must be evaluated in an analytical way, given that this intervention area has barely come out of the study and setting up phase and that there is certainly not enough hindsight to assess its successes or failures and characterize the lasting and effective results.

Several conclusions can be formulated at this stage:

a The operations carried out with PRU support in older housing, when the local communities embark on the project without hesitation and a pertinent operator can be put in place, have a significant effect on physical requalification and can take into account the quantitative dimension of the issue.

b The return of private investors (owner-occupiers and sponsors, new homeowners and investors) takes place as soon as a comprehensive project is carried out by the local community, a mechanism of technical and financial advice and support is in place, and especially when the process of recycling property carries out the extensive work of consolidating the framework of the physical structures which cannot be undertaken by private investment (for technical, legal or financial reasons).

c The operations in older housing influence the entire range of housing units (see Roubaix and especially Bordeaux for rental products) and it is known that they produce a diversification of supply by developing a private rental supply. HLM organizations can occasionally intervene in a localized way but their intervention is not decisive (and may be counter exemplary for the private sector).

d The social goal of keeping residents in the neighborhood is achieved: where there is political will, the mechanisms to ensure the creditworthiness of low-income owner-occupiers and the rental contracts of investors effectively contribute to preservation.

e The requalification of condominiums has been experimented with results in the older neighborhoods and in small condominiums even though the state's framework of legal and financial intervention is still not highly favorable to it. However, the rehabilitation of large, run down condominiums, turning them into new housing, is still at an impasse.

f It is clear that the subject of private housing (which is marginal in the files *(dossier)* carried by the state) has today emerged as an important aspect in urban renewal. However, the positioning of public action in partnership with the private sector is fragile in terms of national policy and the generalization of the rehabilitation of private housing still encounters obstacles. Based on the results of the PRU, the CDC indeed plays the role of facilitator to ensure the development of the process within the framework of a forthcoming public policy.

Results related to social housing

By authorizing the PRU Loan to fund housing, the CDC program met a need. Overall, 48 percent of the PRU Loan was dedicated to the extensive rehabilitation of social housing, including 2/3 for financial engineering related to demolition/reconstruction. This means that where the local communities had a coherent urban renewal project and/or where they were able to convince the services of the state (even when instructions still involved restriction), the social housing organizations (*Organisme de Logement Sociale*, OLSs) found the resources to fund the operations in the PRU-loan.

Nevertheless, the PRU Loan and the potential state subsidies that the Policy for the City has been able to release, have dealt with the problem in terms of operation (the building or group of buildings) whereas the economic consequences for the OLSs have not been taken into account. This is why the PRU program took charge of a 'high-ratio loan' financed through their own funds in order to smooth out in the medium term the negative effects of demolition and while waiting for the OLSs to restore their operational balance. This intervention has involved a limited number of organizations.

The linkage between the use of loans and the 'comprehensive projects' is however not evident in the interpretation of PRU management. At the local level, the discussions with the project managers (local communities or GIP) show that there is a split at this level. This is due to the fact that the *Grands Projets de Ville* (large urban projects, GPV) did not take up housing in the contractualizion since the project managers would not have been able to monitor the flow of financial resources mobilized by the housing operations. The project managers in general have only qualitatively monitored the demolitions and rehabilitations and the PRU has not changed this established fact.[5] However, the DRs emphasize that the loans were part of the PRU leverages which served to gain entry into the urban renewal project and earn the role of partner. The loans were in a good position next to the co-funding of engineering (and of investments if applicable). Loans and funds went together and the PRU was an important vector in the loan activity, which was lucrative for the CDC.

In terms of effects:
- Locally, the PRU played the role of facilitator for demolition, in general managed within an urban renewal project (Reims), but not always (demolition is also carried out as a curative solution in a crisis as shown, for example, by the case of the south-eastern district of St Etienne); in all the cases studied, the PRU, by gradually defusing the highly critical situations through demolition, gave a new dynamism to urban renewal projects in the social housing neighborhoods.[6]
- The PRU was the operational 'testing ground' for demolition/reconstruction as leverage for urban renewal before being taken back by the ANRU. Through the PRU, the CDC was able to examine step by step the data on the financial package of these operations. The PRU provided the opportunity for a significant reflection on the solutions to bring to the problems encountered. Through the *Fonds Renouvellement Urbain*, FRU, it was possible to experiment with solutions which were innovative in relation to current practice, such as high-ratio loans. The CDC has brought to the ANRU solutions tried out under the PRU.
- The observation of the sample cases which were involved in the restructuring of social housing suggests that the PRU greatly contributed to preparing the ground for the projects which are currently being examined by the ANRU and which did not come to fruition under the GPV. In the social housing sites studied, two out of three cases (St Etienne and Reims) were able to immediately present to the ANRU a project which included a housing strategy, produced with the support of PRU engineering and in continuity with the pioneer operations on housing (including the demolitions).
- The PRU-backed operations represent an opportunity for putting together the typological housing supply in a reasonably solid manner in response to evolving demand. However, the diversification of statuses of housing units is not highly visible even in the case of Reims where the reconstructions are about to be delivered.[7] Rental social housing still predominates in the neighborhoods.

Impacts of the PRU: confirmation of the CDC's innovative action

The *ex post* evaluation of the Urban Renewal Program of *Caisse des Dépôts* highlighted two main operational contributions that the PRU made in two specific areas which are useful for local community projects:

- The diversification of the housing supply through long-term reinvestment:
    - This approach was operationalized for social housing. The CDC supported the demolition by funding engineering and through adapted funding products; the PRU facilitated the action of social housing organizations in the area of extensive restructuring of the housing stock by reinforcing the economic balance of the demolition/reconstruction operations.
    - This approach was tried out with promising success for private older housing. The CDC contributed to the emergence of a new engineering, assembling the tools of public authorities and private investment.
    - In the area of recent private housing in condominiums, the CDC has developed important activity in engineering. The operations conducted under the PRU have contributed to the assessment of the challenge and limitations of current responses by the state and local communities; the CDC has helped to explore a few possible responses even though this experiment did not yield proven results during the length of the program.

- The economic regeneration of problem neighborhoods based on the return of private investment in commercial real estate:
    - This approach led to a significant number of operations in still difficult sites (considered as 'black or grey zones' with little or no private investment in previous years).
    - This approach translated into a wide range of 'products' made up of 'local' real estate investments (local, commercial or service facilities) or real estate investments that accommodate activities included in the territory of the urban region and/or the overall economy (cinemas, health facilities, downtown shopping centers, offices, commercial real estate).
    - This approach was implemented in the context of public - private partnerships where the efforts of the local community were concentrated on improving the physical and social environment (for example, urban transportation, development of public spaces, accessibility, parking and reinforced safety management) and where private investment brought together a broad sample of private, and in particular local, investors.

Through the PRU, the CDC was able to explore on a full scale and within the given time frame, new processes and tools which are now part of its heritage (in the literal sense and the sense of its professional expertise). These new processes and tools attempt to construct, over the long term, responses to two main challenges for urban renewal:
- achieving a social mix through the diversification of the housing supply in a neighborhood;
- putting neighborhoods back into the regular economy and the real estate market through the return of investments in commercial real estate.

The PRU evaluation (given the short implementation period of four years) did not yield an overall result on these two goals, but the operational success of the actions carried out has increased the possibility of achieving them.

Thus, it is perfectly clear that the PRU sought to develop responses that were specific to the CDC in order to meet the challenges of urban renewal; hence, PRU interventions were related to:
- either the overlooked aspects of public policy (for example, commercial real estate, the quest for partnership with private investment, putting the neighborhood back on the market, older private housing);
- aspects related to public policy: the demolition of social housing units as a response to the restructuring of supply (while the state often held up or even blocked the projects which put demolition at the center of the solutions for urban renewal, between 1998 and 2003).

With regard to the national policy, the PRU has also presented itself as an experimental program. It will have served as a testing ground for experimenting with new ways (by relying in particular on its role as banker):
- It sought more to 'make to measure' and to 'open up courses of action' rather than to generalize as is shown, for example, by the specific character of the majority of investment actions and the interventions in the area of older housing.
- It triggered studies, diagnoses and support related to the local systematic and exploratory reflection. Based on quite a broad program theory, the CDC's local teams were invited to work on local urban renewal projects. As regards investment, for example, analyses were systematically developed in all the urban districts affected by the Policy for the City; a small part of this research was used in the first concrete operations implemented by the Program.
- It is also likely that engineering has produced other courses of action than the two sets of operations described above which could be of interest to other levels of urban renewal (the level of the urban region for example) or other areas of collaboration between the public sector and private sector.
- Following this extensive, experimental engineering process, the PRU came up with a requirement for concrete operations.[8] This corresponded to a tightening of action and the issues addressed. However, the process remained without preconceived ideas regarding standardized 'products', and continued to be open to opportunities and projects in the territories concerned.

Today, the CDC is seeking to move from an experimental approach to a more systematized approach to urban renewal:
- Having invested most of its efforts in engineering to serve the urban renewal projects of the ANRU, the CDC has largely lost its capacity for responding to local requests 'outside the norm'.
- It systematizes the process of real estate investment based on a list of 'products' which stem from the PRU, but which are limited, that is, cinemas, health services, offices and shopping centers.
- It seeks to bring out a box of tools that is complete and can be generalized to the field of requalifying rehabilitation and the rehabilitation of condominiums fallen into disrepair, in particular with the *Agence Nationale pour l'Amélioration de l'Habitat* (ANAH).

Logically, then, a shift is taking place from a 'research-development' approach (which is experimental and very open) to a process of 'development' (which is normative and less open).

Conclusion

The Urban Renewal Program of the CDC became all the more important during the year 2000, when the state launched the national program of *Grands Projects de Ville* (large urban projects, GPV) and *Opérations de Renouvellement Urbain* (urban renewal operations, ORU). This turning point in national policy marked a return to an infrastructural approach to the rehabilitation of problem neighborhoods after a long period when social measures were favored (with the 'contracts for the city'). This evolving national policy corresponded with the capabilities of the CDC which had the means and the skills to support investment polices in the urban infrastructure.

The CDC, with the PRU, decided to insist on the necessarily comprehensive dimension of the urban renewal project. To this end, it developed intense support activity related to project engineering and the structuring of partnership-based governance of projects. Alongside a national approach which put priority on urban planning led by public authorities, the CDC also developed complementary courses of action:

- supporting local communities for in-depth restructuring of the housing supply (and supporting, with social housing organizations, the emergence of demolition operations and, with private owners, the requalification of the private housing stock);
- emphasizing the economic revival of problem neighborhoods and attempting to operationalize this goal through the return of private investment to the field of commercial real estate.

Today and since 2004, with the National Urban Renewal Policy (*Programme National de Renouvellement Urbain*, PNRU) and the creation of the National Agency for Urban Renewal (ANRU), the state has again re-oriented its action by putting priority on the approach of restructuring the supply of social housing, in particular through demolition and reconstruction.

The CDC is again working to help achieve this national policy:
- it continues to pursue its efforts in project engineering (but is shifting its focus to the operational phases within ANRU projects);
- it continues to pursue its loan activity (PPU and PRU).

However, the state and its associated partners within the ANRU have taken over, on a full scale, the issue of demolition. And the innovations with which the CDC experimented through the PRU have today become part of the 'common right' of ANRU aids. The CDC's role has lost initiative and creativity. But it can be clearly seen that this new orientation regarding 'urban renewal', although justified and pertinent in the short term, has again overlooked entire areas of the urban renewal issue:
- it has focused its efforts on social housing neighborhoods and has largely overlooked the issue of older neighborhoods (for which it intervenes in a selective and limited way only for the older neighborhoods of the GPV/ORU);
- it has reduced its approach to that of the 'neighborhood project' and has withdrawn from the level of the urban region;
- it has not taken up the entire issue of economic revival and private investment in the area of commercial real estate (that was identified by the PRU).

The state's highly targeted prioritization process called Urban Renewal should not cause us to lose sight of the fact that the purpose of the challenge of urban renewal is broad:
- the problems that public authorities and in particular the local communities have to deal with today, in terms of problem neighborhoods, cannot be reduced solely to projects that are reshaped through aids of the National Urban Renewal Policy and the ANRU;
- the solutions to be brought do not only involve social housing and the development of neighborhoods where the latter predominates.

As in 1999/2000, urban renewal is not limited to the segment on which the state is concentrating its action today. The context has not changed. The CDC, which is attentive to the needs of local communities and is willing to put at their disposal its role as banker and its acquired skills, is maintaining a broad field of action in order to take complementary and useful initiatives related to urban renewal.

References

Sueur, J.-P., 1998, *Demain la ville*, Ministère de l'emploi et de la solidarité, Paris.

Thiveaud, J.-M., 1991, La gestation séculaire de l'Etat dépositaire dans l'Europe des Lumières, *Revue d'économie financière,* Hors-Série: Caisse des dépôts et consignations - 175 ans, pp 13-36.

Trichet, J.-C., 1991, La CDC et l'économie nationale, *Revue d'économie financière,* Hors-Série: Caisse des dépôts et consignations - 175 ans, pp 397-402.

Notes

1. The CDC is represented in 26 French regions by a *Direction Régionale* (regional office, DR).

2. However, it should be recognized that the problem is slightly different concerning housing units (for homeowners for example) because the social status of those living in the neighborhood and the socio-cultural image of the district (school, facilities) have a much greater influence on the value of the 'residential address' than is the case for production activities. Social housing neighborhoods are sometimes 'black zones' which are more difficult to overcome when it comes to the home ownership market.

3. New homeowners are not first-time homeowners. These are not households who own their home for the first time but households who are about to buy in the neighborhood and represent a potential for social diversification. This involves encouraging new homeowners, who will participate in the requalification process as soon as they have bought their home, by assisting them to create a rehabilitation file while buying (and, in particular assisting them to construct their funding plan by including the work that will need to be carried out).

4. This term is used here for lack of a better one. The use of the term 'reference' here means that there should be a developer-operator responsible for the entire 'chain' of rehabilitation of housing units and the successful completion of the series of procedures; it does not mean that there should not be a group of operators who are specialized in the various segments of the project.

5. In the various intervention areas of the PRU (FRU and PRU/PPU Loan), the same split is observed between the project managers responsible for the physical and social aspects and the financial managers who negotiate funding with the CDC. Funds based on loans and also on subsidies from the PRU are not necessarily known by the local project managers who have difficulty in refunding the PRU interventions in this area.

6. The effect is premonitory of the ANRU's current success as can be observed in the sample studied. By striving to put housing and its funding at the center of the mechanism to support the projects, and by being permissive about demolition, the ANRU today provides an operational perspective to the urban renewal projects of the GPV/ORU.

7. But Reims is an exceptional case in terms of the weight of social housing in relation to total housing in the city and in terms of the concentration of the buildings of only three social housing organizations in the rental supply (dominating the housing stock).

8. It is mainly this one that the evaluation reports on today.

13 The Case of Jerusalem: a Study in Complexity

Rami Nasrallah and Amin Amin

Introduction

The Madrid Conference of October 1991 is widely recognized as the beginning of the Middle East peace process. Negotiations have stuttered fitfully forward, and backward, now for well over a decade. And perhaps no issue has been so nettlesome as the status of Jerusalem which was introduced in the direct negotiations between the Palestinian Liberation Organization (PLO) and Israel at Oslo in 1993. There, the future of Jerusalem was raised by the Palestinian delegation as part of its negotiation agenda that included other seemingly intractable issues such as refugees, settlements, borders and water rights. However, the Israeli side refused to deal with the Jerusalem question, and through the intervention of the international community, it was postponed to the final status negotiations.

Since that time, many attempts were made by Palestinians and Israelis to discuss the plight of the Holy City, and their efforts have basically focused on reaching a formula of solution for peace making. The complexity of the situation in Jerusalem - where Palestinians and Israelis live in one urban fabric, which is physically undivided but functionally, socially, and culturally deeply divided - is daunting. This reality brought a group of Palestinian and Israeli professionals - urban planners, architects, engineers, social and political scientists, civil society leaders, representatives of decision makers in the public and private sectors - together to explore ways in which they might serve Jerusalem better and to examine whether a solution for the Jerusalem problem could be rather distinct from the resolution of the overall conflict.

In the beginning there were many doubts in the group whether it would be possible to bring Palestinians and Israelis to discuss Jerusalem. A deeply ingrained belief on the Israeli side, the settled perception that Jerusalem is the unified eternal capital of the Jewish state, made Jerusalem a taboo topic for the Israelis, even though the issue lay at the heart of the conflict. On the other hand, the Palestinians considered East Jerusalem as an integral part of the occupied West Bank, and they believed that in any peace settlement, Israeli should end its occupation and domination of the Eastern section, occupied since 1967. It took the two sides quite some time to conclude that despite the disagreement and the gap between basic assumptions, there was still something to discuss for the benefit of both sides and the benefit of the city. This conviction led them to accept the invitation of the Swedish Olof Palme International Center in early summer of 1996 to a conference in the Woods of Bommersvik close to Stockholm. The parties met six days from June 5 through June 10. They found it difficult to agree even on the name of the conference. The Israelis did not want to give it any name that might suggest that the discussions were back channel negotiations. Finally, both sides agreed to designate the meeting as the 'Conference about the Current and Future Urban Problems in the Area of Jerusalem'. This title was a compromise between the desire of the Israelis to talk only about the problems of daily life and the Palestinian insistence on discussing the political future of the city. Despite this gap from day one, both sides agreed during the conference that the urban problems of Jerusalem needed to be addressed, and detailed functional solutions need to be developed in order to facilitate the implementation of a peace agreement concerning the city's future. Both sides presumed that the final peace agreement on the conflict would in all probability address only the broad important political sovereignty issues and would not address the mechanisms and practical solutions related to the urban functions of the city as a whole.

The current reality in Jerusalem was the main factor behind the large gap that existed between the two sides; Israeli participants reflected the majority feeling among Israelis that Israel is the dominant party that controlled the city and its future by means of military and economic force. Israel is the strong party on the ground that transformed the occupation of the East part of the city in an annexation plan and a new reality with a Jewish majority. Meanwhile the Palestinian participants' stand point also reflected the majority of Palestinian being the weak party that is under Israeli domination, and that their existence and aspiration is controlled by means of military force. The reality of unbalanced power between Palestinians and Israelis was reflected clearly, especially in the first meetings.

This entire process eventually engaged more than one hundred Palestinian and Israeli participants. Rather amazingly, they kept their co-operation in a continuous accumulative process despite the cycles of political unrest which the city and the region have endured over the years that have elapsed since that first meeting in Bommersvik in 1996. This Chapter documents the process of Palestinian/Israeli co-operation from that date through the years till the end of 2005. It also documents the development of ideas and materials over the course of the discussions, including a consensus on transforming the city from an area of conflict to an innovative urban space that is shared on the functional level, and divided politically and ethno-nationally.

The writers' personal involvement and participation in organizing the activities of this process since its beginning gave us the opportunity to review all the work done by both teams and to identify dynamics and developments that can be offered as a general framework to be shared as an experience with other world cities. Underlying this Chapter are more than eighty unpublished papers, manuscripts and reports documenting this process, in addition to personal interviews and discussions with participants, and publications that appeared in a later stage of this process.

The first move

Jerusalem is considered one of the most attractive cultural, historical and religious places in the world, and because of its cultural and religious connotations, the city has high emotional value and political significance to millions of Jews, Christians and Moslems all over the world. This makes reaching peace in the region conditioned on attaining peace in Jerusalem. Indeed, Jerusalem may well be the core issue around which the region will either see a secured peace or continue to experience violence and wars.

All who care about the future of the city must recognize the absolute necessity of resolving the conflict over Jerusalem in a way that leads to the peaceful existence of both national groups; the Israelis and the Palestinians. Further, given the city's volatile impact on the national, regional and international arenas, the sincere efforts of all are required.

In a spirit of optimism, and after signing the Oslo agreement in September 1993, and the Oslo B ('Oslo 2') in 1995, joint teams of seventeen Palestinian and seventeen Israeli academics, decision makers, practitioners and civil society activists, worked together in the period from 1996 to 2001 on the conflict in Jerusalem and its future perspective. They focused on different urban aspects of the Jerusalem issue and they sought to provide practical solutions that would support peace-building and prepare both sides for living together the 'day after' reaching a peace settlement.

The two groups represented a joint endeavor of concerned parties drawn from civil society and academia. They operated under the umbrella of two think tanks, the International Peace and Co-operation Center (IPCC), a Palestinian organization based in East Jerusalem, and the Jerusalem Institute for Israel Studies (JIIS), an Israeli body sited in West Jerusalem. A Swedish partner to the project, the Olof Palme International Center, provided financial support and facilitated the sensitive coming together of the Palestinians and Israelis who rarely co-operate around the issue of Jerusalem's future.

The first meeting was a week-long conference held in the summer of 1996 at Bommersvik, a resort in the woods and near a small lake outside Stockholm. The venue is regularly used by the leaders of the Swedish Social Democratic Party and is owned by the party's youth organization. Bommersvik was the site of heated discussions. The dialogue was characterized, at the beginning, by strong mutual suspicion and caution. Each side considered the other to be the opposition. It began in the mode of a polarizing negotiating session, but soon interaction and candid discussions began to take place as the participants became comfortable with the unique circumstances of being with the 'enemy' for the first time to discuss the most complicated issues of the ethno-national conflict on the macro level and on the level of the city of Jerusalem. The symbolic value of Jerusalem caused the first meetings to be more complicated; each party considered any move in the direction of the other party as renouncing the gained symbolic rights in Jerusalem.

The discussion focused on the general state of affairs, the status of various urban functions, and the future of Jerusalem. Inevitably, these topics led to the discussion of the relations between the two conflicting parties on all levels and into such areas as the Israeli settlements, territorial compromise, and the refugee issue. The interaction on these subjects was not confined to the formal meetings but also continued in breaks and during social activities.

This first conference in the summer of 1996 was more or less an exploration of the past causes and results of the conflict. The conference was effectively the kick-off of an accumulative process in which the Palestinian and Israeli think tanks continued to work closely on issues identified by the participants in their initial gathering. These issues included city planning, housing, legal aspects of residency, physical infrastructure as well as social, economic, cultural, environmental and human resource development problems. The aim was to work on themes related to various functional aspects of the city, and to the relationship between the two national groups when the political future of the city has been determined. It also addressed the way the city would perform its functions after a partial or comprehensive political solution has been reached by the leaders of the two national groups.

The basic assumption of the Bommersvik group at that time was that a political solution for future Jerusalem must be based on an undivided and open city functioning as an integrative urban unit. The joint teams agreed on the goal of their work, which was to initiate and maintain a long-term constructive process through which Palestinian and Israeli civil society, Jerusalem experts from both sides, could together develop practical solutions for the current and future political, social, economic and urban issues of Jerusalem and its surrounding area.

The joint team believed that, unlike other negotiation issues, resolving the Jerusalem question lies in recognizing a number of common needs and sharing interests that could not be achieved without co-operation and the joining of Palestinian and Israeli efforts. It was recognized that resolving the conflict over Jerusalem necessitated an in-depth exploration of its various aspects, and a detailed understanding of the city's dynamics and an assessment of the potential effect of ongoing processes and future trends. This sort of inquiry would stimulate initiating models for a mutually accepted constructive and positive relationship in the city. The overarching questions, then, were what life quality are we to share and how wiil that contribute to peace-building in the city.

The Bommersvik group certainly did not intend to introduce or launch a political negotiation framework or a back channel negotiation. Rather, the teams sought to contribute to developing a mutual understanding that would support joint planning for a peaceful future in the city, where Palestinians and Israelis live 'together separately' in one urban unit divided on the basis of national affiliation.

The joint work

In the days following the first conference, the Palestinian and Israeli members of the joint teams worked in subgroups and met regularly once every three weeks to exchange ideas and report on their progress. Seven different subgroups were formed, each handling a different topic related to Jerusalem and its future. The subgroups gathered in joint meetings four times before attending subsequent annual conferences in Bommersvik, in which they presented their findings and recommendations.

At the beginning of this process, discussions were based on negation on the existence of 'the other'. The subgroups adopted a confrontational attitude in which each side blamed the other for the deteriorating conditions in the Jerusalem area. However, over time, the atmosphere improved. Discussions came to focus on existing situations, and exploring the scope of problems and challenges encountered. Dialogs over the current situation have also faced difficulties in justifying the existing gap between urban development processes in Eastern and Western Jerusalem. Both sides explored the deteriorating conditions and identified the different factors connecting development processes and dependency relationships between the two conflicting parties.

The shift from confrontation to a more co-operative interaction that developed throughout the Bommersvik process between 1996 and 2000 was evident in nature of the issues addressed, the quality of the presented papers, and in the way the relationship between the participants matured. Together, they have concluded researches and studies; they have identified problems facing social, economic, infrastructure, cultural, environmental and human resource development in the Jerusalem area; they have proposed rectifying policies and modes of action that would serve the accommodation of the additional needs and aspirations; and they addressed the need for transforming the conflict.

There were more than 30 topics in the 1997 Bommersvik conference; most of the presented papers were jointly written. The joint papers analyzed the urban functional problems and proposed policies and modes of actions that would help in bridging the gap in the standards of living between Palestinians and Israelis in the city, and consequently in facilitating the urban peace building in Jerusalem.

The following chart (Illustration 13.1) indicates the different levels of political and urban division of Jerusalem between the two national groups. These levels were the guiding principles of the work of the joint teams, which were developed following the third conference in 1998. This chart was modified as the work progressed. In the initial stage, the Israeli team wanted to focus, basically, on the daily life in Jerusalem and considered the political future of the city a taboo not to be discussed with the Palestinian counterpart. On the other side, Palestinians raised the political demand of East Jerusalem and the Palestinian sovereignty as a basic need, and stated that in the absence of a political solution, the functionality in the city and its daily life would be irrelevant.

Each year, after the conclusion of the annual conference, each organization then presented, to key decision-makers and politicians, the findings and recommendations of each conference. Public meetings with the community were organized to share the conference conclusions with the citizenry, to gather and consider their input and feedback and to raise their knowledge on key vital issues for the future of Jerusalem.

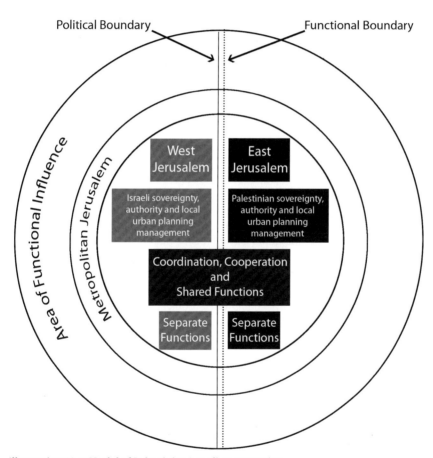

Illustration 13.1: Model of Palestinian Israeli co-operation

Chapter 13: The Case of Jerusalem: a Study in Complexity

Early vision

Over the course of almost six years of joint endeavor, Palestinians and Israeli participants did not only started a process of mutual understanding, but also developed personal relationships that facilitated the formation of a permanent, harmonized core team of intellectuals, civil society representatives, and professionals who have mutually built confidence among themselves. This has anchored the basis for sharing the city in a way that responds to the needs and interests of each national group. Consequently, the group members and organizers realized that together they could articulate a comprehensive vision for the city. The new vision focused on involving the community in its formulation, influencing decision makers and different stakeholders and raising the public awareness on different issues within the formulated vision. This is considered a key turning point and crucial development of a continuous genuine process, geared toward effectuating positive change in the relationship between Palestinians and Israelis in the city for the sake of attaining a durable peace.

The debate of the Bommersvik annual conference held in August 1999 produced a major shift away from discussing the consequences of the conflict and its implications on Jerusalem's realities, to actively analyzing its causes and trying to find solutions of mutual interest. Thus, the joint teams were able to address very sensitive issues such as the geopolitical borders of the city and explore alternative frameworks for the urban future in Jerusalem. In this conference, it was agreed to draft principles for a joint vision on the future of Jerusalem between Palestinians and Israelis and to examine the vision in relation to three possible scenarios:
- An open city, with Palestinian sovereignty in East Jerusalem and Israeli sovereignty over West Jerusalem;
- A politically and physically divided city;
- An open city with functional sovereignty.

The year 2000 conference witnessed another positive move. Most of the papers presented by the teams focused on the future and less on the past and present. The two national groups were more open than ever in discussing the geopolitical solutions. The fact that the Jerusalem Institute for Israeli Studies materials were used during the Camp David II peace negotiations by the Israeli delegation gave more viability for the long-term partnership. Some of these materials had been developed through the Bommersvik process and the joint work had been preserved as a 'support system' for the negotiations on the future of the city. The debate shifted from how to facilitate reaching a solution, to how to effect a change in the image of Jerusalem from a conflict city to a city of peace.

The joint teams developed a matrix summarizing vision components and their functions that needed to be worked out by the joint teams and presented in the Bommersvik 2001 summer conference: Illustration 13.2. The three main components of the vision, agreed on by the joint team were that Jerusalem will be a capital city, an open complex viable city and a world city.
The outcome of the 1996-2001 Bommersvik process had two outputs: a 'learning by doing' process and a content and knowledge base which formed the foundation for the analysis and typology of models for the development of the city in the peace era. The joint teams established a rich database of information, ideas that will help in setting the agenda for the city's future. The products of this process were diverse; they included academic papers, background information papers, and policy or position papers.

		Capital City	Complex Viable and Open City	World city
Functions		Boundaries	Tourism and services	Multiculturalism
		National symbols	Local and international investment	Images
		Religious sites	Higher education and human capitals	Relation with regional and global centers
		Government compound	Transportation and integrated infrastructure	International institutions
		Legislative and judicial institutions	Relation with the hinterland	Religious institutions
		Diplomatic representation	Relation with the other urban centers	
		Municipal organizational structures	Transfer of technologies	Global economic base
		Local and national political structures	Joint strategic plan for Jerusalem	
		Educational system	Shared Urban Functions	
		Civil society	Green areas and parks	
		Planning and land use	Environment, water and sewage	
		Infrastructure	Umbrella municipality governing two municipalities: Palestinian and Israeli	
		Images and landscape	Social and ethnic spatial distribution	International education on conflict, peace and interfaith
		National economic base	Dialogue and co-operation between Palestinian and Israeli civil societies	

Illustration 13.2: General matrix summarizing vision components according to functions

Some of the annual conferences were attended by politicians and key advisers of political leaders. This made the discussions much more relevant to the decision making process. The group argued that peace agreements will not be detailed enough to include urban functions and practical solutions for the urban fabric and its sustainability. During this process, the joint teams worked with politicians and decision makers to convince them to adopt a multidimensional approach to a solution for Jerusalem - not just a political resolution but solutions for the economic, infrastructural, environmental, urban planning and social mobility aspects also. This will contribute to the mechanisms which bring peace and foster urban peace building (Illustration 13.3).

Chapter 13: The Case of Jerusalem: a Study in Complexity

Overall vision	Images, culture and religion	Economic Development	Civil society
Jerusalem/Al Quds will become a capital for both; Israel and the Palestine. It will develop into a viable open and complex city as well as becoming a world city.	An inter-religious vision for Jerusalem based on recognizing the expression and practices of rituals, customs and beliefs of each community group in Jerusalem.	Jerusalem as a center for regional and international economic prosperity and sustainable development.	Centrality of the civil society in attaining a peacefully shared future in the city.
Conflict free; environment, steadily growing economy, flourishing civil society and public-private partnership are the major pillars for a viable future in the city.	General guidelines for preserving the cultural heritage in a way that responds to the needs of the people and the international importance of Jerusalem.	Innovation of new tourist attractions and products.	Develop mechanisms that contribute to the creation of peace between the two national groups that live in Jerusalem parallel to pursuing principles of sustainable development.
Build images of a future characterized by a shared peace, a democratic and economically developed city.	Guiding principles for rectifying the negative influence on architectural images.	Marketing plan for tourism reflects Jerusalem as a peace promoting city.	High investment in education and in developing human capital.
Peace building process in Jerusalem necessitates the initiation of a bottom-up promotion campaign that focuses on feasibility of peace and enlightening the public on vital issues for just, and equitable and lasting coexistence in the city.		Developing new economic sectors specially IT, applied research and financial services.	
		Housing is a main economic sector. Planning and a financing scheme will be developed to offer the city residents high standards of living.	

Illustration 13.3: Points of agreement between the Palestinians and Israelis at Bommersvik (1996-2001)

Back to Jerusalem

The collapse of the Camp David II negotiations and the onset of the second Intifada in September 2000, followed by Israeli and American declarations that the elected Palestinian leadership was an irrelevant non-eligible partner, has effected Palestinian/ Israeli co-operation, especially in relation to Jerusalem issues that had been the focus of the Camp David summit. The fact that the Camp David negotiations failed, due to the high emphasis on religious and national symbols rather than dealing with territorial and functional issues, had two somewhat contradictory impacts on the work of the Bommersvik group: on the one hand, its knowledge base became an important repository of information relevant to understanding the issue, and on the other hand, the work became irrelevant to the peace process itself, which almost stopped.

The uncertainty and the escalation of the conflict created a new reality; from one national side, the whole discussion on an open city shifted to separation. The Israeli public came to favor separation. Concerns over security and a perceived demographic threat combined to serve as justification for this trend.

Israeli voices for an open city were mostly silenced. The restriction of Palestinian mobility increased and entry to Jerusalem became impossible, thus thwarting any positive Palestinian-Israeli contacts. Because of the Israeli closure policies, access to Jerusalem became almost impossible for members of the Palestinian teams living in Ramallah, Bethlehem and other West Bank areas.

The positive atmosphere of preparing for 'the day after' the signing of a peace agreement totally vanished. The raising power of the right wing in Israel and the cycles of successive retaliation, targeted killings and suicide attacks fueled a downward spiral toward greater polarization. The mutual destruction and violence made it more difficult to proceed and to convince our Swedish partner to continue to support our co-operation in the absence of a peace process. Nevertheless, the two organizations; the IPCC and the JIIS, continued to co-operate. A lot of effort was put together to convince European partners to support the continuity of the joint work on Jerusalem, and to avoid the termination of this co-operation. The two sides invested resources and good will. Regretfully, these efforts did not succeed.

The TU Delft Jerusalem Urban Peace Building project

With the knowledge and experience of the Bommersvik meetings, and the willingness to go on, both organizations approached Delft University of Technology (TU Delft) for partnering with them in a peace-building project at the end of year 2000. The involvement of the TU Delft, through CICAT (TU Delft management center for international co-operation) and the Faculty of Architecture, and the participation of Amin, one of the authors of this Chapter, a member of IPCC think tank and the Middle East Senior project manager at TU Delft at the same time, created the opportunity for discussions about ways to develop mechanisms to assist the urban peace transformation in Jerusalem.

The basic assumption reached by the three partners was that peace is not possible unless a mechanism of urban peace building can be developed as an action-oriented plan through trilateral professional

intervention. The three partners developed a proposal in which the mechanism of urban peace building focused on four main clusters:
- Urban and Architectural Images;
- Housing;
- Conservation of Architecture and Urban Heritage;
- Urban Economy and Sustainable Urban Development in three main qualities: Design, Environment and Process Qualities.

These clusters expressed the city's needs and interests of all its residents, and were supposed to provide politicians and stakeholders from both sides with new urban development scenarios that are based on equality, mutual acceptance and participation of the public.

As a part of the project, a two-day kickoff workshop in Delft was organized in March 2001. Palestinians, Israelis and international experts on ethno-national divided cities worked together on the 'Case of Jerusalem', within the framework of a project that addressed various urban planning issues in the Divided City. In this workshop, the participants spent the two days analyzing the Jerusalem case as a divided city and compared the urban dynamics of Jerusalem with other divided cities, especially Belfast (Northern Ireland), Nicosia (Cyprus), Mostar (Bosnia and Herzegovina) and Johannesberg (Germany).

The three partners failed to convince the Dutch foreign ministry to support this initiative. The deadlock of the peace process and the sensitivity of the issue of Jerusalem seemed to be the reason behind this decision. After the failure of several attempts to raise funding to support this initiative, the project was placed on hold.

Learning from Berlin

The period between September 2000 and October 2001 witnessed clashes and escalation of the conflict in which Palestinian and Israeli civilians were killed in a vicious circle of violence and counter-violence. This situation did not stop the two partners from continuing their co-operation and attempting to involve a third 'knowledge' partner in their efforts. In other words, the group shifted from searching for a venue, like the case of Bommersvik experience, to attempting to engage international partners in sharing experience and knowledge, especially exploring the experience of other divided and formerly divided cities from which Jerusalem can draw negative and positive lessons for any possible peace transformation.

The idea of learning from Berlin was raised for the first time in Jerusalem with the former director of the Friedrich Ebert Stiftung in the summer of 2000. At the beginning, there were many doubts about what Israelis and Palestinians could learn from the German capital. However, after the first familiarization visit to Berlin, at the end of summer 2001, the Jerusalem participants came to believe there is much that can be garnered from the experience of this European city. The processes of political, administrative and physical integration have advanced faster in Berlin than have the processes of social, cultural and economic integration. Thus the first Berlin workshop put its central emphasis on explaining this phenomenon, specifically the disconnection between the general frame of unification and the everyday lives of the people.

As a result of this first visit, the Jerusalem Berlin Forum (JBF) was founded in October 2001; it brought together 10 experts, planners and local decision-makers from a formerly divided city – Berlin – and a team of 16 experts and planners from Jerusalem (8 Palestinians and 8 Israelis) most of which took part in the Bommersvik process. The Berlin experts explored the mechanisms of integration in Berlin, and furthermore, the obstacles to the functioning and unification of the city. Thus, they aimed to assist the Jerusalem group's goal of transforming Jerusalem from being a city of conflict to becoming a city of peace.

The JBF has held four joint workshops since 2001, two workshops in Berlin, and two in Jerusalem. Moreover, in 2003 the JBF published its first book, *Divided Cities in Transition I* (Friedman & Nasrallah, 2003) in which the various participants of the JBF discussed their often diverse assessments of how processes of integration and separation have affected both cities. The book contained 26 articles, in two main parts. The first part contained the Jerusalem Palestinian and Israeli perspectives; 8 articles were by the Palestinian members of the team, and 8 by the Israeli members. In these articles, both teams mixed two interests. A desire to learn from the experience of other divided and formerly divided cities, lessons that would assist both the Palestinians and the Israelis to identify solutions and develop multi-dimensional models of transformation applicable to Jerusalem. Their second desire was to promote a realistic dialogue on the issues they believed to have the greatest impact on the success or failure of the peace-building process in Jerusalem. They discussed different aspects of Jerusalem's reality, and future scenarios between being an open city and one of physical division. This included the fields of economics, geography, urban and spatial dynamics, socio-economic and social development, education, population and boundaries, transition, separation and integration as opposed to co-operation, and the reciprocal relationship of the city with its surroundings.

The second part of the book consisted of 9 articles by the Berlin-team members. In this section, the Berlin team explained the situation in 1990 and the mode of operation of the City Forum '*Stadtforum*', founded in 1991. They illustrated their personal and collective experiences and activities in the formerly divided Berlin and their contributions to the management of transition to a unified Berlin. They also illustrated the 'Social City' program, which was founded to combat socio-geographical division in Berlin.

In July 2005, the second volume of this series, *Divided Cities in Transition II* (Auga, Hasson, Nasrallah & Stetter, 2005) was published. In this book, the German, Israeli and Palestinian participants of the JBF analyzed in further detail the complex processes of transition which affect their respective cities. The aim of the book was to investigate developments in Jerusalem and Berlin, systematically, in order to provide a potential framework for Jerusalem's transformation from a city of conflict to one of peace. It consisted of 12 articles in two main parts. The first part contained 10 articles by the Jerusalem team; 5 of which were presented by the Palestinian team, and 5 by the Israeli team. In these articles, they concluded that the political solution is not sufficient to reach peace transformation; both sides should look at Jerusalem's potential as a world center, which can be the leverage for enhancing the city's centrality for both sides, and that this can only be done through respecting the claims of both parties. They theorized that the only viable approach to the Jerusalem problem is political separation alongside socio-economic and physical integration, and that it can be a positive model of peaceful equal real partnership co-operation, which could transform it from a frontier city into a metropolitan center of the region (Illustration 13.4).

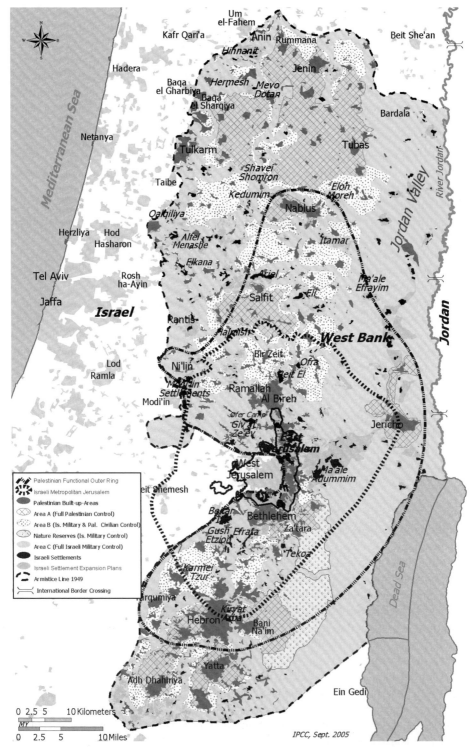

Illustration 13.4: The Palestinian and Israeli metropolitan Jerusalem (Source: Nasrallah, Khamaisi & Youhan, 2003)

The second part of this volume consisted of two articles written collectively by the Berlin team. They discussed the management of transition in Berlin; Berlin between co-operation and division; reconstructing the past via fragmentary analyses of errors and missed opportunities in German unification. The dialogue between and within the Jerusalem and Berlin teams encouraged the Berliners to develop their discourse based on the future issues affecting the two cities. The result has been not only the proposal of models for peaceful transformation in Jerusalem, but has prompted the teams to question for the first time: what went wrong with the unification, and what mistakes can we learn from the past experience? This exercise of reassessing the unification and the integration process has generated a fresh perspective for Berlin.

In the third workshop of the JBF in Berlin, August 2003, we launched the 'Scenario Building' project, incorporating Palestinian and Israeli participants. The dramatic change on the ground by the construction of the Israeli Separation Wall in the Jerusalem area changed the whole atmosphere between the two partners. The Bommersvik process had been focusing on 'the day after' reaching the peace agreement, where the JBF process has been focusing on positive transformation from the current conflict to the peace situation. The deterioration of the situation, where prospects for a renewed peace process seem more distant than ever, has forced both partners to rethink their co-operation. They decided to deal with the negative transformation of the conflict, as well as working to identify factors that will foster the peace transformation and avoid the continuous mutual destruction and escalation of the conflict.

Scenario Building

Jerusalem Scenario Building has become a part of the JBF project. It is an intensive program that started in May 2004 in order to develop scenarios for the future of Jerusalem and strategies of intervention. A group of 12 Palestinian and Israeli planners, economists and social scientists dealt with the complex dimensions of the conflict around Jerusalem, including its ethno-national, political, social, economic and urban consequences. The program has been facilitated by Mr. Dirk Jung, a German expert in developing future scenarios and strategies of intervention from the *Denkmodell* in Berlin.

The participants identified the factors that are supposed to affect the city of Jerusalem and its future, developed matrix relations between the different factors and their driving forces and developed the structure scenario for Jerusalem. The initial scenarios for Jerusalem were developed by the end of December, 2004. It required intensive work to further develop these scenarios and to workout the details and the modifications. The year 2005 was dedicated to this work.

Against this background, this project intended to examine through scenario building different possible futures for Jerusalem. In this way, we enabled the public to review a variety of possible futures and to ask critical questions concerning the future of Jerusalem. Following the 2005 development, we developed a detailed vision for the city of Jerusalem. The difference between the scenarios and the vision are quite clear (Nasrallah, Rassem, Amin, Hidmi, Abu Ghazallah, Wa'ary, Hasson, Fishel, Maoz, Goren, Prince-Gibson & Garb, 2005). Illustration 13.5 shows the scenarios that were developed by the two groups in the Scenario Building 2005 workshop. The groups identified four possible scenarios for the future of Jerusalem, illustrating each by variations of four main factors that affect the future of Jerusalem and its people. These factors are: Strength of Governments, Occupation, Role of Civil Society and International Intervention. The four scenarios varied from a worst-case scenario, to a best-case scenario.

Factor \ Scenario	Strength of government	Occupation	Role of civil society	International intervention
1. The Besieged City (Perpetuation of the Status Quo)	The Palestinian Authority is weak and the Israeli government is strong but lacks a future perspective for a final status agreement. Both governments focus almost exclusively on internal issues.	Israeli occupation continues. Palestinians in the city continue to live between the Israeli and Palestinian systems while belonging to neither.	Civil society is collapsing due to the flight of the elite and middle classes out of both the East and West Jerusalem.	The international community continues to support the Palestinian Authority, avoiding significant support for Jerusalem.
2. The City of Bridges (The Best-Case Scenario)	The two strong governments are able to reach final status agreement and control the peace spoilers.	The final status agreement brings an end to the Israeli occupation and defines two distinct capitals in Jerusalem for the two states.	NGOs engage in cross-border co-operation in the fields of economic development, service provision, planning, conservation and preservation of the Old City.	The international community facilitates the implementation of the agreement and assists in developing Jerusalem as a world center.
3. The Fortress City (The Intermediate-Case Scenario)	The two governments are strong enough to control peace spoilers but are not yet able to reach a final status agreement. They manage to sign a partial agreement within the framework of the road map.	According to this partial agreement, Palestinians have functional autonomy in Jerusalem in the form of a borough with limited security and planning responsibilities.	Moderates and peace entrepreneurs proliferate and are active, but play a marginal role.	The international community attempts to contain the situation by acting as a facilitator and supporter of peace entrepreneur activities.
4. The Scorched Earth (The Worst-Case Scenario)	The two weak governments are unable to reach any political agreement.	Occupation continues and intensifies. Jerusalem is walled-off and 'soft' ethnic cleansing occurs.	Civil society is weak. Moderates and peace entrepreneurs are regarded as traitors, and extremists become the leading force.	The international community retreats.

Illustration 13.5: The four scenarios for the future of Jerusalem, developed by the Palestinian and Israeli groups in the Scenario Building Program

The shared vision

The development of these scenarios had been a great help in articulating a shared vision for the future of the city. The scenarios outline possible futures for the city, whereas the vision depicts the desired future. The scenarios examine what might happen and as such, they are supposed to explore different options of change and transformation. On the other hand, the vision describes the dreams, wishes and desires of the participants.

Both groups were determined to avoid the worst-case scenario and were very willing to promote the best-case scenario, which would be achieved by implementing strategies of intervention (in 2006). To test the group's scenarios and vision, they were presented to different civil society groups and to policy makers in order to solicit their views on our work. For the main elements of the future vision reached by Palestinians and Israelis, see Illustration 13.6.

At Some Point in the Future, Jerusalem will be:
- The unique capital of two states: the State of Palestine, and the State of Israel;
- An open city, politically divided and physically undivided;
- A city which people and goods flow freely between different sectors and the surrounding areas environs;
- A city of peaceful coexistence;
- A viable complex city with a high quality of life;
- A city of diversity and equality;
- Empowered as a world city and an international center of peace and conflict resolution: part of the global network of world cities;
- Jerusalem will combine the strengths of its cultural and religious heritage with tourism, financial services and information technology.

Illustration 13.6: The main elements of the future vision developed by Palestinians and Israelis

Summary and Conclusions

The Palestinian/Israeli Jerusalem process clearly witnessed different phases, each with its own focus and a distinctive outreach addressing different stakeholders.

The period between 1996 and 2001, which was basically in Bommersvik, focused on developing a knowledge base and outlining plans for practical functional solutions which could foster peace-building on the day after reaching a peace settlement. The joint teams focused on the functional boundaries of Jerusalem which have to be considered under any geopolitical solution. The group, at that time, shared its knowledge and work with decision makers and politicians. The prevailing assumption in the group at that stage was that Jerusalem would be an open city. This solution was accepted by many politicians on both sides and was considered to be the best solution.

After the onset of the Second Intifada in September 2000, which was just a month after the fifth annual conference of Bommersvik, the group retreated back from the positive focus on preparations for 'the day after' and began to deal with the realities of the conflict and the need to work on a process of conflict transforming to peace making. The group considered the practical experiences of other divided cities relevant to the Jerusalem situation. Focusing on conflict transformation identified the work in the period between 2001 and 2003.

The third phase of the overall process emerged coincidently with the peak of construction of the wall separating Jerusalem from its hinterland and isolating it from the rest of the West Bank (Illustration 13.7). The wall caused both sides to realize that the positive thinking of peacemaking and peacebuilding was irrelevant and had no horizon. This forced the group to focus on the possibility of further deterioration in the conflict as well, and the impact of that on the city, and the obstacles and barriers these developments represented to achieving the desired vision. This stance resulted in the development of four scenarios for the future of Jerusalem, scenarios which the group analyzed in terms of the costs and benefits of each and the factors that determined the move from one scenario to another. In a later stage of this phase, a shared vision was developed and it still reflects the spirit of the process developed by this group. This phase of the formulation of the scenarios and the shared vision was executed with the participation of the community and different stakeholders. The scenarios and the vision were both modified in response to feedback received from them (Illustration 13.8).

To be sure, the erection of the wall in and around Jerusalem places the group today in a somewhat surreal dilemma: How useful was is it to continue the encounters about Jerusalem's future, while the Israeli bulldozers are demarking the route of the wall and the Israeli policies of house demolition and settlement building are ongoing and increasing? The new realities created by the wall, the facts on the ground imposed by Israel and the threat to the security of both Palestinians and Israelis, made this co-operation seem both necessary and irrelevant. There seemed to be no space for talking rationally about a future perspective. Nevertheless, it is a testament to both sides that this sense of pessimism and futility did not prevent the group from continuing its work. We will not speak for the Israeli perception of the situation, but Palestinians went forward believing that all the solutions that Israel has tried to impose unilaterally are based on the immediate realities and threats of the day and that responding to these will not provide any medium or long term solution for the conflict. The lives and destiny of Palestinians and Jews in Jerusalem is so intertwined for the simple reason that hegemony of one side of the conflict and the denial of the other can not bring any peace or stability for the whole region. Jerusalem holds the key for either a prosperous city that reflects its international significance, or, absent a peaceful solution here, for a total collapse and war. That is the reason why the vision and work developed by this group will continue to be relevant if both Palestinians and Israelis decide to build a better life for both.

The group may take some encouragement from the fact that the Israeli partners of this co-operation continue to believe that Jerusalem should be a city with no walls or physical separation of any kind between its parts. This has convinced the Palestinian side to continue its efforts and to involve the Palestinian and Israeli public as well as the international community in the process to seek an innovative sharing of an urban space which is not based on the challenges and threats of today, but on the potential of tomorrow. This group continues to believe that Jerusalem should be a city divided politically but not functionally, and this belief is manifested in the shared vision developed by the two sides and their best case scenario.

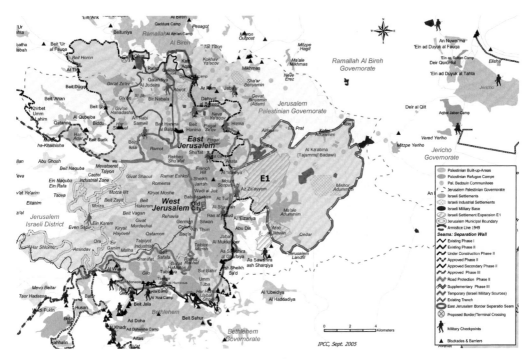

Illustration 13. 7: The wall in the Jerusalem area (Source: Brooks, 2007:10)

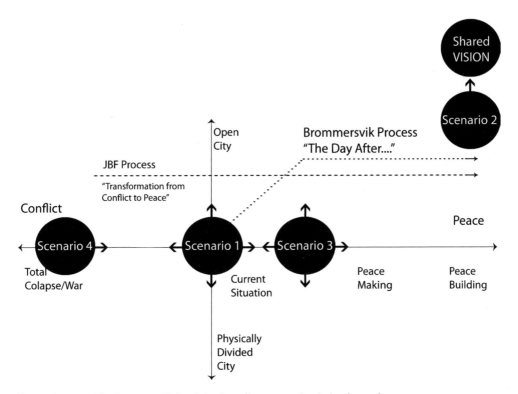

Illustration 13.8: The Process of Palestinian Israeli co-operation in its three phases

Chapter 13: The Case of Jerusalem: a Study in Complexity

Finally, we wish to remark that we think three useful lessons are implicit in the experience of the group, lessons that might impact on how others approach the problems of creating peace in divided cities. We think of these lessons as rational expectations:

1 The peace process clearly is not linear and progressive; it circles back on itself, responding to changes in the environment, and then having to refocus on new realities before moving forward again. With this awareness, we were able to proceed from a posture that viewed the subject of the future of Jerusalem as politically taboo, to a position of shared visions.
2 Ironically, talk, i.e. negotiations, can be an important 'fact on the ground'. While the conditions of today are aggressive and oppressive, we believe the situation would be even worse if the fact of our ongoing talks did not implicitly remind leaders that there is an engaged set of parties striving for peace and equitable solutions.
3 Scenario building may not solve problems but its efficacy lies in structuring a common vision and identifying the consequences of remaining on destructive paths.

References

Auga, M., S. Hasson, R. Nasrallah & S. Stetter (eds), 2005, *Divided Cities in Transition II: Challenges Facing Jerusalem and Berlin*, Friedrich Ebert Stiftung, IPCC and JIIS, Jerusalem.
Brooks, R. D. (ed.), 2007, T*he Wall: Fragmenting the Palestinian Fabric in Jerusalem*, IPCC, Jerusalem.
Friedman, A. & R. Nasrallah (eds), 2003, *Divided Cities In Transition I*, Friedrich Ebert Stiftung, IPCC and JIIS, Jerusalem.
Nasrallah, R., R. Khamaisi & M. Youhan, 2003, *Jerusalem on the Map*, IPCC, Jerusalem.
Nasrallah, R., K. Rassem, A. Amin, A. Hidmi, R. Abu Ghazallah, S. Wa'ary, S. Hasson, R. Fishel, Y. Maoz, N. Goren, E. Prince-Gibson & Y. Garb, 2005, *Jerusalem in the Future: Scenarios and a Shared Vision*, IPCC, the Floersheimer Institute for Policy Studies and Friedrich Ebert Stiftung, Jerusalem.

Unpublished manuscripts

Choshen, Maya, Rassem Khamaisi, Moshe Hirsch & Rami Nasrallah, Planning, Building, and Development in the Jerusalem Metropolitan Area, Bommersvik Conference, 1998.
Tamari, Salim, Jerusalem: Issues of Governance and Subordination, Bommersvik Conference, 1998.
Reiter, Yitzhak, Jewish-Muslim Saint Tombs in Jerusalem between Coexistence and Confrontation: The Case of Nabi Samwil/Kever Shmuel, Bommersvik Conference, 1998.
Ramon, Amnon, Tour Routes between King Solomon's Pools, Bethlehem and Jerusalem for the Christian Pilgrim and Tourist in the Year 2000, Bommersvik Conference, 1998.
Abu Daya, Hani, Israel Kimhi, Fahmi Nashashibi & Amnon Ramon, Preparations for Tourism in the Jerusalem and Bethlehem Region in the Year 2000, Bommersvik Conference, 1998.
Shahwan, Usama, Public Municipal Services in Jerusalem, Bommersvik Conference, 1999.
Tamari, Salim, Development of Human Resources, Bommersvik Conference, 1999.
Abdelkarim, Naser, Financial Services in Jerusalem: Present Status and Prospects for Development., Bommersvik Conference, 1999.
Nasrallah, Rami, NGOs in Jerusalem as a Resource of Peace-Building, Bommersvik Conference, 1999.
Nasrallah, Rami, The Resettlement of Palestinian Refugees: An Approach to a Plan, Bommersvik Conference, 1999.
Choshen, Maya, Rassem Khamaisi, Moshe Hirsch & Rami Nasrallah, Municipal Management in Metropolitan Jerusalem, Bommersvik Conference, 1999.
Tamari, Salim, Jerusalem's Religious Syncretism, Bommersvik Conference, 2000.
Abdelkarim, Naser, A Finance Scheme for Housing in Jerusalem: A Proposal, Bommersvik Conference, 2000.

Choshen, Maya, Rassem Khamaisi, Moshe Hirsch & Rami Nasrallah, City Management: Vision, Day to day life, Peace building, Bommersvik Conference 2000.

Al Khaldi, Ahmad Mubarak, Palestinian Citizens of Jerusalem; Acknowledging or Denying Their Rights: Key Issue to Peace and War, Bommersvik Conference, 2000.

Nasrallah, Rami, A Vision of the NGOs' Role in the Peace Building Process in Jerusalem, Bommersvik Conference, 2000.

Bommersvik Urban Management Team, Activating the Planning System in Jerusalem Area in Aftermath Political Arrangement, Bommersvik Conference , 2000.

Ramon, Amnon & Yitzhak Reiter, An Inter-religious Vision for Jerusalem and The Vision, Bommersvik Conference, 2000.

Tamari, Salim, Jerusalem's Religious Syncretism, Bommersvik Conference, 2000.

Abokhder, Emad, Ahmad AlKhaldi, Rassem Khamaisi & Usama Shahwan, Jerusalem/ al-Quds a capital city for two states; Palestine and Israel, Bommersvik Conference, 2001.

Hazboun, Samir, Jerusalem (Al-Quds): What we need to do and how we can do it together, Bommersvik Conference, 2001.

Hazboun, Samir, Al-Quds – Jerusalem Economic Engines: A Palestinian Perspective for Developing Regional Center, Bommersvik Conference, 2001.

Younan, Michael, Jerusalem a Shared Trust: A Palestinian Perspective for Developing Religious and International Affairs, Bommersvik Conference, 2001.

Tamari, Salim, Development of Human Resources, Bommersvik Conference, 2001.

Tamari, Salim, Jerusalem: Issues of Governance and Subordination, Bommersvik Conference, 2001.

Hasson, Shlomo, The Syntax of Jerusalem: Urban Morphology, Culture and Power, Bommersvik Conference, 2001.

Websites (May 2007)

www.ipcc-jerusalem.org
www.jiis.org.il
www.fips.org.il
www.fespal.org

14 Thinking about Transfer from the Mondragón Experience

Hervé Grellier, Jean Michel Larrasquet, Sain Lopez Perez and Luxio Ugarte

Introduction

The Mondragón co-operative experience is certainly a good example of how results of innovative practice can contribute to the improvement of the depth and contents of the Triple Helix (university, industry, government relationship). The 'Mondragón Group', which became some years ago the *Mondragón Corporación Cooperativa* (Mondragón co-operative corporation) is a kind of cluster, or local production system, developed in the last fifty years in the small region of Mondragón, in the Spanish Basque Country. Some of the main characteristics of this experience constitute, in our opinion, an interesting basis to find out what could be passed on from this experience.

In this contribution the authors will present the Mondragón experience, in order to point out what might be useful for other regions in the world. Our ambition is to consider the concept of transfer, on a concrete basis, in order to define 'good practices' in this matter. The combined action between the productive dimension (creating or developing businesses), the institutions of training, research and knowledge transfer (that is to say labs and university) and the administrative dimension (that is to say political or territorial development authorities or agencies) is certainly central to a successful area development. Our conviction is that passing on experience is always, at least partially, a matter of knowledge and learning (Argyris & Schön, 1978), and that it only may be done under the condition of an effective collaboration between relevant actors. However, our conviction is also that under such a condition of effective collaboration between partners that respect each other, all kinds of transfer are possible and desirable, with developed regions as well as with developing regions. The question is to build the right 'tuning', and obviously, this only can be achieved in the frame of a respectful collaboration, by the sincere and equilibrated engagement of each. This is another reason why the presence of the university as an active partner is needed, in order to find these modes of tuning and to work out the necessary adaptation of transfer practices.

Our Chapter is structured in three parts. We will first present the Mondragón experience. We will present the main features of its historical development and what it has become today, in terms of the present main activities, structure, successes and weaknesses, as well as in terms of today's tendencies (globalization, local concerns, evolution of co-operative values, concept of a 'place based development', role of persons, of innovation, of technology, of management models).

We would like to highlight more precisely, why and how the 'Mondragón Group' has developed on its own a particular class of activities related to innovation and learning, namely research laboratories and higher education schools (the latter becoming a university ten years ago). We also would like to better understand how these institutions have impacted and go on impacting on the above mentioned local productive system, particularly in terms of capacities of innovation and transfer. We also want to understand how the activities of labs and university, in their turn, are conditioned by these strong links with companies and how they generate very specific training and research modes. We will also focus on the territorial dimension, in relation with the concept of a 'place based development'[1], trying to understand the historical dynamics and the characteristics (idiosyncratic on the one hand and susceptible to be transferred on the other hand) that have generated such a successful local production system. More particularly, the role of social capital and social networks, the role of local authorities, of ideology, etc. will be examined in order to understand how such a 'community of destiny', may be worked out.

Finally, all this reflection will lead us to conclusions related to the concept of transfer. Or better, starting from the Mondragón example, we will have to think about the concept of transferability in order to begin thinking about methods and guidelines for organizing and working out effective transfer actions in different contexts. Our purpose in this Chapter is essentially to foresee from the point of view of a university being a part of the Mondragón Co-operative Group, what can be done in the future, starting from today's situation, particularly thinking of the role of such a university (very specific indeed) in the frame of the Triple Helix philosophy. In particular, as far as transfer is increasingly considered an important issue, we will particularly focus on the new specific role that the university will have to play, specifically a business and management faculty, in particular as far as the soft issues that transfer requires are concerned.

The Mondragón experience in history

Origins of the Mondragón experience

The Co-operative Movement in Mondragón (Ormaetxea, 1998), a small industrial valley located in the Basque Country, north-eastern Spain, was initiated in 1956 with the foundation of a small domestic appliances factory, starting what is known today as the 'Mondragón Co-operative Experience' (MCC). The Mondragón region was traditionally recognized for its metal-mechanical industry. The Mondragón group was based on the improvement and consolidation of connections between participants, drawing its centripetal energy from a common set of values, objectives and organizational structure (MCC, 1999; 2001). A co-operative firm differs from a capitalist one in that it supports itself through the balance of two forces: the obtaining of profits, and the development of its social labor, materialized in internal democracy, participation and solidarity. The main characteristic of the co-operatives is that their workers are simultaneously owners of the company, the democratic process for the decision making is based on the simple rule of 'one-person = one vote'.

The first actors

In the first years of the 'co-operative experience', as its founder Father Jose Maria Arizmendiarrieta liked to call it, Mondragón was a depleted community substantially lacking goods to meet basic needs, as food, clothing, education or means to provide for one's household. Fifty years later, the same small region, where there is no real unemployment, is the wealthiest one in one of the wealthiest provinces in Spain (Irizar & Cid, 2004). The main characteristic of the MCC is that being an association of persons both forming a co-operative and forming a group of co-operatives. The MCC is an association of co-operatives in the same way that a co-operative is an association of persons. This idea of the association of persons was very meaningful in the first days of the MCC, when wage solidarity and sharing a common project led to strong cohesion in the human group that sustained each co-operative (Irizar & Cid, 2004).

Historical milestones (MCC, 2001)

Everything begins with Arizmendiarrieta, a young 26-year-old priest who, dynamic, enterprising and bursting with ideas, arrived in Mondragón in 1941 to look after the youth of the parish. Fourteen years later the first manufacturing company appears: *Talleres Ulgor,* founded by five young people decided to turning the often vague and sketchy ideas of their mentor into tangible and successful business realities. Two years after his arrival in Mondragón, Father José María founded the Professional School (Leibar & Azcarate, 1994), the seed which would later become *Mondragón Unibertsitatea* - the University of Mondragón. This institution has demonstrated a vital role over the decades, training many of those who later became key figures in the development of the co-operative project.

The history of the Corporation can be divided into the three principal stages outlined below:

First stage: 1956-1970

The first fifteen years were characterized by a development boom, which, in response to the long awaited revival of the Spanish economy during the second half of the 1950s, resulted in the creation of a large number of co-operatives. We should also remark growing numbers of people concerned about the development of their town or region that approached the organization with the aim of identifying products that, after being subjected to the corresponding viability studies, would then form the basis for the constitution of a co-operative. Some important co-operatives were set up during this period. They would later play a key role in the development of MCC. Two of them are particularly relevant:
- *Caja Laboral*: a financial entity which would channel public savings into co-operative development and play the role of the bank of the MCC system.
- *Lagun Aro*: An insurance company set up to solve the problem that arose when the government refused to allow co-operative members to qualify for Social Security benefits, maintaining that they were owners as opposed to employees.

Second stage 1970-1990

Initially, the second stage was characterized by the same dynamism as the first, with extraordinary improvements in sales and employment rates as well as in the number of co-operatives. *Ikerlan* was set up during this period, in 1974, as a research center whose objective was to study technological progress regarding to their integration in industrial applications. The boom which, in general terms, the co-operatives had enjoyed since their creation came to an abrupt end at the beginning of the eighties with the onset of the economic recession. One of the most distressing symptoms of this period was the emergence of the hitherto unknown concept of mass unemployment, which rose to over 20 percent. The co-operatives did not escape from the effects of the economic crisis. A significant number of negative profits and labor surpluses became, for the first time, a variable to be taken into account. A few companies were even forced to close down. Luckily, not all the co-operatives were affected to the same degree, and those who had the foresight to develop their export activities managed, after a fashion, to weather the storm.

Third stage: 1990 - 2006

The third and current stage in the development of MCC is strongly influenced, and perhaps even characterized by, the organizational process that turned the Group into a Corporation, structuring its business areas according to sector criteria as opposed to geographical location. The development of the new organization required that the Corporation as a whole began to deal with areas that had, until then, been the exclusive responsibility of each individual co-operative. One such area was the development of a Management Model designed to help improve management performance and establish common references which would give coherence to general analyses. The Management Model was, of course, based on the co-operative principles and values adopted by MCC. However, it also made use of modern management concepts, as well as cutting edge methods and techniques used by state-of-the-art organizations.

Co-operative values

The business philosophy of MCC is reflected in its four corporative values which are: Co-operation (being both proprietors and protagonists), Participation (commitment to the management), Social Responsibility (shared distribution of wealth) and Innovation (permanent renovation). Co-operative principles have to do with the question of how co-operatives and more precisely their members behave in relation to their environment, as far as their interrelations are concerned (modes of governance, modes of co-operation, relation to sustainable development, self help, democracy, equality, solidarity) and to the ethical values of honesty, transparency, responsibility and calling for service.

As a co-operative association the MCC has its own principles that have great resemblance with the seven principles of the International Co-operative Alliance (ICA). The basic principles of Mondragón established in 1991 are (MCC, 2001):
1. Open membership
2. Democratic organization
3. Worker sovereignty
4. Instrumental or subordinate nature of capital
5. Participation in management
6. Wage solidarity
7. Co-operation between co-operatives
8. Social transformation
9. Universal nature
10. Education

Mondragón today

Structure and business activities

Mondragón Co-operative Corporation (MCC) employed in 2006 nearly 82.000 people, combining several classes of activities (Illustration 14.1). The MCC core characteristic is its large job creation. In 1995, it employed about 28.000 people, but two decades before, in 1975 this number was a mere 13.000. Today MCC is the largest business group in the Basque Country and the seventh largest in Spain.

MCC consists of three groups: the Financial Group, the Industrial Group and the Distribution Group, as Illustration 14.2 shows. The Financial Group includes activities such as banking, social welfare and insurance. The Industrial Group comprises seven Divisions dedicated to the production of goods and services. The Distribution Group is made up of various commercial distribution and agricultural-food companies. There are also Research, Vocational Training and Teaching centers, including the Mondragón University with more than 4,000 students and the Garaia Innovation Centre, recently constituted, where university and enterprise laboratories will be brought together in the same geographic area.

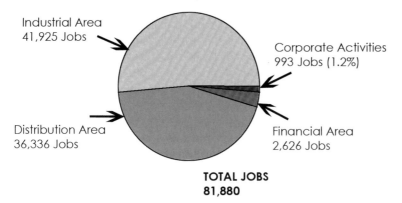

Illustration 14.1. MCC Personnel (at the end of 2006)

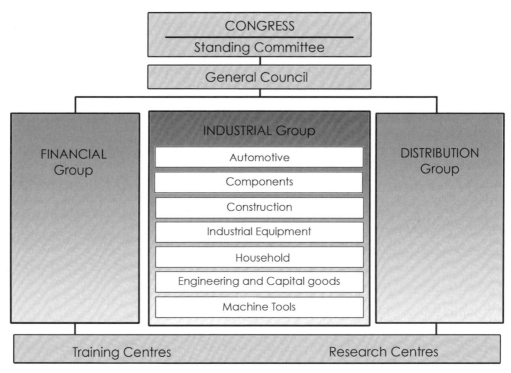

Illustration 14.2 MCC Organizational structure

Chapter 14: Thinking about Transfer from the Mondragón Experience

Elements of success

Due to its foundation of continuous adhesion and formation of co-operatives of diverse size and activity, MCC is a very diversified corporation, that simultaneously counts on support superstructures in financial intermediation (Caja Laboral-banking entity, Aro Leasing, Lagun Aro Insurances), social welfare (Lagun Aro), education (*Mondragón Unibertsitatea*, Otalora Executive Training) and research (Ikerlan, Ideko, Garaia and others). With the involvement of all the actors affecting enterprise management, MCC has created an organizational structure that seeks self-sufficiency in providing the resources that favor improvement in performance.

The current enterprise tendency is to establish a reduced scope of activity (concentration-specialization). In the case of MCC, its success in managing diversity, diversification and heterogeneity underlines a special characteristic of this group that unlike other cases, is developed by the aggregation of enterprise efforts and not by strategic top-down decision-making in search of benefits (López & Irizar, 2002).

Some other characteristics can be summed up as follows:
- Constant reinvestment of benefits in the productive system. The benefits-after-taxes in a co-operative are distributed as follows: 90 percent to the Company Equity Capital; of this, 45 percent is undistributed and the other 45 percent awarded to the partner-workers. Therefore only 10 percent is going outside the company, being channeled through the Social Fund for Social Formation, Research and other activities.
- Inter-business co-operation. Strong synergies exist between the companies of MCC with multi-company projects that promote innovation, through a flexible and adaptable structure. In MCC both diversity and homogeneity are combined, which gives it the advantage of being, at the same time, both large and small.
- Workers participation and social orientation. The co-operative model, in which workers are also owner-partners, promotes the workers' value contribution. The MCC social orientation promotes the generation of new jobs in growth periods and to continue maintaining them in recession periods through inter-business mobility.

Changes in management styles

The new industrial and organizational structures require new forms of direction from the outset. MCC has included the most advanced techniques and tools in its management style, facilitating flexibility in the management of people and processes, attracting and retaining intelligent, motivated and self-managed partners that interact in groups and harmonious networks. MCC involves its employees in the evaluation, understanding and definition of the distinctive competencies of the group and in the development of its strategies, by means of its Strategic Planning System, designed in tune with the corporation's specific characteristics.

The central management of MCC co-ordinates and leads the development of strategies of the co-operative unit (component of MCC) and combines its results in an overall strategy that conditions the behavior of the group. Moreover, the central management tries to exploit the synergy developed between business relationships to promote and improve their overall performance.

Future tendencies

Synergy and inter-group, inter-division and inter-co-operative integration

The creation of MCC centers dealing with the interrelationship and inter-co-operation of their partners is a central element of the synergy building. Actions such as the creation of superstructure organizations, unification of cultures and internal commitments through shared models of management, convergent autonomies, management tools and compatible planning systems, are steering of the development of such integration.

To our mind, it is evident that the set of linkages that provide the strong alliance and the knowledge sharing nature of the Mondragón world is a core characteristic of the success of the group (see Kogut & Zander, 1992). Such linkages may be seen as co-operation links between co-operative companies, but also as interpersonal relationships. From the point of view we take, they may be understood as inter-firm relationships generating a kind of Cluster or Local Productive System. It may also be considered a set of (or a network of) social networks (or social capital), if we stress our analysis on the interpersonal networks in the region (and of course, out of it) (Allen, Tushman & Lee, 1979), and if we focus on cultural and identity issues (ICA, CSCE-EKGK, 1996; Lafleur, 2003). The idea that all of them are sharing the very same project, which seems, indeed, effectively shared, even if it remains relatively fuzzy in the minds of a good number of the involved persons. We would propose the idea that they are building from day to day a kind of 'community of destiny' and that they are aware of this dimension. That is why politics, considering its noble meaning, has a lot to do with the issue of endogenous development. Relations between firms, social networks and cultural and cognitive aspects are the very core of the capacity of this 'nebula' to develop common actions and to strongly tighten internal co-operation links. No doubt these are aspects to be taken into account in order to understand the experience in its whole depth and complexity.

Globalization

The global economy, the trans-national competition and the need for success, based on acquired and dominating competencies have ceased to be a simple theoretical perspective and have become challenges and concerns relevant to any company on a worldwide scale. Currently, the large national or multinational companies are taking an increasingly relevant position within this global economy, but simultaneously the small and medium-sized companies, by their very structural flexibility and adaptability, are showing they are better enabled to carry out processes of innovation and renovation, as shown by Rothwell (1988).

Several questions arise then. Is it possible to combine the advantages of both types of companies? Are the local corporations or groupings, those that unite small and medium-sized enterprises (SMEs) and large companies under the same central co-ordination, command and/or control, a type of answer to this inconsistency? Analyzing the Italian ceramic tile cluster, Porter (1991) pointed out that companies facing this kind of grouping (such as the MCC case), shouldn't compete against an individual company, nor even against a group of companies, but against an entire subculture, whose very organic nature is what makes it more difficult to imitate and therefore, it has a more sustainable competitive advantage.

Today, the MCC industrial group has more than 5 percent of overseas production and nearly 52 percent of the sales are international. Recently, the aggressive internationalization policy of MCC has been one of the keys to its expansion and overall growth. In Illustration 14.3 MCC's corporate delegations and manufacturing subsidiaries worldwide are shown. Even so, it is necessary to recognize that it still has a long way to go before it will really count as an industrial group on a world-wide scale.

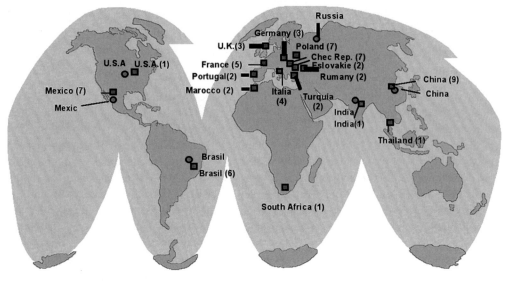

○ Corporate Delegations (6)
■ Manufacturing Subsidiaries (65)

Illustration 14.3. MCC Worldwide

In the opinion of the authors of this Chapter, the heterogeneity is an opportunity and also a threat for MCC, unquestionably fissures can appear in this co-ordination effort. Besides, the continuity of the co-operative model is in doubt along with the co-operative principles in the present and future group businesses, in addition to the threats that a globalization process would bring to the social and participating structure of MCC.

Relationships between education, research, territory and development in the Mondragón experience

Place based development and social capital in Mondragón

A significant characteristic of the Mondragón experience is that until very recently, the whole creation of jobs has been made in a concrete circle around the city of Mondragón or at least in the Basque Country. Only very recently the distribution division and some other co-operatives have begun opening delegations in the rest of Spain, and then, very recently, created delegations in the rest of the world, certainly one of the new characteristics of the group. It is probably one of the main reasons for its dynamic development in the last period, and certainly also the source of a set of new challenges and issues that the group and the companies will have to face in the next future.

As has been underlined above, one of the motors of the group as a whole is not the valorization of capital by the means of maximizing short term profit, but certainly the search of profitability in order to develop the companies and the region (the birthplace) and its society, and particularly to favor the creation of jobs, in particular in the birthplace of the experience. As we will explain further, the concept of a 'place-based development' appears to us as particularly in tune with such a phenomenon.

The links with the region (the birthplace) are therefore very strong. Strong in a double way: firstly because people, managers and workers are particularly attached to their land, no doubt that it has to do with local culture and identity, and secondly because local authorities and influent institutions, of course institutional authorities, but also private and moral authorities like the local catholic church in particular, but also Basque nationalist parties, etc., have played and go on playing a very important role in helping such a development. It is obvious that politicians have an important role to play at the beginning. It is also obvious that when the experience has reached its 'cruising speed' and its social importance, local and regional politicians cannot ignore or fight against the experience. They are obliged to add power and resources to it. The institutional organization of innovation, research and development and the high level of professional training are of a huge importance in the dynamics of a region, particularly the ability to develop private - public partnerships in this field (Gertler & Wolfe, 2002; Rousseau, 2004).

We think that the Basque identity and its political expressions have a lot to do with the success of the experience. Basque nationalism, social Christian doctrine (Itçaina, 2000), industrial tradition and also an anti-franquist attitude of the population, partly explain the movement and the beginning of the experience. In this sense, development is also a political issue. But on the other hand, such characteristics existed in other areas, at least in the whole Spanish Basque country, and the fact is that only one Mondragón was born. There is not another one fifty kilometers around!

So, it is also important to understand the idiosyncratic side of the experience and how this experience may also be understood as a self-production process, and what have been the concrete conditions, the concrete persons, the concrete projects, the concrete relationships and networks that have permitted each step to be the basis of the next one. It is obviously of a huge importance if we are interested in the experience transfer.

Education, learning and research, basic elements of the MCC experience

A significant event that occurred during the nineties was the foundation of *Mondragón Unibertsitatea*, the University of Mondragón, in 1997, by integrating three higher education schools immersed in the co-operative movement, located in a radius of less than ten kilometers around Mondragón. The project marked the pinnacle of a long development process and cleared the way for a bright future in a whole new area.

Given that training has played a vital role in the experience right from the beginning, the creation of a university seems a fitting development, which in addition to other advantages, enables MCC to work toward achieving its own training objectives within the general educational framework. The university plays a central role in the Triple Helix model through its capacity to generate knowledge and interact with the other two helices. In the case of Mondragón, the university has been created with such a purpose, after a deep reflection in some of the companies of the group and in the proper

MCC headquarters. A small sized university was wished for (5000 students were assumed to be the limit) in which the challenge is to train young people and workers to professionalized skills, to develop and pass on applied knowledge (in three major applied fields, namely engineering, management and applied human sciences). A close relationship to companies and regional authorities is also thought as an important feature.

For that purpose, training, research and transference are obviously developed in relation with the companies of the group but in a non-exclusive way, the university being obviously free to define and develop its own research and training issues, working on more or less generic topics, as far as they have some relation with applied knowledge. From this point of view, another epistemological aspect must be underlined: one of the foundations of this challenge is that applied sciences are 'true sciences' and that the question is not only the question of 'defining' suitable solutions, but also the question of implementing solutions in companies and regions. This issue is a point of a tremendous complexity. The university considers it useful to develop specific knowledge on this aspect. In our opinion, this posture is of an extreme importance as knowledge transfer and university - enterprise - regional linkages are our central preoccupation, and in particular in the Triple Helix perspective.

The university is well known at international level in engineering on the one hand, but also in co-operativism, collaborative management and social economy. It has developed a number of international collaboration projects (students exchange; off shore training; including the Masters level; research and transfer projects), obviously in relation with its size. It is obvious that the success and the fame of the Mondragón experience as a whole help its international recognition.

Although integrating interests, needs and actions is a difficult task and goes against current business practices, MCC tries to establish between its co-operatives a transparent relationship based on exchanges of knowledge, technologies, experience, persons and in essence, sources of competence that allow for a kind of interactive growth for the whole Group. An example of this initiative is the effort of the Corporation to the develop a Science and Technology Plan. This has been linked to the science and technology plans of the regional government, by determining on the one hand future technologies and applications for each business, and on the other hand the generic lines and technological areas where they belong. This is done in order to be able to gather the compatible technologies and overlapping areas between businesses. However, the fact that the economic decision power remains fundamentally in basic co-operatives must not be forgotten. The construction and implementation of such a plan is therefore a complex exercise of crossing top-down and bottom-up initiatives. This exercise allows for the compilation of a complete technological database for MCC, from which any interested co-operative can benefit in promoting technological competence.

Another element related to the promotion of knowledge sharing is the constant and direct relationship between the companies, the university and the engineering and technological research centers of MCC. This synergy works in diverse ways. Through contracts, some joint programs of research-development are set up. On the initiative of the university, of the research centers, of the corporation itself or of some companies belonging to the MCC or not, some research programs are set up focusing on regional, cross-border, bilateral or European funding. This integrated relationship has been cultivated throughout three decades and is certainly today one of the main sources for innovation and development for MCC co-operatives, as far as products, services and processes are concerned. It is also an important source for both technical and management staff development, as far as they are trained and prepared according to the very needs of the group.

Dealing with transfer issues

Introduction

As applied scientists in the field of management, we are interested in how things can be done. We also believe that universities are key actors in such dynamics. We assume that the universities which are acting in a particular Triple Helix experiences may be local or foreign universities. This is particularly relevant from the point of view of the University of Mondragón, in the case of local or international co-operation on transfer issues. The Triple Helix theory must be put into practice, and this practical implementation is difficult. Even if the Triple Helix is working in the interrelationships between firms, universities and public authorities, our reflection is made from the perspective of a concrete university, and more precisely from the one of its units which is specialized in management. We start this reflection from what we are, from what we know and with the idea that our contribution may essentially concern transfer from the Mondragón experience.

We will first have to consider what 'good practices' and what modes of doing things are useful in terms of transfer, that is to say to what extent and under what conditions they may be of interest for others. And *de facto*, the second point of our reflection consists in thinking about the modes that could be proposed in order to better organize our transfer activity. That means that we will have to take into account that our intention is not to 'export the Mondragón model', but to organize 'transfer' activities, starting from the Mondragón experience and working with the interested partners to the common construction of solutions adapted to their own characteristics.

What may be transferred?

The first focus we will propose is on the practices that appear to us as particularly useful as far as transfer is concerned. We think that several aspects of the Mondragón experience must be underlined in order to work out some possibilities for the development of an organized transfer activity.

Co-operative management and governance systems

The first focus concerning the transfer question, from Mondragón, is on the implementation of the *co-operative governance and management systems*. It is obvious that implementing in the day-to-day management and control of a firm the principles of co-operativism is not that simple. Mondragón has an experience in this field as far as management and governance are concerned; the MCC group and the companies which compose it have invented, developed and implemented solutions and systems, in the course of their fifty years history. These systems seem to work relatively satisfactorily in the context, culture and particular history of Mondragón. To what extent are these transferable to other contexts?

The question of transferring such models is particularly topical, even in affairs that today concern MCC group's own development. The question of the development of co-operative governance and management systems and the future of co-operative values in the businesses set up in foreign countries by MCC groups companies (which are usually not co-operatives, globalization is at work!) is a crucial issue in MCC's own world today.

Another strategic core issue evidently related to transfer-related issues is the other side of the same medal. At present, some managers of the group are become aware of this problem. It is related to the companies' own future(even of those localized in Mondragón) as co-operatives, as far as the continuity of their strong co-operative spirit and values, may be damaged by the relationships with the capitalist firms that MCC group companies buy and control: isn't there here a danger of dissolving the genuine and nuclear co-operative spirit, which made Mondragón's strength, in the dramatic improvement of all these international relationships essentially based on markets, competition and business? The danger is that immersed in such a game, in fact one of the two pillars (legs) of the work co-operatives (efficiency) takes the priority on the other one (solidarity / co-operative spirit), and therefore, that the co-operative firm, limping on one of its original 'legs', gets absorbed by capitalist logics.

Territorial development and corporate social responsibility

A second concern is about the link to regional development and corporate social responsibility. One of the main values of the Mondragón experience is related to the involvement of co-operative companies with the development of employment, the creation of jobs in the valley for the local population. The corporate responsibility of the firms is first of all related to creating and sustaining activities in the Basque Country itself, following a 'place based development' approach (see note 1). Up till now, this objective has been particularly well achieved, in as far as that the official unemployment rate is less than 2 percent in the Deba Garaia Valley. That is to say that effective unemployment is zero.

Another characteristic is that the MCC activity is so important for the region that such a relationship necessarily exists and gets organized. It is evident for the Deba Garaia Valley and the cities where important implantations are located (Mondragón itself, 45.000 people, but also Oñati, 15.000, Eskoriatza, 8.000, etc.) but it is also the case for the whole county of Gipuzkoa and for the whole province of Basque Country. The contribution of the Mondragón group to the GDP (Gross Domestic Product) of the Basque Country is estimated at 3,8 percent (Illustration 14.4.).

Heading	Basque Country Total		MCC Total		%/total	
	Total	Industrial	Total	Industrial	Total	Industrial
G.D.P.	51,340	15,028**	1,953	1,253	3.8	8.3
Employment *	951,400	244,600	35,842	21,280	3.7	8.3
Exports	14,225	12,898***	--	1,928	13.6	14.9

In Millions of euros
* Number of people
** Of which 1,743 million euros are not purely industrial as they correspond to the Energy and Water sector.
*** Without exports of energy products.

Illustration 14.4 MCC in the Basque Country

The relationship systems (particularly the public-private partnerships), on several fields of concern (innovation, research programs, training, localization of activities, specific programs on high level new technology and internationalization, etc.), that have been defined and implemented between the co-operative group MCC and the public administration must be systematically defined and formalized (at the moment, we think that this work has not been done). It is evident, in this Chapter also, that a lot of practices (certainly 'good practices' in the context of the Mondragón experience) constitute an interesting basis for transfer and may be elements of interest for a process of reflection toward their adaptation to other specific contexts.

Inter co-operative collaboration and development of the corporation.

A third kind of interesting issue, certainly central if we want to understand the heart of the system, is related to the *inter co-operative and the group effect*.

The *inter co-operative* dimension is related to the capacity that the companies have developed to build together and to share a unit of organization at the sector level (today, this organizational level is called 'division': automotive division, electronic division, consulting and information system division, tool machines division, etc.). This kind of 'clustering' is very important in order to share strategic challenges (thinking about strategy, sharing research, innovation and development, facing internationalization together, etc.). Further, all the networks emerging from such formalized relationships, but also from more informal collaboration (supply chain, collaboration projects, common challenges, the concrete implementation of the 'place-based development' philosophy, etc.) give a concrete existence to the concept of a local productive system (LPS).

The aspects related to the *corporation* (*Mondragón Corporación Cooperativa*, MCC) are very important and must be underlined in this presentation. The Corporation performs a number of functions delegated by the basic co-operative companies in order that they are carried out in the same manner. These functions are of course of a fundamental nature as far as the success of the experience is concerned. In the context of different juridical systems, the following functions are performed at corporation level, giving (selling) service to the basic co-operative companies of the group.
- Group (corporation) level corporate strategy (internationalization, information systems, technology management, etc.);
- Training, research, development and innovation: university, research centers and consulting specialized companies;
- Internationalization: delegations in different countries, co-ordination of international projects (China);
- Solidarity: management of a mutual fund for helping companies in difficulty which have begun a process of restructuring with the help of the corporation and its advising entities;
- Financing: a bank and an insurance company to put together the cash, assets and savings of the group, people and firms, to be able to manage the financing of developments and of strategic challenges and their collective interests.

Trusting in collaborators.

A fourth dimension is about *management models*: the central idea is that persons must be in the center of the companies and their development. This principle is put into practice with a variable intensity, following different modes of organization in the companies of the group. In the most specific cases, the renewing of organization and management modes is really drastic, promoting flat forms of organization, project-based management, variable organization charts, trust-based persons' empowering management modes (Mangematin & Thuderoz, 2003). Well known examples of such emblematic evolutions are companies like the Irizar group (number one in Europe for luxury coaches, 2000 collaborators) or the Orona group (second Spanish lift maker, also more or less 2000 people)[2]. A lot of other interesting experiences from this point of view exist in other companies of the group. All these experiences would deserve a cautious study in order to produce material for transfer in the group itself (some companies have to progress on this way), but also toward other contexts.

Studying 'how' things are done in this field is certainly an interesting challenge promising to strongly enrich management sciences: how people are involved, how the evaluation of persons is done, how membership feelings and community culture are developed, how evolution, innovation and change processes are managed, how responsibility of everyone is worked out and concretely organized, how and why high level managers accept small differences in remuneration (the present scale is from one to four) and, as a consequence, relatively low levels of remuneration, while they may be offered a lot more by capitalist companies, etc.

The development of participative management, of persons' skills and competencies, as well as their empowerment and involvement are basic values in the Mondragón world, in direct relation with the co-operative philosophy. As noticed above, a number of the MCC group's companies have been able to define and put into action, in different ways, forms of organization and governance that allow and favor the implementation of these main values.

These management models must be formalized because they are certainly one of the most important emerging characteristics of the Mondragón experience in the present times, even if a number of people in Mondragón are not totally convinced of that. We, however, are convinced that these forms must be considered as they contain the emergent seed of to-morrow's management modes toward more economic democracy and allowing a development founded on the conscience of people and centered on the culture of sustainability. Such complex dynamics must be considered as 'complex loops', something like a kind of 'virtuous autopoietic loops ' (autopoietic: autonomous and self-maintaining unity) , as far as they are at the same time causes and effects of success for these companies which go ahead developing experiences in these directions. We must consider these experiences like an extremely interesting basis for transfer.

Transferring: defining ethical guidelines

Obviously, to put transfer into practice, two partners (at least!) are needed. This truism opens the door to a serious and ethical reflection on the nature of transfer. The point is that real transfer can only be realized between a partner who is ready for transferring and another one who is interested in this perspective. But such a transfer must be understood in a flexible way and realized under flexible conditions. That is to say, that Mondragón must consider, at least in international co-operation issues, which is the case we are working on, that its model (if there is one, it should be worked out!) is not to be exported on its own, but must be considered more like a source of inspiration (among several), the transfer consisting of building together something new.

We think that transfer itself cannot be a simple technological or organizational 'cut and paste' matter. Transfer and innovation are necessarily a matter of collaboration (Arora, Fosfuri & Gambardella, 2001), as far as knowledge is always not only involved, but also the very heart of such activities. As we know, constructivist postures on learning state that learning is never a single transfer (taking the knowledge from one mind or computer and putting it in another one). But as knowledge is involved (Gorman, 2002) it is a matter of learning, that is to say a matter of social individuals interacting in networks and therefore a matter of socio-cognitive constructions (Larrasquet, 2004). So transferring processes require a real collaboration between partners in order to allow and favor such cognitive building processes. We would even add that the transfer process control should be largely in the hands of the less developed partner or the partner who is in the position of 'taking' something from the experience, know-how, technology or competencies of the other.

Needed in the transfer process is a direction and a 'magnetic north' congruent with the needs of the 'learning' partner in position of development. We know that in a number of cases, for a lot of different reasons, this principle is difficult to put into practice, but we also assume that being ethically attentive to such an 'imperialist danger' in co-operation issues is part of the corporate social responsibility of the firm (Desouza, Mason & Sheffield, 2006).

Conclusion

There is absolutely no doubt that the Mondragón experience is a success for its birthplace region and society. As has been underlined in this Chapter, it has obtained very interesting results. For instance, more than 8 000 jobs have been created in 2005, the rate of unemployment in the valley of Mondragón is less than 2 percent, the level of education is high, etc. It presents also some weaknesses today, mainly perhaps on the ecological side. It is also facing new challenges (particularly linked to globalization). No doubt that the group as a human micro-society, is able to face it, it has resources, it is very dynamic and is able to take dramatic decisions (creation of 2.000 jobs in China next year for instance), its people are able to put its certainties in question, it is able to generate internal solidarity, etc.).

The question we have seen in this Chapter is related to its capacity to transfer its 'good practices' toward other environments, which is certainly one of the main forces which make Triple Helix a reality. It is a question that has not been up to day deeply considered in the Mondragón world itself. It is a question we would like to develop in the next future, mixing theory and practice, that is to say developing some concrete experiences of transfer toward companies, local productive systems or regions. Such experiences will be the basis for our future research on this subject.

References

Allen T.J., M.L. Tushman & D.M.S. Lee, 1979, Technology Transfer as a Function of Position in the Spectrum from Research through Development to Technical Services, *Academy of Management Journal*, Vol. 22, N° 4, pp. 694-708.

Argyris, C., & D. Schön, 1978, *Organisational Learning: A Theory of Action Perspective*, Addison-Wesley, Reading, Massachusetts.

Arora, A., A. Fosfuri & A. Gambardella, 2001, *Markets for Technology, The Economics of Innovation and Corporate Strategy*, The MIT Press, Cambridge, Massachusetts.

Desouza K.C., R.M. Mason & J. Sheffield, 2007, Knowledge Management Systems Track: Ethics and Philosophy in KM, Hawaii International Conference on System Sciences-40, Hawaii.

Gertler, M.S. & D.A. Wolfe (eds), 2002, *Innovation and Social Learning: Institutional Adaptation in an Era of Technological Change*, Macmillan/Palgrave, Basingstoke, UK.

Gorman, M.E., 2002, Types of Knowledge and Their Roles in Technology Transfer, *The Journal of Technology Transfer*, Vol. 27, N° 3, pp. 219 – 231.

Kogut, B. & U. Zander, 1992, Knowledge of the Firm, Combinative Capabilities, and the Replication of Technology, *Organization Science*, Vol. 3, N° 3, pp. 383-397.

ICA, CSCE-EKGK, 1996, *The International Co-operative Alliance Statement on the Co-operative Identity, The Co-operative Principles*, Xabide S.Coop., Vitoria, Spain.

Irizar I. & M. Cid, 2004, Evolution of Network-strategies: The Case of Mondragón Co-operative Corporation, 15th International Co-operative Forum, Muenster, Germany.

Itçaina X., 2000, *Catholicisme et identités basques en France et en Espagne. La construction religieuse de la référence et de la compétence identitaires*, Thèse pour le doctorat en science politique, IEP Bordeaux, France.

Lafleur M., 2003, *La formulation de stratégie chez la coopérative basée sur son identité*, PhD Thesis, Université de Sherbrooke, Québec, Canada.

Larrasquet, J.M. (ed.), 2004 , *TOPIK, Action spécifique* CNRS, RTP 47.

Leibar J. & J. Azcarate, 1994, *Historia de Eskola Politeknikoa José María Arizmendiarrieta*, Caja Laboral and Eskola Politeknikoa José Maria Arizmendiarrieta, Mondragón , Spain.

López S. & I. Irizar, 2002, Industrial corporations and their strategic challenges on technological innovation: Mondragón Cooperative Corporation (MCC) case, 11th International Conference on Management of Technology, IAMOT 2002, Miami, USA.

Mangematin, V. & C. Thuderoz, 2003, *Des mondes de confiance, Un concept à l'épreuve de la réalité sociale*, CNRS Editions, Paris.

MCC, 1999, *MCC Enterprise Policy: 2001-2004*, Mondragón Co-operative Corporation (Política empresarial de MCC: 2001-2004), Mondragón , Spain.

MCC, 2001, *The Mondragón Co-operative Experience: 1956-2000*, Mondragón Co-operative Corporation, Mondragón, Spain.

Ormaetxea, J.M., 1998, *Orígenes y claves del cooperativismo de Mondragón*, Saiolan–Caja Laboral, Mondragón, Spain.

Porter, M.E., 1998, The Competitive Advantage of Nations; Porter, M.E., *On Competition*, Harvard Business School Press, Boston.

Rothwell, R., 1988, Small Firms, Innovation and Industrial Change, *Small Business Economics*, Vol. 1, N° 1, pp. 51-64.

Rousseau, J.M., 2004, The knowledge actors energising regional development implementation of the Lisbon strategy: a crucial task for regions, Sector Regional Aspects, Koszalin, 20 December.

Ugarte, L., 2004, *Sinfonia o jazz? Koldo Saratxaga y el modelo Irizar. Un modelo basado en las personas*, Ed. Granica, Barcelona.

Notes

1   Proposed by Prof. Gregory MacLeod (Cape Breton University, Sydney, Canada, 2006).

2   On these aspects, see the work made by Luxio Ugarte in reference to the Irizar group (Ugarte, 2004).

Cross-Case Analysis

Paul Drewe, Edward Hulsbergen and Juan-Luis Klein

> *"Nous sommes faits pour aider nos contemporains à se reconnaître dans leurs idées et dans leur sentiments beaucoup plus que les gouverner."*
> (E. Durkheim, *L'élite intellectuelle et la démocratie*, 1904)

Introduction

Selecting the case studies for this book, we have put the emphasis on diversity because there is no royal road leading to social innovation; that is to say to finding and implementing new solutions to unsolved social problems. The contexts show considerable differences. They are both Western and Third World. They relate to uncommon roles of the State. Or they are unique, not classifiable. But even adopting a policy of "looking forward and backward and in all directions" – as Platt (1966:134) has put it – one may still want to draw general conclusions. How do the cases compare? Does a case qualify as good practice of social innovation, perhaps transferable to other cities? (Of course, bad practice can also be informative, enlightening and instructive.) To answer these questions, one needs a framework which can also provide guidelines for future case studies of social innovation. The scientific status of the book is that of a collection of single cases with each addressing a specific topic relevant to urban revitalization. The case studies are of a descriptive nature.

Choosing urban revitalization as the target of social innovation, the field of analysis might seem somewhat limited. However, urban revitalization encompasses innovative milieus, local mobilization, empowerment of social actors at the local level, local development policies and new forms of governance (e.g. local governance with the civil society and strategies and tools of local development). This is a far cry from urban revitalization being understood mainly as a change in land use, changes of the built environment or as a social housing issue for that matter. Social innovation in urban revitalization is multidimensional. It is about integrated area development.

Our framework reflects the theoretical avenues of the Introducing Chapter of this book It has also been inspired by the introduction and some chapters of a book published by CRISES that can be considered as a handbook on social innovation (Klein & Harrisson, 2007) and by a special issue of Urban Studies (Moulaert, Martinelli & Swyngedouw, 2005).

Here are the ingredients:

1. Innovations imply changes. What is the *object* of change? How tangible is it? Is it procedural, organizational, institutional? Is it a new or improved product or service? Or is it a new technology?
2. What is the *objective* to be achieved? One could answer this question by quoting lofty goals such as 'to achieve the greatest happiness of the greatest number' or 'to make the worst off group as well off as possible'. More down to earth, it needs to be specified what present problem is supposed to be solved; what future problems are to be prevented; or what aspirations exist for the future. In order to identify whose objectives these are, one must take a closer look at the process.

3   Who are the *actors* or agents of change initiating the search for new ideas? They may belong to the public sector, the private sector or the organized civil society and they may cover local as well as wider geographical scales. This, too, can affect the mobilization of means.
4   Successful social innovations, by definition are accepted socially. Hence the importance of *users* and their *participation* in the process, their active participation beyond pure tokenism. At what stage do the users come in: becoming aware of and defining the problem, creation, implementation, evaluation? Participating in the innovation process, users turn into actors.
5   What *means* are mobilized by public, private and civil actors to achieve the objectives? The resources deployed can be financial ones, but also resources in kind. Means may also be related with social capital that includes influence, networks, solidarity or the like. The question is how actors, objectives and means are interconnected in some kind of stakeholder analysis.
6   The proof of the pudding, that is to say the process, is in the *results* to be checked against the objectives and expressed in terms of objects.
7   If the overall balance of results is positive, this is the right moment to decide whether the label of *good practice* can be attributed to the case under study. Good practice may be transferable to other places – provided it matches or can be adapted to a different context.
8. The key word here is *context*. The diversity of the selected cases makes for a diversity of contexts. In trying to identify contextual variables, on can look for factors constraining the innovation process such as complexity, uncertainty, resistance, tensions, compromise or institutional rigidity. Applying, for example, a social actor analysis, constraints can result from power, interests and legitimacy.

Those are the main variables for the analysis of our nine case studies. The latter have been chosen because of their illustrative value vis-à-vis the process of social innovation and social creativity in urban development. Their comparison shows a wide scope of fields of actions and resources mobilized by social actors implied in the social innovation process. But they all converge into a similar path: applying creative methods to improve the quality of life of deprived collectivities by the implication of civil society based local actors. Let us see them one by one before drawing some general lessons.

Community action in Montreal: local development as social innovation

The case of Montreal is about the socio-economic conversion of two marginalized districts (South West and Rosemont) in the light of the new knowledge-based economy. The *prime target* is employment.
The projects are marked by a specific mix of *actors* or agents of change, starting with Community Economic Development Corporations to promote the partnership of district actors followed by the creation of autonomous organizations composed of local representatives and powerful social economy oriented financial partners such as *Fondaction*, a union retirement fund created to generate local investment and local jobs. Among the actors (in particular in the case of Angus Technopole) are trade unions; city, provincial and central governments; and supportive outside organizations such as universities (including the *Université du Québec à Montréal*).
The main *means* of achieving socio-economic conversion have been: collective actions, land ownership, trade union retirement fund and government financial aid (for example fiscal advantages obtained from the provincial government) and socio-economic networking. The so-called Angus Development Society has bought land from Canadian Pacific Railway which, at the outset, favored a housing project in the district instead of industrial conversion.
The project has *resulted* in the construction of six buildings (including an industrial mall as well as a building specialized in social economy businesses), housing more than 30 companies creating

more than 800 jobs. One has also founded two companies to assist people with their reintegration in the labor market (an integrated environmental training and computer recycling center and a wood recycling shop).

The positive *results* are due to a successful 'third sector' approach combining social enterprises, private firms and public-sector initiatives; this beyond a pure local dimension.

The extended local dimension has surely provided a positive *context* together with the financial commitment of trade unions to urban regeneration.

The Eldonian Village in Liverpool: from the opposition to a local re-housing program in a sustainable community approach

In Liverpool's inner area the residents of Eldon Street opposed the municipality's policy of demolition and re-housing with the *objective* of ending the decline of the area (both physically and socially) and the erosion of employment, aggravated by the collapse of the Liverpool economy.

The residents were also the main *actors* who developed a local partnership with a clear leadership organization. Links with outside actors were only established at a later stage.

A diversity of *means* were brought into action from the end of the 1970s, like organizing the community, ensuing community cohesion and community solidarity, realizing housing, services projects and the creation of jobs, and, eventually, governance arrangements with the municipality of Liverpool.

Also the *results* are diverse and many. These include: some hundreds of affordable homes, a day nursery, sports center, village hall, neighborhood wardens and eight community businesses, jobs for hundreds of residents, a large asset base and large private investments, social sector services, master planning, and the creation of two companies to assist in reintegrating in the labor market, of importance for the local economy. All this transformed the physical environment and stabilized the social relations.

These results can be evaluated as *good practice*, nominated for the World Habitat Award 2004. The Eldonian experience offers a model of how to fit the sustainable community approach to a failing neighborhood although the Eldonian Village does not fully meet all of the sustainable communities aspirations.

The Eldonians have launched a 'Beyond the Boundaries' project for direct collaboration, including other parts of Liverpool, Merseyside and North West England. Its success depends on whether the *context* elsewhere equals that of Eldon Street: a shared identity at an early point in time, a collective strategic vision combined with pragmatism, drawing upon local sources of expertise and capabilities, sharing lessons of both positive and negative experience, training of local people for professional functions, determination and long-term succession planning. But the Eldonians are willing to assist other communities in realizing their potential.

Activity center in Gouda: minority integration by voluntary mobilization

The Dutch case concerns the district Gouda-East and its regeneration. The focus here is on a design atelier activity as part of the R&M Activity Center. This Center has as *objective* to benefit all residents although the core objective is the integration of the Moroccan youth.

The initiative is combined Moroccan-Dutch and so are the main *actors*. That is why the case has been labeled bottom-up. This approach has collided for quite some time with municipal agencies and municipality-related welfare organizations rather practicing a top-down approach. The struggle until 2006 is about recognition and some financial support. In the course of 2006, however, part of the initiatives has been included in the neighborhood transformation plan.

The bulk of the *means* are means in kind, i.e. the work of volunteers with little financial costs. Limited additional support, financial or otherwise, has been received from the neighborhood organization, the local police, various private parties, and the municipality.

The volunteers have succeeded in creating the so-called R&M Activity Center. It provides a number of activities – club, support and leisure – in a former school building in the central part of the district. The center offers the residents a place to meet, to socialize, and to try to get a better understanding of education and work in Dutch society in order to improve opportunities. Apart from the daily and weekly activities, occasional conferences are organized about subjects of interest for the neighborhood as well as meetings to inform about work. These extra activities are usually supported by local or national institutions. Furthermore, a debate about the future of the district has been structured as a design studio in 2003 in which the residents have participated involving a national institute for multicultural development. Together they have recently produced a structural plan for Gouda East especially for its central part.

The positive *results* have been achieved thanks to volunteer work with little financial support, providing – for the time being – a solution for a sensitive issue in the Netherlands.

The *context* has not always been favorable. Those who develop bottom-up initiatives elsewhere should prepare for struggle and a work requiring patience, time and labor.

Self-help and housing in León: the strengthening effect of decentralized co-operation

Illegal slum settlements and economic development at the outskirt of the city are the main *objects* or targets of this experience of urban development in León, Nicaragua.

The *objective* is, with focus on the neighborhood scale, to realize a new strategy for León's economic development, to create opportunities for connecting population, income and work, to improve the effectiveness of urban policy, to solve problems by strengthening local potentials, to diminish urban poverty, and to promote sustainable urban and rural development including infrastructure and basis urban services, with local participation.

The *actors* are self-help housing groups, inhabitants and entrepreneurs, local businesses and associations with their skills of self-help construction and self-organization, the municipality, NGOs, and supporting city links with Hamburg, Zaragoza and Utrecht.

The *means* are land development for access to (own) housing and for economic activities, by active land policy, also for low income households without alternative in the housing market, and the development of local knowledge in municipal organizations, together with inhabitants, entrepreneurs and associations.

The *results* before 2000 were very limited with little support of Nicaragua's central government. After 2000 the projects became supported by Hamburg, Zaragoza and Utrecht, and in 2005 the municipality started implementing a local housing policy in view of the new national housing strategy, the so-called Plots Program. Major results still have to come.

Therefore, as a *good practice* case, urban development and self-help in León is at best a promise with the present focus on knowledge development, professional work, closer connection to actual needs, and social and economic emancipation.

But one has to work in a *context* representing a mix of opposing forces. On the one hand, there is support from NGOs and foreign municipalities against, on the other hand, local landowners resisting selling and private developers not favoring self-help and, of course, the overwhelming precarious economic context.

The *cabinas* case in Lima: the innovative potential of the informal economy

The *object* of the *cabinas* study case in Lima is the rise of informal little shops that offer Internet services in poor neighborhoods. Poor neighborhoods are suffering from an important lack of cultural and communication services due to the absence of interest of private corporations to provide this kind of services to the poor and the absence of governmental concern to give an answer to this problem. *Cabinas* do not represent an organized movement nor are they a tight network. They rather correspond to a spontaneous response to the strong inequity between social classes and between neighborhoods that characterize the city of Lima.

If individually the *objective* of each one of these informal enterprises is to get some private revenue, as a global phenomenon they contribute to Internet access and other cultural services for the lower classes, specially the youth.

The *actors* are principally private entrepreneurs, most of them informal, who provide Internet services where the formal businesses do not (yet) invest, but also the youth who massively uses their services.

The *means* are often very limited, and the start is usually an entrepreneur who has a computer and access to the Internet.

The *result* is that, by means of simple equipment and small investment, *cabinas* contribute to reduce the vulnerability and deprivation that characterize informal neighborhoods, especially the youth, for who using internet has turned out to be the main recreation activity. The use of Internet *cabinas* allows young people to connect with the global world and culture, which is a challenge to individualism, crime and violence. Consequently, thanks to the *cabinas* Internet access service constitutes a crucial asset to improve the living as well in informal neighborhoods as in the whole city.

This case illustrates the role that informal entrepreneurship can play in finding solutions that meet social needs. Even if *cabinas* are not anchored in a social movement, nor constitute collective actions as such, they represent a social experience that gives great services to the poor. *Cabinas* are the outcome of the initiative of lower income groups to find a solution to their needs.

Their example can be adapted to any *context* where service institutions are oriented to the rich people and where poor neighborhoods are deprived.

The URBAN Initiative of EU: a European partnership

The *object* of change in the URBAN Initiative is the revitalization of deprived urban areas in European cities: inner city areas, historic city centers, peripheral and mixed urban areas (in 15 member states).

The *objective* is to tackle multiple deprivation by an integrated area approach with active citizen participation to solve problems 'at grass root level'.

The agents or *actors* are local, sometimes regional authorities, national governments and the European Union. As to citizen participation, its role depends on the implementation strategy adopted. Only the so-called 'community focused approach', adopted mainly in the UK, aims to integrate community groups, voluntary groups and residents' associations into the design, management and implementation of the program and its projects.

The *means* in URBAN I are 118 programs, with 900 million euros EU-funding, targeting 3 million inhabitants. In URBAN II there were 70 programs, with 700 million euros EU-funding, targeting 2.2 million inhabitants. Both programs have also triggered additional investment.

The *results*, apart from the 'Community value' added which reflects the interest of the EU, are 'measured' in terms of major impacts such as impacts on the physical environment, improvements in socio-economic conditions, social capital impacts, and institutional impacts. Locally, these results depend on the existing policies in the member states and have to be judged per area, because of differences in integrated approach, strength of leadership, private sector support, co-operation, community participation, and, in line with the principle of subsidiary, the facilitation of local (regional) authorities. According to the evaluators, the overall effect is successful in the majority of the evaluated programs. But does the URBAN Initiative qualify as a *good practice* experience? URBAN seems to have raised the consciousness of the urgency of tackling social inclusion and its basic rationale still holds: multiple deprivation asks for an integrated area approach and active city participation. However, URBAN has hardly been commensurate with the magnitude of multiple deprivation in EU-15 cities. What are the prospects for 'needy' cities in the past-2006 period and what are the urban problems faced by the new members?

There are important lessons to be learned from the European as well as the local *context* of implementation of the URBAN Initiative: from the success factors as well as from hindering factors. It is also important that local (regional) authorities and national governments share in the EU learning.

The *Caisse des Dépôts et Consignations'* Urban Renewal Program in France: the match of public action and local commitment

The *object* of the Urban Renewal Program (*Programme de Renouvellement Urbain*), were sensitive urban neighborhoods in France. This program was implemented from 1998 to 2003 by the *Caisse des Dépôts et Consignations* in the context of a top-down public program.

The *objective* of the program was to regenerate and put sensitive neighborhoods back on the market and, by doing that, to put in action a virtuous cycle of local development. The *Caisse des Dépôts et Consignations* program attempted to make local projects more feasible, giving them credibility and encouraging other actors to participate in them and to apply a comprehensive perspective.

Main *actors* participating in the acting implementation of Urban Renewal Program actions were the *Caisse des Dépôts et Consignations*, a public agency, and local partners as operators.

The program happened to be a trigger to launch local actions and a mediator between local actors on one hand and on the other between the local actors and the government by the *mean* of combining different public funds and adapting them to local investment operations, the Urban Renewal Program focused on new perspectives for intervention areas. Main *users* were local residents and stakeholders.

The program *resulted* in restoring the local market which benefits local residents, without provoking gentrification.

Even though it refers to a governmental action, Urban Renewal Program interventions can be characterized as *good practice* and a source of inspiration for local actions. They demonstrated how the State can succeed in helping local communities to find innovative solutions for achieving urban renewal (without provoking gentrification), and for making neighborhoods more attractive for real estate and commercial investors.

As the key for success lied in finding and mobilizing pertinent local partners, the lessons that can be drawn from the Urban Renewal Program case could be applied in *contexts* where local actors are strong enough as to act as local operators, and are committed to collective local wellbeing.

Towards an open city of Jerusalem: an urban approach to construct peace

The *object* is this case study is Jerusalem, a divided city. Peace building is the prime *objective*, a precondition for urban development.

There are two kinds of *actors*: inside and outside of Jerusalem. On the one hand there are Israeli and Palestinian NGOs, non-governmental practitioners and academics as well as civil society activists. On the other hand there are Swedish, Dutch and German NGOs and universities.

The *means* invested are the Israeli and Palestinian commitment to a dialogue supported financially by the outside parties.

The *results* are four scenarios for the future of Jerusalem:
- 'Besieged City' (status quo)
- 'City of Bridges' (best case)
- 'Fortress City' (intermediate case)
- 'Scorched Earth' (worst case)

But it is still a long way to peace…

The lessons to be learned so far are that the peace process is not linear, but cyclical (the partners in the dialogue were nevertheless able to move from a political taboo to a shared vision). Talk and negotiation can be an important fact, without them the situation would even be worse. And, finally, scenario building may not solve problems, but it can help to structure a common vision and to pinpoint the consequences of remaining on a destructive path. The scenarios can be used to identify strategic levers of intervention, starting from the status quo and moving stepwise toward the intermediate case.

An *open question* is whether lessons can be learned from Jerusalem for other divided cities or vice versa, particularly starting from the recent experience in Belfast.

Mondragón in the Basque country: a co-operative experience at the global scale

The case of Mondragón is from the Basque country in Spain. The main *object* at the start in the 1940s was to revitalize a poor Basque community, which had suffered from the Spanish Civil War.

The *objective* was to stop deprivation, poverty and unemployment in this rural based economy. The roots of the Mondragón experience can be found in co-operative development ideas disseminated by a priest who arrived in Mondragón during the 1940s. He founded a professional school that served as an incubator for co-operative ideas. The very beginning of the experience was when some local entrepreneurs decided to put into action these co-operative ideas during the 1950s.

Since then, the *means* implemented by Mondragón have been numerous such as the creation of a network of co-operatives, a banking system, an insurance company, and a research center linked with co-operatives. A high education center, specialized in modern management, has been the base for innovative spatial interventions and economic activities.

The *results* after 50 years of existence are noteworthy. The Mondragón Group has become a large, internationalized co-operative holding that counts some 78 000 jobs and has turned into the largest business group in the Basque country as well as one of the largest in Spain.

This is why the Mondragón experience has been recognized as one of the *best practices* in local development. Mondragón has become a regional and co-operative innovation system based on inter-business co-operation and synergy, on participative governance, and on strong links with the regional territory, taking advantage of personal skills and competences.

The *context* in which the Mondragón experience has developed is particular; hence the experience can not be replicated. Nevertheless, lessons can be drawn. Firstly, co-operatives values can be combined with a wealthy experience. Secondly, education and knowledge activities are vital for building innovative strategies. Thirdly, the Triple Helix approaches which are often invoked by territorial agencies and actors can be enriched with co-operative and participative values. Even if Mondragón leaders have to face some important challenges, such as the danger of exploding because of the heterogeneity of the experience and the danger of being corrupted by the capitalistic logic because of the size of the whole enterprise, Mondragón experience can be considered as a demonstration of the possibility of replacing the pervasive cycle of poverty by a virtuous local based development cycle.

Finally

By way of final conclusion, one may ask whether a common denominator exists for territorial social innovation. It seems to be the creation of an *innovative milieu*, originally linked to technological innovation (Camagni & Maillat, 2006), but in spite of different aims also relevant to social innovation (see Matteaccioli in Chapter 2).

An innovative milieu or environment – according to Maillat (1994) – has the following characteristics:
- Group of actors (from business firms, research and educational institutions, public authorities; from the viewpoint of social innovation the role of citizens or users needs to be stressed as those for whom the urban regeneration is done)
- Material, immaterial and institutional elements (plants, infrastructure and housing; know-how; public authorities and other organizations including social movements)
- Co-operation (or partnership among actors; networking to make best use of existing resources, thus creating value added or synergy)
- Learning or 'apprenticeship' (enabling actors to modify their behavior in order to develop new solutions, coping with a changing environment).

Both co-operation and learning involve the external environment of a milieu, beyond the local context. Links to the external environment, which may even be international, are ensured by the formation of transterritorial networks.

Both co-operation and learning relate to:
- The creation of know-how required by urban revitalization;
- The development of behavioral norms guiding the co-operation among actors;
- The ability to detect and mobilize specific resources of different actors and the milieu as a whole as opportunities for co-operation. Of particular importance is that those for whom the regeneration is done dispose of resources to achieve their aims which is, after all, the essence of real citizen participation and a far cry from tokenism.

But an innovative milieu is not an end in itself. When urban revitalization is concerned, the final aim is to achieve a *sustainable community* (as described by Roberts in Chapter 7). A sustainable community should be:
- Active, inclusive and safe
- Well run
- Environmentally sensitive
- Well designed and built
- Well connected
- Thriving
- Well served
- Fair for everyone.

In addition, 'placemaking' is called for: "a comprehensive package of measures which is implemented through an appropriate integrated placemaking vision and strategy" (Roberts, see Chapter 7, page 123 in this book). With place making we are back at the integrated area approach, advocated by the URBAN Community Initiative.

References

Camagni, R. & D. Maillat, 2006, *Milieux innovateurs, théorie et politiques*, Economica Anthropos, Paris.

Klein, J.-L. & D. Harrisson (eds), 2007, *L'innovation sociale*, Presses de l'Université du Québec, Sainte-Foy.

Maillat, D., 1994, Comportements spatiaux et milieu innovateurs; in: Auray, J.-P., A. Bailly, P.-H. Derycke & J.-M. Huriot (eds), *Encyclopédie d'économie spatial*, Economica, Paris, pp. 255-262.

Moulaert, F., F. Martinelli & E. Swyngedouw (guest eds), 2005, Special issue: Social Innovation in the Governance of Urban Communities, *Urban Studies*, Vol. 42, N° 11.

Platt, J.R., 1966, *The Step to Man*, John Wiley & Sons, New York, London & Sydney.

Reference Index

A

A.T. Kearny 11, 14
A.T. Kearney and The London School of Economics 78, 84
Abell 53, 61
Abu Ghazallah 227, 232
Ailenei 89, 100
Albeda 64, 84
Alberts 77, 84
Allaert 29, 46
Allen 241, 249
Alter 22, 25, 52, 61
Amable 25, 23
Amesse 22, 26
Amin 103, 106, 114, 227, 232
AMIPCI 171, 180
Apoyo 171, 172, 173, 180
Argyris 235, 248
Arocena 103, 114
Arora 248, 249
Ashkenas 79, 84
Association for Federal Information Resources Management 80, 84
Auclair 40, 46
Auga 225, 232
Avellaneda 180, 181
Aydalot 22, 25, 29, 34, 46
Azcarate 237, 250

B

Bacharach 58, 61
Bamberger 58, 61
Barcelo-Roca 34, 47
Barnett 52, 61
Barré 23, 25
Bastiaansen 11, 14, 63, 68, 69, 84
Becattini 22, 26
Benko 17, 22, 26, 103, 114
Berelson 24, 26
Berger 59, 61
Bernard 43, 46
Bet 146, 149
Bontebal 166
Bordeleau 20, 27
Borja 104, 113, 114
Boulianne 29, 46
Bourque 17, 26, 103, 115
Boyer 23, 25, 26
Braczyk 22, 26, 103, 114
Bramanti 29, 46
Braudel 18, 26
Bredenoord 13, 14, 166
Brenner 106, 114
Brooks 231, 232
Bryant 103, 114
Building and Social Housing Foundation 128, 132
Burwood 121, 130, 132

C

Cabaret 89, 90, 100
Callon 25, 26, 52, 61
Camagni 10, 14, 29, 30, 33, 36, 46, 258, 259
Cameron A. 103, 114
Cameron S. 87, 99
Carroll 52, 61
Castells 65, 84, 104, 105, 112, 114
Chambon 22, 23, 24, 26
Checkland 117, 132
Chevrier 20, 27
Chion 168, 180
Christensen 54, 62
Cid 236, 249
Clark 20, 26
Clinton 67, 84
Cloutier 30, 46
Cofsky 103, 114
Coletti 87, 90, 100
Colona 173, 177, 180
Commission of the European Communities 9, 14, 187, 195
Commons 53, 61
Conato 87, 90, 100
Consiglio Comunale di Roma 91, 99
Cooke 22, 26, 103, 114
Cooperación Española 152, 166
Corbo 19, 26
Corolleur 29, 46

Council of Ministers Responsible for Spatial Planning 120, 132
Coxon 130, 132
Crevoisier 29, 34, 46, 47

D

Dadoy 39, 46
Damanpour 88, 99
David 22, 23, 24, 26
De Bernardy 37, 46
De Bresson 22, 26
De Groep van 100 66, 84
De Klerck 29, 46
De Mattos 103, 114
De Muro 87, 99
De Soto 168, 180
Decoster 35, 46
Dekker 77, 84
Delfau 89, 99
Delladetsima 87, 100
Delvainquière 87, 100
Demazière 87, 100
Dennis 124, 132
Department for Communities and Local Government 131, 132
Desouza 249
Deverey 22, 23, 24, 26
Diacon 128, 132
DiMaggio 53, 54, 61, 62
Dionne 105, 115
Doloreux 22, 26
Dosi 20, 26
Douglas 59, 61
Drewe 13, 14, 29, 46, 193, 195
Durkheim 54, 61, 88, 99
Duyvendak 44, 46

E

Eenmalige Commissie ICT en Overheid 66, 84
El Comercioy Apoyo 169, 180
Eppink 77, 84
Esping-Andersen 56, 61
Etty 64, 84
European Commission 183, 188, 195
European Commission, Directorate-Generale Regional Policy 184, 195

F

Favreau 89, 99
Fernández-Maldonado 13, 14, 173, 175, 180
Ferrao 29, 47
Fishel 227, 232
Flichy 22, 26
Fontan 12, 14, 17, 20, 21, 23, 26, 27, 31, 32, 34, 37, 38, 41, 42, 45, 47, 103, 104, 106, 107, 108, 113, 114, 115, 116
Forgues 17, 26, 103, 115
Fosfuri 248, 249
Freeman 20, 26, 60, 61
Friedman 13, 14, 225, 232
Frissen 66, 84

G

Gaebler 67, 84
Galbiati 29, 46
Gambardella 248, 249
Garb 227, 232
García Canclini 175, 180
Garfinkel 55, 61
Gaudet 24, 26
Geljon 147, 149
Gemeente Breda 74, 76, 84
Gemeente Gouda 136, 138, 146, 149, 150
Gertler 17, 26, 243, 249
GHK 9, 14, 185, 186, 190, 194, 195
Gonzalez 87, 89, 94, 95, 100
Gore 67, 84
Goren 227, 232
Gorman 248, 249
Government of Nicaragua 154, 166
Greffe 39, 47

H

Hamdouch 87, 89, 99, 100
Hamel 108, 115
Harrisson 17, 25, 26, 113, 115, 251, 259
Hasson 225, 227, 232
Hayes 77, 84
Heidenreich 22, 26, 103, 114
Hidmi 227, 232
Hillier 21, 26, 87, 88, 99, 113, 115
Holbrook 22, 26
Hollingsworth 25, 26, 55, 61
Hopenhayn 176, 180

Houterman 139, 141, 149
Hudson 103, 114
Hulsbergen 12, 13, 14, 139, 141, 147, 149, 150, 195

I

IADB/FAO 180, 181
ICA, CSSE-EKGK 241, 249
INEI 167, 169, 171, 172, 175, 180, 181
Interprovinciaal Overleg 66, 73, 84
Irizar 236, 240, 249, 250
Itçaina 243, 249

J

Jacobs 131, 13
Jeffrey 118, 132
Jick 79, 84
Johnston 120, 132
Joseph Rowntree Foundation 119, 132, 121
Joyal 103, 106, 115

K

Kabinet 68, 84
Katz 24, 26
Kearny
Kerr 79, 84
Khamaisi 226, 232
Klein 12, 14, 17, 20, 21, 23, 25, 26, 27, 31, 32, 34, 37, 38, 41, 42, 45, 47, 103, 104, 105, 106, 107, 113, 114, 115, 116
Kogut 241, 249

L

Lafleur 241, 250
Lallemand 40, 47
Lampron 40, 46
Lane 117, 132
Larrasquet 248, 250
Latendresse 106, 115
Latour 25, 26
Laville 54, 62, 89, 99
Lawrence 52, 62
Lazarfeld 24, 26
Le Bas 20, 21, 26
Lecoq 34, 47
Lee 241, 249
Leeming 124, 125, 126, 128, 132

Leibar 237, 250
Leontidou 87, 100
Lévesque 17, 22, 23, 89, 99, 103, 106, 114
Lipietz 17, 26, 103, 114
Loinger 37, 46
López S. 240, 250
López E. 153, 166
Lorsch 52, 62
Luckmann 59, 61
Ludeña 168, 169, 180
Lundvall 22, 26, 60, 62

M

Maillat 10, 14, 22, 26, 29, 34, 38, 47, 49, 258, 259
Mangematin 247, 250
Mangin 168, 181
Manzagol 107, 115
Maoz 227, 232
March 52, 62
Martín Barbero 177, 180
Martinelli 87, 88, 94, 95, 251, 259
Marty 26, 27
Mason 249
Matteaccioli 10, 14, 29, 31, 34, 35, 46, 47,
MCC 236, 237, 238, 250
Mead 24, 26
Meade 77, 84
Meegan 118, 121, 125, 126, 128, 132
Meller 124, 125, 132
Melucci 105, 115
Merton 54, 62
Mierop 11, 14, 63, 68, 69, 84
Ministerie van LNV 74, 76, 84
Ministerie van VROM 72, 84, 139, 149
Misselwitz 13, 14
Mitchell 118, 121, 125, 126, 128, 132
Moore B. 190, 195
Moore R. 119, 132
Morin 106, 115
Moser 148, 149
Moulaert 17, 21, 22, 26, 87, 88, 89, 84, 90, 94, 95, 97, 99, 100, 103, 113, 115, 251, 259
Mourral 45, 47
Mumford 89, 100
Municipality of León 153, 154, 166

N

Nasrallah 13, 14, 225, 226, 232
Nelson 60, 62
North 54, 62
Nussbaumer 17, 21, 22, 26, 87, 88, 99, 100, 103, 113, 115

O

Office of the Deputy Prime Minister 12, 14, 120, 121, 132
Ormaetxea 236, 250
Osborne 67, 84
OSIPTEL 167, 169, 170, 171, 180
Osservatorio Romano Azioni Contro la Povertà 87, 92, 100

P

Pahl 125, 132
Parazelli 106, 115
Pascó-Font 170, 181
Paugam 9, 14
Pecqueur 103, 115
Penninx 12, 14
Perrin 21, 26, 33, 34, 35, 47, 48
Perroux 21, 27
Pettigrew 52, 62
Phagoe 142, 149
Piore 22, 27
Planque 34, 47
Platt 12, 14, 251, 259
Polanyi 23, 27
Polese 103, 115
Pompili 29, 46
Poole 52, 62
Porter 241, 250
Powell 53, 54, 62
Prince-Gibson 227, 232
Programma bureau Overheidsloket 2000 78, 84
Pröpper 78, 84
Provincie Groningen 74, 76, 84
PUCA 44, 47

Q

Quevit 29, 37, 38, 47
Quiroz 173, 177, 178, 180

R

Rassem 227, 232
Rathenau Instituut 72, 84
Rémy 30, 47
Revilla Diez 22, 26
Revue Autrement 23, 27
Reynaud 55, 62
Rhi-Sausi 87, 90, 100
Rieniets 13, 14
Rieu 44, 47, 49
Roberts 12, 14, 118, 119, 120, 121, 122, 131, 132, 133, 135, 149, 150
Rodriguez 97, 100
Rolland 107, 113, 116
Rostow 21, 27
Rothwell 240, 250
Rousier 29, 47
Rousseau S. 20, 27, 107, 115, 116
Rousseau J.M. 243, 250
Rozas 170, 180
Rufini 87, 90, 100
Ruimtelijk Planbureau 72, 84

S

Sabel 22, 27, 40, 41, 47
San Román 171, 181
Sassen 104, 115
Schön 235, 249
Schroth 170, 181
Schumpeter 17, 19, 27, 52, 62, 89, 100
Scott A.J. 104, 115
Scott R.W. 53, 54, 62
Selznick 53, 56, 62
Senn 29, 46, 47
Shearmur 103, 115
Sheffield 249
Shelter 124, 133
Simon 52, 62
Sociaal en Cultureel Planbureau 64, 84
Soete 20, 26
Sole-Parellada 34, 47
Sonnenstuhl 58, 61
Spires 190, 195
Steenbeek 78, 84
Stetter 225, 232

Stichting R&M Gouda Oost i.s.m. FORUM (Utrecht) en Stuurgroep Wijkontwikkeling Gouda 143, 149
Stöhr 103, 115
Strauss 58, 62
Stuurgroep Wijkontwikkeling Gouda 138, 142, 143, 149
Sueur 198, 213
Swinnen 42, 48
Swyngedouw 87, 89, 94, 95, 96, 97, 100, 105, 106, 115, 251, 259
Sykes 135, 149, 150

T

Tabariés 29, 35, 46, 47, 48
Tamisar 29, 46
Tandonnet 45, 48
Tarde 18, 27
Tardif 104, 115
Tarrow 105, 115
The Eldonian Group 128, 133
The Eldonians 125, 126, 127, 133
Thiveaud 197, 213
Thrift 103, 114
Thuderoz 247, 250
Tilly 105, 115
Torero 170, 181
Tremblay D.-G. 17, 18, 19, 20, 21, 23, 26, 27, 32, 37, 38, 41, 45, 47, 103, 106, 107, 113, 115, 116
Tremblay P.-A. 105, 116
Trichet 197, 213
Truth and Reconciliation Commission 176, 181
Turner 168, 181
Tushman 241, 249

U

Ugarte 250
Ulrich 79, 84
United Nations 154, 166
Universidad de Lima 175, 181

V

Van de Ven 52, 62
Van Doren 37, 38, 47
Van Lindert 166
Van Schendel 107, 116
Van Wijngaarden 69, 84

Veblen 17, 19, 27
Vellinga 12, 14, 147, 149, 150
Veltz 103, 104, 116
Vereniging van Nederlandse Gemeenten 73, 84
Vernon 20, 27
Viard 104, 116
Volberda 78, 85
Voyé 30, 47
VROM-Raad 64, 65, 72, 84

W

Wa'ary 227, 232
Weber 52, 62, 88, 100
Wetenschappelijke Raad voor het Regeringsbeleid 64, 69, 70, 71, 85
Wolfe 17, 22, 26, 27
Woodward 52, 62, 243, 249

Y

Youhan 226, 232

Z

Zander 241, 249
Zoeteman 147, 149
Zwart 65, 85

Geographical Index

Austria:
- Vienna 94, 98

Belgium: 44
- Antwerp 94, 189
- Brussels 94, 96, 189
- Charleroi 37, 38

Bosnia and Herzegovina:
- Mostar 224

Canada:
- Montreal 32, 103-114
- Angus Technopole 109-114
- Canal Lachine Zone 109-114
- Quebec 32, 103-114
- Ville Saint-Laurent 49

Cyprus:
- Nicosia 224

European Union: 64, 162, 182-195, 225

France: 169-180
- Arcueil 201-204
- Aulnay-sous-Bois 9, 193
- Avignon–Marseille–Nice region 34
- Bordeaux 201, 205, 206, 208
- Clichy-sous-Bois 9, 193
- Creil 201, 203, 204
- Grenoble 37
- Lille 11, 87, 98
- Perpignan 201, 205-207
- Reims 201-204, 209, 213
- Roubaix 94, 98
- Saint Etienne 201-206, 209
- Toulouse 201, 203, 204

Germany: 191
- Berlin 43, 94, 98, 224-226
- Johannesberg 224

Israel / Palestine:
- Bethlehem 223
- Jerusalem 215-232, 256-257
- Ramallah 223
- West Bank 215, 223, 230

Italy: 90
- Milan 29, 94, 97, 187
- Naples 94, 98
- Rome 90, 94

Nicaragua:
- León 151-165, 254

Northern Ireland: 118
- Belfast 224, 257

Norway:
- Oslo 215, 216

Peru:
- Lima 167-180

Spain:
- Barcelona 34
- Basque Country 235, 236, 238, 242, 246
- Madrid 215
- Mondragón 235-249

Sweden: 44
- Bommersvik 215-229

Switzerland:
- Swiss Jura region 34

The Netherlands: 44, 63-84, 189, 191
- Breda 74, 76
- Gouda 135-150, 253-254
- Groningen 74, 76

United Kingdom: 103, 187, 189, 191-194, 255
- Liverpool 117-132
  - Eldonian Village 117-132
  - Vauxhall area 124-125, 128-131
  - Merseyside 117-118, 124-131, 253
- Newcastle 87, 94, 97
- Wales 98

United States of America:
- Pittsburg 40

About the Authors

Amin Amin, Change Agent for Arab Development and Education Reform (CADER), Amman, Jordan
http://www.caderco.com
aamin@caderco.com

Patricia Ardiles, Municipality of Utrecht, Department of Social Development; The Netherlands
http://www.utrecht.nl/internationaal

Jan Bredenoord, Urban and Regional Planner and Consultant, Amersfoort, The Netherlands; worked in Nicaragua and Peru
janbredenoord@planet.nl

Stuart Cameron, APL/GURU, University of Newcastle upon Tyne; United Kingdom
s.j.cameron@newcastle.ac.uk

Pasquale De Muro, University of Roma Tre, Human Development Economics; Italy
http://host.uniroma3.it/facolta/economia/vedi_docente.asp?id=33
demuro@eco.uniroma3.it

Paul Drewe, Academic hospitality at the Chair of Spatial Planning, Faculty of Architecture, Delft University of Technology; The Netherlands
http://www.drewe.nl
pauldrewe@wanadoo.nl

Ana María Fernández-Maldonado, Faculty of Architecture, Delft University of Technology, The Netherlands;
http://www.bk.tudelft.nl
http://www.networkcity.bk.tudelft.nl
a.m.fernandezmaldonado@tudelft.nl

Jean-Marc Fontan, Alliance de recherche universités-communautés en économie sociale (ARUC-ÉS) http://www.aruc-es.uqam.ca/; Centre de Recherche sur les Innovations Sociales (CRISES), http://www.crises.uqam.ca/ and Département de sociologie, http://www.socio.uqam.ca/ , Université du Québec à Montréal
fontan.jean-marc@uqam.ca

Hervé Grellier, Department of Strategy, Organization and Entrepreneurship, Faculty of Business Science, Mondragón University, Oñati, Spain
hgrellie@eteo.mondragon.edu

Abdelillah Hamdouch, Faculté des Sciences Economiques et Sociales and CLERSE-IFRESI-CNRS, Université des Sciences et Technologies de Lille (Lille, France); Research Associate of the Economic Research Forum (Cairo, Egypt)
http://hamdouch.monsite.orange.fr
abdel.hamdouch@univ-lille.fr

Denis Harrison, Department of Organization and Human Resources, School of Management and Director of Centre de recherche sur les Innovations sociales (CRISES), Université du Québec à Montréal, Canada
http://www.crises.uqam.ca
harrisson.denis@uqam.ca

Edward Hulsbergen, Faculty of Architecture, Chair of Spatial Planning, Delft University of Technology, The Netherlands
http://www.bk.tudelft.nl
http://www.networkcity.bk.tudelft.nl
e.d.hulsbergen@tudelft.nl

Juan-Luis Klein, Centre de Recherche sur les Innovations Sociales (CRISES) http://www.crises.uqam.ca/ and Département de géographie http://www.geo.uqam.ca/, Université du Québec a Montréal
klein.juan-luis@uquam.ca

Jean Michel Larrasquet, Department of Strategy, Organization and Entrepreneurship, Faculty of Business Science, Mondragón University, Oñati, Spain, and Ecole Supérieure des Technologis Industrielles Avancées, France
j.larrasquet@estia.fr

Sain Lopez Perez, Department of Strategy, Organization and Entrepreneurship, Faculty of Business Science, Mondragón University, Oñati, Spain
smlopez@eteo.mondragon.edu

Andrée Matteaccioli, Maître de conférences honoraire des universités, Université de Paris I-Panthéon-Sorbonne; Researcher at Groupe de Recherche Européen sur les Milieux Innovateurs (GREMI); France
andree.matteaccioli@wanadoo.fr

Roy Mierop, Capgemini Nederland, Public Sector, The Netherlands
roy.mierop@capgemini.com

Frank Moulaert, Chair in European Planning and Development, APL/GURU, University of Newcastle upon Tyne (United Kingdom) and USTL-CLERSE-IFRESI in Lille (France)
http://users.skynet.be/frank.moulaert/frank
frank.moulaert@ncl.ac.uk

Pierre Narring, Directeur de l'Ingénierie Urbaine et de l'Habitat; SCET Conseil, Expertises, Territoires in Paris, France
http://www.scet.fr
pierre.narring@scet.fr

Rami Nasrallah, International Peace and Cooperation Center, East Jerusalem
http://www.ipcc-jerusalem.org
rnasrallah@ipcc-jerusalem.org

Peter Roberts, Professor of Sustainable Spatial Development, Sustainability Research Institute, University of Leeds; Chair of the Board of the Academy for Sustainable Communities, United Kingdom
http://www.see.leeds.ac.uk/research/sri/index.htm
http://www.ascskills.org.uk/pages/about-ASC/the-board

Diane-Gabrielle Tremblay, Chaire sur l'économie du savoir http://www.teluq.uqam.ca/chaireecosavoir; Centre de Recherche sur les Innovations Sociales (CRISES) http://www.crises.uqam.ca/ and Télé-université de l'Université du Québec a Montréal
dgtrembl@teluq.uqam.ca

Luxio Ugarte, Department of Strategy, Organization and Entrepreneurship, Faculty of Business Science, Mondragón University, Oñati, Spain
lugarte@eteo.mondragon.edu

Desiree van de Ven, Municipality of Utrecht; Office of Strategic and International Affairs; The Netherlands
http://www.utrecht.nl/internationaal
d.van.de.ven@utrecht.nl

Previously published in the series Design/**Science**/Planning

Klaasen, I.T., 2004, *Knowledge-based Design: Developing Urban & Regional Design into a Science*

Fernández-Maldonado, A.M., 2004, *ICT-related Transformations in Latin American Metropolises*

Restrepo, J., 2004, *Information Processing in Design*

Salingaros, N.A., 2005, *Principles of Urban Structure*

Hulsbergen, E.D., I.T. Klaasen & I. Kriens (eds), 2005, *Shifting Sense in Spatial Planning: Looking Back to the Future*